PROVIDENCE

PROVIDENCE

A BIBLICAL, HISTORICAL, AND THEOLOGICAL ACCOUNT

Mark W. Elliott

B
Baker Academic
a division of Baker Publishing Group
Grand Rapids, Michigan

© 2020 by Mark W. Elliott

Published by Baker Academic
a division of Baker Publishing Group
PO Box 6287, Grand Rapids, MI 49516-6287
www.bakeracademic.com

Printed in the United States of America

Library of Congress Cataloging-in-Publication Data
Names: Elliott, M. W. (Mark W.), author.
Title: Providence : a biblical, historical, and theological account / Mark W. Elliott.
Description: Grand Rapids : Baker Academic, a division of Baker Publishing Group, 2020. |
    Includes bibliographical references and index.
Identifiers: LCCN 2019031877 | ISBN 9781540960405 (paperback)
Subjects: LCSH: Providence and government of God—Christianity.
Classification: LCC BT135 .E5545 2020 | DDC 231/.5—dc23
LC record available at https://lccn.loc.gov/2019031877

ISBN 978-1-5409-6278-2 (casebound)

20 21 22 23 24 25 26   7 6 5 4 3 2 1

Contents

Preface

This work was begun in Edinburgh, in the summer of 2016, although a preliminary sketch had been made as part of a master's module, "Creation and Providence," taught at St. Andrews. A paper on the New Testament material was given at Alphacrucis College, Sydney, hosted by Paul Oslington. A visit to Keble College, Oxford, with generous hosts Markus Bockmuehl and Nathan Eubank, and time in the Bodleian Library helped me to make a good start on the research. The chance to present something of what is contained in the first chapter as an inaugural professorial lecture at St. Andrews University was very welcome. There was opportunity to communicate another section at the research seminar of Konrad Schmid in the spring of 2017 at the University of Zürich, a place without equal for quality of hospitality. In October 2017 I read a paper at Highland Theological College on some biblical texts and received helpful feedback. I am grateful to Darian Lockett for the opportunity to present material on James at the SBL session he chaired in Boston in November 2017 and to Tinu Rupparel for hosting me in Calgary in January 2018, when I was able to deliver part of what became the final chapter. The National Library of Scotland, New College Library of Edinburgh University, and, of course, that of St. Andrews were the locations where most of the book took shape. Resuming teaching and other responsibilities at St. Andrews in August 2018 necessarily slowed the pace down, but also gave ideas time to percolate. I am grateful to the St. Andrews Laidlaw scheme for allowing me the sharp-eyed copyediting services of Autumn Lambert. Dave Nelson at Baker has been an encouragement at a number of stages in the process. Between delivering the first draft and the second I have changed employment and in early 2019 have taken up positions at the University of Glasgow and at the University of Toronto. I'm grateful to the leadership of both those places and for their close interest in what I do, including this project. However, I'd also like to acknowledge the scholarly and supportive context of my former work place, St. Mary's College, St. Andrews, not least the administrative staff as well as sterling academic colleagues. Fifteen (and a half!) years at a place leave a mark, and I have benefited much. Looking ahead, I hope to be able to work a bit around the confines of overspecialization in academic departments today. I trust that this book offers *one* way of doing this, as I become increasingly aware of the importance of collaboration and theology as part of our common life of worship and wisdom, as response to our *Providentissimus Deus*.

Glasgow, March 2019

Abbreviations

General

//	parallel(s)
AT	author's translation
EV	English version(s)
frg(s).	fragment(s)

Ancient Texts, Text Types, and Versions

LXX	Septuagint
MT	Masoretic Text
Vulg.	Vulgate

Papyri

P.Oxy.	Oxyrhynchus Papyri

Old Testament Pseudepigrapha

1 En.	1 Enoch (Ethiopic Apocalypse)
Jub.	Jubilees

Dead Sea Scrolls and Related Texts

1QS	Rule of the Community
11QPs^a	Psalms Scroll^a
4QSam^a	4QSamuel^a

Apostolic Fathers

Eph.	Ignatius, *To the Ephesians*

Greek and Latin Works

Epictetus

Diatr.	*Diatribai*

Evagrius Ponticus

Schol. Proverb.	*Scholia on Proverbs*

Irenaeus

Haer.	*Adversus haereses*

Josephus

A.J.	*Antiquitates judaicae*

Justin Martyr

Dial.	*Dialogus cum Tryphone*

Origen

Dial.	*Dialogus cum Heraclide*
Or.	*De oratione*

Philo

Decal.	*De decalogo*
Deus	*Quod Deus sit immutabilis*
Fug.	*De fuga et inventione*
Leg.	*Legum allegoriae*
Mos.	*De vita Mosis*
Opif.	*De opificio mundi*
Post.	*De posteritate Caini*

Prov.	*De providentia*
Sacr.	*De sacrificiis Abelis et Caini*
Virt.	*De virtutibus*

Plutarch

| Stoic rep. | *De Stoicorum repugnantiis* |

Seneca

Plato

| Ep. | *Epistulae morales* |

| Resp. | *Respublica* |

Modern Works

AB	Anchor Bible
AGJU	Arbeiten zur Geschichte des antiken Judentums und des Urchistentums
AJEC	Ancient Judaism and Early Christianity
AKG	Arbeiten zur Kirchengeschichte
AnBib	Analecta biblica
ANRW	*Aufstieg und Niedergang der römischen Welt: Geschichte und Kultur Roms im Spiegel der neueren Forschung*. Part 2, *Principat*. Edited by Hildegard Temporini and Wolfgang Haase. Berlin: de Gruyter, 1972–
ATANT	Abhandlungen zur Theologie des Alten und Neuen Testaments
AYB	Anchor Yale Bible
BBB	Bonner biblische Beiträge
BEATAJ	Beiträge zur Erforschung des Alten Testaments und des antiken Judentums
BETL	Bibliotheca ephemeridum theologicarum lovaniensium
BEvT	Beiträge zur evangelischen Theologie
BHT	Beiträge zur historischen Theologie
BKAT	Biblischer Kommentar, Altes Testament
BTCB	Brazos Theological Commentary on the Bible
BTSt	Biblisch-theologische Studien
BWANT	Beiträge zur Wissenschaft vom Alten und Neuen Testament
BZAW	Beihefte zur Zeitschrift für die alttestamentliche Wissenschaft
BZNW	Beihefte zur Zeitschrift für die neutestamentliche Wissenschaft
CBQ	*Catholic Biblical Quarterly*
CC	Continental Commentaries
ConBOT	Coniectanea Biblica: Old Testament Series
DCLS	Deuterocanonical and Cognate Literature Studies
ECC	Eerdmans Critical Commentary
EKKNT	Evangelisch-katholischer Kommentar zum Neuen Testament
EvT	*Evangelische Theologie*
FAT	Forschungen zum Alten Testament
FRLANT	Forschungen zur Religion und Literatur des Alten und Neuen Testaments
FrThSt	Freiburger Theologische Studien
HBM	Hebrew Bible Monographs
HBS	Herders biblische Studien
HBT	*Horizons in Biblical Theology*
HCOT	Historical Commentary on the Old Testament
HNT	Handbuch zum Neuen Testament
HTKAT	Herders theologischer Kommentar zum Alten Testament

HTKNT	Herders theologischer Kommentar zum Neuen Testament
IBC	Interpretation: A Bible Commentary for Teaching and Preaching
ICC	International Critical Commentary
JBL	*Journal of Biblical Literature*
JBTh	*Jahrbuch für biblische Theologie*
JQR	*Jewish Quarterly Review*
JSJSup	Supplements to Journal for the Study of Judaism
JSNT	*Journal for the Study of the New Testament*
JSOT	*Journal for the Study of the Old Testament*
JSOTSup	Journal for the Study of the Old Testament: Supplement Series
JTS	*Journal of Theological Studies*
KEK	Kritisch-exegetischer Kommentar über das Neue Testament (Meyer-Kommentar)
LD	Lectio divina
LHBOTS	The Library of Hebrew Bible/Old Testament Studies
LNTS	The Library of New Testament Studies
LTK	Lexicon für Theologie und Kirche
LW	*Luther's Works*. American Edition. 55 vols. Edited by Jaroslav Pelikan and Helmut Lehmann. St. Louis: Concordia; Philadelphia: Fortress, 1955–86
NA28	*Novum Testamentum Graece*. Edited by [E. and E. Nestle], B. Aland et al., 28th rev. ed. Stuttgart: Deutsche Bibelgesellschaft, 2012
NAC	New American Commentary
NEchtB	Neue Echter Bibel
NICNT	New International Commentary on the New Testament
NIGTC	New International Greek Testament Commentary
NovT	*Novum Testamentum*
NovTSup	Novum Testamentum Supplements
NTD	Das Neue Testament Deutsch
NTL	New Testament Library
NTS	*New Testament Studies*
NZSTh	*Neue Zeitschrift für Systematische Theologie und Religionsphilosophie*
OBO	Orbis biblicus et orientalis
OTE	*Old Testament Essays*
ÖTKNT	Ökumenischer Taschenbuch-Kommentar zum Neuen Testament
OTL	Old Testament Library
OTM	Oxford Theological Monographs
PG	Patrologia Graeca [= *Patrologia Cursus Completus*: Series Graeca]. Edited by Jacques-Paul Migne. 162 vols. Paris, 1857–86
PhB	Philosophische Bibliothek
PTMS	Princeton Theological Monograph Series
QD	Quaestiones disputatae
RAC	*Reallexikon für Antike und Christentum*. Edited by Theodor Klauser et al. Stuttgart: Hiersemann, 1950–
RGG	*Religion in Geschichte und Gegenwart*. Edited by Hermann Gunkel and Leopold Zscharnack. 2nd ed. Tübingen: Mohr, 1927–31
RivB	*Rivista biblica italiana*
RNT	Regensburger Neues Testament

SacEr	*Sacris erudiri: Jaarboek voor Godsdienstwetenschappen*
SBLDS	Society of Biblical Literature Dissertation Series
SBLMS	Society of Biblical Literature Monograph Series
SBT	Studies in Biblical Theology
SHBC	Smyth & Helwys Bible Commentary
SNTSMS	Society for New Testament Studies Monograph Series
SP	Sacra Pagina
STJ	*Stellenbosch Theological Journal*
TANZ	Texte und Arbeiten zum neutestamentlichen Zeitalter
TDOT	*Theological Dictionary of the Old Testament.* Edited by G. J. Botterweck and H. Ringgren. Translated by J. T. Willis, G. W. Bromiley, and D. E. Green. 15 vols. Grand Rapids: Eerdmans, 1974–2006
ThDiss	Theologischen Dissertationen
THOTC	Two Horizons Old Testament Commentary
ThViat	*Theologia viatorum*
TLZ	*Theologische Literaturzeitung*
TRE	*Theologische Realenzyklopädie.* Edited by Gerhard Krause and Gerhard Müller. Berlin: de Gruyter, 1977–
TSAJ	Texte und Studien zum antiken Judentum
TUGAL	Texte und Untersuchungen zur Geschichte der Altchristlichen Literatur
TZ	*Theologische Zeitschrift*
VT	*Vetus Testamentum*
VTSup	Supplements to Vetus Testamentum
VWGTh	Veröffentlichungen der Wissenschaftlichen Gesellschaft für Theologie
WA	*D. Martin Luthers Werke.* Complete critical ed. 60 vols. Weimar: Herman Böhlaus Nachfolger, 1883–1980
WBC	Word Biblical Commentary
WMANT	Wissenschaftliche Monographien zum Alten und Neuen Testament
WTJ	*Westminster Theological Journal*
WUNT	Wissenschaftliche Untersuchungen zum Neuen Testament
ZAW	*Zeitschrift für die alttestamentliche Wissenschaft*
ZNW	*Zeitschrift für die neutestamentliche Wissenschaft und die Kunde der älteren Kirche*
ZTK	*Zeitschrift für Theologie und Kirche*

ONE

Is Providence Topical
or Even Biblical?

This book will treat the idea of providence as one that has a number of guises or expressions: it is the property of providence to operate outside the range of knowledge and full comprehensibility, but also even to elude faith's perception and be beyond or behind revelation. So one has to look for traces of God's action in the stories and expressed philosophies of biblical writers, where the glow of revelation shines more brightly and serves as a pattern for faithful glimpsing of providence today.

One finds these traces in the biblical corpus—and ready to be picked up by subsequent interpreters—in such themes as "the hand of God," "the face of God," "the blessing," "the kingdom," "the plan of God," life, breath, enduring order, judgment, protection, and the hidden God. These will be dealt with in such a way that much of the canon of the Bible across both Testaments is allowed to bear witness. In the final chapter the findings will be made to speak to the concerns of systematic and practical theologians.

In this introductory chapter (1) I commence with looking at why some might object to the idea that providence has any relevance in modern times. Next (2) I deal with the objection that "providence" is not a biblical theme by addressing the biblical evidence and trying to come to a working definition on that basis. Then, (3) elaborating providence as part of the content of faith, which seeks understanding as to what God does and doesn't do, I offer a conception that is neither utopian nor a thing of mere comfort, with

1

PTE 9ay - Tempting Providence

a consideration that if providence implies living meaningfully, prudentially, and carefully, then it is (4) "bigger" than theodicy, since it includes thinking about blessing and gift, freshly dispensed to human agents, that is finally much less theoretical than it is "lived."

Modern Resistance to Any Idea of Providence

Providence is not so much "so last century" as it is "so nineteenth century." The rhetoric of providence accompanied a "Victorian" age of God-led imperialism and colonization, as per the title of Stewart J. Brown's book *Providence and Empire*.[1] From about the middle of the nineteenth century, however, a certain suspicion of providence grew deeper, as reflected in literature, just as in the previous centuries philosophers, many of them less radical than Hume and Voltaire, had questioned its existence. Doubting providence was now in the public domain, as it were. The poet Robert Browning believed one could know the divine only through a collage of insights from various great figures in history. Yet here, according to literary critic J. Hillis Miller, is Browning's gloomy conclusion: "The infinite variety of human lives has one universal meaning: the distance of all lives from God."[2] It seemed that there were losers as well as winners in life and that, in fact, the former were possibly in the majority and the happy minority simply lucky. Of course novelists are meant to write about *this* life and not to be dealing directly with theological or any such matters, but they do have, and moreover often do betray, their background beliefs.

The loss of the traditional sense that there is a providence at one end of life in terms of creation (conception and birth) and at the other end (death and resurrection of just and unjust) can be seen in the fin-de-siècle representation by Thomas Hardy, who appeared to assume that life was in no sense to be considered a gift, and a fortiori there was no gift of a life to come in prospect. Correspondingly there was little room for much blessing in Hardy's kingdom of Wessex. Gillian Beer comments: "Maladaptation, the FAILURE

---

1. Subtitled *Religion, Politics and Society in the United Kingdom, 1815–1914*.
2. Miller, *Disappearance of God*, 143. Miller argues that E.Brontë's *Wuthering Heights* permits a benign God only on the condition of the protagonists atoning by suffering: "Only then can the fierce wind of Wuthering Heights be transformed into the soft breeze which blows on Hareton and the second Cathy and through the open doors and windows at the end of the novel" (210). On G. M. Hopkins in his late "That Nature Is Heraclitean Fire and of the Comfort of the Resurrection," Miller comments: "In the end, after a lifetime spent in God's service, he has not gone beyond his beginning, which was to know God as the deity of Isaiah, the God who hides himself" (358–59).

OF THINGS to be what they are meant to be, obsesses Hardy."[3] And yet, as she goes on to report, there is a loud note of joyous affirmation of what Derrida called "the free play of the world" and even an affirmation of delight in the plenitude of experience. Working, even struggling, against Nature's less-than-benign plot, "happiness and hap form the two poles in his work."[4] This means an ironic or sarcastic version of providence as summed up in Hardy's poem "The Convergence of the Twain," but one without reference to a divine plan or reckoning.

Nearly contemporaneous with Hardy's Wessex novels was Thomas Mann's *Buddenbrooks* (1900), with its foregrounding of the family motto, *Deus providebit* (God will provide), set over the entrance of the offices of the venerable but doomed family firm in Hansestadt Lübeck. Behind the Heidelberg Catechism, whose recitation provides the drama in the opening scene of the novel, stands Matthew 10:19–20//Luke 12:11–12 (when the disciples are on trial, the Spirit will give them the words to say), which, with Genesis 22:8, 14 (God supplying a ram after testing Abraham with a command to offer Isaac) in the background, makes one think of providence in the context of testing and sacrifice.[5] But what happens when the Lord for inscrutable reasons seems *not* to provide, or compensate for, a sacrifice, such as that made by the protagonist, Toni (Antonia) Buddenbrooks, of her beloved? The moral of the novel seems to be that God most helps those who help themselves.[6] Or consider Mark Twain's short story of the drunken man who ascribed both his falling overboard and his rescue to divine providence and who, when reporters asked him about the heroic ship's captain who rescued him, declared that the latter was merely the tool of providence.[7] Honoring human responsibility is a good thing, whether the effect of that responsibility is a cure for disease or a life of service. Yet in assessing the significance of human responsibility, it's essential to get the balance right: those who, whether in literature or life, ascribe sole credit to human agency for their responsible service are often people who ascribe it to people like themselves, and one finds it hard to call them "gracious."

Returning briefly to Hardy: in her conclusion Beer shows little Darwinian sangfroid regarding the greater good of the species when she writes, "Hardy's

3. Beer, *Darwin's Plots*, 248.
4. Beer, *Darwin's Plots*, 246.
5. See Hüffmeier, "Deus providebit?," 239.
6. Likewise Theodor Fontane made much of personal responsibility, whereby those characters like Effi Briest (in his novel *Effi Briest*, admired by Mann), who acted outside the moral code, still had to take up some penance and could rediscover themselves as moral agents.
7. "Providence"; published as chap. 53 in *Roughing It*.

texts pay homage to human scale by ceasing as the hero or heroine dies. The single life span is no longer an absolute but polemical. That is one formal expression of [Hardy's] humanism. It opposes evolutionary meliorism or pessimism by making the single generation carry the freight of signification."[8] One may wish to qualify that judgment. For it seems that what does continue and endure to "carry the freight" is the *place*, Wessex, even as an imaginary, and the idea of the collective will.[9] Indeed, the theme of "a breaking of the nations" that echoes Jeremiah 51 comes to the fore: on Christmas Day 1914 Hardy wrote that "the present times are an absolute negation of Christianity."[10] He meant, however, that war was the opposite of a gospel of peace and that large-scale institutions were destroying civil society as they competed for power. This privatization of meaningfulness into the collective community (*Gemeinschaft*) over against artificial conglomerations, although perhaps in part a protest of late Romanticism, was perhaps as much cause then as it seems effect now of the desolation of twentieth-century mass carnage and the consequent evaporation of meaning from twentieth-century political and popular history. As cause, such privatization seems to have been complicit in the depreciation of civil religion into civic religion, and not only in Germany in the 1920s and '30s. This is hardly to blame providence; it is instead to outline what providence had to contend with.

Yet, as Vernon White observes, for all Hardy's bleakness, one hundred years later providence is not so much mocked as it is simply ignored. "In short, when [Julian] Barnes replaces Hardy, when entropy takes the place of evolution and radical epistemological uncertainty replaces confidence in scientific method, the outcome for any purpose in history seems bleaker than ever."[11] Charles Taylor and John Gray have noticed a prevalent popular disgust with explanation of things too: if the economic crash of 2008 is disputed in terms of causes and effects, what chance for giving any sense to the phrase "the meaning of life"?

After the Second World War the Swiss theologian Karl Barth held (appropriately) fairly sober claims for providence: God's activity in the world as the history of the covenantal relationship (not continuous creation nor the history of humanity as such)[12] meant limiting the evidence for providence to a few "in-house" things: the history and preservation of the Bible, the church,

8. Beer, *Darwin's Plots*, 239.

9. See Hardy to Caleb Saleeby, December 21, 1914, in Hardy, *Collected Letters*, 5:69–70.

10. Hardy, *Collected Letters*, 5:72, quoted in Vance, *Bible & Novel*, 134.

11. White, *Purpose and Providence*, 59. This despite Barnes's famous "I don't believe in God, but I miss him."

12. Barth, *Kirchliche Dogmatik*, IV/3, 154–62 (S.57).

and the Jewish people, as well as, curiously, the temporal limit of human life. "Providence" meant a possibility for individuals rather than a universal actuality. "Therefore my life consists in the possibilities offered by this movement [of ascent and descent]."[13] One says too much, Barth claims, when one says the creation is the theater or mirror or parabolic likeness, or even a parable, of God's action,[14] for in the world as it is, too much negativity ("das Nichtige") presses in against God's action for any such clear reflection to be possible. Yet one can at least say that in one's own life the Word of God's power holds things in place, and also that God accompanies his creatures ("das göttliche Begleiten").[15] As Barth puts it punchily: "Es geht ihm als Herr zur Seite [He is the Lord who is happy to accompany]."[16] God "accompanies" each of us, as the Lord beside us. At the beginning and the end of life there is not yet or no longer any place for "self-determination," and Barth uses this as the reminder to every person that at both points there is a disposing ("Fügung") or limitation ("Begrenzung"), with reference to Psalm 31:15 and Job 14:5, such that even in life as it runs its course one is subject to the forces of coming and of going. Barth's main point is that although the framework of life and death or beginning and end of an eon matter for a right understanding of providence, the operation of providence is firmly located in the here and now, not moments in the future or past that can be joined together in a trajectory. Barth may justifiably be criticized for some slippage of meaning in his favored terms of "propulsion" (*Antrieb*) and "decline" (*Gefälle*), or for implying that death is purely to be understood as something neutral, even good, in that it gives one a sense of a fixed amount of time to help one to recognize "possibilities." It might well be that life in its systole and diastole simply seems to witness to the dispensability of individual human lives, not their meaningfulness. Yet raising the issue of mortality should at the very least cause us to be humble before the possibilities for what might constitute the framework into which human lives and human history fit.

The great Jewish philosopher of the Holocaust of the 1940s, Emil Fackenheim, presented an understandably even starker view of things when he wrote: "And the modern Jewish and Christian theologian cannot affirm God's *presence* in history but at most only His *providence over* it—a providence caused by a God who may somehow use nature and man in history, but who is Himself absent from history."[17] In such an account God has retreated to

---

13. *Church Dogmatics*, III/3, 232.
14. *Kirchliche Dogmatik*, III/3, 60.
15. *Kirchliche Dogmatik*, III/3, 102.
16. *Kirchliche Dogmatik*, III/3, 105.
17. Fackenheim, *God's Presence in History*, 5.

watch over events from a safe distance, such that divine providence in the sense of action has given way to self-care by the human race: "There is no externally superintending divine Providence, compelling human freedom and using evil for its own good purposes. Divine Providence is *immanent in* human freedom and consists of its progressive realization. Meaning in history lies in its forward direction—one in which human freedom raises itself ever higher toward Divinity, and evil comes ever closer to being conquered. There is either *this* kind of meaning in history, or else there is no meaning in it at all."[18]

From the founders of the state of Israel, who took matters into their own hands, through to those who work today to eradicate disease on the planet, human beings seek to fill the situation left vacant by the deity. Of course in Fackenheim's Zionist solution there is a Utopia, albeit of a particular sort, in which humans promise to build Jerusalem—literally. And yet this view of providence resonates not only with that of Barth but also with that of ancient Israel—as we shall see in later chapters—in one respect at least: providence is not about reaching a universal goal of history; it is about a particular people being kept safe in a particular place, with their example possibly providing some benefit to the rest of the world.

It is not uninteresting that Fackenheim, while dismissing any idea of divine *presence* in such a dark world, nevertheless, wished to hold on to some notion of divine *providence*, if only providence by proxy. With Christian theologians it is normally the other way around: if there is such a thing as providence, it cannot be pointed to and named; nevertheless, God is somehow present, albeit in a passive or a neutral voice. For Frances Young, "God's presence and providence are to be seen as themselves aspects of the divine otherness. Neither can be like the presence or purposive action of created beings."[19] What she wants to resist is the idea of an intervening or an "interventionist" God, and so she argues in favor of One who holds things together and makes space for each: "The absence or withdrawal of God . . . is not meant to imply deism—with the cosmos wound up and left to get on with it. Rather, it is presented as the prior condition for the existence of beings other than God, and therefore the necessary condition for relationship between 'others,' as distinct from the coercive absorption of creatures within the deity."[20] Even presence itself is reduced to a "presence in absence," the traces or clues left by one who has long since fled the scene of the crime. The note of noncoercion in classic liberal, if not quite Hegelian, phrasing is made to serve the notion of the freedom of mutual love.

18. Fackenheim, *God's Presence in History*, 5.
19. Young, *God's Presence*, 405.
20. Young, *God's Presence*, 406.

Or, to hear the words of recent Christian apologist David Bentley Hart: "Providence, then—and this is what it is most important to grasp—is not the same thing as a universal teleology."[21] Hart is crystal clear that innocent suffering can never be a means justifiable by an end, no matter how worthy the end. In other words, one cannot "like-click" the bon mot wrongly attributed to Stalin that an omelet necessitates the breaking of a few eggs, especially if these metaphorical eggs are the lives of young children. "That there is a transcendent providence that will bring God's good ends out of the darkness of history—in spite of every evil—no Christian can fail to affirm. But providence (as even Voltaire seems to have understood) is not simply a 'total sum' or 'infinite equation' that leaves nothing behind."[22] However—and here Hart announces his alternative—"The Christian eye sees (or should see) a deeper truth in the world than mere 'nature,' and it is a truth that gives rise not to optimism but to joy."[23] Reality is not what it seems, and it is much better than visible circumstances.

However, surely even more than this delight in an invisible reality or higher world that hides Platonically behind our actual world, to be inhaled like a comforting ether, providence means a care that guards and preserves and guides on to safer places, and particularly rather than universally. Something is done on the ground or to a piece of it. Now, of course, as both the "Wisdom" books of the Hebrew Bible and the more reflective ones of the New Testament affirm, if there is a purpose to divine active care, it is not something that can be pointed to as a goal of a project or a mission or a movement: so-called goals will always be in some sense subordinate, and means rather than ends, not least because they tend to be inchoate, corrupted, and deflected. Perhaps the best that can be hoped for is to be kept safe long enough for some human flourishing to take place, and some good and surprising things might then happen. So one can accord with Hart's suspicion of teleology without thinking that God is not moving things around in order to protect and correct. This action by God is not teleological in the sense of a merely this-worldly goal, but it is still purposeful, with a purpose in the here and now. Granted, God did not seem obviously all that active between, say, 1940 and 1945, and also at many other times and places in the remote and recent past; but what made things better then was at least a concerted trust by those who opposed chaos and evil that (without self-righteousness) they could put their hand in the hand of a just and higher cause that God would enlist one for, a cause

21. Hart, *Doors of the Sea*, 85.
22. Hart, *Doors of the Sea*, 29.
23. Hart, *Doors of the Sea*, 58.

bigger than pure national self-interest, even if that just cause was not fully aware of the horrors of the Shoah.[24]

As we seek to formulate definitions of a term like *providence*, we should not expect ancient texts and their writers to have exactly the same conceptual furniture as we do or to understand *providence* as what we might mean by it. However, we do next need to consider the source of our understanding of the term before concluding with a working definition.

The Biblical Evidence for Providence

At first glance it seems that the God of the Bible initiates a number of things; other things he anticipates and responds to. Although God on several occasions is recorded as changing his mind, there is in biblical narrative little sense of God being taken by surprise or so shocked that he is prompted to declare: "This isn't what I expected." The fact that Old Testament prophecy is taken seriously by later parts of the Old Testament and by the New Testament as having declared things well in advance goes hand in hand with the belief that God anticipates future outcomes as well as giving some people a glimpse of these.

"Providence" in Early Postbiblical Judaism

Leaving a detailed consideration of the Hebrew Bible or Old Testament for now, we find a reading of the biblical material that is markedly not Christian but is close in time to the New Testament in Philo of Alexandria, some point just before the New Testament was written. Philo is quite prepared to use the term πρόνοια. Prior to Philo, as a technical term for "divine providence," *pronoia* goes back to Herodotus (3.108.2), then appears in Sophocles (*Oedipus at Colonus* 1180), then famously in book 10 of Plato's *The Laws*, and in Hellenistic Jewish writings it is present in Sirach and Wisdom of Solomon. For Philo in his treatise on providence *pronoia* is not the idea of God's being transcendent simply as voyeur, but transcendent as an observer and as an (efficient) cause.[25] Abraham "first grasped a firm and unswerving conception of the truth that there is one Cause above all (ἓν αἴτιον τὸ ἀνωτάτω), and that it exercises providence (προνοέω) for the world and all that is therein."[26] Here

24. One is put in mind of the lines of the poem "God Knows" by Minnie Haskins, quoted by King George VI at Christmas 1939: "Go out into the darkness and put your hand into the hand of God. That shall be to you better than light, and safer than a known way."

25. Aitken, "Divine Will and Providence," 288.

26. Philo, *Virt.* 216, quoted in Frick, *Divine Providence in Philo*, 44.

divine action is "the efficient cause of creation," with divine activity being in a sense separable from God's transcendent nature. The well-run cosmos makes a prima facie case that God is provident. In Philo's *Quaestiones et solutions in Genesin* 4.87 the combination is apparent: foresight and care (τὴν πρόνοιαν καὶ ἐπιμέλειαν); but in his *De opificio mundi* 171 it seems that "providence" is defined by care: "God exercises forethought on the world's behalf. For that the Maker should care [ἐπιμελέομαι] for the thing made is required by the laws and ordinances of Nature, and it is in accordance with these that parents take thought beforehand for children."[27] This "on the world's behalf" is the direct opposite of Fackenheim's conception, which one might call "providence by proxy." The last clause gives it away: caring means or demands "foresight." The two aspects are mutually dependent: God foresees because God cares. The fact that creation has a beginning confirms its "orderliness," even if matter is somehow preexistent. For Philo God's action of forming, as a transcendent cause, is always about doing something with what is before him. Yet as a Jew he adds that what God creates he also can destroy: this is "providence as judgement."[28] The biblically revealed God is "moral" and takes history (i.e., what humans do with creation and how they respond to guidance) seriously, as if God is One who "takes it personally."

Now when Philo is discussing his own contemporary situation in his *Legatio ad Gaium*, he makes it clear that although providence exists universally for creation, it acts particularly for God's people. It was no abstract doctrine for Israel. The theme of divine providence is sometimes more generally described by Philo as divine help, or perhaps "protection," as in *Legatio* 220, whereas according to *In Flaccum* (170), writes Peter Frick, providence is equated with God as "Champion and Defender."[29] This protection might actually be what salvation amounts to, at least at a visible level. In Philo's account, the Word of God or Logos, who in place of Plato's demiurge has shaped and executed creation, gives insight—whether through prophecy or intellect.[30] (*Pneuma*

27. Translation from Colson, *Philo*, 1:137. Unless otherwise indicated, all English quotations of Philo are based on this edition, with my own adjustments.
28. Runia, "From Stoicism to Platonism," 169–73. He argues (176) that Philo uses Stoic terminology in his discourse of total cosmic destruction, yet this is not so foreign, as an idea, to the Bible (e.g., Isa. 24–27), and, as Runia notes, for Philo cosmic destruction will be non-total, in the sense that some will benefit from the education (177). One might want to speak of a Platonizing then Christianizing of Stoicism, but part of that was a spiritualizing of OT historical concepts of divine action.
29. Cf. Frick, *Divine Providence in Philo*, 187–89.
30. Philo says as much at the conclusion of *Quis rerum divinarum heres sit*: "The wise man, therefore, is presented as the legitimate heir of the knowledge of the things here mentioned. Scripture affirms: 'On that day God established a covenant with Abraham, saying, "to your descendants I will give this land."' What land is indicated, if not the one mentioned before, to

seems to integrate creation at a lower level.) Philo did not want to leave the biblical history out of account, and he aimed to tie protology to his present day by means of Israel's history.[31] God is (*Leg.* 1.18) continually creative because the world decays. Salvation history is part of providence, and it provides lessons: the patriarch Joseph is a type of Moses, and what their characters have in common is valuable. In other words, Philo's is an Old Testament–informed view of history, and one wonders whether the New Testament writers would have thought very much differently. As he himself put it in *De opificio mundi* 10, the Father had in view the preservation of his children.[32] The context would suggest that he is referring to all creatures. *Opificio* 24.77 speaks of a particular care for humans, God's providing within creation; 46.135 speaks of how the intellect relates all humans to God. God works for the benefit of all humanity (*Prov.* 2.43); for example, natural motions like eclipses can serve as warnings (2.50). Creation is providence in the sense of God using things for the benefit of humanity according to an original plan. In *De providentia* Philo emphasizes the abundance of created good things (2.6). "So in the same manner, God, who is the father of all rational understanding, takes care of all those beings who are endowed with reason, and exercises a providential power for the protection even of those who are living in a blameworthy manner, giving them at the same time opportunity of correcting their errors, and nevertheless not violating the dictates of his own merciful nature, of which virtue and humanity are the regular attendants, being willing to have their dwelling in the God-created world."[33] God provided manna even for those grumbling and rebelling in the desert. One may here see Philo taking principles from the Old Testament concerning God's actions toward Israel and applying them to humans and the wider world more generally, and more abstractly; for example, the soul is to migrate as Abraham did physically, and providence includes a spiritual leading into transcendence. Philo is concerned that material abundance might be received in the wrong way and lead to greed and

---

which Scripture now makes reference? The fruit of this land is the firm and certain apprehension of the wisdom of God, by which he, through his powers which divide, separating all things, keeps the good things away from evil" (3.2, 4:445).

31. Siegert, "Philo and the New Testament," 180: "It would appear that only the Alexandrian crisis at the time of the governor Flaccus made Philo think of the concrete dangers and changes in world history, especially regarding his people."

32. *Opif.* 10: "For reason proves that the father and creator has a care for that which has been created; for a father is anxious for the life of his children, and a workman aims at the duration of his works, and employs every device imaginable to ward off everything that is pernicious or injurious, and is desirous by every means in his power to provide everything which is useful or profitable for them" (AT).

33. *Prov.* 2.6, 9:461–63; cf. *Decal.* 16–17. See Kaiser, *Studien zu Philo von Alexandrien*, 44.

pride (*Prov.* 12). As Peter Frick illustrates, Philo can take an incident from salvation history and draw from it a lesson about providence more generally. For example, regarding Exodus 3:3, in which an angel appeared within the flames of the bush, Philo supposes that "the angel was a symbol of God's providence (προνοίας ἐκ θεοῦ), which all silently brings relief to the greatest dangers, exceeding every hope."[34] It seems that in the passage Philo prefers this understanding of the angel as a symbol of a divine real presence to any notion that the angel was an image of "him who is" as such. In other words, providence is about God being immediately present and active to creation rather than about something mediated through a created agent—as equally "transcendent and immanent" (so, Frick). Moreover, God is present in his power (6.397b16–20), not in his essence. A summary definition appears at *De providentia* 2.3, where Philo writes: "God combines the two finest features of nature on the ground of fixed law in unbreakable union, that is, the leading and the caring for."[35]

To offer a simple stock definition with the help of Philo, himself relying on the Old Testament and the story of the people of Israel: providence is God taking care of things, which involves responding to humans in need and difficulty as well as ongoing supply of the goods of creation, and this according to some intentional, even planned action. Also, in Hellenistic Jewish literature from the period the order and harmony of creation is confidence-giving. Sirach agrees with the Stoics that *all things* have a purpose; and this appears to be a *novum* over against the Old Testament. God is no immanent principle, but one who exercises influence on the world, in the sense of a potter working on a pot from outside it toward something reshaped.[36] On this model God is in charge of the cosmos, although how world history comes under divine control is still a moot point. In the *Letter of Aristeas* we find a Greek philosopher praising the Jewish concept of providence (201), and the concept plays a role in the Greek "extra" sections of Daniel and 2 Maccabees (and even more so in 4 Maccabees' theology of martyrdom). However, by the time of Philo and Josephus *pronoia* had become a catchword to explain the actions of God and the cause of historical events (more generally or universally). Equally important, however, is the metaphor of the kingship of God, which seems to fulfill the same role, with a healthy amount of space for human free will in moral matters, as per the Hebrew חפץ, whereas רצון is the word in the Dead Sea Scrolls "to denote the guidance of God over

34. Philo, *Mos.* 1.66–67, quoted in Frick, *Divine Providence in Philo*, 53.
35. Colson, *Philo*, 9:461, altered.
36. Wicke-Reuter, "Ben Sira und die Frühe Stoa," 277. See, more fully, her *Göttliche Providenz*, 277.

human affairs. . . . God's care over humanity but not necessarily a predetermined order," and it seems to have the more basic meaning of "that state
of affairs acceptable in God's sight."[37] With reference to Sirach 33:7–15 it
seems that free will is actually encouraged by providence, which assures it
that the moral order exists.[38] By 50:22[39] God's interest seems to extend to
the history of Israel as a generous rule, one that invites human response and
reciprocity. It seems to involve the whole cosmos, through association with
particular Jewish history.

Now the standard line is that by way of contrast the biblical authors of
the New Testament were not particularly interested in thinking about God's
running the cosmos.

But What about "Providence" in the New Testament?

One key word in the New Testament is προνοέω, which one New Testament dictionary defines as "to give attention beforehand, to have in mind to
do, foresight."[40] This means to think about something ahead of time, with
the implication that one can then respond appropriately. In Romans 12:17
Paul uses the verb προνοέω when telling his Roman congregation, "Give attention to what everyone considers good" (AT). However, this does not have
God as the subject. Again, Romans 13:14 has Paul warning the Romans,
"Stop planning ahead so as to satisfy the desires of your sinful nature" (AT).
Likewise there is that element of forward planning in what the noun πρόνοια
conveys. Acts 24:2 has the somewhat sycophantic advocate Tertullus praising
the Roman governor Felix: "Your foresight has brought many reforms to our
[literally "this"] nation" (AT). In these three cases we have the word, but none
of these are very relevant to theological purposes.

Yet it might be argued that even if the word πρόνοια does not appear very
much in the New Testament, nonetheless a number of words in the New
Testament begin with the προ- suffix, used with God as subject, probably
owing to some influence of Hellenistic Jewish "wisdom" thinking. Indeed, a
series of words in the New Testament all beginning with pro- strongly implies
that the will and plan of God lead up to the taking-place of the events themselves.[41] Yet, contends Wolfgang Schrage, all the pro-suffixed verbs in the New

---

37. Aitken, "Divine Will and Providence," 292.
38. Wicke-Reuter, *Göttliche Providenz*, 284; *pace* Prato, *Il problema della teodicea*, 40. Cf.
Prato, "L'universo come ordine e come disordine."
39. Καὶ νῦν εὐλογήσατε τὸν θεὸν πάντων τὸν μεγάλα ποιοῦντα πάντη, τὸν ὑψοῦντα ἡμέρας ἡμῶν
ἐκ μήτρας καὶ ποιοῦντα μεθ' ἡμῶν κατὰ τὸ ἔλεος αὐτοῦ. Cf. Sirach 36:22.
40. Louw and Nida, *Lexicon of the New Testament*, 30.47.
41. Feldmeier, *Der Höchste*, 201.

Testament *are to do with Christ*, either in his first or second coming, and hence not with providence as such, which would be a creation-derived planned care for some in actuality and all in potentiality. Any hint of "divine care" has to do not with God's rule over creation nor even with special providence toward individuals, Schrage claims, but simply and solely with the special arrangement of the "Christ event."[42] If one is to speak of the idea of providence in the New Testament, then one may speak of it only with reference to the Easter resurrection event specifically as an intervention that was predetermined, which thus "proves" God was at work in Christ.[43]

By way of response to Schrage's reservations, first of all, one might object to his excluding Easter Sunday's divine activity from the overarching category of providence, undoubtedly special though it is. Second, the total domination of the New Testament by Christology in Schrage's treatment is also open to question. Schrage finds it hard to see any notion of providence in Romans 1:3 or 3:25, which seems right enough, but when it comes to Romans 8:28 ("We know that all things work together for good to those who love God, those being called according to purpose" [AT]),[44] the Christocentricity seems less clear. Although the "according to purpose" refers to the planned calling, the working-out concerns believers' lives in their wider focus, and for a brief moment Christ is not mentioned: all things work out for good to those indwelling that calling. As for the three relevant verses from Ephesians 1, the evidence is mixed. The first two of these, with their clear reference, at first sight support Schrage's case for Christocentricity (v. 5: "He destined us for adoption as his children through Jesus Christ, according to the good pleasure of his will"; v. 9: "He has made known to us the mystery of his will, according to his good pleasure that he set forth in Christ," where ἐν αὐτῷ, "in him," is clearly "Christ"). Yet it could be argued that these verses taken together contribute an account of something like a final cause ("sonship") and an efficient cause (Christ). The third of the three verses (v. 11: "In Christ we have also obtained an inheritance, having been destined according to the purpose of him . . .") is open to an interpretation that understands it as having to do with a cosmic power at work, a power not restricted to that which flows from the resurrection of Christ, albeit very much caught up with that source. God's specific work in Christ undergirds a wider providential plan.

42. Schrage, *Vorsehung Gottes?*, 137; see also my *Heart of Biblical Theology*. Unless otherwise noted, all translations are my own.
43. Schrage, *Vorsehung Gottes?*, 138.
44. Οἴδαμεν δὲ ὅτι τοῖς ἀγαπῶσιν τὸν θεὸν πάντα συνεργεῖ εἰς ἀγαθόν, τοῖς κατὰ πρόθεσιν κλητοῖς οὖσιν. Unless otherwise noted, all quotations of the Greek New Testament are from NA28.

In any case, James Barr's call to all theologians in the 1960s not to mistake words for concepts[45] reminds us that, of course, word studies can only be a starting place, not an ending. It could well be that a good number of images and semantic domains correspond to something that the philosophical tradition contemporaneous with the late Old Testament and the early New Testament and the later Christian and Jewish (in their different ways) theological traditions have understood as divine providence. Nevertheless, if the lexical evidence is so scant, it might also be the case that the conceptual furniture of the New Testament leaves no space for "providence" as an idea.[46] Indeed, according to Schrage, what the New Testament is about is a sudden change from one age, world, and order into another, very different one, in which conceptuality changes with a sea change of understanding. There is neither progress in history nor decline, neither in the ancient world nor now.[47] In short, not creation but instead "new creation" is the dominant theme of the New Testament.[48]

In any case, perhaps the lexical cupboard is not quite so bare. There are other ways of saying things similar to "providence" without using words with the prefix *pro-*. Semantically speaking, the verb ἐπισκοπέω, "to give careful attention to, to consider carefully, to guard against," is close in meaning to "to act providentially," as in Hebrews 12:15 ("see to it") and 1 Peter 5:2 ("watching over them" [NIV]).[49] These of course are examples of equivalents that are used of human, not divine agents, who, not least in the case of shepherd-pastors, stand in for God as he acts through them. Another semantically related verb is that which means "to be concerned for" (μέλει/ἐπιμελέομαι) and crops up at 1 Corinthians 9:9 ("Is it about oxen that God is concerned?" [NIV]) or in 1 Timothy 3:5 ("How can he look after / be concerned for God's church?" [AT]). Admittedly these two verses concern human agents principally, but again, they are about tasks delegated to human agents by God. Also, in Luke 15:8 (in the parable of the widow seeking diligently [ἐπιμελῶς] until she finds the coin), this is a parabolic representation of God's compassionate search for the lost.

Then there are the verbs that mean "seeing" with the extended sense of "seeing to" / "concern" (ἐπιβλέπω),[50] as in Luke 1:48 ("For He has looked [kindly] upon the lowliness of his maidservant" [AT]) or in Luke 9:38, where

45. Barr, *Semantics of Biblical Language*.
46. See Watson, *Text and Truth*.
47. Schrage, *Vorsehung Gottes?*, 268.
48. Schrage, *Vorsehung Gottes?*, 184.
49. Louw and Nida, *Lexicon of the New Testament*, 30.46.
50. Louw and Nida, *Lexicon of the New Testament*, 30.45.

the same verb is used by a man who asks Jesus to look kindly upon his son, for he's his only one. Then there is ἐφοράω ("look") in Acts 4:29, where the context is that of the apostles asking God to "look at their [the apostles' enemies'] threats": the sense is that of God's watching in order to protect the church, and "the focus is actually upon [divine] intellectual activity and concern."[51] Or sometimes the verb is just "to make," but in the sense of "to arrange" like the French *faire* plus verb, or the German *lassen*, and this can also have the sense of providential activity (Luke 1:25, where Elizabeth says: "This is what the Lord has done for me when he looked favorably on me and took away the disgrace I have endured among my people").[52]

If one thinks of a semantic map, then, to extend the discussion of Louw and Nida, somewhere between words for providence and words for divine will or decision lies the technical term οἰκονομία (household management),[53] literally indicating that which pertains to the law of the household. In 1 Corinthians 4:1 Paul styles himself as one of the managers (οἰκονόμους), bringing his congregations into line, and yet the context is that he is moreover a manager of the mysteries of God: for he is one of the stewards "of the mysteries of God," presumably working for the right distribution of spiritual goods for persons. This does not simply mean Paul's preaching of the kerygma about Christ; it also involves his channeling of the power of the kingdom. Gerhard Richter wants to privilege the patristic interpretation whereby this larger sense is taken seriously: it is not simply the ministry of salvation as such that *oikonomia* is about.[54] Rather, God takes responsibility for every member and for making sure this ministry all works together, by distribution and provision: in the parable of the wise steward in Luke 16:1–8 one can see an allusion to the "generous person" referred to in the Septuagint version of Psalm 111:5 (EV 112:5),[55] one who lends compassionately and will "economize" his words in judgment (or with the Hebrew: "conduct affairs with justice"). Richter resists seeing any eschatological sense of the parable,

51. Louw and Nida, *Lexicon of the New Testament*, 30.45. This brings to mind a question as to whether the Hebrew *yādaʿ* has a significant role in the Old Testament in developing the idea of providence. E.g., Ps. 1:6: "The LORD watches over the way of the righteous" (NIV; RSV: "The LORD knows the way of the righteous"). My thanks to Robert Banning for this observation.

52. Sterling, *Historiography and Self-Definition*, 358nn241–43. Sterling notes that ὁρίζω is used six times in Luke-Acts with the sense of "foreseeing": προορίζω appears only once, but significantly in Acts 4:28, and προοράω three times, "but only once in the sense of God's plan (Acts 2:31)." Cf. also Acts 2:25 (citing Ps. 15:8 LXX [the only reference to divine foreseeing in the LXX]) and 21:29. It should be observed that Ps. 138:3 also has the sense of divine foresight.

53. Louw and Nida, *Lexicon of the New Testament*, 30.68.

54. Richter, *Der Gebrauch des Wortes* oikonomia, 40–44, against the "heilsgeschichtliche" interpretation by Reumann, "*Oikonomia* = 'Covenant.'"

55. χρηστὸς ἀνὴρ ὁ οἰκτίρων καὶ κιχρῶν, οἰκονομήσει τοὺς λόγους αὐτοῦ ἐν κρίσει.

which is more simply about the "manager" God's generosity in the present,[56] and he notes that the Jerusalem Synod under Patriarch Dositheos took Psalm 111:5 to be a caution to right speech. The term seems to have connoted acting in a moderate, considered way and even to mean modesty in the context of dress and manners. As for the church as specific object, *oikonomia* more widely denoted the pastoral care of the church under God. Just as Joseph did in Genesis 50:19–20, so too in 1 Corinthians 9:17[57] Paul declares that he has been entrusted with the *oikonomia* or planned care and that even if this activity is his own, he is compelled to carry out God's plan in the service of God. One can speak of divine economy—that is, the carrying out of some intended sequence of events.

In the later Pauline Letters the term *oikonomia* is not restricted to the meaning of "apostolic proclamation of the gospel"[58] and has a theological use, as at 1 Timothy 1:4, where one is reminded that the teaching of the economy of God accords with faith (οἰκονομίαν θεοῦ τὴν ἐν πίστει) and not myths. This "economy" could indicate Christian practices (Dibelius, Bauer) or the plan of salvation (Jeremias, Cullmann) or, simply and more likely, God's "housekeeping" or action to manage the world and its events—for humans to recognize.[59] God is putting things into order as he rules over them, in the sense of Ephesians 1:10, fulfilling all this salvation in Christ for the furthering of another purpose—that is, the management or administering (*oikonomia*) of the fullness of the ages. Although not to be totally identified with a plan of salvation, and not limited to the salvation of individuals, this *oikonomia* relates to what Ephesians 1:10 declared, that God purposed to sum up all things in Christ.[60] In Ephesians 3:9 Paul says he was commissioned to preach the gospel and make clear the *oikonomia* of the mystery and other things designated by "plan" words. This mystery, unlike other myths, seems something available to be known in its outworking, unpacking, and consequently in its articulate expression. Of course the word *oikonomia* shifted its meaning when it was used theologically, for God is more "Lord" of the universe even as he is manager of it, and hence his managing overlaps with this kingdom rule. Yet in the cosmos the biblical God takes the place of Nature from within the Stoic system and redefines it in a "personalist" direction.[61] Paul could have

56. Richter, *Gebrauch des Wortes* oikonomia, 37. (He relies on Hans Weder's reading here in *Die Gleichnisse Jesu als Metaphern*, 265–66.)

57. εἰ γὰρ ἑκὼν τοῦτο πράσσω, μισθὸν ἔχω· εἰ δὲ ἄκων, οἰκονομίαν πεπίστευμαι.

58. Richter, *Gebrauch des Wortes* oikonomia, 89.

59. Richter, *Gebrauch des Wortes* oikonomia, 83.

60. Eph. 1:10: εἰς οἰκονομίαν τοῦ πληρώματος τῶν καιρῶν, ἀνακεφαλαιώσασθαι τὰ πάντα ἐν τῷ Χριστῷ.

61. Richter, *Gebrauch des Wortes* oikonomia, 85.

picked up the Stoic understanding[62] from the atmosphere surrounding him, even if not necessarily through reading Stoic texts, although one should not underestimate his studies at Tarsus, depending on how one reads Acts 22:3, for it seems Paul's education was not only in Jerusalem. (Or, alternatively, did he make a late acquaintance with Stoicism while in Rome?) Hence *oikonomia* is the special action of God, not the history of salvation as a process, yet it is more deliberate in its correction and guidance of world-in-event than any mere "Stoic" ordering of the cosmos.

The bringing about of the fulfillment of the ages is something that relies on the recapitulation (ἀνακεφαλαίωσις) of the past. Richter emphasizes that any providential cosmic ordering of the present-future builds on the obedient death of Christ, but surely it does not march quickly and directly from the cross to the eschaton as between two points on a plan or roadmap, as he seems to imply.[63] Just why Richter wants to play the cross and soteriology off against the incarnation, wherein Creator and creature are united in a way that reinforces the idea of God's care for humanity, is hard to discern. It is surely better to see the two aspects (salvation of humans in the church and divine activity to rule over creation) to be concurrent and in parallel, rather than in series. This is in keeping with what began with Luke (Acts) but was made more manifest by Eusebius, that whereas Old Testament history was part of universal history and preserved wisdom throughout its course, universal history was "larger" than Old Testament history, even though after the coming of Christ universal history became tagged and tied to church history.[64] Yet the fullness of providence goes through cross, resurrection, and Pentecost in a way that transforms what providence is, even that of "the Lord will provide" at Genesis 22:8, 14. Ever since the patriarchs existed, salvation and providence have been related; ever since the church existed, they are so close as to be intertwined.

So much for the objection concerning the paucity of the term *pronoia*, given the presence of other terminology. As for the burning theological concern that the New Testament witnesses to a new creation introduced by Christ rather than a corrected and enhanced old one that belongs to the doctrine of ongoing providence, Reinhard Feldmeier is right that Jesus's teaching of the Father's care for creation has less to do with the reliability of a fixed creation order being maintained than with the power of God to sustain and remake, a power that Jesus would in turn reveal in more focus. Similarly to Schrage,

---

62. For *oikonomia*, see, e.g., Epictetus, *Diatr.* 3.22.4; Plutarch, *Stoic rep.* 1049F–1050B. See also Malherbe, *Light from the Gentiles*, 306.
63. Richter, *Gebrauch des Wortes* oikonomia, 55.
64. See Löhr, "Heilsgeschichte und Universalgeschichte," 535–58.

Feldmeier concludes from this that one who has faith and confidence, even a hermeneutic of trust in what was expected and promised by the Son of God, can see creation as a place of God's continuous activity, not with respect to a teleological ordering of the world, but only with respect to an exceptional divine salvific action in the "end-time" season (καιρός).[65] In other words, this is a belief not in an unmodified continuous creation, but rather in creation's being rebuilt since Christ and to be perfected in the age to come, into a creation that only the believing beholder can see, once she is inspired by the example of Christ's resurrection. Schrage is equally clear that this is not quite the same as standard versions of "providence in the here and now." Again, he insists that New Testament writers clearly avoid the "Middle Platonic" notion of *pronoia* with its idea that humans all participate inasmuch as they can recognize cosmic order; rather, in the Christian gospel the divine will comes to question and upset reality, which is itself a perversion of order.

Nonetheless, it can be contended that the summons to people in the gospel is to begin with themselves and a skewed vision, so that they may better see creation as it was intended and may repent of mis-seeing it. This includes less thinking of a purpose inherent to creation and more thinking of God's consistent purpose for it, mysterious no doubt, but vital and including much refashioning and revising, but, *pace* Feldmeier, that renewing work did not only begin with Christ. And so, while one might be justified in including this "correcting" of the world and its ways as true providence, distinguishing it from mere continuous creation, with all that idea's connotation of predictability and effortless development, one should not devalue creation by thinking "new creation" has superseded and replaced "old creation." Better to see creation as joined on to God's providential action, to transform it by relating it to concern for the people of God, a special providence that corrects even as it directs and sustains.

Providence, Christ, and Living Meaningfully

Part of what Schrage and Feldmeier object to in the idea that a doctrine of providence can be found in the New Testament is an understandable reluctance to classify Christology under a more generic heading of "providence." After all, if Christology were allowed to control providence and not the other way round, then nobody would find Hitler's claim to be chosen by providence the tiniest bit plausible. Yet, first of all, that is not how "doctrine" works:

65. Feldmeier, *Der Höchste*, 200.

within the doctrine of the church the doctrine of the sacraments might use-
fully be listed, but that does not make the sacraments or the section on them
subordinate to what is said in the material on the church, and much less
is sacramentology merely an expression of ecclesiology. So when it comes
to Christ, to say that his advent, life, death, resurrection, exaltation, and
promised return are "providential" or belong to divine providence does not
mean that Jesus is just some expression of the idea of providence in story
form and that his coming cannot do anything to make a difference to things,
providence included.[66] Of course, as I shall discuss later, the very being of
Jesus, his life, his death, and his resurrection are providential, and they contain providential elements, but not in such a way as to remove the mystery,
initiative, and singularity from Christ, as though he could be explained in
terms of primary and secondary causality or be reduced to being a species
of a genus (God's care for creation). Still, the concern in speaking of "new
creation" is to link Christ's saving history with ongoing providence in the
not-so-obviously "religious" parts of life of believers and unbelievers, and
Barth is right to remind us that a God who is not a living God, available in
the seemingly smaller things, is not God at all.

Part of the problem can be viewed in what John Barclay says about Paul
in contrast to Philo. He thinks, quite understandably, that Christ makes the
difference:

> For Paul, God does not just "name" those whom he blesses (in the sense that
> he recognizes some preexistent value, even one created by himself), he "calls
> them into existence," in the sense that he creates them *ex nihilo*, by a process of
> election that *transforms* those whom it chooses, ungodly though they be. The
> problem in Paul's eyes is not just that there is no such natural "worth" (creation,
> and humanity within it, is radically subject to sin, Rom. 3.22), but that to bring
> in here the category of "worth," even if it is as diverse and qualified as we find
> it in Philo, would be to make the Christ-event (and the election of Israel) a
> socially, morally or legally explicable event. But for Paul it is precisely because
> it does not fit into any such schema that God's grace-in-Christ is a peculiar and
> radical form of grace—radically threatening and radically hopeful.[67]

Yet this should not obscure the fact that providence, which moves from
the past to the future through the present, even when it is given a particular
color by a soteriological twist that includes the name and reality of Jesus,

66. This is something that Albrecht Ritschl seemed to come close to saying in *Die christliche Lehre*.
67. Barclay, "Grace within and beyond Reason," 18.

↘ both includes *and* is transformed by the salvation story of Jesus. Or, put conversely, the "Christ-event" does not fit any schema, true, but neither does it stand outside of the schema (in terms of morals, laws, salvation-historical patterns, and customs). As Christ in the person of his Spirit enters into the realm of providence and reshapes it, perhaps breaks and remakes it in places, not simply calling to it but redirecting our vision and then our wills to God's seeing and will that are given form in Jesus himself, he refers his hearers backward and forward to the living God of Exodus 3:14.

↘ What might be called "ethical implications" also arise from a belief in providence, a belief that there is such a thing, even if the details are sketchy. The apostle Paul's own remarks about being "poured out like an offering" (of incense perhaps) in Philippians 2:17 and 2 Timothy 4:6 (AT) are illuminating when one considers that Paul has less interest in his own life span than in the stages of his apostolic mission as part of God's universal plan for the gospel.[68] Yet this selflessness means a metaethical awareness for all who would be prudent in the way the gospel redefines "prudence": "What does it advantage a person to gain the whole world, yet lose their soul?" (Mark 8:36 AT; see also parallels). "Soul," or whatever *psychē* means in the Gospels, sounds like something that extends beyond the duration of the "individual life-project." This has a corresponding subjective (and ethical) side: prudence of that redefined kind trusts in its *Gegenüber* (foil) of divine providence and is an image of that careful divine foreseeing. Unlike the man in the parable (Matt. 25:24–25 AT), it does not say, to paraphrase: "I knew you were a hard man, . . . so I buried the one talent you gave me." For, having God as the personal, ultimate, and sense-making principle that will bring one salvation and redemption in the here and now, one can do no other than clasp the furthest-removed citizen of the earth as one's brother and make a real effort with foresight.[69]

And yet behind Paul stand Christ and God, who are themselves prodigal and profligate in love, while allowing a fair bit of room to creatures to maneuver, even while offering moral guidance. As William Hasker puts it, "Now, I maintain that if it were generally believed that things are really like that [God simply won't allow harm to happen], this would have a very serious effect on our incentive to live morally good lives and to take responsibility for the welfare of those around us."[70] It is not reasonable to expect routine intervention. God's persuasive activity is en route to the final rest promised in Ephesians 1:11 (NIV): "In him we were also chosen, having been predestined

---

68. Avemarie, "Heilsgeschichte und Lebensgeschichte bei Paulus," 381.
69. Platzer, *Geschichte, Heilsgeschichte, Hermeneutik*, 275.
70. Hasker, *Triumph of God over Evil*, 192. However, his target—that God is entirely pleased with the world exactly as it is, that there is no single fact he would wish to alter—is a straw man.

according to the plan of him who works out everything in conformity with the purpose of his will." As things stand, God is not yet totally in control: yet he is progressively controlling. To hear Hasker again: "God, who potentially has absolute, meticulous control exactly as posited by theological determinism, has willingly chosen to become self-limited by creating free persons on whom he bestows limited but nevertheless quite significant powers to affect both their own lives and the world around them."[71] That is true, but along with "self-emptying" kenosis and descent go ascent and fullness or pleroma: with God, what goes down must come up. Providence is a struggle for God, just as Jon Levenson insisted in writing about the creation narrative in Genesis. It is not about God's easy mastery but his limiting of the destructive powers within a now-flawed creation: a theology of omnipotence *in potentia*, a power that is already working through and helping transcendence, which is not the same as escape.[72] God provides a providential pattern for prudence to work with and within.

Now, to speak of providence is not quite the same as the theology of "graced creation" after the manner of *nouvelle théologie*, according to which creation by nature includes a relation of dependence for being sustained and growing, with a mystical lien or connection existing in creation as part of the image; here grace is part of nature's capacity that is brought to life through Christian baptism/conversion. This is much more than just a potential; it is part of our actual nature even before conversion. "Grace was not so much an additional story built upon the already complete house of nature as an inner nourishing sap that drove the seeds of nature from the dark earth through the obstacles of sin upward to the vivifying light of God."[73] Yet providence does not mean a force acting within creatures but rather a power and a presence that come from outside even if alongside, usually through some other creature or event.[74] For Karl Barth, the economy of grace is visible ("whose will is done and is to be seen in His election of grace, and therefore in the history of the covenant between Himself and man, and therefore in Jesus Christ"),[75] whereas providence is mostly invisible, whether in the everyday or uncanny.[76] The point is to believe that there is a providence, rather than knowing what it is.[77] It is

71. Hasker, *Providence, Evil and the Openness of God*, 153.
72. Levenson, *Creation and the Persistence of Evil*, xvi.
73. McDermott, *Love and Understanding*, 2.
74. We shall return to this in the closing chapter.
75. Barth, *Church Dogmatics*, III/3, 3.
76. A point well made by Duthie in his very useful "Providence in the Theology of Karl Barth."
77. Duthie, "Providence in the Theology of Karl Barth," 70, with reference to Barth, *Church Dogmatics*, III/3, 243.

something intelligent working behind the "grace-events" of miracle and healing and conversion, baptism and proclamation. This should inculcate a spirit
of "astonishment." It is not so much about God's occasional intervention as
it is about supervising a course of events even while being present within it.

If God cares and does so in such a way that he plans ahead but is flexible
enough to accommodate how his gifts and his plans are to be received, then
those who are believers should do likewise. One sees God's intentional and
purposeful activity combined with an openness to interruption and objection,
accommodating but still guiding and directing. To think like God here is to
think *with the grain of the universe*, a phrase from John Howard Yoder that
Stanley Hauerwas drew on as the title of his 2001 Gifford Lectures, "The Grain
of the Universe."[78] The church, then, is to think more in terms of responsibility than of rights, because a lot has been given to believers, in grace, pardon,
and restoration. Communities as well as individuals are encouraged in the
Lord's Prayer to invite God down and in, but the attitude of prayer then may
hopefully become simply a prayerful attitude, operating even when one is not
actively at prayer. God takes the initiative, as when Christ says prophetically
in the Apocalypse of John, "I stand at the door and knock," yet conversely
there is the command to disciples by Jesus in the Sermon on the Mount to
"seek, ask, knock": these two images reinforce each other rather than cancel
each other out, as with Jacob, who by wrestling with the angel grew stronger
through repeated exercise.

John Webster has commented: "Providence is an aspect of the wonder
of the overflow of God's abundant life."[79] Yet that profligacy is and is to be
understood as informed and qualified by other truths. "Moreover, distributed
in this way, providence is informed by other tracts of Christian teaching—
most of all the doctrine of God, but also, for example, creation, soteriology
and anthropology."[80] This helps to keep the doctrine's Christian flavor. For
example, linking it to a sound doctrine of creation means that providence
is not something precarious; it is not a matter of trying to keep something
going that does not have stable foundations. That should give one confidence
to invest in creation's story with one's story, giving one's life to order and
yet movement.

As a reality, then, the doctrine of providence is also bridging or connecting
doctrine or mind-set "backward" to creation as well as "forward" to soteriology. As well as objective, a belief in it is "subjective" as an interpretation

78. Published as Hauerwas, *With the Grain*.
79. Webster, "On the Theology of Providence," 166.
80. Webster, "On the Theology of Providence," 160.

of and attitude toward the world. We cannot really approach it immediately objectively, as Webster would, as "revelation" or derived from revelation[81] or say that this moment is where all other moments have been leading to (as with Wolfhart Pannenberg). In Webster's account it sounds as though God's activity in the world and his gift of the eyes to see it are one and the same motion. However, often a fuller account of God's ordered activity takes a while to discern, and written accounts in Scripture usually belong to some considerable distance "after the fact." The point is that God's objective providence is worked out inductively from faith-filled observation, even if such an observation struggles to give a universal account of things.[82]

This inductive process depends on a growing vision that is more local and personal and hence less prone to skepticism for attempting to give a "God's-eye view." In a sense that is how things work. Should one pray for peace in the Middle East if one hasn't had some sense of answered prayer in smaller matters? Should giving an account of a practice precede the performance of it? Is not having a sense of a thing prior to an explanation of it? Well yes, in the sense that one needs to understand something for oneself before explaining it.[83] So providence is an article of faith, not of sight, but on the other hand it is faith in something other than itself. It is not that providence "exists inside a believer's head." Rather, the life-form of faith receives providence as a living thing and has an impression of it and insight into its wider-scale form and vitality. To quote Oliver O'Donovan: "It is the mark of true freedom that it can see the moral law from a new vantage point as a witness to God's purpose to order and bless the life of the human race. . . . As we call God 'Abba! Father!' our agent-identity is united with that of the Son."[84]

However, the divine action in the world need not be salvific as such, exclusively for the conversion of believers or about-to-be-believers only. To take an obvious case: the New Testament does not present the resurrection of Jesus

81. "Providence is knowledge of God, and known as God is known, in the act of faith. The creaturely act of faith is the work of the Holy Spirit, a point at which reason is caught up in an antecedent gracious causality which enables the intellect to see God and all things in God by locating its operations *coram Deo*. This is why faith in providence is only derivatively 'subjective,' an interpretation of and attitude towards the world. Primarily and strictly it is objective, generated and sustained by a movement from outside reason. Its objectivity is of a special kind, in that it is derived from 'revelation,' that is, from those acts in which God makes himself present to disordered creatures in such a way that they are caused to know that against which they have blinded themselves." Webster, "On the Theology of Providence," 163.

82. Bernhardt, *Was heißt "Handeln Gottes"?*, 480.

83. *Verstehen* as part of making sense of something in one's life precedes *Erklären*, the conceptual and verbal explanation or interpretation after all. This distinction is associated with Wilhelm Dilthey (1833–1911), professor at Basel, from his *Poetics* (1887).

84. O'Donovan, *Finding and Seeking*, 8, 12.

as having happened only for those who witnessed and accepted it and hence were saved by it in some sense. The characters who disbelieve it are presented as willfully refusing to look at the facts rather than those who believe being presented as being gullible, but it affected all of them and the course of world history, and whatever their response, they are caught up in it. To hear Eric Gregory: "We must not champion 'saving history' so zealously that the kingdom of God ceases to be the purpose and destiny of *all* history."[85] That is not a totalizing claim for the Christian church, but a recognition that the one who creates humans and history can be trusted in his claim to the creation in its movement. Providential action is wider than salvation action, even while including it. Faith that sees providence takes a wider picture into account, while never thinking that its viewpoint is universal.

Bigger Than Theodicy

But it can't be all about ethics. Let us consider humor; *not* humor that is a means to an end, sarcasm or mockery to demean an opponent, to deflect serious matters, or to undermine a friend. No, humor that is almost an end in itself. What is often needed for soul-healing is not just time to get over tragic events, but time to see what can be learned from those events and in a good enough humor, a peaceful state of mind to be able to think clearly. And this is not so much to explore the relationship of tragedy to comedy as, rather, to think in terms of the religious aesthetic of appreciation and thankfulness. The believer who is thankful for her salvation through Jesus Christ and is thankful for sunshine or for toast with honey is thankful to the same source of blessing and in the same manner: this can take place at moments of, or moments just after, pain and sorrow. The very idea of joy in ordinary matters (humor) moves us to a place that is not simply the sphere of moral philosophy or theology but to something prior to that: the sense of being grasped and given a foundation. This carries the risk of delusion and a false foundationalism, but it should be remembered that joy is not the vindication of innocence in pain and sorrow— "I was right after all!"—but a reward that is gratis, for that has no particular correspondence to moral endeavor, as Job found out, but does contain a proportionate relation to the outreaching of the God of creation and providence to him, although there is probably an indirect correlation. Job is vindicated for caring about moral order, his own and that of God and the cosmos, and joy comes from knowing that an order exists and a Sovereign behind it.

85. Gregory, "Boldness of Analogy," 76, quoting O'Donovan, *Resurrection and Moral Order*, 65–66.

Barth insisted that one must answer the question of providence from within, with reference to Jesus Christ, and, as Luther did with all doctrines, Barth made it answer the seemingly pointless suffering of the innocent by emphasizing not meek acceptance but a place for protest as well as faith, to struggle with contradictions.[86] As with Job, questions and attempted answers to our deepest questions are not silenced; in fact they are given room, yet they do not have the last word. Life is to be wondered at, grieved over, then wondered at again.

The question of theodicy (why does God allow evil?) arises where the disaster is either natural or is of such a scale that attributing it to people's immorality seems somehow irrelevant, no matter how much human beings contribute to a natural disaster by careless stewardship of resources or faulty building specifications. God by definition (Love, All-Goodness) cannot be the moral cause of evil, although, inasmuch as he is responsible for making creation and creatures in the first place, he is the ontological cause of the instruments of evil and the agents of sin. To be human means above all that we have active agency that works along with God's creative and active presence (as in the German Enlightenment, from Leibniz to Goethe to Hegel), an agency that pays respect to "I" and to "Thou" as meaningful units, and not so much attention to atoms and molecular chains.[87] Attempts to speculate about the problem of metaphysical evil, to say, for example, that God kenotically allows creation to continue in its imperfections, are all very well, but they stand on the speculative side of the river staring at the darkness of mystery, rather than at the positive power of the God of life. Rather than just hoping for time to make things feel less significant, providence and past faith, present love and future hope give a perspective to tragedy, even where there is as yet no obvious resolution of tragic events.

86. Barth, *Kirchliche Dogmatik*, III/3, 252.
87. Hildebrandt, *Leibniz und das Reich der Gnade*, 197.

TWO

Alternative Themes to Providence in the Bible

In this chapter we examine biblical themes that overlap with providence but that do receive much more attention in contemporary theologies of the biblical material—namely, (1) God as the source of life, (2) continuing creation, (3) divine rest, and (4) the eschatological bringing of all to perfection. I will argue that viewing these things from the standpoint of "providence" gives a better account of the biblical witness.

God of the Living

It is already the best part of a decade since Reinhard Feldmeier and Hermann Spieckermann issued a book-length statement proposing that what unites the biblical witness is an insistence that God is an ever-active source of life.[1] The title *Der Gott der Lebendigen* alludes to Jesus's famous appeal to the "God of the living" ("He is God not of the dead, but of the living" [Mark 12:27]), after telling the Sadducees that God is the God of Abraham, Isaac, and Jacob, and thus offering a thoroughly axiomatic definition of God as he does so.[2] Likewise for Paul the "God who justifies" (Rom. 8:33) is just as much the God

---

1. Feldmeier and Spieckermann, *Der Gott der Lebendigen*; ET, *God of the Living: A Biblical Theology*.
2. Feldmeier and Spieckermann, *Der Gott der Lebendigen*, 516.

who "calls into existence" (4:17). This New Testament teaching intensifies the Old Testament message, for Deuteronomy 30:15–16 offers a choice between life and death or between good and evil, before stating plainly in verse 20, "The LORD is your life" (NIV), not just the giver of life.[3] The people of God certainly receive life from him; the Song of Hannah in 1 Samuel 2 carries a note of protection in life, and Psalm 118:17 says, "I will not die but live" (NIV). These are expressions of trust that demonstrate that in and through God life may endure through death.[4]

Yet Jesus's "spin" on the issue is intriguing. He names three *dead* people to make the case that God is God of the living! In his Matthew commentary Ulrich Luz spots a reference back to Exodus 3:6, in spite of the absence of "(burning) bush" in the Matthean version, and he writes of a continuation of meaning ("Sinnkontinuum") between that verse in the Torah and the New Testament's use of it here. To that end Luz takes the first and second of the Eighteen Benedictions ("God of the patriarchs," "God who makes alive the dead")[5] as part of that "continuum of meaning," albeit their provenance might be later. "God is the God of the living" is not the second premise (so that those patriarchs of whom God is the God who must be alive), but rather the conclusion—that he is God of the living even now. I agree that this conclusion is implied in the text of Matthew, but on simpler grounds—namely, that the present tense of "I am" (Matt. 22:32), drawing on the Septuagint text of Exodus 3:6 as glossed by that of 3:14 ("I am who is"—Ἐγώ εἰμι ὁ ὤν), uses Exodus to reinforce the present nature of God, who draws all those in relation to him into the present.

It takes Luke to make things more *explicit* by adding four little words: πάντες γὰρ αὐτῷ ζῶσιν ("for all are alive to him"; Luke 20:38), possibly an explanation, just in case his gentile readers would not get the tight rabbinic logic. God tells Moses that the patriarchs are still alive. It might not be that they are alive in the full bodily sense of a future resurrection, but their existence and, more significantly, the ongoing existence of *all* human beings (*if* that is the referent of "all") are what the Sadducees must realize.[6] R. T. France sees in Matthew a restriction of the resurrection to those within the covenant, and certainly one could argue that the Lukan πάντες refers in an exclusive manner to these. This restricts providence to a special providence,

3. Feldmeier and Spieckermann, *Der Gott der Lebendigen*, 540.
4. Feldmeier and Spieckermann, *Der Gott der Lebendigen*, 546.
5. Luz, *Das Evangelium nach Matthäus (Mt 18–25)*, 266. Philo, *Sacr.* 5, speaks of Abraham gaining imperishability, "being the same as the angels."
6. Even if the life to come is in some ways very different from life before death: Michael Wolter, *Das Lukas-Evangelium*, 657.

delivered in terms of ongoing existence of a protected sort. Nevertheless, however many people this applies to, the point is that "the covenant by which [God] binds himself to them is too strong to be terminated by their death. To be associated with the living God is to be taken beyond the temporary life of earth into a relationship which lasts as long as God lasts."[7] John Nolland points to the detail here that "'God of' in connection with the Patriarchs points to God in *his role* of savior, protector, and deliverer."[8] There does seem to be some connection between God relating to individuals (not just to a nation) and those particular, named people being preserved in life. This might be close to the meaning of Wisdom of Solomon 3:1 ("But the souls of the righteous are in the hand of God"), without our having to specify that these are the righteous already in heaven, as distinct from being "in purgatory" or anywhere else.

To focus more directly on the theme of "living" as a key one for understanding divine providence, in a review of Feldmeier and Spieckermann's book, Georg Fischer affirms that the coauthored work "presents *systematically many major aspects* of the biblical God, e.g., his name(s), love, omnipotence . . . , always dealing with both parts of the Bible. . . . Their concentration on the aspect of God giving *life* ('Gott der *Lebendigen*') is appropriate for the biblical God."[9] Fischer concludes by suggesting that the joint approach safeguards the "rightful place" of the Old Testament in a way (he opines) it gets lost in Brevard Childs's biblical theology, where the Old Testament is viewed in too much of a Christian perspective. Whether or not Fischer is right to object to Childs here, the way in which the biblical evidence is treated in *Der Gott der Lebendigen* reflects a refreshing nonconfessionalism, almost to the point that the book is more a description of theological experience of others long ago than an attempt to affirm a present-day conception about God. If the emphasis is more on human religious experience reflecting God, one does wonder a little, however, if the step still has to be taken that outlines just how God is indeed reflected and what he "looks like" in that mirror of human believing experience. Clearly God is not identical with that experience. To perceive God in that experience one might need to be still and silent, abstaining from naming God so that the Word might speak what he wants heard at any particular moment, emerging from his powers (only in *that* sense is God "plural") out of that silence. Franz Rosenzweig put it well: instead of his name we call him Lord ("Statt seines Namens nennen

7. France, *Gospel of Matthew*, 840.
8. Nolland, *Luke 18:35–24:53*, 967, quoted in Nolland, *Gospel of Matthew*, 906, emphasis added.
9. Fischer, "Biblical Theology in Transition," 83.

wir ihn Herr").[10] Certainly the term *life* cannot be used of God unequivo-
cally, but only analogically.

Also, as Walter Klaiber notes in another review, in *Der Gott der Lebendigen* any unity of the two Testaments is *contrastive*, to use Bernd Janowski's term, which avoids any unwelcome suspicion of *heilsgeschichtlich* or
salvation-historical continuity. However, surely there is a *conceptual* continuity between the Testaments in that Old Testament concepts get thickened
("verdichtet") in the New Testament, developed from what the Old Testament
announces. In *Der Gott der Lebendigen* it is mostly the Old Testament where
the themes start, so it takes the initiative and sets the agenda, as it were. There
is perhaps a sense that the New Testament makes the Old Testament themes
more generalized and abstract, not least that of *life/living*, but *that* could be
understood as seeing the Old Testament's concern with life in the present to
give a distinctive quality to talk of *everlasting* life in the New. The two parts
of the canon are in a relationship of both correlation and contrast. Klaiber
also puts his finger on something of substantive theological importance: for
Feldmeier and Spieckermann, humans can perceive their lives rightly only
when looking in the light or context of God.[11] Yet if this insight is theologically important, how does the work of Feldmeier and Spieckermann and
others of the guild illuminate the *God* of the living? And hence the God
who gives life *today*? A flurry of biblical anthropology has arisen in recent
European scholarship. Again scholars are looking to the Bible for things it
might tell us about *us*.

Now, of course the names of God do show God *in relation* to creatures.
Even *pantokratōr* in its earlier usage in the Septuagint is relational (toward a
heavenly host, if the nuance of the Hebrew original *ṣəbāôt* is understood to
be at all preserved), thus linking to the sharing of lordship between God the
Father and the Son (in the NT, 2 Cor. 6:18; Rev. 1:8; 4:8; 11:17; 15:3).[12] Also relational, the name *kyrios* now (with the NT) refers in the first instance to how
Jesus participates in God's honor. Philippians 2:5–11 speaks of a transfer of
name to the Son from the Father: both Father and Son can be called "Lord."

Moreover, along with names come qualities: *ḥesed* could be translated
as "steadfast love," but just what is the difference between *'ahăbâ* (the more
common name for love) and *ḥesed*? The point is that *ḥesed* gets taken in a
direction away from *'ahăbâ* to a point that *ḥesed* becomes something that
God has chosen (by his *'ahăbâ*) to lock himself into, as it were. Yet *'ahăbâ*

---

10. Rosenzweig, *Der Stern der Erlösung*, 427, cited in Dalferth and Stoellger, introduction
to Dalferth and Stoellger, *Gott Nennen*, 18.
11. Klaiber, review of *Der Gott der Lebendigen*, 653, with reference to Janowski, *Ein Gott*.
12. Hartenstein, "Die Geschichte JHWHs."

frames this and is always the ground for God's affective sense of faithfulness toward his people.

A number of scholars of the Hebrew Bible would balk at any talk of God so binding himself. Thus in Friedhelm Hartenstein's programmatic essay "JHWHs Wesen im Wandel,"[13] the Munich Old Testament scholar argues that it requires the standpoint of the Christian church to make a biblical theology out of the Old Testament, to reconcile inconsistencies and contradictions, and ultimately to try to "fix" or pin down the untrackable God of the Hebrew Bible. Accordingly, he considers the approach of Feldmeier and Spieckermann as too "normative" regarding the original meaning of the various texts, which he thinks is rather loose until a confession (or even a New Testament) steps in to tighten it. He feels the Bible to be both more complicated and more demanding than the coauthors would have us believe. The witness in the biblical text points to some events outside it and bigger than it, whatever these were. Therefore, one should think of a dialectic of sense experience and the evidence of traces of God in history, even looking for the identity of God manifested in his activity. What we can say, as Walter Zimmerli once admitted, is that the biblical God in fact *does change*. Even if God's essence and will remain somehow as constants, he reveals himself in connection to an increasingly widening total reality, and even as he becomes more transcendent as the biblical traditions develop, so too his relationality invites questions about himself.[14] Again, this call for a biblical theology, while rightly concerned to say something about God, can be interpreted (as by Feldmeier and Spieckermann) as too complicated to be understood by human minds. Fine, but it is not too far a stretch from this position to the conclusion that if God can be everything, then what he is means nothing, and that obviously is a counsel of despair.

How could it be otherwise? Well, if we regard statements about God produced from experience not to be reducible to that experience and as something Israel still believes, even when the experience is different and difficult, and something that forms the core of a transformed belief in the universal God of the gentiles (with the NT), what about God's working to give life in the present? It is very easy to have a biblical theology of God that is stretched between past events and future salvation. Is God any less real and focused in his being for being *now* (temporarily) absent and ungraspable? Yet, one might add, if the primary datum, the people's *experience of God* past to

---

13. Hartenstein, "JHWHs Wesen im Wandel," 12–13. In this programmatic article, Hartenstein develops further the theme of these two aspects of the biblical God. The same volume of *TLZ* contains Klaiber's review of *Gott der Lebendigen*.

14. Hartenstein, "JHWHs Wesen im Wandel," 13.

present, undergoes change of fortune, that does not mean that God himself does in his activity, since he is the one who decides to reveal himself or hide himself (even when apparently or truly in re-action), in such a way that he is not directly himself bound up in the action. Even where God appears to be "suffering alongside," this is not usually understood as limiting or qualifying his capacity to show his power simultaneously, and in doing so to reveal himself, becoming spoken of "cataphatically."

Perhaps what Fischer complained about in his review of *Der Gott der Lebendigen*, the losing sight of the discrete layers of textual growth, does not matter so much if one is content to arrange the sequence of material not so much sequentially as synchronically, as the "literary" snapshots or "impressions" of God.[15] Why should the imagery of these texts in their slight abstraction from their historical context not continue to be valid through centuries and even across Testaments, albeit like camera filters laid on top of each other, so that, as Childs insisted, the earlier view does not get trumped by the later?[16] Something like this seems to have motivated the biblical theology of Feldmeier and Spieckermann in that their book actually traces themes much less than one might expect, but more often presents sketches of theological moments. In other words, this approach does not *oppose* O. H. Steck's insistence that the change in theologies is essential for understanding a God in successive actions through the redactional "Fortsetzung" (continuation) of traditions, but this approach emphasizes more the symphonic theme-likeness of the biblical message, as themes pop up again and again.[17] God's revelation does not then matter so much for what it says about human religious *history*—no matter how fascinating—as for what it says about God toward the world, although one will seek illumination from understanding the different times, emphases, and ideologies of the biblical writers. Steck repeatedly insisted on the impact of the Word of God in terms of the effect on political and social life-networks ("Lebenskonstellationen").[18] Theological expression comes from the whole range of life experience from different points, in the time-conditioned, hermeneutical reception of the

15. If Isa. 28:16 is very late in the sequence, then when 28:15 speaks of a "covenant with death" that presumably separates from God and declares in v. 16 that "a hard stone of judgment is laid" (AT), that is the end of hope until one learns that life breaks through in the NT's death of death. Perhaps Isa. 26:18 ("covenant with death shall be annulled") and Dan. 12:2 hint at this in the very brief glimmers of hope they each supply.

16. Childs, *Biblical Theology of the Old and New Testaments*, 70.

17. Steck, *Gott in der Zeit entdecken*, 70–71, refers to "Gott und sein zugewandtes Wirken, da ist der tragende, durchgängige Inhalt der biblischen Überlieferung" (God and his associated effects, the major consistent content of the biblical tradition).

18. Steck, *Gott in der Zeit entdecken*, 18.

Word by places and generations.[19] It means looking at the effecting of divine decisions, as these are captured in the narratives of the prophetic books, as, for example, Isaiah 13 to 27 moves from the judgment of nations to the judgment of the world, or as Isaiah 33 to 39 prepares the way for the rise of Zion, or with Jeremiah 21 to 24—that is, from God giving the chance to avoid total destruction by Nebuchadnezzar to his setting apart of those hostages taken with Jeconiah to Babylon.[20] What one might want to *add* to Steck's outline is to highlight both the universal range of God's reach and the power of his word—for example, Jeremiah 23:23–24: "Am I a God near by, says the LORD, and not a God far off? Who can hide in secret places so that I cannot see them? says the LORD. Do I not fill heaven and earth? says the LORD." Then verse 29: "Is not my word like fire, says the LORD, and like a hammer that breaks a rock in pieces?" God comes close in order to make things happen through his powerful word.

This is, then, indeed politics as theology. Yet there is surely a place for what Steck too quickly calls "abstract, textual memes connected by catch-word."[21] Jeremiah 30:10 ("Jacob shall return and have quiet and ease") helps interpret the rejected promise of Isaiah 30:15 ("In returning and rest you shall be saved; in quietness and in trust shall be your strength. But you refused"), which in that context has no sense of hope or "second chance." Prophetic books and episodes are linked thematically, and this reinforces the sense of God's being in control, as promise and prophecy get reapplied. The note of planning is also to the fore, not least at Isaiah 28:28–29 ("Grain is crushed for bread, but one does not thresh it forever; one drives the cart wheel and horses over it, but does not pulverize it. This also comes from the LORD of hosts; he is wonderful in counsel, and excellent in wisdom.").[22] Here a parable concerning the natural world gets applied to Israel's history.[23] Just as Amos 3:7 notes that nothing happens without YHWH telling his prophets, so, according to Isaiah 44:25–26, God's Word and announced plan work in all things.[24] By

19. Steck, *Gott in der Zeit entdecken*, 134.
20. Steck, *Gott in der Zeit entdecken*, 180.
21. Steck, *Gott in der Zeit entdecken*, 175–76: Steck reports that Childs and Claire Matthews both dismiss Steck's work *Gottesknecht und Zion* for not understanding that "Zion" is metaphorical. Steck replies that he prefers to anchor "Zion" to history because the prophetic God is very much involved in history and politics.
22. "Wenn der Bauer in seiner Arbeit planvoll vorgeht, dann verweist das auf eine allumfassende göttliche Ordnung." (When the farmer proceeds according to a plan, then it points to an all-encompassing divine order.) Steck, *Gott in der Zeit entdecken*, 175–76.
23. Werner, *Studien zur alttestamentlichen Vorstellung vom Plan Jahwes*, 29.
24. Werner spots a recurring theme: "Die Erkenntnis, daß das Leben des Einzelnen, das Leben des Volkes nach einem göttlichen Plan gelenkt wird, und der Glaube, daß Jahwes Geschichtssouveränität die eschatologische Heilszeit herbeiführen wird, sind an ihren Ursprüngen das

working together, Word and Act perform a dance of mutual reinforcement and interpretation. We can be grateful to this more recent scholarship for refusing to see history as all about great men and high politics and insisting, instead, on seeing it as about the collected (second-person plural) people.

As long ago as Walther Eichrodt's seminal article, the ordinary Israelite's experience of "being saved" and "being kept in life and guided" have belonged together. Hence providence is something that has meaning for the experience of the people of God from the exodus onward. The study of it is not a speculative science.[25] Really it can often mean simply coincidence from the viewpoint of humans, until on reflection a triangulation of these observations suggests inferences that allow for a "higher" explanation. This can include things that don't make a lot of sense to people, as in the asylum protection ordered in the law of Exodus 21:13 (48). For Eichrodt, the divine care could be grasped only in individual events; it could not be grasped in biographies—as though whole ordinary life-stories made a shapely sense; one could say that only of the God-chosen leaders (49) in the Bible (cf. historical books or Acts). Now, putting it that way in 1934, when history as shaped by personalities was hardly a salubrious matter, was grimly ironic, even if it was meant to be about Moses, David, and Jeremiah. According to Isaiah, providence is to be found in the individual event as experienced locally; it is there that one can see the meaning of the whole history, not in some (fictional) whole *Gestalt*. Even negative events have their part to contribute (53), leading to a faith in God's steering of the history of humanity with reference to the law, especially the Noachic covenant, as some sort of "algorithm," requiring no direct intervention from God (55–56). In this sense, theoretical theodicy or any claims to see great continuities of God's action within people along a continuum of a march through time are ultra vires. Jeremiah 15:15–21 and Psalm 16 show how the doctrine of providence requires momentary experience as the true substance of one's being (55–56). Job's message is that revelation is required for any comforting-if-oblique answers—to one's own questions arising out of one's own experience, eventually. Again, Eichrodt thinks this is rather rare in the Bible. There is no sense of a comfort of being caught up in the emanation of the divine being from which creation takes shape; there is no talk even of

---

Ergebnis einer Reflexion über die individuelle Lebens- bzw. die Volksgeschichte." (The recognition that the individual's life, the life of the people are steered by a divine plan, and the faith that Yahweh's sovereignty over history will usher in the eschatological time of salvation, are in their origins the result of reflection on the life of the individual or people.) Werner, *Studien zur alttestamentlichen Vorstellung vom Plan Jahwes*, 302.

25. Eichrodt, "Vorsehungsglaube und Theodizee im AT." Subsequent citations to this work in this section are in parentheses in the text.

God's taking humans into his counsel. There is just providence. Eichrodt, however, by his focus on "famous individuals," has overlooked the importance of the ongoing, if sporadic, experience of God's action as witnessed to by the prophetic books regarding the people as a whole.

Rightly, then, Steck will not deny the place of the existential thematic,[26] and he reaffirms that in the classical prophets the themes are not as "individualized" or as "timeless" as perhaps in Psalms / Wisdom of Solomon or preclassical prophecy. According to the Prophets, as things change, God reserves the freedom to persist or surprise peoples and families. Theology, therefore, too, is in motion as God teaches his universal plan through his action.[27] As to whether the vision at the end of Isaiah concerns only a small remnant to be saved is open to debate. Actually, in Isaiah 66:22–24 the vision seems positive and generously inclusive,[28] with a number of "rebels" receiving exemplary chastisement:

> For as the new heavens and the new earth,
>   which I will make,
> shall remain before me, says the LORD;
>   so shall your descendants and your name remain.
> From new moon to new moon,
>   and from sabbath to sabbath,
> all flesh shall come to worship before me,
> says the LORD.

And they shall go out and look at the dead bodies of the people who have rebelled against me.

The vision seems on the whole a rather positive one for those in receipt of special providence. Although less so for those outside this sphere, it appears that these constitute a minority (as rebels) who lose out through providence being universal in its extension. Likewise a good case can be made that Isaiah 24–27, although it deals specifically with Israel, has a theology of history that can hardly be termed "apocalyptic."[29] Instead, it is a positive message of hope

---

26. Steck, *Gott in der Zeit entdecken*, 189.

27. The content of the classical prophetic books for Steck is nothing less than "the announced and set-out plan or way of God that he made with Israel and the nations through obstacles, rebellions, negations, and delays in the time-frame of creation but especially from the Assyrian to Persian times (Isa. 40–55, Hag., Zech. 1–8), a way that he has taken and takes and will take until a future completion." Steck, *Gott in der Zeit entdecken*, 188 (AT).

28. Feldmeier and Spieckermann, *Der Gott der Lebendigen*, 414, on Isa. 66:24 and Dan. 12:2.

29. See D. G. Johnson, *From Chaos to Restoration*, 99: "But our study has demonstrated that the author of Isa. 24–27 was decidedly positive about Yahweh's activity within this world. He

within the political and historical frame, of the revival of a nation and others, by God's initiative. In the darkest reaches of the canon, hope in God is not forlorn.

One could read the text of, say, Jeremiah in sequential order so as to follow the historical development of God's purpose. Jeremiah 44:15–23's oracle concerning Ishtar affirms a stability in creation that is already thematized in Jeremiah 7:5–7's discourse on household and nurturing and feeding, which looks back to an ideal in Manasseh's time, and arguably to a creation idyll, a "given," which might not be wholly lost.[30] One wonders whether once a crisis has passed, the Lord of hosts might just be God of the everyday. Yet that is the ideal of restoration. As is pithily expressed in Micah 4:4 ("Everyone will sit under his own grapevine and fig tree" [AT]), this helps one to grasp that creation faith is the basis of all that follows in Israel's belief and that it holds all epochs and developments "timelessly" together. There is much to be commended in H. H. Schmid's argument that Israel's faith did not begin with a salvation-historical credo but rather, like its neighboring belief systems, *moved out from* a shared belief and understanding of creation on its way to becoming "distinctive" as a faith in a God who saved a particular people. At this point one may speak with good reason about a specifically Israelite theology of history (as with Gerhard von Rad). Yet history has theological relevance only and precisely because it gains meaning in the context of thought about the order of the world, which phenomenologically is bound with creation[31] and, one might add, with God as the one who holds these two things together. As we shall see in the next section, creation does not so much continue, whatever one might think of Psalm 104 and Psalm 65:6–8 (where the LXX treats the verbs as present participles), with their word of continuing divine activity. No, salvation hinges on a new creation or an *ever-renewing succession* of new creations. This note is in unison with what one might affirm about Luther's theology, with its joint emphasis on the goods of creation and the requirement of continual shedding of noetic sin. However, the main point is that it is creation. Even a word study like that of the *Theological Dictionary of the Old Testament* on *šālôm* will reveal just how much the cessation of distress is the same thing as the reemerging of quiet and order: back to creation and strength and "normality," as fever and disorder die down.

---

believed that the evil city, the historical city of Babylon, would be overthrown (25.1–2; 26.5,6), that there would be a resurrection of the nation (26.19), and that these historical events would mark the beginning of the new age."

30. Cf. McKane, *Jeremiah*, 2:1089.

31. H. H. Schmid, "Schöpfung, Gerechtigkeit und Heil," 19n110. It is not that creation and salvation are different strands to be brought together as von Rad thought in his "Die theologische Stellung des Schöpfungsglaubens bei Deuterojesaja."

It is at the very least implicit that Israel started with "creation" and "life" and on the basis of this developed an awareness of how creation and life might be reaffirmed in the face of destructive forces. Somewhat ironically, H. H. Schmid's approach[32] was vindicated by von Rad's last book (*Wisdom in Israel*); and this move toward the priority of the Universal Creator God was certainly welcomed by Lothar Perlitt and Walter Brueggemann. Spieckermann himself offers the triad of *Schöpfung-Gerechtigkeit-Heil*: *Gerechtigkeit* (roughly "justice" or "righteousness") is here perceived as the mediator of the divine will into the universe and is not itself personal or creaturely righteousness but is the ordering that that state of salvation (*Heil*) presupposes. Yet where that righteousness dwells, there too God is close—and this for the whole world, not just for Israel. After catastrophe this salvation as reordering is indeed needed.[33] Konrad Schmid gives this expression in his (originally 2000) essay "Zeit und Geschichte," where he proposes that the Priestly cultic theology be understood as about setting aside sin (rather than so much as about sin's avoidance), with a stabilizing force deriving from worship, which relativizes time and change in all their chaos: "Thus is the end of history being stabilized through the cult."[34] Likewise, for the New Testament the "surprise" of the incarnation puts an end to any idea of worldly human lordship over history that Daniel 2 might envisage by bringing God into that history. So one might well question whether history has *no* place as part of a happy contingent and everyday life in ideal conditions. Change can be change for the better and part of the gift of renewal. Contra Eichrodt, individual lives are concerned with historical-political realities, and their faith and faithfulness are stretched in believing God is at work in those realities, but also, contra H. H. Schmid, history is not believed to be "objectively" chaotic, and Konrad Schmid's view of cultic stabilization is better glossed as "prayerful and worshipful recognition of God's power to act."

The new heaven and new earth, which together provide the backdrop of the goal of salvation for the new people—this is the new Jerusalem of Isaiah 65. Both creation and new creation need to be thought of with reference to the other. The step that Feldmeier and Spieckermann are unafraid to tread is that of tracing this trajectory of creation–new creation through the "intertestamental" book Wisdom of Solomon. Here the gift of righteousness is redefined as one for those made in God's image who deserve to be kept safe in his hand enjoying immortality.[35] Spieckermann counts this divine activity

---

32. See also H. H. Schmid, *Gerechtigkeit als Weltordnung*.

33. Feldmeier and Spieckermann, *Der Gott der Lebendigen*, 408.

34. K. Schmid, "Zeit und Geschichte," 315.

35. Feldmeier and Spieckermann, *Der Gott der Lebendigen*, 418. Subsequent citations to this work in this section are in parentheses in the text.

as both *creatio continua* (continuous creation) and *Heilsgeschichte* (salvation history), since it is about the story of Israel within that of the nations.

In my view it might be better to see God's story *with creation* as the *providential* story of the nations, in which God acts through Israel, making an offer to Israel (directly) and nations (indirectly) that invites faith and trust, which is something over and above conservation, cooperation, and direction of life: again, it is *renewing* creation. The God of providence is preserving and guiding *toward* salvation, without this story being quite the full salvation history as such. To put it in "history of religion" terms, YHWH "becomes king" (Ps. 46:10). He doesn't start out manifestly as such, but adopts and adapts the properties of *El Elyon*—as in history, so in cult. This is not about God becoming more involved and more dominating of creation (for that is settled with primordial creation), but rather it is about his revealing to Israel in and through their historical sorrows and joys just how wide (the whole cosmos) and far back (to creation) his universal jurisdiction reaches. People are won over as they perceive this power and glory.

What is interesting is that in the second central section of the Feldmeier-Spieckermann theology (entitled "Gottes Zumutung"; literally "God's imposition") the argument clearly shifts to an emphasis on the cultic (*not* the forensic) aspect of "righteousness" (342). Human rejection of God's love brings on wrath, which includes God's hiding of his presence and divine distance. One certainly cannot accuse Feldmeier and Spieckermann of overlooking the issue of sin and alienation and how God deals with (and does not ignore) this in Israel's offerings and institutions.

Indeed, they make it clear that this is different from what Job as a righteous person experienced: his story was *not* about sin, disgrace, and grace (338).[36] Yet, according to Feldmeier and Spieckermann, in the Prophets that *is* the case for sinful and "unclean" Israel-Judah, even if these Scriptures insist that divine wrath is less part of God's person than love is. Moreover, this is explicitly made clear in the New Testament. God's property is to have mercy: that is, his long-suffering (*langmütig*) nature presupposes a prior will to judge that gets restrained. Isaiah 28:14–16 is a key text, demonstrating the "compact with death" that separates the people from God, with a "hard stone of judgment laid," according to Isaiah 28:16 (AT). The idea of the stone, even shorn of its "New Testament" (1 Pet. 2:6) associations, involves sweeping away the compact with death and seems in some sense salvific, even while destructive, in the sense of a negative canceling out a negative. Wrath is more just a force than

36. On p. 361 reference is made to MacGregor, "Concept of the Wrath of God in the New Testament," 103–4.

truly part of the Lord's essential makeup (361), and in the Hebrew Bible this wrath is actually "taken out on" the prophet as God's representative, not least Jeremiah, thus foreshadowing the New Testament's witness of God taking sin and wrath into himself (374). The relevance of all this (largely Christian) soteriology to the wider theme of life is perhaps revealed in the following sentence: the theology of the cross attests the powerful presence of God in the midst of suffering and death (340). The cross witnesses God's creative power calling what has died back into life, in the same way that through it God demonstrated his love according to Romans 5:8. The New Testament's account of what was the case for Jesus Christ and what it is to be "in Christ" is a special, emphatic example of God reasserting his presence. The idea is that God operates in this kind of way with his presence regularly, thus drawing a moribund creation back into life, as in Isaiah 26:19 ("Your dead shall live, their corpses shall rise. O dwellers in the dust, awake and sing for joy! . . . The earth will give birth to those long dead.").

One can certainly read the experience of the psalmist in that way too. What Feldmeier and Spieckermann offer is extremely insightful. Yet perhaps their way sometimes puts things in extremely dramatic terms and seems to hitch the model of God's action to occasions that are exceptional, with a drastic divine response, rather than anything quite like the quiet, hidden work of a *Deus absconditus* (a God who is hidden), who as such is silently trustworthy rather than "dark" (in the sense of a Being to be *feared* while one waits for the *Deus revelatus*, "the God who is revealed"). Reflecting on God's silent but efficacious activity rather than on the themes of divine presence and promise of future hope—with outwardly visible divine action preserved for salvation history, when, as it were, the train of divine operation comes out of the tunnel—could have helped Feldmeier and Spieckermann to more closely and helpfully consider providence as a biblical topos.

To repeat: for *Der Gott der Lebendigen*, between creation and salvation stands not "providence" but "righteousness" (of a "cultic" sort, related to the divine presence, and needing to be called closer by worshipers). Konrad Schmid, too, doubts that any place can be left for *general* providence in this scheme.[37] A soteriology of presence and conscious response is what makes providence providential. The fear that "the ethical" may get lost when people get swept up in providentialism makes these scholars rightly cautious about losing sight of human responsibility. Now, what the biblical prophets appeal to is no longer about individual doing and reward, but has to do with God's initiating and leading the course of history more broadly. Yet surely what God does for his

---

37. K. Schmid, "Wenn die Vorsehung ein Gesicht bekommt."

people has universal effect, as Gamaliel observed at Acts 5:38, indicating that something needs to be the will of God for it to succeed, for that which comes from human initiative is doomed to fail. The focus of providence is on God's leading of Israel, Jesus, and church. Thus while righteousness is what God provides in salvation, such salvation is the particularizing of this providential provision for a peculiar people, and accordingly *there can be, more widely, providence even without righteousness* as the outside penumbra of that core of salvation activity, although the margins will be drawn toward the center and affected by it. Nor should one reduce God's action in the world to its moral ("righteous") aspect, cultic or otherwise, even though his action includes that.

Take, for example, the ark narrative of 1 Samuel 4:1–7, where it seems that God is working in response to sin: that is even the main or first theological "point." Now, this would seem best labeled "soteriological," in the sense of God's being responsive and because the term presupposes some fault or flaw, as per the more general thesis that the Old Testament narratives are more about the history of salvation than about providence. In the psalms God is believed to know all (cf. Ps. 11:4–5), yet in Psalm 139 the psalmist asks God *to* know him / test him (vv. 23–24), and Patrick Miller infers: "There are some things God does not know about us without some process of testing, searching, and probing."[38] It is that activity that is not so much salvific as it is formative of one who wants to go further in life with God. Similarly with Psalm 81:7, where God recalls how he tested Israel in the desert: that is part of what it means for him to provide, just as in the case of his testing of Abraham in Genesis 22. Salvation might need to be involved, but possibly not, whether for the speaker of Psalm 139 or that of Psalm 81 or even Abraham: Abraham had obedient faith, and that saved him, even if this was a response to God-driven initiatives.

The second theological point is that of upholding or restoring the balance of a *moral* order—in a manner on the one hand similar to the Anselmian or even Grotian atonement theory, in that it is the order, not God himself, that needs "restoring." Yet there is not *always* in the Old Testament a clear presupposition of sin, or of enemies to be saved from, just as not all Levitical sacrifices are for sin or disorder. "In a number of Psalms we find reference to or praise of God's creative activity alongside or intimately associated with the Lord's salvific work and the maintenance of justice in the universe."[39] The Lord's upholding life and upholding order are interlinked, right down to the level of the person, as in Proverbs 16:1: "yet from the LORD comes the answer to the tongue" (AT). The point of Proverbs is that even in an everyday context

38. Miller, *Lord of the Psalms*, 13.
39. Miller, *Lord of the Psalms*, 55.

God is not haughtily "above" ordering things for his sake and glory.[40] Disappointment and pain often lead the psalmist(s) to ask God in to take charge, in order to overcome the imbalance of negativity in the universe. The psalms are of the genre of *təhillâ*, in the sense of drawing up a case, but also that of *təhinnâ*—a pleading for grace, with an appeal to consistency of God: "for your name's sake." If this sounds as though human prayer is in some fashion a part of the dynamic of divine activity in the universe, that is just the point.[41] The Bible speaks of God's providential activity under the rubric of blessing, and it knows a continual provision of the matrix of nature and history in which "the world and those therein" may exist. The Bible also knows a veiled but real providential activity to preserve and enhance human life. The absence of intercessory prayer in the Joseph story is an important clue.[42] God acts anyway, and many beneficiaries are none the wiser concerning his activity. One can trust creation only inasmuch as God is sustaining it, even repairing it. There is a need for the covenantal pole or axis and a liberating soteriology, to some extent, but part of the saving purpose is to put the creation order back on course, even as the believer is led by a mysterious plot sequence to confess his or her sin, offer a sacrifice, and ask for mercy.

Providence is thus both God's onlooking of human activity *and* his work in the fashioning of hearts, which might not necessarily involve *metanoia* (conversion). Psalm 33:13–15 ("The One who looks down . . . on the inhabitants of the earth, who fashions the hearts of them, and observes all their deeds . . ." [AT]) stands at the center of things, theologically positioned midway between Isaiah 40–45 and the later development in Wisdom of Solomon and Sirach. The Lord is in control of the world right down to the matter of human hearts, whether these acknowledge him and are participants in covenantal salvation or not.[43] Moreover, according to Spieckermann, the world takes concrete shape in God's reconciling and redeeming. We might paraphrase: God has work to do, he is active toward creation, and he is intelligently monitoring it in order to redeem it in the future. The important thing is not to talk too much, in Romantic fashion, of the world being God's temple to indwell, or of the earth having the power in itself to restore itself, or even of something

---

40. Miller, *Israelite Religion and Biblical Theology*, 77.

41. Miller, "Prayer as Persuasion," 352. Also, in a chapter in *Israelite Religion and Biblical Theology* entitled "Prayer and Divine Action": "Several texts attest to the fact that God is not simply open to prayer at this point but depends *upon such prayer to affect and effect God's actions*. The instances in Jeremiah where the Lord forbids Jeremiah to intercede suggest this indirectly" (453). Cf. Balentine, "Poet as Intercessor."

42. Miller, *Israelite Religion and Biblical Theology*, 461.

43. Cf. Ps. 32:15 LXX (EV 33:15): ὁ πλάσας κατὰ μόνας τὰς καρδίας αὐτῶν, ὁ συνιεὶς εἰς πάντα τὰ ἔργα αὐτῶν.

called Mother Nature or the planet as a partner with rights. Konrad Schmid rightly opposes those who would wish to keep God—and, for that matter, "the natural realm viewed as creation"—out of their considerations of ecology and conservation and who proceed as though the human species were the measure of all things, even as it chastises itself.[44] Schmid singles out the resolutions of the World Council of Churches at Vancouver in 1983 for critical attention. Humans arrogantly try to pretend that their own works can spring them high above creation, high enough to be independent of it.

The Hebrew Bible, where it deals with "creation," is much more ready than its ancient Near Eastern equivalents to accentuate the Creator/creation distinction and to put *Homo sapiens* firmly in the latter category, and hence "in its place." For Luther, "creation out of nothing" was a doctrine that was easier than the incarnation to believe in and hence was fundamental, more suited for beginners and holding first place in the Apostles' Creed. But we cannot speak of creation without a Creator, and hence faith in the Creator is first required to grasp that God's activity in the world (providence) is mediated through the "given" of creation and created order. Creation is no "mere metaphor," another vague way of loosely saying that God is present in the world, although worryingly. The theology of providence today has largely retreated to this position. As both Barth and Dietrich Bonhoeffer in the last century emphasized, a biblical theology's task is not one of spiritualizing the world but of perceiving its worldliness—that is, its dependent autonomy in all its *Weltlichkeit* (worldliness or secularity), as something created and established as an "other" vis-à-vis God. One might simply want to add that God's providence includes God's affirming faithfulness toward the world, while also judging wickedness and unbelief. Providence keeps the gift of creation pristine through ongoing renewal, and so there is less an ontology of (continuous) creation than a phenomenology of providential action toward creation. Even if one avoids the risk of emanationism and pantheism, it is not enough to affirm that God is the source of life, for one needs to say, *positively*, that God is powerfully and voluntarily active in his world on the basis of creation as "already given."

Creatio Continua and Providence

Despite Genesis 1 having no place for the vocabulary of the eternal (*'ôlām*), Psalm 136 does speak of creation as God's act of eternal love.[45] Some sort of

---

44. K. Schmid, "Einführung," 9. Also see, in the same volume, "Zum Alten Testament" and "Zusammenschau."

45. Feldmeier and Spieckermann, *Der Gott der Lebendigen*, 38.

"continuous creation" (*creatio continua*) here seems fundamental: creation out of nothing (*ex nihilo*) less so, since overemphasizing the latter would tend to push "creation" away, back into the distant past, and make it seem not immediately relevant. Hence in his concluding essay in *Schöpfung: Themen der Theologie*, Schmid contends that *creatio ex nihilo* in no way should be allowed to overshadow *creatio continua* as that which the Bible cares about.[46] It would be better, he thinks, if we lost the idea of creation as "first cause" (*causa prima*), since this reinforces the tendency to see even God the Creator as one who is stuck back in the long-gone past, with his best days and work very much behind him. In any case, creation is not once and for all completed, but is necessarily repeated, time and again, lest creation fall back into nothingness.[47] The Bible never says that the earth was created holy.[48] Even the early chapters of Genesis were never written for ethical instruction nor to provide a romantic ideal or idyll to get back to. There is no place for sacralized romanticism of Enuma Elish–style.

Schmid is quite happy to mix natural and graced categories together: the world owes its (continued) existence to God's coming to it—a thought that Spieckermann had also taken up in *Der Gott der Lebendigen* with the section heading "Gottes Zuwendung" (God's attention). The idea is that creation is an ongoing field for the exercise of God's power, which is "saving" in the sense that it presupposes chaos, in order to overcome it. As we have just seen, Schmid would insist that one must maintain the biblical vision of the "worldliness" ("Weltlichkeit") of the creation, its "worldliness" if not quite "secularity." To speak truly, creation is somewhat "accidental," yet despite its being not "necessary," it is nevertheless "worthy." According to Schmid, the discovery of vital, natural forces in the early modern age has encouraged a kind of reenchantment of the world that seemed to have gone missing in the later Middle Ages.[49] Our care for the planet is predicated on its fragility and also—what might at first sight appear a paradox—on its God-given ability to self-repair through its own regenerative powers. God's self is already there to be seen in creation. He gives his creation space but is ready to come to it. According to 4 Ezra, God provided a second age for humans that would suit their fallenness. *Creatio prima* comes only after a belief in *creatio continua* has been established: one works one's way back to what creation is by considering what God has done with it.

There is a lot to agree with here in Schmid's argument. Yet, if one is to stick with the rather bland category of *creatio continua*, does one not miss a

46. K. Schmid, "Zusammenschau," 328.
47. K. Schmid, "Zusammenschau," 328.
48. R. Anselm, "Systematische Theologie," 225–94.
49. See Lauster, *Die Verzauberung der Welt*.

sense of the need for re-creation to be radically new and at the same time a free work of God in preserving, working with, and directing? It is unclear just what these natural forces are that can amount to assistance to human beings in time of need. Surely God works anew with what is the case, rather than merely extending a creating action continuously. God's "act of eternal love" in Psalm 136 is perhaps not the same thing as God's "eternal act of love." One might venture that it is not a "real relation" in God, but more some gift-like action calling for reciprocal response from creatures.

Two other contributions, the first that is important for the collection *Schöpfung: Themen der Theologie*, may warrant reference here. Friedrich Graf's article "Von der creatio ex nihilo zur Bewahrung der Schöpfung"[50] traces how "creation" as a doctrine has been stamped by that of divine sovereignty as part of the doctrine of God. Graf's claim is that for the Lutheran orthodox, creation extended to God's ruling action in the present: thus, *creatio continua*. He noted (on the basis of Carl Heinz Ratschow's work) that the Reformer Melanchthon was more concerned with this present divine action than he was with matters "in the beginning" and any *creatio ex nihilo*. This emphasis on continuing creation became even more pronounced at a time of crisis: "conservation" in particular, as the first part of the larger tripartite doctrine of "providence in creation," received much attention. Lutherans also emphasized the close coworking of God and humanity (*concursus*). The Reformed, claims Graf, denied this, preferring a *concursus praevisus* (a foreseen concurrence), where human action is only a reflex of the divine initiative. However, as Rainer Anselm argues in his contribution to the same volume, both sides were trying to find a place for God's activity in the aftermath of the *De auxiliis* controversy of the early 1600s.[51] Graf thinks that *concursus Dei* (concurrence of God) was less the second part of a doctrine of "providence" and more a reaction to the demands of the incipient Enlightenment, as represented by Descartes. In other words, there took place a stage-by-stage development: from "creation as God's continual conservation of the world" to "creation as concursus," where it is all about humans and God working together, with God increasingly understood as the junior partner.

Now, Graf might be in danger of creating the wrong impression here, since *concursus* belongs to sixteenth-century theology as much as to that of the eighteenth, and "conservation" is not just the intellectual result of a snap reaction against crisis, change, and uncertainty, but is a doctrine older than Thomas Aquinas. The other thing to say in criticism of Graf is that an

50. Graf, "Von der creatio ex nihilo zur Bewahrung der Schöpfung."
51. R. Anselm, "Schöpfung als Deutung der Lebenswirklichkeit," 239.

interest in providence does not always mean that the idea—far less the terminology—of *creatio continua* was used. If anything, this term was resisted,
since it could connote emanationism, and also suggested in its connotation
of "tinkering" that God's creation was never in any sense settled or "good"
such that it made sense to say that he rested from it and thereby drew a line
under it. Providence has been and is a more pleasing category, one that implies
God's maintenance and redirection of the given creation. It is unlikely that
Lutherans any more than the Reformed thought of God's activity as merely
adding to what creatures were doing anyway or "gracing" it, as Graf implies.
There is a sense, of course, that God's providential action takes the created
realm as he finds it, so that God does work with creation, as well as direct
it (*gubernatio*) in that he also takes fresh, uncalled-for initiative, which God
is not *bound* to take, action that is a good deal more than "enhancement."

To continue with Graf: he observed that the "substance ontology" of the
Lutheran orthodox, criticized by Eberhard Jüngel and Richard Schröder but
defended by W. Sparn,[52] was combined with a strong teleology. Then, with
Schleiermacher, divine action became transposed into becoming the limit of
human subjective apprehension, while the flip side of this anthropocentrism
was a wider and wilder pantheism. On the conservative-reactionary side "creation" was used to buttress the idea of natural order, with God as strongly
subjective (Otto Zöckler), and in representing God in this way, this use of
the doctrine of creation was a new development, unlike anything to be found
in early modernity. Further, what has been lost in most recent developments
(perhaps in Moltmann supremely) is any metaphysical hierarchy: most is
handed over to humans as the agents who allow a divine yet kenotic creative
power as an extra resource. Accordingly, with God no longer "in heaven,"
nothing is guaranteed as safe from destruction anymore. At best, "God"
stands for the limit, or *Grenze*, to human self-transcendence, as a counter-
weight to human hubris. What does have explanatory force in the realm of
this natural providence and continuous creation is the notion that "the whole
makes sense of the parts" and that that "whole" may exercise an influence on
individual decision-making.

One might want to combine this diagnosis with that of Reiner Anselm in
the *Schöpfung: Themen der Theologie* itself. Anselm mistrusts traditional
theology's picture of God in himself as far removed and giving tacit approval
to what goes on below. The problem of early-twentieth-century Protestant
theology in Germany was not, as is often believed, that it posited "two kingdoms," but that God's kingdom was seen as hovering over them both at far too

52. Sparn, review of *Johann Gerhards lutherische Christologie*.

safe a distance. Anselm opposes this with a God as Trinity who is fully in the world, offering his energy for creaturely participation. God affirms "human becoming" as not yet known but something to be worked toward, not set in stone by "nature," for all that given preconditions ("Vorbedingungen") have to be taken into account. While not forgetting self-limitation as part of the future-oriented ethical life, which God wills, with Eberhard Jüngel we seek out future possibilities ("Zukunftsfähigkeiten"), not actualities. Also, Bonhoeffer reminds us that the natural is only provisional en route to redemption, and anything that excludes Jesus is unnatural. Anselm's further talk of trinitarian energy as providing creatures with new possibilities sounds enticing, but it does not seem obviously biblically rooted.[53]

To get back to the biblical evidence, Terence Fretheim is quite right to observe: "There is an ordered freedom in the creation, a degree of openness and unpredictability, wherein God leaves room for genuine human decisions as agents exercise their God-given power. Even more, God gives them powers and responsibilities in such a way that *commits* God to a certain kind of relationship with them. This entails a divine constraint and restraint in the exercise of power in relation to these agents . . . [thus a] relationship of integrity."[54] Philip Clayton adds that while the God-world relation (as Charles Hartshorne saw) is dipolar,[55] it is so only in that there is also much asymmetry, since we are constituted by our free finite relatedness whereas God is not. He can, however, have a consequent nature that is properly "kenotic." In taking the initiative, God gives his all. However, the object and subject of dependence are clear and unidirectional. This is no charter for monergism, as someone like Maximus the Confessor would insist. "Covenant" is an expression of a "continuous" conception of creation, a conception that means that God has built a principle of "new start" into history and life. But is that how God works? There is not much room in the biblical prophets for consultation, even if God lets them into his secrets so that people later on can acknowledge it was God's work, as in the programmatic Amos 3:7 ("nothing happens without YHWH telling his prophets" [AT]).

If creation becomes the basic doctrine among all others, and this gets defined as *creatio continua*, then what place is left for providence? Surely it seems better to think that God supplies the resources and the model but leaves it to creatures to impose it. However, it is hard not to think of "continuous creation" as implying God constantly bringing in new stuff. It is better to

53. R. Anselm, "Schöpfung als Deutung."
54. Fretheim, *Jeremiah*, 39.
55. Clayton, "Creation *ex nihilo* and Intensifying the Vulnerability of God," 21–24.

believe[56] that each new life is not part of a continuum but is created, and wonderfully so, as Psalm 139:14 famously tells us, although the Septuagint interprets this verse as having more to do with the psalmist's awe at the universe around him, perhaps not really understanding the idiom of the Hebrew "to be made miraculously."[57] Yet even if that is so, life has a habit of going "off" and needing to be repaired or "recycled." God needs to do more than be permissive when it comes to creation righting itself.

According to Feldmeier and Spieckermann, "life," when left to fend for itself, at least as per Psalm 39, soon becomes revealed as not just ephemeral ("vergänglich") but even hollow ("nichtig").[58] The human life span is short, and all the psalmist can hope for is a turning away of the Lord's gaze and a few days of happiness. How does this square with the assurance in Genesis 1 that God saw that creation was very good? Does "continuous creation" not resemble someone filling a bath with fresh water even as the old water disappears down the plughole? Or isn't it like resources that need replenishing almost as soon as provided? If that is the case, then there is nothing very stable about things, and there is little sense of *preservation* of the "very good" of Genesis 1:31. If the oracle that Isaiah declares in 43:19 (ESV)—"Behold, I am doing a new thing" (echoed in Isa. 65:17, then Rev. 21:5)—has any plain meaning, then it is about a divine providence renewing in its maintaining and vice versa.

Divine Rest

This brings us to the question of the tension between Genesis 2:2 (God completed on the seventh day his work and rested from all the works he had made), on the one hand, and John 5:27 (Jesus says that the Father and the Son are continuing to work).

Why might it be important to say that God rested? Well, the usual answer is that this truth supports and protects the principle of rest and recreation for humans, and also to set a time for them to contemplate God's work, including his deliverance of his people from slavery. But it is also for the sake of being sure that God acts within a universe that is already very good in its ordering. So when Genesis says that God saw it was very good and rested, it doesn't mean he stopped working forever after creation. Instead, he has creation no longer as an object to complete, but rather to sustain, to work with

---

56. With Calvin, *Institutes*, 1.15.5.

57. אוֹדְךָ עַל כִּי נוֹרָאוֹת נִפְלֵיתִי נִפְלָאִים; Ps. 138:14 LXX (EV 139:14): ἐξομολογήσομαί σοι, ὅτι φοβερῶς ἐθαυμαστώθην.

58. Feldmeier and Spieckermann, *Der Gott der Lebendigen*, 391.

and direct. He rested from the work of *creation*. Exodus 16 is a case where
the Sabbath is connected to providence. God *is* working, and so the Israelites
should trust in the Sabbath supply of manna while being freed from burdens
of labor/yoke. Jesus's teaching echoes this, and he continues with a prayer
for daily bread and the assertion that "today's trouble is enough for today"
(Matt. 6:34). Brueggemann writes of "the restfulness of God"[59] and points to
Exodus 31:17—on the seventh day the Lord rested, and his soul (*nepeš*) was
refreshed—and concludes: "On Sabbath YHWH is 'refreshed'!"[60]

The restful "mindfulness" of God seems odd, as when Brueggemann
claims that God needs it.[61] The biblical author might well have considered it
less strange, of course, but would have been aware of his own analogical or
metaphorical language, language that the Greek translation carefully avoids:
God had finished creating in terms of the fundamental structures of life, and
he could contemplate this order. The idea of "fixed structures" need not be
gainsaid by our modern understanding of evolution, even though that has
surely given some encouragement to the recent preference for "continuous
creation." As Augustine saw and explained with his teaching on *rationes
seminales* (seminal reasons), there is a chance for creation to develop and
change, but not to the extent of forfeiting its fundamental goodness in any
of its component aspects, not to mention its goodness as a whole.

Thus it might be better to say that for God to rest does not mean that he gets
tired and so rests by necessity, but that his pausing shows that he is not merely,
or not essentially, a "doing" God, but one who can be—as if eternally and
atemporally without doing—"contemplative," although we must impose these
categories only with a large pinch of equivocation. As stated above, "on the
seventh day God rested" does not mean that God became inactive in the world
after creating it, but that the groundwork of creation has been settled once
for all and that God will go on working to conserve, empower, and enhance
life. Exodus 16, then, is about trusting, relaxing in the providential Sabbath
supply of manna. "Sabbath" also means a freeing from burdens of labor or
yoked servitude. In Jesus's teaching, too, rest and trust go hand in hand, daily
bread being actually sufficient to confine anxiety to "worry for today," so that
it does not expand to become "worry for tomorrow" (Matt. 6:11, 25–33).

59. Brueggemann, "God Who Gives Rest," 568.
60. Brueggemann, "God Who Gives Rest," 584.
61. Brueggemann, "God Who Gives Rest," 584. Here Brueggemann refers to Exod. 31:17:
"On the seventh day he rested, and was refreshed" (וּבַיּוֹם הַשְּׁבִיעִי שָׁבַת וַיִּנָּפַשׁ; καὶ τῇ ἡμέρᾳ τῇ
ἑβδόμῃ ἐπαύσατο καὶ κατέπαυσεν.) The LXX, in its use of *katepausen*, "ceased," actually gives
a nonpsychological interpretation to the Hebrew word that many of today's English versions
translate as "was refreshed."

So when Jesus says in those "twin" Johannine verses, "My food is to do the will of him who sent me and to finish his work" (John 4:34 NIV) and "My Father is always at his work to this very day, and I too am working" (5:17 NIV), it might be worth remembering, with Hans-Ulrich Weidemann,[62] "the works of the Father and of the Son are 'making alive': their ἐργάζεσθαι is a ζωοποιεῖν." In their joint work, the healing of flaws, correcting, and perfecting are offered, but only for those who permit an encounter—which makes it all properly "consistently eschatological," yet to be grasped in anticipatory fashion especially in the liturgy. The contexts of these two dominical sayings are the signs at Cana and the feeding "sign" or miracle, and these were more "provision" than "nature miracles." It is also striking to see just how positively Jesus speaks about the Creator, how he looks trustingly toward creation as the place that God gives to humans for living and (not least) as a trustworthy resource for his parables of the kingdom:[63] this to the point where it is hard to spot the join between the Creator-Lord of All and the Father of the Lord Jesus Christ. By using the latter title with reference to the God in the Old Testament as heard by Christians, Brevard Childs was keen to reduce any huge difference between the God of the two Testaments, even though one hears such a distinction espoused in Martin Hengel and repeated in Reinhold Feldmeier—that God "became" father only in the New Testament, since in the Old Testament the attribution was avoided, quite possibly in rejection of any idea of humans' natural kinship with the divine.[64] So creation as very good and in a sense complete can be relied on as a given, a gift, not needing to be worked toward. If the category of "creation" has become popular in theology again, then one also needs to be aware that God is not still at rest in and toward creation.

This also allows the theologian not to separate creation from the doctrines of providence and grace but to distinguish them, before joining them, or showing how they are joined. Creation is not "continuous" in the sense that it has been going on always, with no distinct beginning, which might be called the creation or creating. From the point of view of earthly time, there does seem to be not only a period when sentient life emerged but also a time when basic matter itself came into being. The main thing is that it is good, and that includes a certain freedom to be worse or better. From the point of view of God, creation is timeless. Assuredly God continues to work in his creation, without our needing to call *that* work the work

---

62. Weidemann, "Victory of Protology over Eschatology?," 316.
63. H. Klein, "Die Schöpfung in der Botschaft Jesu," 254.
64. Feldmeier, "Gott und die Zeit," 345; cf. Feldmeier, *Der Höchste*, 179.

of creation. Psalm 104 expresses how God renews his power over creation, asserting his kingdom, as that which combines all types of providence. But Genesis 1:1 is a backstop to all that. And of course this is interpreted or glossed by John 1:1 (to paraphrase): in the beginning was not so much the creation as it "always" has been but the Word behind that, whom Irenaeus (in *Haer.* 5.6.1) later would speak of as one of God's two "hands," more the architect than the construction worker or engineer, which is a role assigned to the Spirit.[65] From a human perspective, rest lies in the future (Ps. 95:11// Heb. 4:3) as an eschatological good: it is the paradisal eternity, a cessation of all striving. Psalm 94:11 glosses the pentateuchal narrative, which in turn allows Hebrews 3:11 to emphasize that the fuller sense of the "rest" is *my* (God's) rest, not the resting place of Canaan. As Harold Attridge observes, *katapausis* and *anapausis* are similar, so that the former's meaning is not restricted to "resting *place*";[66] and Philo uses it at *De cherubim* 87 to mean God's sabbath, not man's. The term *katapausis*, translated "rest" in Psalm 95:11 (94:11 LXX) and Hebrews 4:3, indicates there the eternal spiritual destination of those who now have faith—God's own power and presence.[67] Luke T. Johnson offers this explanation: "Here God says in the psalm that he has a rest, *and yet* his works have been done from the start of the world. To make sense of the contrast, then, we must take the aorist passive participle *genēthentōn* not as 'done and finished' at the beginning, but as 'still done and being done' from the time of the world's foundation."[68] "The 'sabbath rest' is therefore to live as God lives. . . . The 'rest' that is God's very being (God's glory) is not disturbed by God's 'working' in the world because all that God does empirically is an outpouring of infinitely rich life rather than an effort to redress a lack."[69]

However, God is perhaps better seen as intentionally always active, in a way analogous to how the planet is at rest through being in continuous motion, or with help from the metaphysics of Maximus the Confessor and his positive construction of "movement as rest." God's might and constant activity are underpinned by his ability to withdraw and rest.[70] On the one hand, "God does not rest but works without ceasing."[71] God is "semper actuosus"

65. Moberly, "On Interpreting the Mind of God," 44–65.
66. This, *pace* Käsemann (*Wandering People of God*, 68) and Hofius (*Katapausis*, 32). Attridge adduces Philo's *Post.* 23, 128–29; *Fug.* 173–76; *Deus* 12–13 and passim (*Epistle to the Hebrews*, 127n59) to argue that another world is meant, not something in the mind or psychological.
67. L. Johnson, *Hebrews*, 126.
68. L. Johnson, *Hebrews*, 127.
69. L. Johnson, *Hebrews*, 130.
70. Kraus, *Theology of the Psalms*, 46, inspired by Luther's insights.
71. Luther, *Commentary on the Magnificat*, WA 7:574. Cf. *LW* 21:295–398.

(always active). His power is "actualis potentia" (active potential).[72] The psalms speak and sing of the power of Yahweh's mercy (*ḥesed*) and of his compassions (*raḥămîm*), and Psalm 79:8 talks of "compassion hastening"; 119:77, of this *ḥesed* coming to give comfort; 119:156 recounts how great his compassions are; and 145:9 proclaims that God has compassion on all he has made. Nevertheless, on the other hand, God is also a "rock-like" shelter who in that sense is unmoving and "at rest" in himself, *ad intra*. The observation of divine "rest" declares that. And it is that "rest" which Hebrews declares to be on offer.[73]

Eschatology and Providence: Ultimate and Penultimate

It has been fashionable to hold the view that creation is open to God's maintaining and eschatological fulfilling (Jürgen Moltmann). God has to open up a system that has become closed in "durch leidende Kommunikation" (through suffering being communicated), which results in an evolutionary cosmos with a happy face; negative energy can be turned positive.[74] Karl Eberlein argues that this is more "natural theology" than anything worthy of the term "biblical," before then proposing his own solution—namely, that, whereas Psalm 19:1 sees the earth as full of divine glorious presence, Romans 8 emphasizes the *suffering* of all creation/creatures in which God shares by means of the cross-resurrection. Moltmann, Eberlein argues, wants too much continuity between creation and eschatology, and this without much place for Christ.[75] The problem with this is that God's glory is *heavenly* for the psalmist, although it is no *theologia gloriae* in the sense of creatures being able to participate therein. Moreover, there is not really in Romans 8:18–30 any real sense of the suffering of God, or the Spirit of God dwelling with creation, and Christ and his cross go unmentioned in those verses. A more general point drawn from the content of Psalms 136 and 148 seems more plausible, that God's action as creator and his efficacy in history can be conceived as a unity.[76] Indeed, Job 34:14–15 ("If he should take back his spirit to himself, and gather to himself his breath, all flesh would perish together, and all mortals return to dust") teaches that life is contingent on the constant provision of God's breath,

---

72. Luther, *On the Bondage of the Will*, WA 18:718. Cf. *LW* 33:3–295.
73. Backhaus, *Der Hebräerbrief*, 165: "Hebrews is the first to coin *sabbatismos*; but this has to be taken as a heavenly resting place" (AT).
74. Moltmann, *Gott in der Schöpfung*, 218. Cf. Moltmann, "Gespräch mit Christian Link"; Moltmann, "Schöpfung, Bund und Herrlichkeit."
75. Eberlein, *Gott der Schöpfer*, 482.
76. Eberlein, *Gott der Schöpfer*, 264.

but this seems less like creation as an activity that God has to maintain and more like God's working with creation than the transmission of God's essence. If God is at work in creation, it is not without reference to the cross and resurrection; however, it might be better to see Easter resurrection as that part of providence that provides for all true earthly needs and desires. If God is to intervene at all in the natural order, then he will do it in such a quiet, unobtrusive yet possibly persuasive way, using his spokespersons, or through his people more generally (cf. Isa. 11:1–5; Zech. 9:9–10).[77] The resurrection shares this subterranean, subversive quality, as it breaks into the open from deeply concealed realms.

The Old Testament does see God repair and renew as part of his sustaining maintenance. Yet the idea that life doesn't really get repaired prior to the Christian era, when we arrive at the New Testament with its note of eschatology, is popular among New Testament scholars like Jürgen Becker.[78] He flirts with the idea that life expressed in the form of a human person is that in which the image of God consists, but is clear that with the New Testament it is a case of something more than life as looking back to its origins, as in the case of the genealogies of Genesis.[79] The present situation, according to Becker, is that God is no longer merely the God who is the source of life, but that he can now be creative in giving every human life a new start and is there to fix human beings in light of their future-pointing identity in the Second Adam.[80] On this view all divine input begins with the New Testament and in parsing life as something quite other than any former life, and without overlap with it.

The problem with this is that it is supersessionist toward creation as well as toward the Old Testament witness. It is not only that the creational substructure is seen to belong, along with the law, to a prototypical dispensation, but also that there is no place for the "orders" of the ongoing march of human life as illustrated in the first part of the canon. Of course Christ's commands might well question, qualify, and override these structures and institutions, but they have to be recognizable and meaningful since they are still in force this side of the resurrection. The eschatological call and the possibility of alternative living patterns need to have something to call to and be called out of. The particular acts of the economy of God embrace the more general, ongoing shepherding of creation through history, although

77. Janowski, *Gott des Lebens*, 192.
78. Becker, "'Bei dir ist die Quelle des Lebens' (Ps 36,10)," 63.
79. Yet cf. Hieke, *Die Genealogien der Genesis*, which presents a quite different raison d'être for the genealogies.
80. Becker, "'Bei dir ist die Quelle des Lebens' (Ps 36,10)," 62–63.

this is very hard to know and define.[81] The New Testament in particular does not so much express a general reality as it speaks of a remaking of it, yet in this form-giving according to the will of God the "ethical" cooperation of human agents also receives its content from the matter of what creation has been and is also becoming: again, the ordinary world as mirror image of the kingdom in Jesus's parables. The point is less the possibilities for gaining knowledge through such wisdom (a modern obsession) than the possibility of becoming aware that quietly God is getting things done. This is not to take over Bonhoeffer's "penultimate" things as though creation and providential orders will pass away and be superseded by some*thing* new: even if the earth *might* pass away, heaven will too: and all that remains is "my words" (Mark 13:31//), with the new heaven *and the new earth* reserved for a future age.

The idea that there was an eschatologizing of Wisdom[82] in Second Temple Judaism is useful here.[83] This implies that any expectation of survival after death is bound up with the notion of God himself as the giver and guarantor of life rather than with some "new place."[84] Bernd Schipper views this as the God of the living opening up new opportunities from death (cf. 2 Cor. 1:9), but one might want to add that the more usual way is opening up new possibilities *from within life*. The point is that there is a God of created life over death (Ps. 74) who is also Lord over history, bringing otherwise precarious life to fulfillment, not dissolution (Ps. 114).[85] One may speak instead of a sapientialization or "wisdoming" of eschatology.

God is needed by his creatures to be continuously active: in between the theoretical affirmation that "the earth cannot shake" (Ps. 93:1 AT) and Israel's actual experience of its shaking (Ps. 75 and Ps. 82), the conclusion that the whole world is precarious and very much prone to being shaken owing to experience of perpetual injustice sounds the message and reality of God's rule over the world and his preservation.[86] God only *seems* to have withdrawn. Amos 1:8, with its promise of justice to come, is quite different from Psalm 104, yet is no less valid for faith. This means that God's activity is required

---

81. Eberlein, *Gott der Schöpfer*, 70–72. The issue of subjectivity versus objectivity—which Pannenberg (*Wissenschaftstheorie und Theologie*, 267) accused Barth of too much favoring the former—is hardly a biblical theme, as Eberlein observes.

82. Witte, *Von Ewigkeit zu Ewigkeit*, 60.

83. Cf. Schipper, *Hermeneutik der Tora*, where Schipper argues that by adding Prov. 10–30 and Prov. 2 to Prov. 1–9, Second Temple Judaism could find no way to theologize wisdom, only apply it; wisdom can only serve for practical living. Salvation requires intervention.

84. Schipper, *Hermeneutik der Tora*, 112.

85. Witte, *Von Ewigkeit zu Ewigkeit*, 112, on Ps. 73, which speaks of the Creator overcoming death; see also 171.

86. Jeremias, *Studien zur Theologie des Alten Testaments*, 235.

not just for the sake of consolation but also for that of an objective basis for hope. God has shared himself with humanity in history but in a way that is covenantal in form, offering, at least with the new covenant but quite possibly earlier, a true sense of free commerce between God and humans and among humans.[87]

God is the one who begins things but also in acting on creation persists in giving freedom to it in the moral order. If creatures are to participate in creating, they will do so covenantally, hence morally, responding to an infinite love rather than to infinity itself. God as covenant partner allows himself to shape events and look for moral reactions. So when John Rogerson concludes that God looked after Israel to give it *shalom* but not to lead history to a goal, with Psalm 105:16–22 and Genesis 50:20 as his texts of reference, surely that is underplaying what Joseph meant for Egypt.[88] With Joseph, providence seems modern in the sense of an individual bildungsroman or educative-vocational story,[89] although it can also be for a people. Eichrodt with his Reformed covenantal reading of history stressed that this covenant becomes a purpose for all nations through Israel only in the Prophets, but such a purpose is already at least implicit in the Pentateuch. A goal of history that includes the nations becomes real only when they come into contact with Israel: only then does God exert more direct control of the nations analogous to his leading of Israel, albeit without their having much idea of it, as with Cyrus and Xerxes.[90]

Ancient Israel had a more limited view of God's purposes, and so it seems fitting to lower the expectations of or broaden the criteria for providence, where they are like those of John Rogerson, as when he concludes that he can find *Heilsgeschichte* (salvation history) for Israel in the Old Testament but nothing more, not least because history is a process, not a system. For Rogerson, providence seems concerned with international politics and *Heilsgeschichte* only in an obvious sense: Baruch got his life as a ransom, even as the diasporic exile was set to continue (Jer. 45:5; cf. Zech. 4:10 [NIV]: "Who dares despise the day of small things?").

87. Essen, "Gottes Treue zu uns," 390.
88. Rogerson, "Can a Doctrine of Providence Be Based on the Old Testament?"
89. Gunkel, *Genesis*, 459.
90. G. Fohrer denied a plan and saw the OT history as one of "Entscheidungsgeschichte," which sounds like "making it up as one goes along." J. Vollmer and F. Huber agreed, in common with more recent "open theists." Rogerson ("Can a Doctrine of Providence Be Based on the Old Testament?," 542–43) argues that as the Israelites looked forward, they worried about a threat to existence. As elect they thought God would provide a place for them and arrange things with other nations: "Only towards the end of the Old Testament period did they begin to comprehend series of events in terms of a divine plan, as in Daniel, at which point it became necessary to have a seer who was granted heavenly revelation so that events could be understood" (543).

My difficulty is that increasingly, I doubt whether it is possible to talk about history as a thing, and whether, in that case, it is possible to speak about God controlling history, or whether there is a goal of history that will explain or make sense of the whole process. . . . It has become increasingly questionable to me that I should be required to accept that the atrocities of the twentieth century and the injustices of the present-day world are part of a process that will ultimately be seen to be meaningful in all its details.[91]

Here we are back with Zimmerli's "providence for the individual," a curious "two kingdoms" type of doctrine for scholars from decidedly non-Lutheran traditions. Rather, the witness of Job—granted with the wisdom of hindsight and revelation—and the witness of the Deuteronomistic History indicate that providence is a secret history, an object for faith, not for the sight that Rogerson supposes, a God "clearly on our side." Perhaps *Heilsgeschichte* is a subset of providence, or, as already implied (above), it is perhaps best understood as providence when it comes above ground for a while, before disappearing on its course underground.

The psalmist, however, reassures us that divine care is constitutive of being human. As Janowski puts it: "The human being is human, according to Psalm 8:4/5, because YHWH is mindful of the person and benevolently looks after each one (cf. Ps. 144:3)."[92] The verb *pqd* (to care for, to see to) is an intensification of *zkr* (to remember). The person is one who is growing into a space made for her by God: one should remember the dialogic quality of the human being in the Hebrew Bible. "This idea is well expressed in Psalm 8, when the question of the nature of human beings—'What are human beings?' (v. 4/5a)—is answered in reference to 'remembering' (בַזְקָר) by YHWH. . . . Human beings live and are human because God remembers them and cares for them (cf. Ps. 144:3) or because they examine their 'heart' and direct it toward God, characteristically adapting the idea of God's remembering, as in Job 7:17–18."[93] In all this there is no possibility of objectification, but only of an openness toward God. "Mindfulness" means "providential mindfulness."[94] But is it not that humans are something, for God remembers them? Surely divine provision, God's "added extra" in lives, is only part of who/what humans are: by creation humans are granted a degree of self-determination within that providence according to some creaturely autonomy. On the basis

---

91. Rogerson, "Can a Doctrine of Providence Be Based on the Old Testament?," 538, with reference to Platzer, *Geschichte, Heilsgeschichte, Hermeneutik.* Also Baumgartner, *Kontinuität und Geschichte.*

92. Janowski, *Arguing with God,* 53.

93. Janowski, *Arguing with God,* 12–13.

94. Janowski, *Arguing with God,* 53.

of this created worth God is mindful toward his creation, gives worth to it first through his remembrance and care.

To conclude this part: as we shall see in the final chapter, there has been recently in German-speaking literature a fair bit of discussion of the theme of *Vertrauen* (trust) and of *fides* as *fiducia* (faith as trust). Connected to this is an appreciation of phenomenology's insistence on taking things, if not at face value, then at least as prima facie truthful.[95] God is thus the basis of all our activity and is behind our experience of life as guarantor, and not just in the sense of initially bringing creation into being or even of giving new starts, but in molding what he has made. The hymn verse comes to mind: "Father-like he tends and spares us; / Well our feeble frame he knows. / In his hands he gently bears us, / Rescues us from all our foes." Providence supports salvation history and its higher purpose, but it is a lived and storied providence and somewhat meaningful in glimpses. Sometimes those lower-purpose affairs are more important, as we see, if we may return to Jesus at Mark 12:26–27, where, in answering the question of marriage in the resurrection, he refers to Exodus 3:6, 14–15 ("the LORD, the God of the patriarchs") and says: "He is not the God of the dead, but of the living. You are badly mistaken!" (NIV). Theology is not to be dominated by speculation over the eschatological but by continuing trusting faith in the continuation of vivifying providential action in human life, which may in turn have salvific and lasting consequences.

95. Held, "Phänomenologische Begründung," 26. Biblically speaking, one must get away from the idea of God as pure power; this needs to be refined by telos of the Good (Husserl).

THREE

Providence and Divine Action, Viewed Biblically

Philosophies and Biblical Theology

When it comes to drawing parallels between Paul and Platonic and Stoic philosophy, Reinhard Feldmeier has expressed a certain amount of caution. To begin with, Platonizing philosophy held God and humans to be in direct and personal relationships, whereas Paul spoke about adoption and election, not some natural kinship, but one of grace and mediation.[1] The point of Paul's mentioning the heavenly Father is to emphasize eschatology rather than protology, a movement of divine initiation and human response in faith and baptism. Yet as to the verses to which Feldmeier refers, Philippians 3:20 and 1 Corinthians 15:35–37, in the first there is no word "father," and the verse relates to citizenship in heaven, not to spiritual sonship, while in 1 Corinthians 15 the issue is more that of the resurrection body. "Heaven" might well indicate an eschatological context, but one will not find "the Father" linked to the end times when referred to as "heavenly father." Likewise Galatians 4:6 and Romans 8:14–17 bear the sense of something occurring in the present rather than anything eschatological, with the believer crying to his "Abba," who is in the "here and now." Feldmeier appears to base his "eschatological" interpretation of divine fatherhood in Paul on 1 Corinthians 8:6:[2] God the

1. Feldmeier, *Der Höchste*, 192.
2. Feldmeier, *Der Höchste*, 193.

Father is ground and *goal* of creation, with the Son as Mediator of creation and new creation. Yet the Father here is just as much the ground as he is the goal of creation, and there is no referring of "new creation" to him. Add to this Ephesians 4:5–6: "one Lord, one faith, one baptism, one God and Father of all, who is for [ἐπὶ] all things and through all things and in all things" (AT). Yet rather than a statement of eschatology, properly understood these latter two passages concern the fatherhood of God in relation to what has happened before now, to what is for now and this life, and beyond it.

Like Christians, Stoics believed in the rule of the high God over the world, but, remarks Feldmeier, unlike the Stoics' teaching, Paul's message was not one of following God ethically in order to "realize a nature." Others have noted further keen differences between the New Testament and the Stoics, for whom newness is but the different combination of the matter that is, which will come about through cycles of purifying conflagration. Also, God as reason is the grain of the Stoic cosmos. "Providence equips the soul to withstand Fortune, so as not to become hostages to Fortuna."[3] Ancients did see their lives and ideas enmeshed, as Pierre Hadot has gone to pains to show. However, the Stoics did not have an answer for why we are ignorant.[4] As Kavin Rowe puts it, Luke means that we discover who God is—God as Father of Jesus—not by any historical unfolding,[5] but through a special historical revelation. Reason cannot repair itself; wisdom comes only through being known by God. "The Christians are innocent of the act of *stasis*, says Luke (Acts 26:31 et passim)," in contradistinction to Stoic views.[6] Rebeginning in Christ is key for the story that God gives, and that corresponds to a mode of life, which in turn orients one so as to be able to make sense of things.

Yet neither Paul nor Epictetus saw any real opposition between divine "external" agency and human autonomous agency. "On the contrary, both thinkers operate with the idea of an *overlap between divine and human agency* that trades on the specific character of human cognition. . . . In both Paul and Stoicism, cognition—operating through the pneuma—*aligns* human beings with God, *thereby* giving them a freedom of genuine agency that is also always in accordance with God."[7] On some accounts, and in the mature Stoicism of Epictetus,[8]

3. Rowe, *One True Life*, 26, with reference to Seneca, *Ep.* 9 and 98.
4. Rowe, *One True Life*, 307n50.
5. Rowe, *One True Life*, 124.
6. Rowe, *One True Life*, 221. Yet different modes of life reinforce the idea of different theologies, after the manner of Pierre Hadot, somewhat ironically, given what the great French scholar thought of mutual contamination of systems.
7. Engberg-Pedersen, *Cosmology and Self in the Apostle Paul*, 108.
8. Long, *Epictetus*, 26. Yet Long continues: "Although he starts by justifying divine providence, the real focus of the discourse is less on this than on what it means to be endowed, as

there is a personal relation of divine to human according to a belief in the world's divine governor, and the fact that Stoicism's God is unpredictable is perhaps a sign that Stoic "providence" is not at all mechanistic, but is predicated on the notion of a quasi-personal will. Thus, Troels Engberg-Pedersen: "In addition to identifying fate (physical discourse) with Zeus (personal discourse), they also ascribed 'providence' (that is, cognitive discourse) to Zeus, taking it that God's providence was operative *through* fate, which they even called 'the *mind* of God.'"[9] "But we must also now say that *once* human beings have acquired the proper knowledge—through God's unpredictable agency—they will have a knowledge that will either dissolve this unpredictability or at least push it into a subsidiary position."[10] Engberg-Pedersen appeals here to Philippians 3:12 ("I press on to grasp because I have also been grasped by Christ" [AT]) and to 1 Corinthians 13:12 ("then I will know fully, just as I am fully known" [AT]). However, is it not the case for Paul that the active human grasping and knowing lie in the future, such that for this present life the *being grasped* or known is fuller than the grasping or knowing? In other words, there seems an asymmetry in Paul that is missing in Stoicism. As Engberg-Pedersen himself admits, "Paul has apparently *already* been *fully known*, but will only himself come to *know fully* in the future."[11] And of course this being grasped and known is something very much like "providence," even where knowledge of guidance seems opaque.

There is one little key difference, however. Engberg-Pedersen writes: "Pauline freedom is the Stoic freedom of understanding God's acts that lifts human beings out of any form of servitude to the powers of the present world—and indeed to God himself. Instead, it *aligns* them with the new world that is literally to come—and *with* God."[12] This idea of freedom as self-transcending by some sort of ascesis, in order to stand tall spiritually and be lifted by one's mind out of "servitude . . . to God himself," hardly seems reminiscent of Paul's message in any part of his writings. It sounds more like Hegel (in

humans are, with the capacity to oversee themselves and to acknowledge their internal divinity . . . , which is also the voice of objective reason and integrity, as their only authority." For Chrysippus, "universal reason," that is, right reason pervading everything, was also "Zeus, who directs the organization of reality." For Epictetus, one must commit one's daimon to the good or "God" (4.12.11–12), which guarantees right choices; see Long, *Epictetus*, 163–68. Likewise (2.16.28) the divine law is to be happy with what has been allotted and not resentful when that allotment is removed.

9. Engberg-Pedersen, *Cosmology and Self in the Apostle Paul*, 81.

10. Engberg-Pedersen, *Cosmology and Self in the Apostle Paul*, 136.

11. Engberg-Pedersen, *Cosmology and Self in the Apostle Paul*, 238n35.

12. Engberg-Pedersen, *Cosmology and Self in the Apostle Paul*, 138. Also, Chrysippus saw the problem of not being able to act ethically since nature lets us down as a way to better self-understanding. Cf. Paul in Rom. 7 (Engberg-Pedersen, *Cosmology and Self in the Apostle Paul*, 136).

his *Philosophy of History*), putting the faith-cart before the grace-horse. For Paul, there something real with a special providence, something that is not merely a way of seeing things but is something for faith to lock on to, as is the case with grace.

What *may* be affirmed is that Paul's vision for redemption includes the cosmos and its providential ordering. This is not to say that Paul thinks in terms of cosmology in its most expansive sense, but he does affirm in Romans 8 that all creatures are linked together in a common destiny that is touched by resurrection.[13] All creatures are in the same boat: Paul doesn't teach so much cosmology as the humbling but gratitude-inducing lesson of human identification with beasts, and so on. It can be argued that Paul had a perception of the fragility of creation and that his sensitivity on the matter is analogous to that required in today's ecological crisis.[14] Theologically speaking, in Samuel Vollenweider's terms, God's future, promised renewal of creation will build on his present care for a dying and evanescent creation. The new experience in Christ will rise above both the contingency and the rules and move away from classic teleological order. Paul did not share the world-subject diastasis beloved of moderns, so he developed an "apocalyptic" connection of humanity with creation, argues Vollenweider.[15] Now, that seems a lot to get out of Romans 8:19–21, a passage that Vollenweider calls "quasi-cosmic."[16] This passage is not about freedom as emancipation from creation, letting it die so as to resurrect something new that is better, but is rather a promise of new life for all of it. Perceiving God in the cosmic realms is a nice idea, but awareness of one's place in the cosmos just as much as Luke located his readers in history tends to obscure any such confident vision of the cosmic.[17] One may only affirm *that* God will remain faithful to it. One could argue that much of the discussion of Romans 9–11 about what it might mean that "all Israel shall be saved" in the light of the promises to gentiles rather misses the point.[18] One must believe in order to be grafted back in (11:22–24), but the door is open. "All Israel" does seem to be the combination of part of the Jews and part of the gentiles added together to make a whole, although verse 32 might persuade one that all who rebelled and were shut up might have mercy. Yet on balance the "all" means the sum of rebellious Jews and rebellious gentiles, with little sense of a Pauline theology of a "remnant" being found suitable for

13. Grässer, "Das Seufzen der Kreatur," 111.
14. Vollenweider, *Freiheit als neue Schöpfung*, 392–93.
15. Vollenweider, *Freiheit als neue Schöpfung*, 404.
16. Vollenweider, *Freiheit als neue Schöpfung*, 382.
17. Vollenweider, "Wahrnehmungen der Schöpfung im Neuen Testament," 250.
18. See, e.g., Still, *God and Israel*.

God to work with, whatever Luke 1–2 might suggest. Whatever the answer, God's providence has arranged a sequence of events at the level of "peoples" (less so "individuals") that is marked by gracious generosity and a "cosmic" range of active authority. This is confirmed by the doxological "from him and through him and to him . . . all things" of Romans 11:36.

With Easter comes a perception of a present reality of creation: faith perceives a divine creativity at work that natural eyes cannot see as anything other than "business as usual," since they expect God's activity to be more "marvelous" and obvious. Oda Wischmeyer has reported on the same locus classicus in Romans 8.[19] The theme of preservation of creation shows a parallel story to the history of God's people; both are being delivered from slavery of what is passing toward glory, and natural creation is kept for that end-point transformation. It is all part of a bold reworking of the glory of creation. Wischmeyer claims that Paul uses the term *physis* to connote the idea of ethical or "fitting" behavior, as also in 1 Corinthians 11:13–16.[20] Certainly in Stoic terms that which has to do with "origin" is understood as setting the way of being, as per Romans 11:24.[21] Her insightful point is that Paul is not like that, since creation is freer to change than "nature," and believing in creation in the new age that Christ brings does not mean believing in a status quo that has to be abandoned.[22] Creation as it is in the present is being moved on the way to its final reordering.[23]

Creation and eschatology are thus not opposed but connected. This is clear from how Jesus works with the natural world in his parables: one's experience of how God is in creation can suggest how he will act eschatologically: a fortiori, not *au contraire*. This is not to say that nothing is different; in fact, one can say that God's action is new. But it is better to use the term "renewal," since otherwise it is hard to speak of the kingdom of God "breaking in": for into what does it break? Thus it is not as radical as destroying and starting completely anew.[24]

Kavin Rowe suggests that even if there are some resemblances between Christians and Stoics, there is something about the Christian claim of universal epistemological blindness that vitiates or undermines all such apparent commonalities. "*Providence*, for example, no more names a shared conviction

19. Wischmeyer, "PHYSIS und KTISIS bei Paulus."
20. Wischmeyer, "PHYSIS und KTISIS bei Paulus," 361. Cf. Opelt, "Erde."
21. εἰ γὰρ σὺ ἐκ τῆς κατὰ φύσιν ἐξεκόπης ἀγριελαίου καὶ παρὰ φύσιν ἐνεκεντρίσθης εἰς καλλιέλαιον, πόσῳ μᾶλλον οὗτοι οἱ κατὰ φύσιν ἐγκεντρισθήσονται τῇ ἰδίᾳ ἐλαίᾳ.
22. Wischmeyer, "PHYSIS und KTISIS bei Paulus," 374.
23. Wischmeyer, "PHYSIS und KTISIS bei Paulus," 365.
24. Wischmeyer, "PHYSIS und KTISIS bei Paulus," 365.

about a God/world relation than it does a shared sense of what God or world is." For example, Stoics (with no doctrine of sin) do not have an answer for why we are ignorant.[25] Rowe goes on to claim that for Stoics, God is not something other than the world so as to be able even to say that God locates himself in it. True, he adds, Stoics, like Christians, speak of a direction in the cosmos, yet there is no divine will to intend that direction.

One can be grateful to Rowe's close readings here. Yet something in them seems a bit self-contradictory: Epictetus, too, never loses confidence in the guidance of providence, and Seneca even wrote an entire treatise on the topic (*De providentia*). When he comes to counsel Lucilius, he says his pupil ought to recall that "the whole universe about us go[es] by turns, that whatever has been put together is broken up again, that whatever has been broken up is put together again, and that the eternal craftsmanship of God, who controls all things, is working at this task" (*Ep.* 71.14). This sounds rather like intentional direction.

In Sirach 15:19 God is said to be watching for the sake of judgment: "The eyes of God behold his works, and he understands every human deed" (AT). One might also compare the passage at 39:16–25, where the use of πρόσταγμα (in v. 16) and ἔκτισται (in vv. 21, 25) indicates that God's gaze spans all the ages. True, unlike the Stoics, Sirach indeed has a sense of coming individual judgment as part of the harmony of the whole,[26] yet the harmony of creation should inspire the people of God with confidence. The stars not only are regular in their purpose but also provide a beauty that is part of theodicy (Sir. 39:13–25; 42:15–43:33).[27] For Sirach, God is no immanent principle as the Stoics would have it, but he would have agreed with them that all things have a purpose, and in doing that, he moves beyond what the Hebrew books of the Old Testament would imagine, although not in such a way that providence is equally in everything or that physical evil contributes the overall harmony. Yet there *is* a harmony.[28]

Although much is made of the torah by Sirach, the law's strength lies in the making known of the wisdom therein that communicates the reason of the whole creation and represents (and makes present) the world to God.[29] What Judaism adds to philosophy is a special and privileged connection to this universal wisdom in earthly terms. This of course means that as with the Stoics, so too in Judaism the ethical is decisive—for example, at Sirach

25. Rowe, *One True Life*, 307n50.
26. Wicke-Reuter, "Ben Sira und die Frühe Stoa," 279.
27. Sir. 39:16: Τὰ ἔργα κυρίου πάντα ὅτι καλὰ σφόδρα, καὶ πᾶν πρόσταγμα ἐν καιρῷ αὐτοῦ ἔσται· οὐκ ἔστιν εἰπεῖν Τί τοῦτο; εἰς τί τοῦτο; πάντα γὰρ ἐν καιρῷ αὐτοῦ ζητηθήσεται.
28. Wicke-Reuter, "Zusammenfassung," 277, 280.
29. Wicke-Reuter, "Zusammenfassung," 281–82.

33:7–15.[30] Humans still have freedom, and God works with that, having already set up the possible ways (v. 11). God freely adopts or rejects according to human behavior.

In the case of the Middle Platonic (hence Stoicizing) Philo, one can discern how accepting a moral order makes one's action fit with God's will. "In a fragment of the lost treatise *Legum Allegoriae* [frag. 8], Philo says that, 'strictly speaking, the human mind does not choose the good through itself, but in accordance with the providence (ἐπιφροσύνη) of God, since he bestows the fairest things upon the worthy.'"[31] Likewise for Sirach, the knowledge of mortality is a good thing, for it allows preparation for a peaceful death, and trusting God helps one in bad days.[32]

Providence for the Stoics was not the word for the guiding hand of a sentient God who as superintendent works upon the eternal dissolution-reconstitution cycle of the cosmos from without. Providence, rather, is the Stoic word for the ordering principle inherent within. It seems supremely important for Rowe, then, that the Christian God must be transcendent and in himself remain at a distance from creation so as to work on it "from without," which enables him to be viewed as somehow personal rather than "simply written into what is." Stoic "prayers" are not, despite a surface reading of their texts, addressed to someone in particular. Yet what does this spatial language mean? And is it not in fact contradicted or at least qualified by Paul's insistence that the human heart is the dwelling place of the divine Spirit, who interprets God to humans and interprets humans to God (Rom. 8:27: "And God, who searches the heart, knows what is the mind of the Spirit, because the Spirit intercedes for the saints according to the will of God"; or 1 Cor. 2:10: "The Spirit searches all things, even the deep things of God" [AT]). In Romans the Spirit's role is less one of communicating from God to humanity than the other way round, and what is "personal" seems to have to do with the human speaker, with the Father needing the Spirit to interpret. The Father may well be a person, but it is the Spirit within creation who works meaningfully with him for the sake of connection. Conversely yet correspondingly, Engberg-Pedersen contrasts Philo and John: "What Philo does, then, is to construct a layer between a remote God and the sensible world. In other words, he separates God and the sensible world from one another. John, by contrast, apparently aims to connect them."[33] John was not a good Platonist as Philo was, but rather imbibed

---

30. Kaiser, *Des Menschen Glück und Gottes Gerechtigkeit*, 149.

31. Frick, *Divine Providence in Philo*, 174.

32. Kaiser, *Des Menschen Glück und Gottes Gerechtigkeit*, 229, concerning Sir. 11:28; see also 229n174.

33. Engberg-Pedersen, *John and Philosophy*, 57.

a Jewish Stoicism as one might find in Wisdom of Solomon.[34] In short, the gospel is that God communicates a divine *pneuma* to people through Christ so that they too do the works of God (John 6:28), as stewards of renewed creation. Further, receiving the *pneuma* and becoming pneumatic means being more than, not less than, corporeal.

Paul's very mention of "creation groaning" (cf. Eccles. 12:5!) shows how much that which is "old" extends into the present and the eschatological age. Even if creation has been affected by a fallen cosmos, and any new creation requires the presence of the Spirit by faith to produce obedience in a new ecclesiological reality, there is, nevertheless, still a place for the old creation.[35] There is no sense in which the new creation (meant metaphorically to describe believers) implies the termination of old, groaning creation. The "glorified" of Romans 8:30 is aorist, even if "gnomic" (i.e., drawn from experience that "God tends to glorify"). Yet the point is that renewal means adding something, not taking anything away (except that which is defective, which, strictly speaking, is a lack).

As for the famous passage in Romans 8:28–32, Paul is much more interested in a radical "conformity to Christ" as in verse 29, which goes further than the Platonic parallel,[36] which speaks only of "friendship" with the divine through an upward path. For πρόθεσις means a "preexistent" divine decree with the sense of intention, and the Spirit gives power to grasp present sufferings as participation in Christ and as experiences that are (surprisingly for the natural mind) all part of the plan. "All things" includes the present sufferings, as mentioned in verse 18. The Spirit of verse 27 is clearly a mediator between God and Christians.[37] The phrase ἐραυνῶν τὰς καρδίας ("who searches the hearts") is well attested in the Old Testament, not least in historical books: 1 Samuel 16:7; 1 Kings 8:39; 1 Chronicles 28:9; Psalms 17:3; 26:2; 139:23;

34. "Here there is no unbridgeable gap between the logos understood as God's active power in creating the world and the idea that this logos came to be present in all its fullness in a single individual. (a) The Stoic logos is present as the world's active power in everything that is, operating as it does in the whole world as an energy that guides and maintains it. (b) It is also present, at the level of consciousness, in human beings as a power ('reason' or nous) that makes them capable of understanding the world's order, for which the logos was responsible in the first place. (c) That power, however, is insufficient in ordinary human beings. And so the Stoic logos is finally present in the world in its most powerful form in one being who may be as rare as the phoenix: the Stoic sage or 'wise man.'. . . The idea is certainly not that 'John is a Stoic,' only that the picture one finds in Stoicism helps to give precise meaning to John's claim. We also saw that there is at least one other claim in the Prologue that does not immediately fit with Stoicism, namely, the claim that the logos was 'with' God" (Engberg-Pedersen, *John and Philosophy*, 61–62).

35. Cf. Beinert, "Weltgericht und Weltvollendung bei Paulus."

36. Plato, *Resp.* 613a (10.621C). Cf. Hommel, "Erwägungen zu Römer 8,28."

37. Wolter, *Der Brief an die Römer*, 525.

Sirach 42:18. Yet the idea is also found in Proverbs 20:27: the lamp of the Lord is the breath of humans, he who searches the chambers of the innards (LXX: *ereuna tamieia koilias*).[38]

The verb ὑπερεντυγχάνει in Romans 8:26 is exclusively Christian and means to intercede, as in Shepherd of Hermas, Similitude 2.8. The Spirit seems to replace angels' role in Jewish texts. However, Paul then extends this idea of the Spirit's interceding to all creation, for the Lord in being the eschatological Redeemer is the Creator continuing to work, just as he is Creator in his being Redeemer and as the Creator he realizes his care for his creation in that he finally renews it.[39] This is related to the following verse (27): God knows his mind, yet communicates a measure of knowledge sufficient for believers, a knowledge believers possess from experience of individual cases. The next sentence (v. 28) begins "for we know." If a passage like 1 Corinthians 2:10 is more explicit about the transmission of God's knowledge into human minds, nevertheless there is a trace of that in the "we know" of Romans 8:28.[40]

Should Romans 8:28 be translated "all things work together" or "God works all things"?[41] It is likely that God is the one working, even if one reads the variant that has "all things" as the subject of the clause. However, one's preference of variants might have implications for theology. C. H. Dodd argued that to think "all things work together" is to be too optimistic, or one could say also: too deterministic. As Carroll Osburn summarized the case:

> Stoicism, then, advocated a resignation to one's Fate; whatever happens must be construed as "good," the will of God (Cicero, *De finibus* 2.34; 3.14). Thus when Plutarch (*De Stoic. repugn.* 1050e) and Seneca (*Ep.* 74, 20) proclaim the Stoic view that "all things work unto good," it is meant by them that everything happens through universal reason, or Fate, and one therefore should live in harmony with universal nature, resigning himself to whatever happens as "good." As Epictetus (*Discourses* 2.14.7) put it, "We must put our will in harmony with events so that whatever happens will be to our liking." Dodd's observation that such "universal optimism" is un-Pauline is cogent.[42]

38. Wolter, *Der Brief an die Römer*, 526.

39. Wilckens, *Der Brief an die Römer*, 166, with reference to Steck, *Welt und Umwelt*. The fathers and Aquinas point out that it cannot be the case that material creation is literally groaning.

40. οἴδαμεν δὲ ὅτι τοῖς ἀγαπῶσιν τὸν θεὸν πάντα συνεργεῖ εἰς ἀγαθόν, τοῖς κατὰ πρόθεσιν κλητοῖς οὖσιν.

41. G. Folliet, "Deus omnia cooperatur in bonum." Cf. Vulg.: "Deus omnia cooperantur." But in Augustine's citation of Paul in Rom. 8:28, not least in *De gratia et libero arbitrio*, this is made into "Deus cooperatur" (39). In the sixteenth century Estius saw that Amerbach, Erasmus, and some Benedictines had made this mistake: he retorted with Prosper and Cajetan.

42. Osburn, "Interpretation of Romans 8:28," 100.

Moreover, does God cooperate with the believers for a *wider* good? Well, in fact, yes. The progress of the gospel was what was meant by Paul in Philippians 1:12–13, even where it was hard to see Paul himself benefiting from God's intervention. According to Matthew Black, "the Spirit" is the subject of the sentence in Romans 8:28; yet "God" is clearly the subject of verses 29–30. Now, it could well be that any idea of cooperation is not that between divine and human agency, but rather, with Mark Gignilliat, "the collaborative idea associated with the verb συνεργεί is between the Spirit's activity on behalf of the saints according to God's will (v. 27), and God's *providential* care for his people via the Spirit's activity. God's people in Christ are the beneficiaries of God's working together with the Spirit [in the wider world yet] on their behalf. . . . In all things, God is working together with the Spirit for the good purposes of his people."[43] This of course is another point. Not that all things might be cooperating, but who the beneficiaries of the activity are. As distinct from "God works *in* all things," "God works all things" still sounds quite monist. One could, as Dodd and Osburn have done, argue that even with *panta* it still means "in all things" and that it was placed in the accusative rather than the dative in order to avoid two datives in the sentence,[44] but this seems like special pleading. The decision of the Vulgate to use a plural verb with "all things" as subject does not quite do justice to the odd, anarthrous, almost nominal nature of *panta: scimus autem quoniam diligentibus Deum omnia cooperantur in bonum.*

And is this about predestination—that is, about the destination of individuals? Michael Wolter argues that Paul in Romans 8:28–29 does not mean "predestination" as such but rather, simply, that God has a plan for those who love him. Yet it does seem that the second group of verbs in verse 30 (ἐκάλεσεν-ἐδικαίωσεν-ἐδόξασεν) presuppose the first group (προέγνω-προώρισεν), which are to do with God's decree (πρόθεσις).[45] While not ascribing to Paul the doctrine that "predestination" came later to be, we can say that it might well be the apostle's doctrine that God's preparing his chosen *people* as a unit is something that is prior, even "predetermined," and that hence divine providence at least includes within it some form of "predestination." This is not to say

43. Gignilliat, "Working Together with Whom?," 514, with reference to Black, "Interpretation of Romans viii 28."

44. Osburn, "Interpretation of Romans 8:28," 104: "Accordingly, Black is led to suggest that if God is the understood subject in v. 28, one is not bound to take the verb as transitive (as did Sanday) and that πάντα could well be taken here as an Inner Accusative ("*in* all things"), thus rendering, 'works for good in all things for those who love God,' as Dodd proposes. One problem Black finds with this reading comes from Zahn's critique that if this were Paul's meaning he would surely have written ἐν πᾶσιν rather than πάντα. To this it might be objected that ἐν πᾶσιν could then be taken confusedly with τοῖς ἀγαπῶσιν rather than with the verb."

45. Wolter, *Der Brief an die Römer*, 531.

that it means what it has come to mean in parts of the Augustinian-Reformed tradition, but that "those" who respond are responding *to* an initiative that is grounded "prehistorically" in God's will.

Something similar is sounded in Romans 11:33–36 (everything "from him and through him and to him").[46] Here it is less Christocentric and more focused on divine power in creation: but there is also a *new creation* for faith to take hold of; and *that* is something ecclesial, a special providence, and this is, of course, related to the idea of "a new heaven and a new earth" (Isa. 65:17; 66:22; 1 En. 91.16). If one understands "in Christ" spatially, then it becomes a "pneumatic sphere of salvation." Of course Colossians 1:15b tells us that Christ is *over* creation even as it is in and through him, but it is Christ as the risen one, since all creation is also "to him" (τὰ πάντα δι' αὐτοῦ καὶ εἰς αὐτὸν ἔκτισται [1:16b]), and thus these verses show a certain continuity or bridging between creation and new creation, with Christ operating in that hinge. The hope in Christ and renewal of the world are based on trust in God the Creator as Lord of that creation and Savior of it in a "new" dimension.[47]

For many New Testament scholars, Stoicism's problem is its inherent conservatism, preferring personal morality to any challenge to world systems, a philosophy meant for the private realm only. (Balthasar Gracian, and in turn many Jansenists and Oratorians, explored the idea of pious self-development, with spiritual forces coming from above, which the individual has to harness.)[48] Admittedly that is not so very different from some classical versions of Christian providence. Yet the New Testament message of the kingdom of God is not so "private" and at the very least involves the self's being directed toward a common goal. This indeed might be the issue that distinguishes the Stoic from the Christian. The other distinguishing mark is that of the person of Christ. In terms of the understanding of the Mediator in creation, with the later New Testament—for example, in Colossians 1—there is an epochal change (*Wende*) of some sort. And it is slightly later still, with the older piece of "tradition" preserved in Ignatius (*Eph.* 19) and in John's Gospel, that things become fully clear. What is new is not so much the elevation of the Mediator of creation into the place he always has, but rather his epiphany, which started on earth and ended in heaven, so that the church is raised above the malevolent powers of the heavenly realm.[49] The (deutero-)Pauline Mediator is conceived of in his historic-salvific work as being of a concrete angelic form.

---

46. Konradt, "Schöpfung und Neuschöpfung im Neuen Testament," 157. Cf. Yates, *Spirit and Creation in Paul.*
47. Konradt, "Schöpfung und Neuschöpfung im Neuen Testament," 177.
48. Colish, *Stoic Tradition*; Colish, "Stoicism and the New Testament."
49. Hegermann, *Die Vorstellung vom Schöpfungsmittler*, 200.

The locus classicus of 1 Corinthians 8:6 is worth considering in full: "Yet for us there is one God, the Father, from whom are all things and for whom we exist, and one Lord, Jesus Christ, through whom are all things and through whom we exist."[50]

Humans are "to" or "for" the Father and through the Son: it is that *reditus* (returning) part which joins on to the *exitus* (going out) of creation. In this sense, Pauline cosmological thought, for all that it is rarely expressed in the epistles, works in teleological and providential terms in ways not very different from Philo. Indeed, Schrage sees evidence here—in the use of εἰς αὐτόν—of eschatological thinking, according to which the end lies ahead in time, rather than there being any present glorification of God,[51] and Schrage also sees traces of soteriological thinking, whereby Christ is the beginning and end of the mediation of both creation and salvation: that is the force of the two *dia*-phrases.[52] The traditional translation of 1 Corinthians 8:6—"Thus we have only one God, the Father, . . . and only one Lord, Jesus Christ"—makes "to us" (ἡμῖν) stand out and gives it an existential flavor like the Latin "pro nobis," which might not have been Paul's emphasis.[53] Really this verse is a reaffirmation of the Shema of Deuteronomy 6:4: "There is no other God," *not just* "There are no other gods to those who love him." The dative *hēmin* really belongs to the phrase itself. This is a truth to be taken in faith by "us," but in its content it is not principally a truth that includes our experience.

"The bountiful activity is initiated by the Father, but it is mediated by the Lord."[54] As Joseph Fitzmyer in the Anchor Yale Bible commentary on 1 Corinthians suggests, part of the human condition is that for which we are created: "He [Christ] is . . . understood not only as the mediator through whom (*di' hou*) Christians attain the goal of their existence, that toward which Christians are tending or are destined (viz., the *eis auton* of v. 6b). The two prep. phrases express instrumental causality with reference to origin and goal."[55] Christ is mediator of creation before he is mediator of salvation, although of course he is that too: in fact there is a sense that the two functions are mutually enhancing. One might speak of Christ's providential work in uniting these two strands. Of course the person of the Mediator is none other than the Son of God, or the Lord Sabaoth even. But he also dwells and works as

---

50. ἀλλ' ἡμῖν εἷς θεὸς ὁ πατὴρ ἐξ οὗ τὰ πάντα καὶ ἡμεῖς εἰς αὐτόν, καὶ εἷς κύριος Ἰησοῦς Χριστὸς δι' οὗ τὰ πάντα καὶ ἡμεῖς δι' αὐτοῦ.

51. Schrage, *Der erste Brief an die Korinther*, 2:243.

52. Schrage, *Der erste Brief an die Korinther*, 2:244.

53. Hofius, "Einer ist Gott—Einer ist Herr," which takes ἡμῖν as a *dativus iudicantis*.

54. Fitzmyer, *First Corinthians*, 343.

55. Fitzmyer, *First Corinthians*, 343.

one who comes from below, working in and through providential history, as part of his "kenotic" and exocentric mission.

Providence and the Kingdom of God

According to the recent study by Martin Leuenberger,[56] there are communal and individual dimensions to enjoying the protective divine kingship; familial-style protection is how kingship is "felt." In Psalm 90:1 the Lord is proclaimed as the dwelling place for the righteous, and in Psalm 93 it is clear that he watches over the right outcome and restored order. These psalms lead into book 4 of the Psalter, in which Psalms 93–100 give a positive answer to the question whether Israel can live without an earthly king and with YHWH as king.[57] In summary, Psalm 93 tells us the Lord has reigned over the whole earth since early times, while Psalm 94 handles the question of revenge and payback, which can be entrusted to God. After the praise of God as king in Psalm 95, Psalm 96 sounds a proclamation of salvation, including participation in cult and judgment open to the nations too. Psalm 97 contains the theophany of YHWH the king in the realms of nature, Israel and the nations, and the individual. In Psalm 98 Israel and the nations praise King YHWH's wonders, and in Psalm 99 a priestly account of right order is provided.[58] Finally, in Psalm 99 what matters to nations is the order he brings.

In the phrase *YHWH mālāk* the verb is stative, yet it could mean that he actually becomes the king as well as he is the king. This is the basis of all discourse about the *action* of God in the inbreaking of the kingdom (e.g., Isa. 52:7), a presence that has effect.[59] Yet the state of his "being king" is predicated on activity, so one might want to speak of a mutual dependence of state and activity, without prioritizing one over the other.[60]

It seems that providence is God's work, provisional to his final salvation and future judgment on the nations / all the universe (Israel included). His power is too great to be caught between past and present, for it stretches into the future as well as across the earth.[61] Leuenberger demonstrates how "lovingkindness" and kingship are combined, especially in Psalm 103.[62] These two seem to reinforce each other.

56. Leuenberger, *Konzeptionen des Königtums Gottes im Psalter*.
57. Leuenberger, *Konzeptionen des Königtums Gottes im Psalter*, 89.
58. Leuenberger, *Konzeptionen des Königtums Gottes im Psalter*, 136–40.
59. Leuenberger, *Konzeptionen des Königtums Gottes im Psalter*, 141.
60. Leuenberger, *Konzeptionen des Königtums Gottes im Psalter*, 141.
61. Leuenberger, *Konzeptionen des Königtums Gottes im Psalter*, 182.
62. Leuenberger, *Konzeptionen des Königtums Gottes im Psalter*, 87.

This does not mean that the biblical providence is monergistic. If Luke 12:22b–31 is to be properly classified as "wisdom teaching," there is a small problem with the Textus Receptus: "They do not spin." "Jesus' assurance that God will provide [for lilies that do nothing] seems to contradict worldly experience where human beings generally earn a living by the 'sweat of their brow.' What *kind* of 'wisdom,' therefore, is being offered here?"[63] It could be the preferable reading is "they grow" (αὐξάνουσιν) rather than the rather surreal-sounding "they do not spin" (οὐδὲ νήθει), as suggested by the alternative reading preserved in P.Oxy. 655 and Codex Sinaiticus at Matthew 6:28. As creatures live out what they are made to be, God will provide and protect. Also, the original version seems to have stopped at Luke 12:29b with the mentions of providence, and only later was it adapted into teaching on prayer. Similar-sounding teaching can be found in Sirach 4:11–12. However, in the gospel it is no longer "wisdom" that one is to seek but the kingdom. One is "to give oneself unreservedly to the pursuit of the Kingdom."[64] All that the human being or community, like lower life-forms, has to do is that which "deep down" comes naturally. It is dependent action: as they do what they do, God will sustain. It is not quietism.

There is more to Jesus's ethical teaching than simply the giving of alms to the poor, as though that were some set piece without any connection to a larger purpose and plan.[65] Heavenly riches are what matter, even for the poor, and for that reason showing mercy must have a spiritual dimension to it, such as in releasing from debts that are not just economic but moral. For the heavenly economy, as part of the Father's will to be done on earth, combines material and spiritual goods. Luke 22:36 with its enigmatic symbolism of buying a sword makes disciples realize the kingdom is a matter of life and death.[66] Jesus and his followers will appear as brigands, with a possible allusion to Isaiah 53:12 ("reckoned with robbers" [AT]). Yet behind that is an allusion parallel to that of Matthew 11:12 concerning a warfare that is spiritual in essence and cause, yet all too physical in operation. The kingdom in Luke 16:16 is "forcefully entered into" (AT), requiring effort and resistance of evil.[67] Matthew 11:12, similarly, has the kingdom that passively suffers force.[68]

63. Joseph, "Seek His Kingdom," 397.
64. Guelich, *Sermon the Mount*, 344, quoted in Joseph, "Seek His Kingdom," 400. Cf. also Piper, "Wealth, Poverty, and Subsistence in Q."
65. Wolter, *Das Lukas-Evangelium*, 432, on Luke 11:40. See Heligenthal, "Werke der Barmherzigkeit oder Almosen?"
66. Wolter, *Das Lukas-Evangelium*, 718.
67. Marcus, "Entering into the Kingly Power of God," 670.
68. Ilaria Ramelli makes a somewhat confused or at least confusing attempt ("Luke 16:16: The Good News of God's Kingdom," 739) with reference to Luke 16:16 (πᾶς εἰς αὐτὴν βιάζεται)

It is often assumed that *basileia* (kingdom) very much belongs in an eschatological context, indeed too much for it to be understood as denoting "God's constant care" in and resulting from creation. However, according to James Robinson, Jesus's teaching was originally a message of providence, not of eschatology, and where Jesus's instruction is "eschatologized" by Luke, the message becomes one of "don't worry" in the face of an uncertain threat and changes its tenor from what Jesus first intended. That is only to stretch the meaning: God provides now, so he will go on providing, up to the end, and *that* is the context and framework for meaningful and ethical activity.

For some scholars like Simon Joseph, one should not place providence and eschatology in opposition. "The admonition of the collection is to trust in God's providence. Yet the introduction of the 'kingdom' at the climax indicates that seeking the kingdom is the critical factor in receiving God's providence."[69] It might be concluded that since it can also be found "within" or "among you" (Luke 17:21), notwithstanding the "yet to come" conceptions, as in Luke 14:15 ("until [the blessed] eat in the kingdom of God"—and that is the comment of a bystander, not of Jesus), "the 'kingdom' should not be defined in an exclusively futuristic sense: the 'reign of God' is a 'way' of being."[70] There is with Jesus a reversal of the fallen condition of life, a new covenant of divine providence: to live in the kingdom is to be reborn into a world where God took control of one's affairs. Here then it can be proposed that the eschatology of Jesus's proclamation is a means to an end of "living under providence." Jesus is presented as the new Adam, as "son of God" in that sense. This kind of interpretation might be viewed as deficient in "imagination," but where scholars who believe that the kingdom is something "ahead," "new" and unknown, their descriptions or sketches of such a state of affairs are so thin as to not even to deserve the epithet "speculative."

As for Palestinian Jewish literature roughly contemporaneous with Jesus, one might compare the providentialism of Psalms of Solomon 5.10, where there is a perceived tension between the "sapiential" (including Genesis 3's) insistence that humans work "by the sweat of [their] brow" and a certain "eschatological" passivity. Yet is that particular chapter really so "eschatological" in character? Is it not rather just a case of wise counsel that one should be happy with what one is given by the provident God, so that one ought not to

---

and 14:23 (*compelle intrare*) to argue that βιάζεται is a divine passive and that everyone is pushed by God through the preaching of the kingdom into the kingdom, which is how the Vetus Syra has it and how Cyril of Alexandria has it (754). She admits that in post-NT Greek the middle voice is common, and indeed the sense of reflexive action—i.e., "forcing themselves"—is more suitable.

69. Joseph, "Seek His Kingdom," 402.

70. Joseph, "Seek His Kingdom," 402.

go looking to possess more? It is a passivity required of people living under providence, which is the content of the "kingdom." The uncertainty of life (James 4:14), quite apart from the awareness of the present world standing under judgment with its days numbered, is enough to motivate a search for reassurance in the eternal truth and merciful provision of God. For Psalms of Solomon 5.17 tells the reader to be "satisfied with righteousness," and 5.18 has "May those who fear the Lord be happy with good things; in your kingdom your goodness [is] upon Israel." In this long paean to providence the discourses of individual salvation and creation providence are mixed, as in Psalms of Solomon 5.7: "Even if You do not convert us, we will not remain distant, but will come to You." Note also 5.8: "For if I am hungry, I will cry out to You, O God, and You will give me [something]." This is somewhat reminiscent of Karl Barth's remark that prayer focused on the kingdom is the most fitting human action correlative to divine providence.

As Israel began to understand its history in terms of the kingdom of God, the concept became determinate, yet all-reaching. While the nations soon come to embody chaos, "the Lord" takes over from Baal the role of giver of life toward created and historical realities.[71] By the end of the Psalter we can see how the kingdom of God is both a present and a future reality. This sense of permanence and continuity (*lə'ōlām*) in this reign is expressed magnificently in the Hebrew of Psalm 145:13: "Your kingdom is an everlasting kingdom, and your dominion endures throughout all generations." The gloss in 11QPs[a] ("Reliable is YHWH in all his words and faithful in all his deeds") reinforces what Frank-Lothar Hossfeld has called "the immanence of God in his deeds on behalf of human beings."[72] There was no hard-and-fast line between present and future. The conclusion drawn by Odo Camponovo with regard to texts from Wisdom of Solomon, that the idea of eschatological divine rule proceeds forth from "the present" and stretching into the future, is borne out.[73]

But also at Psalm 146:4 "on that day" stresses the eschatological dimension in the sense of the climax of a providential rhythm, as the end of a process, not a sudden interruption.[74] The idea of the kingdom of God expands from creation order to local history to universal history to cosmic restoration; we can see this at work in how the old hymns—as in Psalm 68:29, where he becomes the Lord from Sinai (as per Deut. 33)—were redacted for future use.[75]

71. Jeremias, *Das Königtum Gottes in den Psalmen*, 152.
72. Hossfeld and Zenger, *Psalms 3*, 593.
73. Camponovo, *Königtum, Königsherrschaft und Reich Gottes*, 376.
74. Ps. 145:4 LXX: ἐξελεύσεται τὸ πνεῦμα αὐτοῦ, καὶ ἐπιστρέψει εἰς τὴν γῆν αὐτοῦ· ἐν ἐκείνῃ τῇ ἡμέρᾳ ἀπολοῦνται πάντες οἱ διαλογισμοὶ αὐτῶν.
75. Jeremias, *Das Königtum Gottes in den Psalmen*, 93.

In Psalms the Lord as king is consistently protecting Israel and Zion, but one day he will settle things for lasting peace. God is the mighty king, especially in Jeremiah 46:18; 48:15; 51:57, with the idea of a monarch who has left in order to return in Micah 2:13 and 4:7, which connect with Ezekiel 20:33: "As I live, says the Lord GOD, surely with a mighty hand and an outstretched arm, and with wrath poured out, I will be king over you." The reference to a future— that is, "on that day"—is found, first, in the prophetic material of Isaiah 24:21–23, Zechariah 14:9, and Obadiah 8. Although not "marginal" to some other "core" meaning, the futuristic use depends on a core sense that refers to the Lord's ongoing activity in time and space. There is fulfillment of Isaiah 25:8 ("[The LORD] will swallow up death forever.[76] Then the Lord GOD will wipe away tears from all faces")[77] that does not exhaust the prophecy: according to Thomas Hieke, it is fulfilled ("erfüllt") but not completed ("erledigt") in 1 Corinthians 15:54 (death swallowed up into victory [*eis nikos*]) and Revelation 21:4 ("he will wipe away every tear from their eyes"), for it is not yet defeated "forever" (since *eis nikos* can mean "forever"). Hence Hieke argues for a promissory surplus that is not exhausted but taken up and renewed.[78]

These passages emphasize *malkût* (*basileia*, "kingdom") as kingly power, hence a "dynamic" and temporal rather than a spatial or "local" category in the sense of denoting an area of territory. However, only in Daniel is the "kingdom" theme a controlling one, just as it also frames Sibylline Oracles 3. Otherwise it was not very significant in Jewish literature and soon became viewed as a marginal and old-fashioned idea.[79] Jesus's preaching indicates a place or sphere "here and now," *not* an action in the future when God will assemble the faithful. However, there is no use of the term *kingdom* where the discourse about the present lordship of the risen Lord is used instead, doing service for it. "Kingdom" is implicit in Christ's risen, exalted presence, which can come close in the present and can even be entered into by submission, although it will be wholly visible or tangible only in the eschaton.[80] For now it

---

76. Both the Hebrew and Greek have "death" as subject in this clause, and the NRSV's "he" attempts to make sense of it in light of the overall sense of the whole verse, which has a positive-sounding outcome, as well as Paul's version of it in 1 Cor. 15:54's passive verb ("death will be swallowed up"). One might well render it, while being truer to the letter of the text, as follows: "Death being powerful swallowed / will swallow up, but the Lord will wipe away the tears." Whether death or God has agency in the process of dying, the Lord's will is supreme in the outcome. God reigns through, even by, death.

77. בִּלַּע הַמָּוֶת לָנֶצַח; Vulg.: "praecipitabit mortem in sempiternum"; LXX: κατέπιεν ὁ θάνατος ἰσχύσας (death being strong swallowed).

78. Hieke, "Er verschlingt den Tod für immer."

79. Camponovo, *Königtum, Königsherrschaft und Reich Gottes*, 441.

80. Gäckle, *Das Reich Gottes im Neuen Testament*, 244–46. The kingdom grows slowly out of the mustard-seed-like Word planted within (Mark 13:19). See also 251.

is translated into believing hearts as well as minds. From that the concept then got transformed into "salvation" and "eternal life," as being more acceptable to gentile or diasporic contexts. In other words, the futuristic conception of *exousia* (authority) is somewhat secondary, and the place of the kingdom of God, latent in the current affairs of the present order, is primary.

Credo and *Heilsgeschichte* may indeed have come into being only with the exile, apart from a few fragments such as Exodus 15; and yet Psalm 78 contains an awful lot of it that would need to be marked as "redactional" in order to make sense of it in that psalm. To put it plainly, the idea of salvation history (*Heilsgeschichte*) has from the exile onward been overlaid on the "presence of salvation" (*Heilsgegenwart*) theme in Israel's consciousness. However, Dietmar Mathias has argued that the two categories are mutually dependent. Remembering God's deeds is fundamental to the psalms as such, as Psalm 78 (but also Pss. 105; 106; 135; 136) confirms, with Psalm 135:18 giving evidence that the Israelites also had a history of forgetting the Lord.[81] These summaries of history in Psalms that relate salvation history as the experience of saving events are not so much about Israel's origins as about God's provision in the middle of things, with significance for the present and ethical consequences (Ps. 106:35–38).[82] As Spieckermann rightly notes, it is in the themes of "presence" and "the house of the Lord" wherein the protecting agency of the Lord God is foregrounded. He is clear that it provides a theology of God's transcendent glory: divine glory, not that of humans.[83] Likewise with doxologies that give Psalms structure, with "bless the Lord": these serve to accentuate the theocentric character of the Psalter.[84] Time and vicissitude seems less problematic, the more one regards the Lord.

One of Israel's chosen images was that of the ideal king: yet this is not sharply defined, but is sketched in story form, with allusions ("assoziative Redeweise") that play with ideas from past Scripture.[85] This image was more about an expression of God's salvific will for Israel being extended to be that for all of the world, and making it a future thing makes it also "conditional" on human response. That being said, there is yet no real thinking about the difference between present and future kingdom—until targumim and rabbinic literature. Once again, although at "Qumran" the theme is more of

81. Mathias, *Die Geschichtstheologie der Geschichtssummarien in den Psalmen*, 209.
82. Mathias, *Die Geschichtstheologie der Geschichtssummarien in den Psalmen*, 212.
83. Spieckermann, *Heilsgegenwart*, 28. Cf. Krüger, *Das Lob des Schöpfers*. (Cf. Pss. 93:1; 96:10.)
84. Kreuzer, *Der lebendige Gott*, 193.
85. Kreuzer, *Der lebendige Gott*, 438.

looking backward to God's past glories, in the canonical biblical material of the pre-Christian dispensation, what matters is an extension of a reality already built into history. Overly to identify this extension as being one of a covenant evolving into a kingdom is perhaps just too "evolutionary" and even idealist. The biblical material nowhere suggests that the covenantal structure is something to pass away, with the kingdom coming into full force in its wake. These conceptions are mutually overlapping.

If one is to attempt to give a working definition of the concept at the time of Jesus, then *malkût* includes both the power and the institutional framework—or, one might say, mediating agency; it is not a geographical "area."[86] However, Jesus made the kingdom central to his preaching and gave content to the form.[87] In Jesus's preaching the theme of judgment does seem to retreat behind an announcement of salvation, yet it is never absent. In a sense the preached reality is the symmetrical reverse mirror image of the everyday, experienced reality, of salvation being obscured by a closer sense of tribulation, with any providence being of an *absconditus* form. Dynamic activity in God's reaching out is what is emphasized, rather than a "nineteenth-century" understanding of kingdom as an ethical matter for human endeavor. For all the eschatological anticipation, God rules perpetually in the present, and his rule both precedes and corresponds to a future salvation.

It is only because God goes into the temple that worshipers are able to enter. By "the kingdom," similarly, Jesus is talking of entering into a presence as power. Joel Marcus possibly overstates his case when he writes that Zechariah 14:9, 16[88] "contains the picture of the kingdom in the context of an eschatological celebration of Tabernacle, with people entering into an action."[89] For while there is no doubting the "entering into" element in verse 16, it is not clear that this is what is to the fore there. The people enter in order to praise a God who is actively king over all the land and recognized as such, rather than in order to experience this action as their own. They are the beneficiaries of it, yet this can mean they also reflect and mediate that powerful presence. But they are not part of the action of "the show."

The kingdom is something that is a "given," even if it is to be entered into. "Mark 10:15 leaves us in no doubt about the absolute priority of gift over call to faithful service. Jesus does not say, 'Unless you strive to enter God's

---

86. Kreuzer, *Der lebendige Gott*, 443.
87. Kreuzer, *Der lebendige Gott*, 444.
88. (14:9). וְהָיָה יְהוָה לְמֶלֶךְ עַל־כָּל־הָאָרֶץ בַּיּוֹם הַהוּא יִהְיֶה יְהוָה אֶחָד וּשְׁמוֹ אֶחָד:
89. Marcus, "Entering into the Kingly Power of God," 667. Cf. Marcus, *The Way of the Lord*, 156–58; Schnackenburg, *Das Johannesevangelium* (ET *The Gospel according to John*), on John 4:38b, "Others have labored, and you have entered into their labor."

basileia, you will never receive it,' but exactly the opposite."[90] Receiving it like a little child, like one dependent, is more apt. The original sense of Jesus's teaching, as expressed in Mark 10, might be that there will be an earthly kingdom of Christ, but what is clear is that the end state is almost deliberately obscure, as one might expect of something otherworldly, and the kingdom that takes one there is rather mysterious.[91] Indeed, a transcendence of the earthly dimension should be expected for just and unjust, which can be seen in Mark 9:43, and its reference back to the very end of Isaiah 66. However, as Jacques Schlosser makes clear, there is a present moment of salvation leading up to final deliverance in the age to come. Luke 20:38 curiously mingles soteriological with creation-providential categories: "God is not of the dead, but of the living, *for all live in him*" (AT). This Lukan *Sondergut* (material exclusive to Luke) (πάντες γὰρ αὐτῷ ζῶσιν; cf. Mark 12:27; Matt. 22:32) is echoed in Acts 17:28. Matthew, as we have seen at the start of chapter 2, ties it to the present, whereas Luke (20:33–36) keeps the context of the divine saying—to Moses at the burning bush.[92] The idea is that God considered the patriarchs still to be alive. "The argument is that God will not have continued to represent himself as their God if he had finished his work with them and abandoned them to the grave."[93] Of course, as Michael Wolter points out,[94] life in the resurrection is seen as completely different from human life, yet it can be seen as an expansion (see Nolland's discussion) of what is good in life (the friendship in marriage into a nonexclusive, nonbiological register).

However, the point is that God is king and in control, and he cares, even about basic human needs (Luke 12:20–24), so that humans do not have to, yet from verse 31 it is clear that there is more to life than these things.[95] But it is

90. Marcus, "Entering into the Kingly Power of God," 675.

91. Cf. Schlosser, "Die Vollendung des Heils in der Sicht Jesu," 82.

92. In his commentary on this verse in his *Das Evangelium nach Matthäus* Luz claims a reference to Exod. 3:6, the absence of "(burning) bush" notwithstanding, and speaks of a "Sinnkontinuum" (continuum of meaning) between that verse and the NT use of it. To that end he takes the first and second of the Eighteen Benedictions ("God of the patriarchs," "God who makes alive the dead") as part of that "continuum of meaning." "'God is the God of the living' is not the second premise (so that those patriarchs of whom God is the God must be alive), but rather the conclusion—that he is God of the living even now" (Luz, *Das Evangelium nach Matthäus*, 266; see also 266n33).

93. Nolland, *Luke 18:35–24:53*, 967, quoted in Nolland, *Gospel of Matthew*, 906: "'God of' in connection with the Patriarchs points to God in his role of savior, protector, and deliverer." Note also France, *Gospel of Matthew*, 840: "The covenant by which he binds himself to them is too strong to be terminated by their death. To be associated with the living God is to be taken beyond the temporary life of earth into a relationship which lasts as long as God lasts." Philo, *Sacr.* 5, speaks of Abraham "gaining imperishability, being the same as the angels."

94. Wolter, *Lukas-Evangelium*, 657.

95. Konradt, "Schöpfung und Neuschöpfung im Neuen Testament," 128.

the reassurance of divine care in basic things that encourages humans to seek God's kingdom. With Schlosser, it might be appropriate to speak of the two poles of the kingdom of God: theology and eschatology.[96] According to one pole, believers are in the position of children toward a providential father, and according to the other, slaves toward a Master who needs their submission if they are to be delivered. God has possession, but his title is a double one. The one accused by conscience of being a poor servant is invited by Jesus to lift his eyes toward the Father, who from that point onward pardons and takes care of him. To support this, Schlosser points to the parable of the prodigal son (Luke 15:11–32) and the injunctions "not to worry" in Luke 12:22–30.[97]

Schlosser's work was itself built on that of Anton Vögtle, who argued that this preaching of the kingdom was not a "theology of God in himself," but rather that Jesus's message of trust was one predicated on an eschatological kingdom that builds on God's intervention in past and present history. As Schlosser puts it: *basileia* is God's eschatological intervention already inaugurated. One is to see in the present the gathering of an eschatological intervention: a process starting in the present. According to Vögtle, Heinz Schürmann was wrong to establish a distinction between (1) the "present" presence of the *eschaton* and (2) the kingdom, by postponing, hence relegating, the latter into the future. Vögtle thought that theocentrism and eschatology were held together in Jesus's preaching: there are definitely two poles, but these are not poles in tension with each other. Yet Schürmann makes a valuable contribution in emphasizing that Jesus did believe in a transcendent coming of the kingdom that related closely to an "Abba Father" God, rather than an alien one. The Son descended *as* the presence of the kingdom, making total ownership of it possible in the future. This is a secret kingdom that nevertheless becomes open to membership with Easter and the epiphany of Jesus as the kingdom in the post-Easter proclamation.[98] The "Son of Man" sayings are from a later, second stage of tradition. Before that, Jesus was already known as the proclaimer of the kingdom. But he was proclaimer of God's protection at the worst times, with even his own death-resurrection being a witness to divine reversal of fortunes.

One might well say that the eschaton, in its reaching backward to the present, *is* the kingdom and that in doing so it meets the providential care of God halfway in the present. For Schürmann, the kingdom is indeed yet to come, but Jesus announces a "coming" of God into and through creation,

96. See Schlosser's summary at *Le règne de Dieu dans les dits de Jésus*, 680.
97. This following Schürmann, "Das hermeneutische Hauptproblem."
98. Schürmann, *Gottes Reich—Jesu Geschick*.

a coming that is present in his providential care, such that Vögtle's concerns about any dichotomy between the presence of eschatological reality and future kingdom are met. Although other Jewish sources express this notion of care and appeal for corresponding trust, Jesus was unusual in extending this virtue of trust in God's taking care of justice (entrusting justice to God in Deut. 32:35: "Vengeance is mine") to the virtue of forgiving enemies as evidence of a deeper trust in the eventual righting of the moral order. Early Christian ethics not only responded to the expectation of a coming kingdom but also simply sought to align itself with the unfeigned will and manner of God.[99] "Seeking the kingdom" as such is quite unique to Jesus. Yet Schürmann seems to admit that the two movements ("waiting" and "seeking God's will") join forces, so as to form a "living indwelling."[100] Vögtle accused Schürmann of losing sight of the future and expected action of God due to a high christological reductionism; in turn Vögtle has to argue that "give us this day our daily bread" and "forgive us our debts" relate to a future eschatological reality, as though little material and practical aid is to be expected this side of the future eschaton.[101] Actually, Schürmann's "presentist" reading seems preferable. However, Vögtle is very helpful in showing the seamless connection between the prayer for daily needs and the forgiveness of sins in Matthew 6, even if the logic he discerns is rather convoluted.[102] François Bovon has written of providence becoming clearer to the disciple the more eschatological it gets. In Luke at least, eschatological reality is neither separated from nor identified with the created reality. God's kingdom, will, and name are the most important of life's realities, and not the lusts that would too readily identify with consumption.[103]

In his book already referred to above (*Vorsehung Gottes?*) Wolfgang Schrage disagrees with what he calls "Dogmatics, and its claim that Matthew 10:29 and Matthew 6:26 have much to do with the maintenance (*conservatio*) or government (*gubernatio*) of the universe." No, he contests, these two verses are about God's care for his own (here, disciples or little flock), what one might traditionally call "special providence," whether with reference to Israel or to Christians. Any reference to the natural world and order is merely as analogy for the sake of the reassurance for the little flock, not an assurance that this order will endure. It is strange that Schrage feels the need to oppose the "in-breaking kingdom" to the care of God for his creation, which is all too visible

99. Vögtle, "'Theologie' und 'Eschatologie,'" 20.
100. Vögtle, "'Theologie' und 'Eschatologie,'" 25.
101. Vögtle, "Der 'eschatologische' Bezug der Wir-Bitten des Vaterunser," 41–42.
102. Vögtle, "Der 'eschatologische' Bezug der Wir-Bitten des Vaterunser," 47–48.
103. Bovon, *Das Evangelium nach Lukas II*, 311.

in Jesus's teaching, and something on which Christ's a fortiori arguments rest.[104] One supposes that Schrage does this because the idea of in-breaking seems to connote an overriding entity or even something destructive in its "sweeping away." Indeed, God's coming is not to be felt in the natural world, thinks Schrage. Yet Schrage also admits that the *psychē* (which one is not to worry about [e.g., Luke 12:22]) means "life," and that in an earthly sense.[105] It is not just one's "spiritual life" that one is not to worry about, but what matters deeply to people "here and now." While determined to oppose any immanent built-in progressive principle, he is prepared to say that the vision is not totally pessimistic.[106] In Deuteronomy 30:15–16 *zōē* means obviously more than just bare physical life, but as a life associated with blessing and flourishing, it is not *less than* physical in its scope, and both of these predicated on love for the Lord.[107] The Lord sustains life, as in the use of "staff" in Psalm 23:4 as a metaphor for support (with "rod" denoting "guidance").[108] Protection, not guiding, is indicated, although these are hardly mutually exclusive.[109]

Spiritual Life, Light, and "Ethical" Presence of God

Light and life are strongly connected in Scripture, beginning in Psalms and echoed in John's Gospel and Epistles. Also, in Job 3:16 ("Or why was I not buried like a stillborn child, like an infant that never sees the light?") there is a paralleled opposition of death and light, but light and life are linked more obviously in Job 33:30 ("to bring back their souls from the Pit, so that they may see the light of life"). The imagery is clearly that of womb and underground versus living in the sun and air. The face of God seems to supply extra light: here a number of psalms are helpful: Psalms 4:7; 31:17; 67:2; 80:3, 7, 19.[110] Deuteronomy and Proverbs—Torah and Wisdom, respectively—forge a strong link between light and life, as a means to life made stronger.

What is important here is the idea of the *spirit* of life. The two notions, those of sustaining creation and of Pentecost, combine in the one reality. The Spirit is the same who starts in creation and who then becomes part of

104. See Schrage, *Voreshung Gottes?*, 208.
105. Schrage, *Vorsehung Gottes?*, 209n752.
106. Schrage, *Vorsehung Gottes?*, 268.
107. See Feldmeier and Spieckermann, *Der Gott der Lebendigen*, 538–40.
108. Liess, *Der Weg des Lebens.*
109. Kreuzer, *Der lebendige Gott*, 41, quoting Kraus, *Psalmen*, 2:722. So, Exod. 13:21–22 and Ps. 78:14, not Exod. 14:19 or Wis. 10:17.
110. Cf. Grohmann, *Fruchtbarkeit und Geburt in den Psalmen*; Pola, 'Was ist 'Leben' im Alten Testament?,' 251–52. Also, K. Schmid, "Fülle des Lebens oder erfülltes Leben?"

creaturely experience. "The Holy Spirit is called 'holy' because it sanctifies life and renews the face of the earth."[111] This means that the spiritual is not "the inward." The community is the location of an awareness of Shekinah. "If we become one with ourselves, the Shekinah comes to rest."[112] One might think of Rilke's "to be here is glorious" or Bergson's "élan vital"—that is, a love of life, "life against death." And yet the Spirit also generates a centrifugal, or extroverting, force, creating freedom to serve. To experience the *rûaḥ* is to experience what is divine not only as a person, and not merely as a force, but also as *space*—as the space of freedom in which the living being can unfold. That is the experience of the Spirit: "Thou has set my feet in a broad place" (Ps. 31:8 RSV). "You also he allured out of distress into a broad place where there is no cramping" (Job 36:16 AT). Yet just as the metaphors for the Spirit in creation and in the coming of Christ have to do with reconciliation and the maternal (principally "the brooding dove"), it is unfounded to see the Spirit as an "it" or simply as a "force."

This is where "presence" comes in[113]—for example, in Psalm 91 and Isaiah 41:10 ("Fear not, I am with you" [AT]). Katrin Liess claims that Psalm 73 gently inverts the subject and the object of this prayer, and she has the one who is praying reassuring God of *his* presence. She points to verses 23 and 28: "Nevertheless, I am continually with you; you hold my right hand" (v. 23); "But for me it is good to be near God; I have made the Lord GOD my refuge, to tell of all your works" (v. 28). Certainly the note here is that the psalmist comes close to God to find the divine presence coming to meet him, which indicates that there is both a reciprocal element and a subjective one, of *feeling* or *sensing* supportive presence, as in Psalm 16:8: there God "at my right hand" is predicated on God's care as expressed in v. 5 ("You are my choice portion and cup; you hold my lot" [AT]). Providence *may* include a sense of being provided for, but more essentially, at its heart is the divine action in presence.

This means that since God becomes present, he often acts in an unannounced and unpredictable way, though this is not the same thing as predicating arbitrariness or capriciousness of him. "The knowledge of this free and sovereign God," writes Samuel Terrien, "informs Israel's standard of faith. . . . Such knowledge stems from a single factor: the Hebraic theology of presence. . . . Divine intervention in human affairs is generally, if not exclusively, represented as sudden, unexpected, unwanted, unsettling, and often devastating."[114] Terrien later adds: "Biblical Hebrew did not apparently

111. Moltmann, *Spirit of Life*, 7–8.
112. Moltmann, *Spirit of Life*, 50.
113. See Liess, *Der Weg des Lebens*, 357.
114. Terrien, *Elusive Presence*, 28.

possess an abstract word meaning 'presence.'" Instead, *panîm* is used "to designate a sense of immediate proximity,"[115] as when Deuteronomy 34:10 speaks of "Moses, whom YHWH knew face to face." Yet that is a particular idiom, whereas *panîm* on its own seems to mean something that might well be described as "abstract." What it connotes, however, is the speaking and the hearing of the Word of God.[116]

The Lutheran roots of Terrien's thinking appear in his footnotes and excursuses.[117] In the conclusion he turns to Isaiah 45:15a and comments: "While the Latin version with its passive participle led to the often abused theme of 'the hidden God,' the Hebrew original, with its verbal reflexive, stressed divine freedom and sovereignty: 'Verily, thou art a God that hidest thyself!'"[118] One might wonder what difference the voice of the participle makes to theology at this point, or what Terrien has in mind by "the often abused theme." What he seems to imply is that, far from the bleak theologies of God's absence, God can be present precisely *because* he is hidden, moving close so as to whisper a word.

> Faded presence became a memory and a hope, but it burnt into an alloy of inward certitude, which was *emunah*, "faith." When God no longer overwhelmed the senses of perception and concealed himself behind the adversity of historical existence, those who accepted the promise were still aware of God's nearness in the very veil of his seeming absence. For them, the center of life was a *Deus absconditus atque praesens*.
>
> The erection of the tent and the ark in the wilderness, the sanctuaries in Canaan, and the temple in Jerusalem testified to the elusiveness of theophany and vision and stressed the paradox of a hiddenness which was not an absence.[119]

Even in salvation God's effects are "under the contradictory," *sub contrario*: not just in Christ but also in Israel acts God in a subtle way.[120] The God of Israel, Jesus, and Auschwitz is one and the same God.

This accords well with what has been said about the Israelite form of skepticism. "The negative side of a skeptic's mental outlook consists of the doubting thought, whereas the positive affirmation of a hidden reality indicates that it is

115. Terrien, *Elusive Presence*, 65.
116. Terrien, *Elusive Presence*, 95: "The *anamnesis* or liturgical rehearsal of the word became the distinctive factor of Hebrew cultus."
117. Terrien, *Elusive Presence*, 103n88, quotes Luther (WA 43:220): "We say, 'In the midst of life we die.' God answers, 'Nay, in the midst of death we live.'"
118. Terrien, *Elusive Presence*, 474.
119. Terrien, *Elusive Presence*, 470–71.
120. Mußner, "JHWH, der sub contrario handelnde Gott Israels."

altogether inappropriate to accuse skeptics of unbelief. This vision of a better world is inherent in skepticism."[121] Might God be closer if his people were holier? "It seems that Terrien has perhaps been too ready to follow the traditional understanding that God's hiding is always and in every case a response to sin." There are psalms other than Psalms 22 and 51 where sin simply does not come into the matter of God's hiddenness. It could simply be that God relates to humanity as creation in a somewhat "up close but impersonal" way. "It is rather an integral part of the nature of God which is not to be explained away by theological exposition of human failures or human limitations. God is hidden just as he is present; he is far away just as he is near."[122]

There does seem to be some change between the Prophets, on the one hand, and Psalms and Wisdom literature, on the other. In the former, divine distance is viewed as largely caused by the sin of the people.[123] This can be explained as the difference of situation, with sin being punished or about to be punished, or sin having been punished.[124] The very fact that questions are raised in the nonprophetic literature suggests that it is not obvious that God's disfavor is due to collective sin. Such questions are posed in Proverbs 6:9 and 25:8 but are even more poignant in Job 13:24, along with Psalms 44:25 and 88:15. There was perhaps a season in Israel's life when sin had been atoned for through exile and cult, enabling a genuine questioning. However, for theological purposes, it might be better to see things in terms of epochal changes, with theology being ruled by circumstance (as distinct from application to it), rather than in terms of progress or decline,[125] or even simply change (Samuel

121. Crenshaw, "Birth of Skepticism in Ancient Israel," 1.

122. Balentine, *Hidden God*, 175.

123. Balentine, *Hidden God*, 122. Balentine argues that it is wrong to see laments as always preliminary to a resolution as per Westermann (*Praise of God in the Psalms*, 60–63) and Brueggemann ("From Hurt to Joy"). Where Brueggemann sees much trust in YHWH to transform situations, Balentine finds plenty of continuing anxiety, as in Pss. 42 and 43.

124. In Balentine's estimation, the psalms come before the prophets, and the original sense of the verbs is to be more found in the psalms. In the prophets the distance is due to the people's abandonment of God. Ezekiel 8:6 contrasts with Ps. 22:12–20 or Ps. 10:1; see also Ps. 27:7; 28:1—"answer me!"—whereas Mic. 3:1–5 is about judgment. The same goes with God's forgetting (שכח). "In effect the prophets take over the basic import of the lament but reverse its application. What had been the people's complaint against God became God's complaint against the people" (*Hidden God*, 161).

125. It is common to affirm that there was a time when questioning ("suspending of belief") was allowed but that it was cut short, oppressed, as per Dell, *Book of Job as Sceptical Literature*, 215–16: "It is parody not wisdom, thus more radical than Eccles. . . . By his use of parody the author deliberately stepped outside literary conventions to make a protest. 'Parody' does not necessarily contain a comic element, as in modern definitions." This means "suspending judgement rather than coming down fully against the orthodox position. . . . The final form of the books as the author intended it is deliberately contradictory. . . . There was a short stage

Balentine's preference). Whether "dialectical" is the right word to use, there may be a tension between prophets and psalmists, just as one sees within the book of Job, a "dialectic between prologue and speeches."[126] The psalmist in Psalms 42–43 does not mention sin, true, but nor does his questioning exclude the idea that sin has been involved. That said, it is right to remember that the relationship between sin and suffering is not a straightforward one. To bring Job into the discussion, that book does not defend a creation order so much as demonstrate God's radical freedom to Job and the reader.[127] That is what encounter teaches—that God is active but without revealing, despite Elihu's claim in Job 36:3, that he gets his knowledge "from afar."[128]

Indeed, "the face" means blessing, rather than its having anything to do with theophany/seeing the form of God,[129] as in Exodus 33:13. Lothar Perlitt has written an important and influential essay on this,[130] arguing that only in Israel is the language of "hiding" used, even though the ancient Near Eastern gods can also be silent. It is important to affirm that God is mindful and that therefore his initiatives and responses are not automatic but intentional.[131] The self-withdrawing (*str* in the hiphil) can be felt even within the cult, where one cannot literally look on God, as the prohibition of images confirms. Yet when Psalm 69:18 MT has "Hide not your face" (AT),[132] what might that mean in an aniconic setting, assuming that Psalm 69 presupposes this? The sense must likely be metaphorical, such that for God to hide his face had something to do

---

in Hebrew thought, which was not allowed to develop, where moral ambiguities were present and where sceptical questioning endangered traditionally held beliefs."

126. Hoffman, "Relation between the Prologue and the Speech-Cycles in Job," 169.

127. Van Oorschot, *Gott als Grenze*, 205, *pace* Loader, who wrote of the finale of Job setting forth "the profoundly planned order of the creation of god—a harmony in the midst of mystery" ("Job—Answer or Enigma?," 22).

128. Van Oorschot, *Gott als Grenze*, 208.

129. M. Smith, "'Seeing God' in the Psalms," 177: "'The Lord came from Sinai, and dawned (*zāraḥ*) from Seir upon us; he shone forth (*hôpîʿa*) from Mount Paran' [Deut. 33:2]. As C. Meyers has noted, the language is patently solar. In this passage, the verb for the rising of the sun, *zrḥ*, is used to describe the divine procession. In Isa 60:1, the verb is also applied to the going forth of God. This verb appears as well in Biblical Hebrew and inscriptional personal names with the theophoric element. Thus, solar language is used to describe God's own light. Solar imagery for God is found also in Ps 84:12, which calls God 'a sun and a shield' (*šemeš ûmāgēn*). While this language is figurative, it assumes that the divine could be described in solar terms." Note also 181: "The language of seeing God in Ps 11:7 expresses the traditional wisdom that seeing God was a mark of divine blessing or approval (as in Psalms 4, 31, 80, etc.). Ps 17:15 describes the expectation of seeing the divine 'face.'"

130. Perlitt, "Die Verborgenheit Gottes," 367.

131. Perlitt, "Die Verborgenheit Gottes," 370.

132. Fornara, in *La vision contraddetta*, writes that where Job says, "Now I have seen God," this is really "vedere senza vedere" (a seeing without seeing) (482), and it really means "to be in conversation with," involving some kind of perception, when God decides to reveal. See also 229.

with not making Israel's condition any better, or letting it deteriorate. Hence in Psalm 30:8b MT it is as a singer before the Lord that the psalmist experiences the hiding of God's face. However, that seems to mean that the cult is not the fail-safe way of restoring one's fortunes. In Psalm 104:29a God is seen to be hiding his face from all creation. The lesson is one of creaturely contingency and divine omniscience: humans cannot hide, as per Jeremiah 23:24a and Job 34:22, and this affects them not just in their ignorance in the faculty of cognition but in their affliction through their whole being.[133] It is the God of Israel who does this, even as individuals complain. It is not that he doesn't exist, but that he has just withdrawn and thus is not fulfilling the role as the Lord of Israel. It is Isaiah who says God can withdraw due to human guilt, leaving behind "darkness" as judgment (8:17: "I will wait for the LORD, who is hiding his face from the house of Jacob, and I will hope in him"). Here God seems to be testing his prophet, requiring him to wait for any revelation, as also in Psalm 18:11–12. Perlitt notes that by Deuteronomy 29:28[134] and 31:16–18 Israel's relationship with God has become rather mechanistic: Israel sins and the presence withdraws. "My anger will be kindled against them in that day. I will forsake them and hide my face from them; they will become easy prey, and many terrible troubles will come upon them. In that day they will say, 'Have not these troubles come upon us because our God is not in our midst?'" (Deut. 31:17). This helps to clarify that the loss of presence is seen on the outside, as symptoms of a cause. That is what hiding the face means, even if the remedy has more to do with inner attitude and cultic repentance. Moreover, his majesty does not prevent him from revealing in action (cf. Isa. 55:6–11).[135] Yet it is that God who saves them, even while not revealing himself to them.

The semantic range of the metaphor "hand of God" should be considered next to that of "face of God." In the paragraph above, it is the psalmist's hand rather than that of God himself. When "God's hand" is employed, of the 115 cases, it stands for "sickness" only in 15 cases. Some of the examples of a "positive," salutary signification have to do with "care" rather than "salvation," since there is more about help for individuals than is the case in the corresponding ancient Near Eastern material. It is not so much about the divine singling out individuals as in the ancient Near Eastern context, where "hand of God" almost means "illness" or "misfortune."[136]

133. See Perlitt, "Die Verborgenheit Gottes," 372.
134. Cf. Deut. 29:29: "The secret things belong to the LORD our God, but the revealed things belong to us and to our children forever, to observe all the words of this law."
135. "Seek the LORD while he may be found, call upon him while he is near; let the wicked forsake their way, and the unrighteous their thoughts" (Isa. 55:6).
136. Norin, "Das Hand Gottes im Alten Testament," 59.

Thus in Psalms God's hand is largely seen as a positive thing in its effects, for its use in judgment is a means to the end of saving the people as a whole.[137] Job provides a difference in that he is a singular recipient of God's hand understood in terms of its effects, both favorable and negative.[138] It is the same hand, but over time the protecting hand comes heavier to bear. In the Hebrew Bible the left hand is never mentioned on its own but only when two hands are. Is the *yād* (hand) in Psalms 89:13 and 138:7 to be understood as left hand, when *yamîn* (right hand) comes second in the parallel?[139] If so, providence could be understood to be a sequence of woe followed by restorative weal. Indeed, Job himself is unaware of Satan and so experiences his suffering as provided from the chastising hand of God.[140] Again, in Isaiah 1–11 and in Jeremiah the use of "hand" is mostly negative. Amos 9:2 has an anthropomorphic way in its depiction of God's digging so as to be able to reach the people with his hand wherever they hide, even in death. By the time of Deuteronomy and Chronicles the metaphor is "dead," and it simply means might or authority. Yet in the Pentateuch and Ezekiel (and then Second Isaiah)[141] is where one finds the hand of God as an active and positive thing to be considered.

Lastly, the notion of "the way" has to do with making choices to improve morally one's lifestyle yet does not aim toward salvation. There is no sense of merit that puts God in one's debt, and yet merit is connected to reaching the will of God and so is of high importance. This of course is ethical, but the ethics presupposes not merely a metaphysical framework but even a covenantal framework, in that an active will of God is reaching out into history, to which the decision is a response.[142] Fear of the Lord connects people to the law in terms of motivation even if that fear should turn to trust, joy, and love for God as one walks according to the law. An easy path is not at all guaranteed if the right move *is* made, but eventual, guaranteed destruction looms if a wrong step is taken.

The collective use of *way* for the walk of the people of Israel is rare. Unlike in parallel Egyptian literature, there is no mention of "way" beyond death or anything so cosmic. Nor is there anything mantic about finding it. "Way" simply means God's instruction, and in some cases God's action. Occasionally God's own going forth is meant, as in Nahum 1:3 ("in the storm is his way")

137. Mies, "Job et la main de Dieu," 62–63.
138. Mies, "Job et la main de Dieu," 70.
139. The targumim spell this out; see Philonenko, "Main gauche et main droite de Dieu," 135–40.
140. Mies, "Job et la main de Dieu," 81.
141. Norin, "Das Hand Gottes im Alten Testament," 60.
142. Zehnder, *Wegmetaphorik*, 609.

and Habakkuk 3:6 (*hălikôt*, ways); God's spatial movement when frequently mentioned as in Exodus is usually only in connection with his people, and little is made of any divine movement in heaven or underworld.[143] There is no hint of the military-ritual procession usage of "way" as in Akkadian, and no water metaphor is brought into association, unlike in the Egyptian sources. No opening of a way for a god by means of a human subject is mentioned: the emphasis is very much on humans acting to be ethical in correspondence to divine will and "prodding."[144] One might therefore speak of an ethical "sphere" that God provides, as part of an "ethical ontology" of sorts, or a sphere of holiness, as perhaps best illustrated by the "H" (Holiness Code)— additions to the Levitical cultic instructions, which serve to take "holiness" outside the sanctuary (Lev. 17–25).

Holy Life

Life is the direction God gives, and eternal life is a participation in the livingness of God, in a spiritual sense now, and in a complete sense in the life to come. The God who raised Jesus from the dead was a key part of early Christian preaching, and indeed crucial even as far back as Abraham's faith, according to Romans 4:17: "the God who makes alive the living" (AT). This is used metaphorically or is what one might call "spiritually applied," not least in Colossians-Ephesians. Christ is usually spoken of as "resurrected," and only in 1 Peter 3:18 is "made alive" used, but the usage is significant for what it affirms about created life. God taking an interest in lives is indeed providential.

There is also the note of "protection" in Psalm 63:9, but in Psalm 73:24b this gets elevated to lifelong accompaniment in the very path of life. However, by the time Psalm 73 is apparently written, the deed-result connection (*Tun-Ergehen-Zusammenhang*) has fallen into disrepute in Hebrew thought, such that there is a resort to future postmortem restoration, in full fellowship with God (as foreshadowed in Psalm 49:13–16's reference to deliverance from Sheol), as the end of a continuous process throughout life. It is not quite clear that the afterlife is explicit in Psalm 73, not least because the Septuagint interprets the verb in verse 24b as an aorist: "With glory you took me" (AT).[145] Yet for both this and the earlier Psalm 16 the nature of

143. Zehnder, *Wegmetaphorik*, 612.
144. Zehnder, *Wegmetaphorik*, 613.
145. Cf. Ps. 72:24b LXX: καὶ μετὰ δόξης προσελάβου με. Vulg.: "et tenebas manum dexteram meam in consilium tuum deduces me et postea in gloria suscipies me."

the relationship between psalmist and God as an enduring one is key.[146] In Psalm 121:3–6 a guarantee is given to Israel: God is said to offer both spiritual shade-like protection and company in this life, a homely sense of belonging. Therefore the future darkness for the psalmist is illuminated by the assurance that the Lord is Creator of heaven and earth, that his power—in that he "neither slumbers nor sleeps"—is effective in what he does to save, and that the Lord is the protector of Israel watching over every member at all times. One might wish to issue a small comment: Does God act only to *save*? No doubt he does that, but the keeping watch in these verses is more preventive of worse evils than salvific as such.

Likewise with that most famous of psalms, Psalm 23, the Septuagint renders the second verse beautifully: "he will make me to dwell in a green place, by the waters of rest he will nourish me" (MT: "guide me").[147] The Hebrew text alludes to Exodus 15:13 with its mention of guidance into holy pastures, yet also to that interim resting place of Numbers 10:33 and its peaceful waters.[148] Frank-Lothar Hossfeld and Erich Zenger add that Isaiah 35:6–7 and 41:18 should be kept in mind, with "rest" as a promise for the future.[149] Guidance to places of nourishment and rest is a good thing. God as shepherd is also a king on the move, whose role is to care and protect, yet to bring to a place of stability: the nature imagery is just that—metaphorical, as in Lamentations 1:11, 19's "seeking food to revive . . . strength." The temple is the Lord's sphere of influence (*Machtsphär*),[150] and what is on offer is more objective protection and encouragement than consolation, as per Isaiah 40 and Lamentations 1–2, where one is still without power for anything to change. The Lord supplies power for the present to overcome difficulty, rather than rescue completely out of the adverse situation, and that is what makes his action "providential" rather than typically "soteriological" at base.

Numbers 20:1–13 tells of Meribah, where Moses and Aaron are about to be suspended from their roles for not believing that God would provide—that is, that God could operate directly, when they struck the rock.[151] It would appear that the story originally emphasized divine care and provision, with the

---

146. See Zehnder, *Wegmetaphorik*, 396, 402.

147. Ps. 22:2 LXX (EV 23:2): εἰς τόπον χλόης, ἐκεῖ με κατεσκήνωσεν, ἐπὶ ὕδατος ἀναπαύσεως ἐξέθρεψέν με.

148. Craigie, *Psalms 1–50*, 207: "The undertones of the Exodus indicate that [the psalmist's] expectation is established on the bedrock of Israel's faith, namely the precedent of God's refreshment and guidance in the Exodus and wilderness journeys."

149. Hossfeld and Zenger, *Die Psalmen I: Psalm 1–50*, 154, points to Ps. 95:11 for entering into rest.

150. Spieckermann, *Heilsgegenwart*, 273.

151. Seebass, *Numeri*, 270. Frevel, *Mit Blick auf das Land die Schöpfung erinnern*.

"murmuring" motif a later addition.[152] As Katharine Doob Sakenfeld puts it, there is "a failure to sanctify God before the people. For God's chosen leaders, no sin could be more serious than that which by lack of trust impedes God's mercy to the community."[153] For its part Numbers 10:33 relates the daily journey to the resting place of the ark: the *Deus praesens* (present God),[154] which gives rest just as the pillar of cloud gives protection.

This direct and active presence in the Pentateuch may be confirmed by what Rogerson has noticed; with reference to Genesis 18 and to the burning bush of Exodus 3, he writes: "Narratives about God's *presence* seem to be confined to traditions about what happened in Israel before Israel had a king"; yet from Exodus 3 onward, human intermediaries, beginning with Moses, tend to step in to lead the people, yet clearly as God's proxies. "Taken as a whole, these stories about God's power express the conviction that God is in control of the world and the happenings in it."[155] Specifically in the case of Numbers: "The pillar of cloud by day and of fire by night is a symbol for the *presence* of God during the wilderness wanderings. In the Yahwistic source it is a symbol not of an active presence, but of how *God himself* led the Israelites through the wilderness when there was no other leader who knew the way. In the Priestly source, the divine presence seems less active (see especially Numbers 9:15–23)."[156] The idea is that the presence stays still and tells the people to move or stay.

"The fact the conception of the Tabernacle cloud as guide rests on the assumption that the cloud is penetrable—in clear contradiction to Exod. 40.34–35—shows that the entire conception is a late supplement within the priestly stratum."[157] David Frankel here thinks that the idea of the cloud as a guide in Numbers 10 has been superimposed upon the earlier P-stratum's preferred agent of guidance, which is "(by) the word of the Lord" (as in Lev. 24:12; Num. 3:16, 39, 51; 4:37, 41, 45, 49; 13:3; 33:2, 38; 36:5; Josh. 22:9).[158]

152. Frankel, *Murmuring Stories of the Priestly School*, 322: the caring God is not later than the God who demands strict religious obedience, *pace* Knohl, *Sanctuary of Silence*, even if the Priestly narration keeps God a "hidden agent" (92–94); but what about Deut. 29:5, which tells of discipline in the desert, as Zakovitch has observed in *On the Conception of Miracle in the Bible*? Presumably that meant after the provision of manna and the ungrateful response there was plenty of time for want and "discipline."
153. Sakenfeld, "Theological and Redactional Problems in Numbers 20.2–13," 151.
154. Seebass, *Numeri*, 17.
155. Rogerson, *Supernatural in the Old Testament*, 14, 15.
156. Rogerson, *Supernatural in the Old Testament*, 42.
157. Frankel, "Two Priestly Conceptions of Guidance in the Wilderness," 32.
158. "This is clearly indicated by the strikingly parallel opening statement of Exod. 17:1— The whole Israelite community travelled on their journeys from the wilderness of Sin by the word of God." Frankel, "Two Priestly Conceptions of Guidance in the Wilderness," 33–34.

Frankel draws support from Israel Knohl[159] to propose P and H "sources" and concludes: "To a certain extent we might even say that the late priestly polemic shows a degree of sympathy for the sentiments of Korah: 'all the congregation is holy for God is in their midst, so why do you [namely, Moses and Aaron] raise yourselves above the community of God?' (Num. 16.3)."[160] However, it might be that while the people saw something (the cloud), Moses's ears were also employed (for the Word), and that these sense organs reinforce each other, as in Numbers 9:18, or at least that they do not form theologies too different in content, but rather are mutually complementary. God creates the conditions for hearing as well as directing the people through Moses and prophets like him.

Contrary to any "progress" myth, ancient or modern, "the priestly writing envisions the world not as something thrusting dynamically forward, but as a system that moves from dynamism to stability."[161] Hence, "once the world and humanity have arrived at their full dimensions and proper order, the world can and should *remain as it is*. . . . According to the priestly writing, salvation is primarily a successful creation: the good life of the nations in their lands."[162] Also, "salvation is also the immanence of the transcendent God in a creation extended by human labor: the encounter with God in cultic worship."[163] One wonders about salvation as the category here that includes both the good life of the nation and the encounter with God. Norbert Lohfink does not show just how God's inhabiting the "man-made" extension of creation relates to meeting God in creation. Salvation seems to be God's being present in the world and available for encounter, which actually sounds more like a statement about God's constant presence and providence as a presupposition (present, waiting) than a statement about anything soteriological (encountering), even if the latter is Lohfink's preferred term.

Providence and Soteriology: God's Fatherhood

In Jesus's teaching one feels a strong sense of being caught up in something bigger, as well as purer and sanctifying. This does not exclude but rather demands ethical obedience to the will of God—as that which explicates the kingdom's coming in Matthew 6:10. The background to this might be

159. Knohl, *Sanctuary of Silence*.
160. Frankel, "Two Priestly Conceptions of Guidance in the Wilderness," 36.
161. N. Lohfink, *Theology of the Pentateuch*, 120. Further: what is "dynamizing" is "deviation from the God-given order of things" (123).
162. N. Lohfink, *Theology of the Pentateuch*, 125.
163. N. Lohfink, *Theology of the Pentateuch*, 128.

Psalm 103:21 ("Bless the LORD, all his hosts, his ministers that do his will").[164] This involves discerning the will of God, which seeks a good outcome in historical circumstances, in places where obedience is not obvious. Schürmann notes that whereas the Septuagint preferred *boulē* (or *logismos*), the New Testament prefers *thelēma*, as in Acts 22:14 ("God . . . has chosen you [Paul] to know his will") and in Acts 26:16 (Paul's being appointed to be servant and witness to the things seen and to be seen)[165]—although there is no mention of *thelēma* in that passage and in Acts 22:14 *thelēma* actually means the salvation of gentiles, not simply God's providential will as such. Matthew 26:42 ("your will be done" as the conclusion of Jesus's prayer in Gethsemane) and 18:14 ("It is not the will of your heavenly father that one of these little ones go astray" [AT]) may well argue for this will's having a very wide range and eclectic targets.[166] When the Lord's Prayer has "will be done," it could be that Psalm 103:21 (with its use of *rāṣôn*) is at least alluded to.[167] Again, is the will of God then something ethical (what humans do in obedience to the commandments) or something directive in the sense of God's (by means of his ministers) bringing about the ends of salvation? It would seem from Beate Ego's research that a Jewish interpretation would stress more God putting his own will in motion than it being a question of his relying on improved human ethical performance in obedience to commands.

It is not clear that either the fatherhood of God or the kingdom of God takes "priority" over the other. It is as provider of sustenance that God is Father to those who would belong to the kingdom, which Jesus, like many a prophet before him, sees as ahead of his hearers, future in the sense that it is not a "given."[168] Jesus's message is distinctive because in it God has care even for the sinner, the lowest of life forms. One might conclude that fatherly mercy and lordly kingdom overlap almost to the point of being indistinguishable.[169] Both terms remind one that the relational Lord (as Father) also has to (as King) overrule and override recalcitrant creatures for the sake of their "sonship." "In fact, the Matthean phrases 'birds of the air' and 'grass of the field' adorn the whole sequence that includes creation (Gen. 1:26–30; 2:5), the naming of creatures (Gen 2:19–20), and fallen man's punishment

164. Schürmann, *Gottes Reich—Jesu Geschick*, 113.
165. προχειρίσασθαί σε ὑπηρέτην καὶ μάρτυρα.
166. Schürmann, *Gottes Reich—Jesu Geschick*, 131.
167. G. Lohfink, "Der praexistente Heilsplan," 113; Ps. 102:21 LXX (103:21 EV): εὐλογεῖτε τὸν κύριον, πᾶσαι αἱ δυνάμεις αὐτοῦ, λειτουργοὶ αὐτοῦ ποιοῦντες τὸ θέλημα αὐτοῦ.
168. Schlosser, *Le règne de Dieu dans les dits de Jésus*, 682.
169. Schlosser, *Le règne de Dieu dans les dits de Jésus*, 683.

(Gen 3:18); and so they could evocatively reinforce the lessons about their grandeur and limits that men and women learn from the first pages of the Bible."[170] On this wider semantic basis, rather than the more indirect verbal similarities suggested by Martin Hengel,[171] it might be legitimate to hear in Jesus's "do not be anxious" a release from the anxious "toil" laid upon both protoparents by their Creator's sentence (Gen. 3:16–17) and epitomized in the career of Cain.[172]

In Jesus's counsel against anxiety (Matt. 6:25–34//Luke 12:22–29), the "greater to lesser" ("how much less") teaches human limits, whereas "lesser to greater" ("how much more") teaches human grandeur. Both insights are indispensable premises to the acceptance of the eschatological reign of God; yet we are prone to overlook this "alternating current" of the original argument, because Luke read the second aphorism in terms of time (Luke 12:25: "Who of you by worrying can add a single hour to your life?") and glossed it with an argument from the lesser ("so small a thing") to the greater (v. 26: "Since you cannot do this very little thing, why do you worry about the rest?"), the same direction as the mature analogies on either side.[173]

Matthew 12:28's rendering of the Lukan "the finger of God" (Luke 11:20) as "the spirit of God"—referring to casting out demons as a sign of the kingdom of God—dominates the early Christian tradition's exegesis of Old Testament passages that refer to the finger of God. For example, Justin Martyr (*Dial.* 114.3) glosses Psalm 8:4's reference to the heavens as "the work of your fingers" (ἔργα τῶν δακτύλων σου) with the phrase "the work of your spirit."[174] This connotes the relative "effortlessness" with which God works. Tertullian spotted the connection with Exodus 8:19, in the account of the third plague, where the Egyptian magi failed and admitted that Moses and Aaron's work came from the finger of God, not from any power of Moses. That the same divine power to inflict and deliver was in Jesus, even if in a punctiliar, focused way and for a short while, seems patent.[175] The Septuagint translated the "minicredal" Exodus 15:18[176] in the present tense, to denote God's ongoing rule. Hence God has been recognized by Israel as king since the crossing at the Red Sea, and forever onward. Jesus, as part of the epiphany of the kingdom of God, does not exclude the future realization.

170. Dillon, "Ravens, Lilies, and the Kingdom of God," 614.
171. Schlosser, *Le règne de Dieu dans les dits de Jésus*, 683n34.
172. Dillon, "Ravens, Lilies, and the Kingdom of God," 614.
173. Dillon, "Ravens, Lilies, and the Kingdom of God," 614n29.
174. Hengel, "Die Finger und die Herrschaft Gottes in Lk 11,20."
175. Hengel, "Die Finger und die Herrschaft Gottes in Lk 11,20," 103.
176. יְהוָה יִמְלֹךְ לְעֹלָם וָעֶד.

But the associated idea of the Father's hand protecting even while his finger provides power appears in the Gospels as well, not least in John. In Acts the "hand" is about "healing."[177]

One extremely important issue in early Christian interpretation, a concern lasting into Byzantine times, is that of the span of one's life. The word ἡλικία can mean simply "span" or "height," as it does in a physical sense for the short Zacchaeus in Luke 19:3. It can just mean "age," as in John 9:21, 23 ("Ask him; he is of age"). However, in Matthew 6:27//Luke 12:25[178] (only differing in word order) the tradition has often taken it to mean the *life* span that cannot be added to. However, *pēchys* usually means "cubit" (e.g., Gen. 7:20 LXX) or "a short amount," such that "life span," while not impossible as the intended meaning in Matthew 6:27//Luke 12:25, seems unlikely. It has more to do with a status of life, or even, taken more literally, the vanity of physical stature.[179] This conclusion is reinforced by the curious verse that is Luke 2:52, "Jesus advanced in wisdom and *hēlikia* and in divine and human favor" (AT), where English versions for the most part render *hēlikia* with either "stature" or simply "age" for the adolescent Jesus.[180] The idea seems to be that God will provide exactly that practical thing, whether appropriate height or seniority, or influence, or fuller flourishing with authority. It is not about life span.

Schrage argues that Matthew 6:10 ("Your kingdom come. Your will be done") presupposes that the divine will does not yet hold total sway everywhere. For God does not will all that happens. Divine will means not only his "saving-will" (*Heilswillen* [Matt. 18:14]) but also simply a moral "will" that instructs the living of life (*Lebenspraxis*). "On earth as it is in heaven" is a way of saying (presumably by merism) that God acts in all spheres everywhere, not that "heaven" is waiting for "earth" to catch up, as per the traditional interpretations. Rolf Knierim sees it differently, albeit tentatively:

> The disciples are to assume that God's will is already being done in heaven, and on this basis they are to pray that it will likewise be done on earth. Does the New Testament assume a cosmic realm in which God's creation has always been intact, over against a realm that is not intact? . . .
>
> Moreover, why was it necessary that Jesus be understood as nothing less than the resurrected one? Above all, the resurrection certainly means that the new creation has come into existence cosmically. But what, then, is the relationship

177. Grappe, "Main de Dieu et mains des apôtres." Also, his *Le royaume de Dieu*.
178. τίς δὲ ἐξ ὑμῶν μεριμνῶν δύναται προσθεῖναι ἐπὶ τὴν ἡλικίαν αὐτοῦ πῆχυν ἕνα;
179. With Nolland, *Gospel of Matthew*, 311: "You cannot by worrying gain the seniority to which you aspire."
180. Knierim, *Task of Old Testament Theology*, 113.

between this new creation and that realm of God's initial creation in which God's will has always been done?[181]

Likewise, in Judaism just before the time of Jesus the heavenly cult was understood as presupposed by the earthly one, until postbiblical times, when the earthly cult seems to have taken back its status of "primary."[182] The heavenly cult, or even "a parallel heavenly world" yet to be revealed, was not merely eschatological but a guarantor of oversight and spiritual protection.[183] In 2 Enoch much attention is given to the supervisory roles of the angels (seasons, waters, crops, peoples) and Michael as Israel's specific angel among the angels of the nations (cf. 1 En. 20.5).

Prayer is not the acceptance of the unacceptable but an expression of trust with respect to the coming kingdom of God or "of heaven." This sublimates anyone's personal life or destiny and all life and limb to God's will in personal self-dedication.[184] This of course is all very "soteriological," yet to overemphasize one aspect of the believer's being carried along as an object by the Spirit[185] is to ignore the fact that material providential operation assists the salvific and "internal" movement of the Spirit, not least in forming and preserving a people, just as the angels ministered to Jesus's physical needs after he fasted and was tempted under the Spirit's guidance (Matt. 4:1–2). One might boldly assert: "Your life [$z\bar{o}\bar{e}$] is hidden with Christ in God" (Col. 3:3); or with Galatians 2:20 we might assert: "The life I now live in the flesh, by faith I live in that [*the flesh*—which the parallel with Col. 3:3 suggests] of the Son of God" (AT).[186] Yet that life in Christ still requires to be lived, for all the nourishment and protection these last two verses imply. The feeding of the five thousand was about material gifting by God's agency, even if it also fed the spiritual imagination of believers. The fate of the martyrs—to take Paul in Acts as representative—was not one of escape from the world but part of God's provision for the church so as to sustain it as it went into the world to witness with risk to itself.

Jesus's message has a material aspect without which the "spiritual" could not take effect. As his own creation, Jesus could build his parables and remake them linguistically as well as express truths another way in his

181. Knierim, *Task of Old Testament Theology*, 223.

182. Ego, *Im Himmel wie auf Erden*.

183. See Barnard, *Mysticism of Hebrews*, which argues that the Epistle to the Hebrews owes a debt to Jewish apocalyptic and has "pre-*Merkabah* tendencies" (19, quoting Hurst, *Epistle to the Hebrews*, 84–85). Awareness of joining in with angelic liturgy is referred to in 1QS XI, 7–9.

184. Schrage, *Vorsehung Gottes?*, 222.

185. Schrage, *Vorsehung Gottes?*, 251.

186. ὃ δὲ νῦν ζῶ ἐν σαρκί, ἐν πίστει ζῶ τῇ τοῦ υἱοῦ τοῦ θεοῦ τοῦ ἀγαπήσαντός.

miracles.[187] The works (*ergazesthai*) of the Father and of the Son are "making alive" (*zōopoiein*).[188] One could argue that the signs at Cana and the feeding miracles are more "provision" than "nature" miracles. Salvation (*Heil*) and well-being (*Wohlsein*) are not very different in meaning. Belief in the promise of well-being comes from saving faith looking to the possibilities for creation: promise is more constitutive than experience. Yet the plea for daily bread in the context of a plea for ending is illustrative of how requesting and receiving penultimate goods builds up trust. As Calvin wrote, seeking the kingdom can be done in the knowledge that God will take care of the everyday, thus allowing more energy to be given to the gospel, kingdom, and ethics.[189] Or we could say, with Ulrich Wilckens: "Submitting to the routine providence of God and holding oneself in fervent expectation of the imminent kingdom of God thus fall completely together into one, according to Jesus' outlook."[190]

The motif of God as shepherd in the Bible appears at first glance to be a soteriological metaphor only. The soothing words of Micah 2:12–13 ("I will surely gather all of you, O Jacob, I will gather the survivors of Israel; I will set them together like sheep in a fold") are tacked on to a judgment oracle, and verbs often used in military context are in some ways used ironically here, to much softer and reassuring effect—*qbṣ* and *'asp* (the word "gather" is often used in the prophets for gathering in; cf. Jer. 8:13, where that ingathering of virtuous "fruit" is one that is full of threat).[191] One may speak of Yahweh's pastoral activity, with a largely favorable attitude to the remnant as ones who have already been refined. Of course "pastor" is a royal title, but the remnant will be protected in such a way that they do not fall under the judgment and loss; one can also think of Micah 7:14–20, where the nourishing and protective functions of the royal shepherd are to the fore.

For God to be "the God of my salvation" (Ps. 18:46) means that he restores one to life or takes life and strengthens it, as in Isaiah 38:16. H. Ringgren, writing about Hezekiah's thanksgiving psalm, comments: "Here the hiphil of *ḥlm*, 'make strong, restore to health,' is used alongside the hiphil of *chāyāh* (only here in this sense, which is elsewhere rendered by the piel), i.e., 'make me strong, let me live.'"[192] This usage is obviously based on the idea that sickness and distress impair the forces of life and represent, as it were, a potential death: deliverance is therefore appropriately termed "life." One might wish to

187. Klein, "Die Schöpfung in der Botschaft Jesu," 254.
188. Weidemann, "Victory of Protology over Eschatology?," 316.
189. Calvin, *Sermons de Iehan Calvin*, sermon 1, on Isa. 5:12 (pp. 22–23).
190. Wilckens, "Das Offenbarungsverständnis," esp. 55–56n35.
191. Cruz, "*Who Is like Yahweh?,*" 182–84.
192. Ringgren, "חָיָה," 334.

compare this with the word *šālôm* (cf. Prov. 3:17 and Mal. 2:5). The message of Isaiah 26–29 is that on that day doom will become salvation, so one should trust in the Lord, for the storm will pass. Specifically, in Isaiah 26:12 *šālôm* means "making intact," undoing the damage done to the created order. Despite the "gloomy" reputation of that part of the Bible, "the author of Isaiah 24–27 was decidedly positive about Yahweh's activity within the world."[193]

Here the notion of the God who rescues from the pit (Isa. 38:17; cf. Ps. 103:4) is the continuation of a shepherd metaphor. The metaphor can be employed in a number of ways: God's rescue of his people from their foes, of an individual from their trouble, and perhaps last in order, of sinners from their sins. The fact of death casts its shadow on all of life: one lives in expectations of limit, for better and for worse.[194] The question that needs to be addressed is, Well, might knowing our limits be possibly for the better, even if the limits we are half aware of are for worse? Humans know that they only have so much time and have no guarantee of having anything like the maximum. Is that condition a factor in creativity, or can it only invite despondency and a sense of futility? Well, Psalm 39 is less sanguine than Psalm 90:5–7 about life's limited duration, in that humans are compared to vulnerable, temporary structures and to vegetation.[195] For the latter psalm teaches that the consciousness of such limitation (v. 12: "Teach us to number our days that we may gain a heart of wisdom" [RSV]) is salutary, and obedience seems the key to some sort of supernatural hope, for the cause of evanescence does seem a moral one, with words for anger and overwhelming wrath being dominant in verses 7 and 11. In the case of Psalm 39, there is nothing to look forward to other than the hope that life might be enjoyed. In my view the difference between the two psalms is less one between optimism and pessimism than between the individual and the people as an entity that outlasts the natural human life span. In both cases appeal is made to God's ability to restore fortune, for some happiness in the remaining years, as per Psalm 39:13. Happiness as an achievable end before dissolution is cast in a melancholic way, yet all the same it is what one might call a natural end, or a penultimate good.

Even at Psalm 78:33–39, where the note of dependence, contingence, and fragility follows a path of breath–fragility–death, there is nevertheless a strong note of "preservation." Janowski has given this threefold motto, which sums up the import of this and associated psalms. Hence Psalm 88, especially as

---

193. D. Johnson, *From Chaos to Restoration*, 74: "[Isaiah] 26:7–10 has to do with the comprehensive created order and humanity's response to it. 24:5, on the other hand, refers to a special people in a special, covenant relationship with Yahweh."

194. Janowski, *Gott des Lebens*, 250, 250n18.

195. Janowski, *Gott des Lebens*, 391.

qualified by Psalm 89, indicates deliverance from living in death's shadow on this side of death and back into community, whereas Psalm 16 emphasizes a newer, closer relationship with God in this life, and only in Psalm 73 (v. 24), which also deals with the theme of God's preservation of his people, does the focus shift to the afterlife.[196]

In the present state of human life the breath of life is in need of a stronger draught. Ecclesiastes speaks of *hebel* (vanity) in apposition to "chasing after the wind" (1:14, 17; 2:11, 17, 26; 4:4, 6, 16; 6:9) or toiling for it (5:16). This frequent phrase seems to express the notion of trying to fix that which is unpredictable, as in Jesus's gnomic analogy: "The wind blows where it wills" (John 3:8 RSV). The teaching of the preacher in Ecclesiastes is that one is in no position to catch the wind—in other words, to control the variable and arbitrary conditions to which human life is subject. Likewise God works by means of something like "wind." Without wishing to use the word *dynamic* too loosely, we can say there is something about the usage of the term translated as "wind" that refers to more than just a share in the breath of life, but rather something that indicates being moved by a power. As S. Tengström puts it: "In the vast majority of instances, therefore, *rûaḥ* in the sense of 'wind' is associated directly with God's active intervention. Some fifteen texts speak explicitly of *rûaḥ yhwh* or *rûaḥ ʾelōhîm*, or use a pronominal suffix" (examples include Isa. 11:15; 27:8; 30:28; 40:7; 59:19).[197] However, it should be noted that spirit is closest to God in the creation and that perhaps only in Amos 4:13[198] is it something created for man to aid him in understanding, if the thought about God creating the *rûaḥ* is to be linked with the idea of imparting thoughts to humans.[199] Staying with Genesis 1: "The P account of creation bespeaks a threefold principle of creation: first the *rûaḥ ʾelōhîm*, which drives back the waters of chaos, then the spoken creative word (*dābār*), and finally light (*ʾôr*). . . . In contrast to Ps. 104, Gen. 1 gives priority to *rûaḥ* and treats light as part of the created world."[200]

"When the constitution of human beings is involved, the word *rûaḥ* proves to be a relational term, comparable to the notion of the 'image of God' used by P."[201] *Rûaḥ* is somewhat ambiguous as to whether "spirit" is created and hence distinct from God (again only Amos 4:13, with the LXX introducing

196. See Janowski, *Gott des Lebens*, 241–42.
197. Tengström, "רוּחַ," 382. He argues that judgment is expressed in Gen. 3:8: YHWH comes to the garden *lǝrûaḥ hayyôm*—not "cool of the evening," but "the day," which implies judgment: "in the wind of the very same day" (384). This seems to stretch things: "day" need not mean "day of judgment"!
198. הִנֵּה יוֹצֵר הָרִים וּבֹרֵא רוּחַ וּמַגִּיד לְאָדָם מַה־שֵּׂחוֹ כִּי.
199. On this verse, see the commentary by Eidevall, *Amos*.
200. Tengström, "רוּחַ," 386.
201. Tengström, "רוּחַ," 387.

the idea of the spirit of a prophecy of the Messiah).[202] The Septuagint seems to hypostasize spirit even to the point of inverting the text so that "he makes his angels spirits" (in Ps. 103:4 LXX [104:4 EV]: ὁ ποιῶν τοὺς ἀγγέλους αὐτοῦ πνεύματα; the Masoretic Text of Ps. 104:4, on the other hand, has "He makes his winds/spirits messengers"), and it is the Greek version which lies behind Hebrews 1:7, 14. The sense of the Hebrew is not too far away from the thought of God's dynamically creative, beneficent, and angry presence communicated or expressed in and through the world itself.

According to Psalm 104:5–9, God sets a limit to waters of chaos and thus makes that water useful—for fertility (v. 10), as it bubbles up from underground, so that chaotic water is made to serve life. The keynote is that all of creation is situated in absolute dependency, but not on the sun, like in the ancient Near East parallel (Aton Hymn), but on the Lord's creative energy.[203] Psalm 104:29–30 reassures one of this: "When you hide your face, they are dismayed; when you take away their breath, they die and return to their dust. When you send forth your spirit, they are created; and you renew the face of the ground." This is some kind of further creation that does not have the idea of delegation (as in "procreation"), nor simply of the Lord's continued efficacy ("fortgesetztes Wirken"). Here is depicted a "system open to the Lord, needy of him." Is this not then "continuous creation" (cf. the use of $b\bar{a}r\bar{a}$' after all) rather than, as Leslie Allen names it, "God's providential control"? Perhaps the idea of governing and governance is the lead one.[204] The setting up of foundations for creation with correspondence to "the temple" need not be too problematic, even if the language is irregular. Any idea that the chaos waters are the presupposition of creation seems more in keeping with Genesis 7:19 than with Genesis 1:6–13, and all the waters should be viewed as within God's plan and control, as is the message of both Genesis chapters.[205]

God's glory beams forth in Psalm 104:31, such that Calvin could speak of the world's foundation in the joy of God.[206] The psalm ends with a formula

202. Amos 4:13 LXX: διότι ἰδοὺ ἐγὼ στερεῶν βροντὴν καὶ κτίζων πνεῦμα καὶ ἀπαγγέλλων εἰς ἀνθρώπους τὸν χριστὸν αὐτοῦ.

203. Kraus, *Psalmen*, 2:714.

204. Allen, *Psalms 101–150*, 48. Cf. Köckert, "Literargeschichtliche und religionsgeschicht-liche Beobachtungen zu Ps 104," 276, which suggests that the psalm extends to the original creator the idea of provider of life on earth. Creation presupposes governance. Psalm 104:5–9 might well be a later insertion regarding the provider of life—as Spieckermann (*Heilsgegen-wart*, 29–32) claims—building on the original affirmation of the creator in the previous verses.

205. Spieckermann, *Heilsgegenwart*, 31.

206. Commenting on Ps. 104:31, Calvin states, "Status mundi in Dei laetitia fundatus est" (The world's condition has been founded in the rejoicing of God). Calvin, *Commentary on the Book of Psalms*, 170.

of woes to be cast upon sinners and with the exclusion of all that is evil. In other words, these psalms describe an ongoing process, with little sense of "Nature" or stability, and H.-J. Kraus is right to conclude that these texts express movement as well as a sense of being addressed in the "here and now."[207] Psalm 104, in its basic form, is a "creation psalm" in the sense of the *conservation* and *governance* of "creation."[208] In other words, it is not really a creation psalm at all, but more a "providence of creation" psalm,[209] and after the initial description of cosmic foundations, indicating that the text will be "an ongoing activity of divine purpose" psalm, with switching between perfect and imperfect verbs perhaps deliberate,[210] the subject matter from verse 10 onward has to do with the life foundation of beasts and humans. Human beings are "spoiled" with God's generous giving, including work, and in enjoying *Lebensraum* with a relational connection to the Lord, although one should be careful not to overplay what is only implicit in the psalm: it is more "connection" than "relationship" here. For, as Spieckermann observes, there is something business-like about humans having a task to accomplish rather than merely waiting on God.[211] Certainly the atmosphere is one of safety, with both night and day equally watched over by God, without light being in any sense "divinized," for the glory in the world's patterns goes to God, on whose immediate activity they depend (vv. 29–30). Hossfeld could argue how the cyclical theme in the psalm relates to the "purposelessness of creation" as found in Matthew 6:26–29: "Is this, as in Lam 5:21, about the restoration of what previously existed, or about a new creation of a different new thing, as in Ps 51:12 [MT] (new creation of heart and spirit), or is it about a new eschatological creation *totaliter aliter* (that is entirely different), as in Isa 65:17 (cf. Isa 66:22)? Here it is probably a matter of comprehensive renewal of life in the middle sense, that is, the renewal of fauna and flora in the one creation constantly sustained by God."[212]

Other psalms show that God's ongoing concern for creation—although the things the psalms mention are things that have been completed once for

207. See Kraus, *Psalmen*, 2:715.
208. Spieckermann, *Heilsgegenwart*, 49, translated in Hossfeld and Zenger, *Psalms 3*, 60. Cf. Miller, *Lord of the Psalms*, 51: "What is very clear from Psalm 104 is that there is little distinction between creation and providence in that God's creative work continues in the provision of water and grass and food and plants (cf. Ps. 65:9–11). Creation is a continuing activity even as it is clear that heaven and earth were made long ago (cf. Ps. 105:25)."
209. Spieckermann, *Heilsgegenwart*, 32, 37.
210. Spieckermann, *Heilsgegenwart*, 32: Spieckermann does not see the stylistic variation within sections of text as raising the question of the unity of each section.
211. Spieckermann, *Heilsgegenwart*, 39.
212. Hossfeld and Zenger, *Psalms 3*, 57.

all—comes as a result of his steadfast love (136:1–3) with everlasting effects. This is not *continuous* creation, but God's constant concern for the world he has made. Despite Genesis 1 having no place for *ʿōlām*, Psalm 136 views creation as an act of eternal love by God, whose "steadfast love endures forever," which in turn, and consequentially, reaches to Israel and through and beyond the exodus. R. Kratz spots the reference to "daily bread" at Psalms 136:25[213] and 104:27 and also mentions Psalms of Solomon 5 (see above, under "Providence and the Kingdom of God") and the Kaddish prayer.[214] There are links between the divine provision that keeps Judah-Israel going in the exile until salvation in the restoration comes into view and what Jesus's prayer "your kingdom come" presupposes but also requests.[215] One may call this reality in between provision and expectation a "kingdom," not in a full, political sense, yet nonetheless in a real and spiritual and moral sense, because of its cultic and cultural expression, realized through the effective presence of God's name and kingdom, as God answers prayer with provision. Psalm 145 expresses *this-worldly* trust, which has a universal resonance.[216] It is *life* that is made the object of God's saving work as something worth saving and hence *Heilsgeschichte*'s raison d'être.[217] "His compassion is over all that he has made" (Ps. 145:9), with creation and salvation in perfect balance. The "everlasting kingdom," enduring "throughout all generations" (v. 13), affirms divine constancy in history. The presence of the Lord with his creation is an actual one, however one is to understand the modes of his activity. Perhaps, as many, including Friedrich Schleiermacher, have argued, too much recourse to causality has not always been helpful. There should be not too much talk of an effortless flow of history: much will be lost, and the struggle will be long. Critical of von Rad and of any suggestion of divine revelation's being "readable" through history, Knierim thought that one could speak of a revealing of "Yahweh" not in the identity of his name, but merely in his presence, yet that seems a thin account of revelation.[218]

213. נָתַן לֶחֶם לְכָל־בָּשָׂר כִּי לְעוֹלָם חַסְדּוֹ.
214. כֻּלָּם אֵלֶיךָ יְשַׂבֵּרוּן לָתֵת אָכְלָם בְּעִתּוֹ.
215. Kratz, "Die Gnade des täglichen Brots," 24.
216. Kratz, "Die Gnade des täglichen Brots," 30.
217. Kratz, "Die Gnade des täglichen Brots," 36.
218. Knierim, "Cosmos and History in Israel's Theology," 121n56, arguing against Kraus: "The notion of the revelation of Yahweh's presence in reality must be distinguished from the notion of the revelation of Yahweh's name. Yahweh's identity in his name is revealed in Israel's history in a particular kind: a word-event. And it remains known through the particular tradition-history of that word-event. It is revealed neither through world-order nor through or as history. However, world order and history reveal, in various kinds, the presence in reality of the God known as Yahweh." Further, see Perlitt, "Die Verborgenheit Gottes."

Psalm 145:15–20 is worth hearing in full.

> The eyes of all look to you,
>   and you give them their food in due season.
> You open your hand,
>   satisfying the desire of every living thing.
> The LORD is just in all his ways,
>   and kind in all his doings.
> The LORD is near to all who call on him,
>   to all who call on him in truth.
> He fulfills the desire of all who fear him;
>   he also hears their cry, and saves them.
> The LORD watches over all who love him,
>   but all the wicked he will destroy.

In Psalm 103:1–2 "blessing" is accorded to God in return for his blessing, like a gift that returns to the giver. In the passage just quoted from Psalm 145, there are twelve words that mean (roughly) "praise," but those who praise the mighty deeds are the faithful, who have had the epistemic "nudge" from their experience of salvation, helping them see God's universal goodness in his provision, and who then point it out to "the children of humanity."[219] The term "just" (v. 17) seems to connote that he will fix things that are out of order for those who ask,[220] even while his hand and love continue to give indiscriminately (cf. Matt. 5:45, which teaches all disciples about God's profligate generosity). Psalm 145 balances the righteousness and the goodness of Exodus 34:5–7, especially in verses 8–9.[221] As the last major psalm of the fifth book of the Davidic psalter, the text evidences a care for the humble. "The aspect of endurance from the present into a continuous future, which especially marks Psalm 145:1, 2, 13, 21, is indicated in typical fashion in Psalms 138:8 and 139:24."[222] As Kratz observes, the use of the abstract *malkût* is found in the Psalter only here (Ps. 145:13) and in Psalm 103:19.[223] The verses after verse 16 of Psalm 145 shift in focus from the animal and human world to God's presence toward those who pray, thus showing the continuity between the species, with each having "desire" or favor. What might such desire be? Possibly the "desires of your heart," as in Psalm 20:5 (AT), in apposition

219. Hossfeld and Zenger, *Psalms 3*, 595–96.
220. What Erich Zenger equates with "genuine JHWH-Theologie" (Not-Rettung). See Zenger, *Mit meinem Gott überspringe ich Mauern*, 164.
221. Zenger, *Mit meinem Gott überspringe ich Mauern*, 598.
222. Zenger, *Mit meinem Gott überspringe ich Mauern*, 601.
223. Kratz, "Das *Shema'* des Psalters." Cf. *Vergänglichkeit und Gottesherrschaft*.

to "your plans," and in Psalm 37:4 (heart's petitions), a situation that von Rad summed up as "relaxing with God" ("Verwöhnenlassen bei Jahweh").[224] Richard Swinburne has written of general providence as including the gift of good stated-knowledge, good desires, and efficacious desires.[225]

It is hard to know whether the exilic and late writings are pessimistic about this world. Whatever the case, God is still active according to their witness, even if not very often clearly and favorably: any pessimism is not that of nihilism. Knierim writes: "Finally, von Rad himself hinted to what he called Yahweh's ever increasing 'hiddenness' and the 'history of God's progressing retreat.' . . . Israel's history did not simply fail as history, it failed because of Yahweh, so that Israel would look and wait for Yahweh and quit hoping for the future reenactment of its past."[226]

Spieckermann believes that Isaiah 40–55's message of hope of salvation for Israel drives the prophet's positive picture of the Lord's activity in creation, leading to an account of creation itself that distinguishes and separates entities and will do so in history.[227]

Throughout many of these psalms metaphors of God in his activity as builder, father, general, and economist are employed. Regarding the fifth part of the Psalter, Hossfeld and Zenger write that it emphasizes "the active and effective presence of the Creator God in his world (*creatio continuata*) and its perfection through God's saving, healing, and transforming royal rule (*gubernatio mundi* [governance of the world])."[228]

Divine protection can go beyond giving faith and keeping the believer in salvation, as in 2 Corinthians 1:8 (where Paul admits to despairing of life [*zēn*] and being delivered) and 1 Peter 4:19 ("Therefore let those who suffer according to God's will entrust their souls [*psychas*] to a faithful Creator while doing good" [ESV]). Although the former passage concerns the life in the body, and the latter the soul, the range of meaning of *psychē* in the latter suggests a much more exact sense: of life continuing in the present dimension and beyond. When a recent German theological handbook enounces that in the New Testament the old must pass away in order for the new to begin,[229]

---

224. Von Rad, *Theologie des Alten Testaments*, 2:380; Kraus, *Psalmen*, 1:288, refers to it as *fruitio Dei* (enjoyment of God).

225. Swinburne, *Providence and the Problem of Evil*, 116.

226. Knierim, *Task of Old Testament Theology*, 174–75.

227. See Spieckermann, *Heilsgegenwart*, 79–81. Prior to that, there was a theology of God and the world that employed terms such as כון and פעל כון as a pairing in Exod. 15:17, and in Ps. 74:16 (in its original sense), where the "enduring" and "guaranteeing" aspect of the deed is emphasized, and the point of view is that of the earth.

228. Hossfeld and Zenger, *Psalms 3*, 7.

229. Berjelung, "Weltbild/Kosmologie," 71.

one wonders whether this thoroughgoing "apocalypticism" has been allowed too much volume. Even if the New Testament at a doctrinal or thematic level is principally about "soteriology," the wider that doctrine becomes, the more it has to be "touched" by other doctrines, such as those of creation and eschatology and the links between them. If one concedes to Schrage, Angelika Berjelung, and others that there are only two "occasional" verses on this issue, such as 2 Corinthians 1:8 and 1 Peter 4:19, that is still enough to found a doctrine on, at least according to the rule of Thomas Aquinas: it cannot just be dismissed as exceptional witness to a minimal doctrine. These verses are like windows onto what was deeply believed. Even a verse like Revelation 6:12, to which Berjelung appeals,[230] says little about the total destruction of the universe—one might be better speaking of a "rearrangement." There is no suggestion of a new creation in the sense of a second creation replacing the first.[231]

How can something that yearns for deliverance end up destroyed or passed over? Schrage is more subtle here. He simply questions how it can be the case that providence is the heart of biblical theology. Indeed, as Wilhelm Hüffmeier has observed, a hiatus has developed between traditional "providence" and soteriology, or a "vacuum" between creation and completion (*Vollendung*).[232] However, Hüffmeier, in opposition to this "gap," criticizes Günther Klein for treating New Testament texts like 1 Peter 2:13–17 and Romans 13:11–14 as having nothing to do with the reign of Christ, as well as for not considering what "conservation" might mean.[233] *Fürsorge*, or *pronoia* understood as *epimeleia* ("care" or "attention"; see John of Damascus, *De fide orthodoxa* 2.29), can be something rather conservative: God works not so much through *creatio continuata* as *creatio preservata*. Hüffmeier invokes Jüngel here: without preservation and world government God cannot be thought of as Creator. However, thinks Hüffmeier, God is to be compared to someone who gives order and guidance rather than to an absolute monarch, which was a "scholastic" notion and one that was not always well differentiated.[234] That preference for a nondespotic deity might well be contained in the best of the tradition, but it can also be argued that it corresponds

230. Berjelung, "Weltbild/Kosmologie," 72.
231. See Hubbard, *New Creation in Paul's Letters and Thought*.
232. Hüffmeier, "Deus providebit?," 243, responding to G. Klein, "Über das Weltregiment Gottes." Cf. the reference in Hüffmeier, "Deus providebit?," 245, to Jüngel, "Gottes ursprüngliches Anfangen." On 247 Hüffmeier, following Johann Friedrich König (d. 1664) and David Hollaz (d. 1713), appeals to Jüngel's erstwhile colleague Wolf Krötke ("Gottes fursorge für die Welt"): God treats each creature according to the need of each.
233. For a summary, see Hüffmeier, "Deus providebit?," 244.
234. Hüffmeier, "Deus providebit?," 251.

better to the biblical material. Luther might have insisted that *providentia Dei specialissima* (God's most special providence) is priority or "special" only according to the order of knowing and that the universal ethical responsibility of humans is part of *all* humans' participation in providence. One cannot simply look at the Old Testament and say that here is a story of what God did *not* will. There is no cross without resurrection: there is no powerlessness of God without power, and both are loving in source and the necessary framework for prayer.[235]

One could see Jesus Christ as the one on whom continuity between creation and eschatology depends.[236] Yet Isaiah 65:17 and 66:22's metaphor of new creation is reused in Revelation 21:1 and 2 Peter 3:13 (cf. Jub. 1.29 and 1 En. 72.1), and that is without particular reference to a particular mediating (or messianic) figure. In some ways, if one is to link the crucified Christ to new creation, then the latter is a reaffirmation of the former creation, as facilitated by Christ, who, as the best of it, absorbs the worst of it. Likewise the book of Revelation[237] refers to Christology less than Paul does, although Christ is there in Revelation 3:14 (*hē archē tēs ktiseōs*) or 22:13, as Alpha and Omega, such that he is presented less as mediator of creation and more as a framer of history, contextualizing it. Some elements of the book of Revelation suggest that the future kingdom is part of the course of history as it unfolds within itself; others suggest that the kingdom is about God intervening and putting an end to history. The text reminds readers what ultimate reality is, behind the "appearance" of Roman dominion and so on.[238] What is given is a panorama (*Zusammenschau*) for believers of the times: that time and eternity have *not* already met up in John. True, Jesus lived out such a melding of these two apparent "opposites," and disciples could glimpse it, but most followers see only a prospect far ahead.[239] Even within Jesus the kingdom is not yet, even though in God's working it is very much present.[240] Let eschatology be eschatology! One might think of the kingdom as that which gives a limit: "nicht als Gegenstandsbegriff, sondern als Bestimmungsbegriff" (a concept that indicated not substance but rather definition).[241] God limits the world by providing a framework for it wherein he can view it and also contain the

---

235. Ebeling, *Dogmatik des christlichen Glaubens*, 1:328; Krötke, *Beten heute*.

236. Kertelge, "'Neue Schöpfung,'" 142.

237. Nicklas, "Schöpfung und Vollendung," 410.

238. Frey, "Was erwartet die Johannesevangelium?," 546. Also Frey, *Die johanneische Eschatologie*, 3:238. Yet see also Frey, Kelhoffer, and Tóth, *Die Johannesapokalypse*, 548. Cf. Engberg-Pedersen, *John and Philosophy*, 359–60.

239. Wolter, "Die Unscheinbarkeit des Reiches Gottes," 115.

240. Wolter, "Die Unscheinbarkeit des Reiches Gottes," 110.

241. Wolter, "Was heisset nu Gottes Reich?," 7.

flow of time.[242] Between them, Psalm 90:4 and 2 Peter 3:8 reaffirm that for God time is made fully objectified through his vision of it—even its past sequences—from outside, without his being affected by it.[243]

The only place where the word *apokalypsis* appears in Revelation is in 1:1, and there it might best be translated as "vision." Christology gives God the place to show himself to church and humanity.[244] In encountering God, Christians also encounter the essence of history, which one might parse as "the power of providence."[245] Addressing the church as a whole, Revelation tells the church of its situation in light of the end times, almost wrapped up by a God who is historical and eternal, yet who is identical to himself in whatever mode.[246] Chapters 4 to 5 of Revelation (also known as the Apocalypse) are in some sense the key to the whole; the throne vision is one of true reality.[247]

Most important is the announcement in Revelation 1:4. This is itself revealing. In this "who is and who was and who is to come" the "isness" of God is not viewed as some "eternal present" but is qualified by "to come," containing that element of divine intervention toward what is the case, putting in a recognizable (to faith) "stage appearance." This is very much "God" that is meant here, for in 1:5 we get someone else introduced: Jesus Christ the witness, faithful one, pledge, "the firstborn of the dead, and the ruler of the kings of the earth," which at first seems slightly surprising given the suspicion of earthly powers and the fact that in the Johannine literature it is the prince of the world (John 12:31; 14:30) who is the enemy. Cosmic jurisdiction is of course greater, being without territorial limitation. But the idea of being the ruler of the kings of the physical, territorial earth implies that Jesus is pretty much at the same level, and is there on earth to replace Satan with all the latter's capricious and malign interference with human affairs and history. What Jesus does among other things, according to the continuation in Revelation 1, is to accord the church a status and function: Jesus "made us a kingdom, priests to God and his father" (v. 6 AT). The peroration in verse 8 is also telling.[248] This would seem to be God speaking about himself, not Jesus about himself. In the two chapters of the Apocalypse of John that follow, God

242. Schnocks, *Vergänglichkeit und Gottesherrschaft*, 160. Cf. Assmann, "Das Doppelgesicht der Zeit," 199–204.

243. Schnocks, *Vergänglichkeit und Gottesherrschaft*, 160.

244. Holtz, *Die Offenbarung des Johannes*, 16.

245. Holtz, *Die Offenbarung des Johannes*, 18.

246. Holtz, *Die Offenbarung des Johannes*, 22. Cf. Rev. 11:17; 16:15; and some interesting grammar.

247. Schimanowski, *Die himmlische Liturgie in der Apokalypse des Johannes*, 273. Also 277. "Lamb" of course is not a messianic title in OT: it means the one who has atoned.

248. Ἐγώ εἰμι τὸ Ἄλφα καὶ τὸ Ὦ, λέγει κύριος ὁ θεός, ὁ ὢν καὶ ὁ ἦν καὶ ὁ ἐρχόμενος, ὁ παντοκράτωρ.

shows himself to be concerned with specific places and their seven churches. Geography as well as history matters.

Yet in 1:17 the one like a son of man says, "Do not fear: I am the first and the last" (AT), thus appropriating the span of history to himself. We need not reconcile apparently competing Christologies, but rather must see the stress on how the heavenly one reaffirms that he belongs to the sphere of time: from first to last and, by force of merism, at the heart of all that takes place in between. Therefore this confirms that God, not merely soteriology, is the driver of providence and the one who contains all that is salvific in event, for God is "located" outside this in a wider bandwidth of history within which salvation history is safely contained. Ezekiel 1:4–28 grounds Revelation 4; yet God is not on the move but on throne; yet God is at work in and through the reigning Christ, not only as protector of the church (cf. Rev. 11–12).[249] Pierre Prigent insists that the titles come from the Old Testament and Judaism, not from Roman paganism—for example, at 4:11.[250] If God rules over history and the world, then Christ is at work between Christians and other humans.[251] All that the coming of Christ does is shorten the time until God reveals himself in judgment, as he leads his own to the "sources of the water of life" (7:17 AT), with true communion of Christ and people reserved for the eschaton.

Christ's titles are less about showing that he is king than about showing that he is God, who deserves a hymn of creation. John's vision is not some mad escape into the future as consolation;[252] rather, it actualizes and makes present, just like John's Gospel. The judgment has come with Christ, so that Christians can identify the signs of judgment and live as those already judged.[253] And one might wager that ethics builds on a sense of embodied care, a care for self. It is only when Hippolytus in *Contra haeresin Noeti* 6 says that it is right to call Christ *pantokratōr* that a wrong turn is taken. This is a mistake, for Christ is "only" *Alpha and Omega*; that is, he is the one who frames world history, not the one who stands in the center of that history. It is not a case of an ideal Christ "up there" and believers down here; rather,

249. Smalley, *Revelation to John*, 378: "Throughout the conflict, the messianic community is shown to be the recipient of divine protection (7.1–12; 12.5–6; 14.1–5, 13), and the antagonism of Satan is demonstrated as being limited in its length and scope (12.12, 16; 13.5; 14.8–11). The scene in Rev. 12–14 is set both in heaven and on earth; and the two dimensions interact closely, as the characters move easily between them."

250. Prigent, *L'Apocalypse de Saint Jean*, 181. Cf. 500.

251. Satake, *Die Offenbarung des Johannes*, 75. See further on 79.

252. As argued by Yarbro Collins, *Apocalypse*; Yarbro Collins, *Combat Myth in the Book of Revelation*.

253. Prigent, *L'Apocalypse de Saint Jean*, 181. And Prigent (at p. 377) comments on Rev. 20:12 as well.

the seven chandeliers, hanging at some height, signify the church in its recent past history.[254] Erik Peterson comments on 4:11 that the God who takes (back) the power will be the same as the one who made matter in creation.[255] John's "symbolism, and Revelation as a whole, cannot be understood as referring solely to what will take place in the future or at the end. The trumpets herald judgement here, as well as hereafter (8.2–6); the gates of the heavenly city stand open now, to welcome believers who have washed their robes already, or will do so in time to come (22.14); and the throne of God's sovereignty is established in this world, as well as in the next (4.2–3; 20.11; 22.1)."[256]

Now, in Revelation 12 John starts the narrative again, this time from the viewpoint of Christ. He begins with the period immediately before the birth of Christ (12:1), continues through the ministry to the death and resurrection of Jesus (12:2–5, 7–10), and concludes with the destiny of the protected messianic community in the age of the church (12:6, 11–17; cf. 14:1–5; 15:3–4).[257] The exalted Christ is just as much creator as God and just as much the telos: the exalted one in Revelation 3:14c is the "origin of God's creation." John 1:3 ("nothing was made without him" [AT]) and Colossians 1:15 ("firstborn of all creation") resonate with this.

The father concept had certain motherly notions integrated into it while remaining the paternal ground for praise, trust, and consideration of what it means for God to be Father to Israel. God is Father both to the Son of David (2 Sam. 7:12–14) and to Israel as God's firstborn.[258] To the former relationship corresponds the faithfulness of the Father, and to the latter, the authority to command obedience.[259] Yet overall the vision is a total one, a benevolent, cosmic monopoly even while keeping the traits of a "family business," from first through second to last stage of its development.

254. See Prigent, *L'Apocalypse de Saint Jean*, 183.
255. See Peterson, *Ausgewählte Schriften*, vol. 4.
256. Smalley, *Revelation to John*, 14. Cf. Beale, *Book of Revelation*.
257. Cf. Hahn, "Die Schöpfungsthematik in der Johannesoffenbarung," 93.
258. Böckler, *Gott als Vater im Alten Testament*, 343.
259. Böckler, *Gott als Vater im Alten Testament*, 165.

FOUR

Finding Providence
across the Old Testament Genres

Having examined the subject of providence in the Bible in terms of other categories and other words than *providence*, we now turn to assess the prevalence and significance of providential thinking and expression in the Former Testament. Just how structural is such thinking, or is it merely epiphenomenal to scriptural concerns?

Narratives

God uses institutions, not least kingship, to do his bidding. His judgment is tempered, and so should that of earthly kings and judges be, as reflections of divine equity, but even when they fall short, they can be the providential sword for evildoers (Jer. 48:10; Rom. 13:4).[1] Exodus 21:13 documents the provision of a city of sanctuary for him whose committing manslaughter was "an act of God" and who harmed another unintentionally. Deuteronomy 19:5 has

1. Leproux, "L'ἐπιείκεια divine ou la mesure du jugement." The *philanthrōpia* of God is viewed as moderation in the exercise of justice in Wis. 11:15–12:27, which is reflecting on God's treatment of those resisting his people in history: it is proportionate (11:16) to their sin (cf. 11:20—measure, number, and weight). Also 12:22 (with Vanhoye) should read not *myriotēti* but *metriotēti*; the idea of education is contained, and not just multiple punishment; cf. Aristotle, *Nichomachean Ethics* 5.1137b, who discusses a mercy that fills in where the letter of the text leaves a gap—*epieikeia* is thus a realization of a universal justice (281).

a more profane explanation, with no explicit reference to God, but one can see this as reflecting a more detailed situation of a case of an ax head falling, where the death is completely accidental; the Exodus case could include "self-defense" along with "accident." The point is that the human actor did not plan and therefore did not function as a true agent. In Numbers 35:22 accidental death of a wider kind is envisaged.[2] These laws might be valuably distinctive, but it is also the existence of functioning law codes in whatever society that the Bible values, because they serve to deal with cases of pure misfortune—hence, in a way, cases of cushioning the effects of life's unpredictability and irrationality.

God in these narratives does not leave institutions to look after themselves. To hear Gunnel André: "What does Hebrew *PQD* in the Old Testament mean? It is the proposal of this dissertation that the basic meaning of *PQD* is 'to determine the destiny' . . . in the sense of *determine the destiny of the congregation according to its fitness to perform a certain task. . . . Piqqûḏîm* are the appointments of the covenant according to which the people's destiny is determined by YHWH."[3] "Muster" or "inspect the army" is the more particular meaning of that verb, which includes "checking up on fitness," quite often following affliction. André concludes: "It is quite possible that these texts prove that *YHWH's determining a good destiny* is the original meaning of *PQD* and that *PQD* in its favourable sense existed prior to and concomitantly with its double cultic development."[4] Of course this includes visiting for purposes of checking to see how things are and for imposing the consequences of obedience or disobedience—and it does seem to carry this negative sense in Exodus 32:34. Thus, canonically speaking, the meaning of "visit" then becomes more positive in contexts where due suffering has already been endured, such that one can rejoice with the psalmist in Psalm 65:10: "You visit the earth and water it" (AT). Michael Widmer observes that often the verb is meant "not in the sense of 'avenging the iniquity of the fathers upon the children . . .' but as *'visiting with view to examine the iniquities of the fathers onto the third and fourth generation. . . .'* In other words, following Scharbert ["Formgeschichte," 139], we have argued that YHWH comes first *to examine* or *to assess* the moral standing of successive generations before

2. Again with no direct reference to God; Num. 35:22 (AT) reads: "But if he pushed him suddenly without enmity, or hurled anything on him without lying in wait, or used a stone that could cause death, and without seeing him dropped it on him, so that he died, though he was not his enemy and did not seek his harm . . ."

3. André, *Determining the Destiny*, 241. Texts are presented from Exod. 3–4; Ruth 1; Gen. 21:3; 1 Sam. 2; Gen. 50.

4. André, *Determining the Destiny*, 240, naming the New Year Festival as the *Sitz im Leben*.

appropriate measures are taken."[5] One ought to consider the complexity or "moral sophistication" of YHWH, who is not like the local gods, who are one-dimensional and situated, who are not even heavenly beings, that they might roam around the globe. God's anger ranges *only* to the third and the fourth generation.[6] He is open to persuasion or his own reassessment and responds to changes of heart and will not always punish. Likewise Hosea 11:9 affirms that, in contrast to humans, God can change his mind. Repentance means God can go back and forth between qualities of anger and love, in proportionate measure, selecting which proportions of combination as he sees just. "According to Exodus 32–34 and Numbers 13–14, divine sovereignty is not so much manifested in YHWH's freedom to act for Himself, but rather in His freedom to honour his relationship with His chosen servant (and His people) and to allow Himself to be persuaded to overcome justified wrath with loving loyalty."[7] God almost expects servants to persuade him, even as he gives a warning. There is a place in the immensity of God to make room for Moses's petitionary prayer, not least when it accords with God's own word. As Norbert Lohfink comments on Exodus 32:7–11,[8] prayer is presented as reflection of God's will in a human soul.

It does not seem to be the case that the point of the *narratives* in the Bible is to demonstrate sanctification.[9] Neither David nor Samson nor Hezekiah appears to be a better person by the time he departs the pages of the sacred text. The story of Samson, marked by great instability and violence, is part of a cycle that begins with the assurance of blessing to the people: "They do not get out what they put in, but get far more, far beyond their deserts: they are blessed. . . . Time is truly not cyclical, but leads somewhere."[10] Samson, then, the personification of Israel, does his share of evil, but even then God intends it for good. Whereas Ahimelech and Jephthah start with nobility but eventually reveal their flaws, Samson's final months (including the time of his genuine and vulnerable love for Delilah), his loss of sight to the one named

5. Widmer, *Moses, God, and the Dynamics of Intercessory Prayer*, 344, with reference to Barth, *Kirchliche Dogmatik*, III/4, 119–20. Cf. Widmer, *Moses, God, and the Dynamics of Intercessory Prayer*, 347: "There is good warrant to argue that God *expects* His servants to avert Him from His circumstantial wrath and to persuade Him to act in accordance with His innermost being and His ultimate will for Israel." That is exactly why God informs the prophets. Cf. N. Lohfink, "Exodus 32,7–11.13–14," 58–59.

6. Döhling, *Der bewegliche Gott*, 517.

7. Widmer, *Moses, God, and the Dynamics of Intercessory Prayer*, 347.

8. N. Lohfink, *Die alttestamentlichen Lesungen*, 59; cf. Eichrodt, *Theology of the Old Testament*, 2:450.

9. Murphy, *Comedy of Revelation*, 42.

10. Jenkins, *Experiment in Providence*, 65–66. He is particularly interested in the minor character Achsah, the daughter of Caleb (Judg. 1:11–16).

"little light" (presumably the lust of the eyes included), and his kamikaze-style death show signs less of moral character as such than of a growing dignity in his opposition to his adversaries, something Hebrews 11:32–36 acknowledges in mentioning him among those of faith who "were made strong out of weakness, became mighty in war" (v. 34), "suffered mocking and flogging, and even chains and imprisonment" (v. 36). Notably, Samson receives the provision of water when he begs God for it in Judges 15:18–19.[11] The point of the stories seems to have less to do with human virtue and more to do with divine glory, yet the judges' mixed-motivated actions are absorbed into divine action. Within this perspective one can point to large portions of material that may be called "comic." There is something of the pathetic about having to learn the hard way to reach out for help. Divine providence presumes human weakness rather than nobility, much less growing nobility. Even the pentateuchal story is not a linear one, in which the past and its murkiness get left behind. As Francesca Murphy writes: "Although temporality is present, there is no story in the Pentateuch in which a temporal tension is uppermost." "So long as one remembers that human beings have stomachs *and* dream of other worlds, one will stay on the right track."[12] Yet one might wish to point to blessing to assert that God's leading is at least somewhat intelligible. Kornelis Miskotte offers something to help here: "It would appear to us that something essential in the acts of God will be misunderstood if we forget that they are not a blessing to us if we cannot distinguish them as acts of God from the events around them. . . . What is experienced in such boundary situations can lead to a glorification of the Name, but as a rule God leads us on a middle way where faith can discern the outlines of God's providence. We are allowed, quite fully, to understand something of his purposes."[13]

Joseph and the Pentateuch

Joseph is a central character and, as such, is never totally far from the remembrance of the author and reader. Yet Joseph is "offstage" for all of Genesis 42:29–43:25, and the use of "bring to pass / came to pass" here, in what Robert Longacre describes as a series of "happens" implies that even he is swept along in the course of events.[14] The denouement comes in Genesis 45 after

11. Thus it seems one-sided of Butler, *Judges*, 469, to say that Samson identifies with and wants to die with the Philistines. In fact, Milton's reading in *Samson Agonistes* seems a useful corrective. Block, *Judges, Ruth*, 472, puts it well: "By the free exercise of his own immoral will, Samson serves as an agent of the Lord's ethical will."

12. Murphy, *Comedy of Revelation*, 80, 83.

13. Miskotte, *When the Gods Are Silent*, 395, 396.

14. Longacre, *Joseph*, 45.

the brothers' refusal to abandon their father's favorite (this time, Benjamin), proving they have learned the lesson.[15] As Michael Fox has demonstrated, "The Joseph story does not adduce Joseph's successes to demonstrate his wisdom. Rather, the author emphasizes that it was Yahweh who brought them about" (Fox cites Gen. 39:2–3, 5, 23).[16] None of the story's readers are going to be able to follow Joseph as model, not least since he received extraordinary information. Fox's general point, that this conception of God's providence, according to which "man proposes, God disposes,"[17] is not restricted to the pages of "Wisdom Literature," is worth hearing more fully:

> Virtually every biblical narrative shows God's plans overriding man's, and numerous statements affirm this principle. Some examples: "My plans are not your plans," God says in Isa. lv 8; cf. vs. 9. Yahweh confounds the plans of the nations (Ps. xxxiii 10). The enemy schemes to gloat over Zion but God has planned to let Zion break them (Mic. iv 11–13). Senacherib plans to vanquish the nations and take Jerusalem, but God will put a hook in his nose and turn him back (2 Kgs. xix 23–28). Balak intended to have Balaam curse Israel, but God nullifies this scheme (Num. xxiii 7, 8; xxii 12; xxiv 1). Gog plans to invade and overwhelm Israel. God will drag Gog's [hordes] to Israel with hooks (Ezek. xxxviii 10–23). In this case, even though the movement to Israel was what Gog intended, the real force behind the event is God's plans of former days (xxxviii 17). God both devises the evil plan and overcomes it. The belief in divine guidance of history is fundamental to theism.[18]

Joseph's brothers serve God and his plan as instruments, without their requiring the knowledge wisdom brings. Hence it is not just God directing, but even using foolish and immoral activity.[19] Again, this indicates that providence is not just about making things better; in fact, the story critiques a stiff concept of deed and reward, since God prodigiously makes blessing out of self-curse. It is not a purely "soteriological" narrative, and in fact the ongoing story might well leave loose ends, giving the appearance of the deterioration of things. Is it really "salvation" for Israel to be in Egypt? To reinforce the point, something like Genesis 38, which is not even worthy of being called a tragedy, but is a tawdry story, is included to demonstrate the bathos of the whole ensemble's interaction. The Judah and Tamar story is added to the

---

15. Longacre, *Joseph*, 51.
16. Fox, "Wisdom in the Joseph Story," 31.
17. Homo proponit, sed Deus disponit. Thus book 1, chap. 19, of Thomas à Kempis, *The Imitation of Christ*, sums up Prov. 16:9 and 19:21.
18. Fox, "Wisdom in the Joseph Story," 36n38.
19. Ruppert, *Genesis*, 553.

rest partly in order to witness that God can and will overrule wicked human plans on a wider scale.[20] God's way is to harness, restrain, and use. Hence by the end of the story lessons have been learned the hard way, for that is what providence brings about. Genesis seems to tell of (1) the (at times) intersecting and (at other times) parallel running of a special providence to a particular people in all their need and desire for salvation and (2) a general providence to a wider humanity. These stories witness to the reality of the contingency of events with divine grace required for survival of unforeseen calamity. Joseph becomes friend to his family only once he has become "accidentally" family of the stranger. Lothar Ruppert is right to emphasize how Genesis 50:20 regards the patriarchs as "tools" in the hand of God, rather than first and foremost moral agents. Yet ultimately God in blessing brings life and good things.[21] The Joseph story is surely one of repeated but mediated and hidden interventions of God, to judge and to bless at the same time, to reverse expectations, to bring the cleverness and latent piety of a Joseph into service of the world. If Genesis 37–50 is a *Bildungsroman* (novel featuring personal formation), then what is formed in Joseph and his brothers is the equipping for service. André Wénin argues that the Joseph story is thus an education in learning the value of service or, perhaps rather, in learning the true nature of friendship, through overcoming the violence of certain desires and thinking of how to consider others in close relationships.[22] No little evil arose out of Jacob's own psychological weakness, and it grew to have disastrous ramifications for many people. Yet there is the chance to amend bad choices by finding where a good has unfortunately given occasion for evil: good rebounds where lessons are learned.[23] Yet the verse to which Wénin appeals, Genesis 50:20, seems, to my ear, rather to envisage the human characters as joyful instruments than cooperating agents.[24] Much of God's providential work is spent on Joseph in a way that touches others through his action in a more "external" manner.

Now, maybe Joseph's assertion of providence in Genesis 45 is just a rhetorical device. He needs to gain the confidence of his brothers if he is ever to get back to Canaan. In verse 7 he says: "God sent me before you to preserve [*lāśûm*] for you a remnant on earth, and to keep alive for you many survivors." And in verse 11: "And I will provide [*wǝkīlkaltî*] for you there [Goshen]."

20. Priebatsch, *Die Josephsgeschichte in der Weltliteratur*; Rosenthal, "Die Josephgeschichte mit den Buchern Ester und Daniel verglichen," 278–84; see also Rosenthal, "Nochmals der Vergleich Ester, Joseph, Daniel."

21. Ruppert, *Genesis*, 552. Cf. Seebass, *Genesis*, 109.

22. Wénin, *Joseph, ou l'invention de la fraternité*, 330.

23. Wénin, *Joseph, ou l'invention de la fraternité*, 329.

24. Lang, *Joseph in Egypt*.

Providence might seem to be overlaid with Joseph's cunning manipulations in the foreground, yet there is a place for it, even when hidden: "The assumption of God's providential activity gives unity to the experience of time, and confers its force upon the experience of evil and the growth of conscience."[25] "What strikes us is that the narrative's conception of providence is not related to the realm of creation. If there is a silent theological supposition to be conceived in *Joseph*, it concerns divine fidelity to the patriarchal promises, and not to creation."[26] True, and yet God has implanted resources within creation and human life as part of providence, not least prudential wisdom, to the extent that Fox is right in what he affirms but not in what he denies. It is not only about God's commitment to his own promises. In the realm of providence, God doesn't have to intervene visibly and directly in the manner he uses in salvation (cf. Jacob's story or Exodus). The word of promise sharpens or thickens the divine purpose, even as it draws human hearts to act.

The message is that God's activity can only be recognized in retrospect as providence, or perhaps the conclusion of a providential sequence can be recognized, just as the weeping Joseph glimpses in the early verses of chapter 45.[27] This is not to say that the whole sweep of God's plans could ever have been discerned by Joseph. One senses that he is *not* a prophet in the way that Daniel (in the latter part of that book) is. Hence Joseph's knowledge is partial and is generated more by inspired reflection on experience than by a prophetic gift.

The subjective side of this providence is both reassurance of divine favor and a confirmation of present and future tasks. Brueggemann calls the Joseph story "the hidden *call* of God": true, there is calling in the use of "sending" (*šālaḥ*) in Genesis 45:7: "God sent me before you to preserve for you a remnant on earth"—this is the first time that this word appears with God as subject. There is something of the sense of a "missionary," who by representation carries out the task. The text praises God's surprise plans, which in turn demand forgiveness as the corresponding human activity. "The two verbs used here נחם and דבר על-לב [speak to the heart] occur also in Is. 40:1, 2"— that is, in the sense of reassurance, with "the forgiveness . . . subsumed into God's action,"[28] yet here this is intended to be understood as applying to "all his creatures,"[29] although the difference seems to be that while all creatures benefit, only God's covenant people can have any real *understanding* of this

25. Hettema, *Reading for Good*, 275.
26. Hettema, *Reading for Good*, 344.
27. G. Fischer, "Die Josefgeschichte als Modell für Versöhnung," 265.
28. Westermann, *Genesis 37–50*, 251.
29. Westermann, *Genesis 37–50*, 251.

forgiveness. For Joseph is not only the messenger of the story of God but also the agent, *once and inasmuch as he is aware of* the plan, although he remains totally in the tow of God's powerful but hidden action. Joseph here anticipates Jesus, as in Acts 7:9–16, 44, 60. Joseph intends care rather than recompense.[30] Joseph works out of a gratitude to God.

Despite all other commentators on Genesis 45:5–8 mentioning providence, Claus Westermann is not so sure. "But one must be quite clear that this is not what the text is talking about. The Joseph story knows nothing of a concept of this kind. . . . To explain the verse as the working of God's providence does not fit the structure of v. 5, which sentence is in the perfect; the explanation could only be described as a reflective conclusion from what has been said."[31] What Westermann seems anxious to rule out here is any sense of Joseph laying claim to knowledge of a divine plan for the present leading into the future.[32] For Joseph, God has acted in the past and has been at work, and that is ground for trusting. It is "not as some sort of abstract belief in providence, but as trust in God who acts to save and preserve."[33] Yet that is exactly what providence is—something that does not have to be believed in, just acknowledged in passing and discerned in retrospect, in the mode of Wisdom. So awareness of providence has to do with a knowledge of degrees, increasing through the wisdom of hindsight as time goes by, *not* a knowledge of the future, nor an abstract belief. It is about divine care in the past and present. After all, "the monotheistic revolution of biblical Israel was a continuing and disquieting one. It left little margin for neat and confident views about God, the created world, history and man as political animal or moral agent, for it repeatedly had to make sense of the intersection of incompatibles—the relative and the absolute, human imperfection and divine perfection, the brawling chaos of historical experience and God's promise to fulfil a design in history."[34]

Westermann argues that providence should be viewed as on a parallel track to soteriology and that the modus operandi of providence is more one of gradualism as opposed to the punctiliar intervention of salvation, and this is no different in the "other" Testament, as he specifies: "What is the relationship in the New Testament between what it says on the one hand about God's activity that is of a punctiliar nature, such as the proclaiming and the hearing

---

30. Seebass, *Genesis*, 200.

31. Westermann, *Genesis 37–50*, 143.

32. Which was obviously what Hitler seemed to understand providence to mean.

33. Westermann, *Genesis 37–50*, 145. The point is, it is not about trust in what God will do but knowing what he has done.

34. Alter, *Art of Biblical Narrative*, 154.

of the Word (proclamation), justification, forgiveness of sins, the Christ event as an eschatological occurrence, and so on, and what it says on the other hand about events that have an entirely different structure, persevering, progressing and declining, growing and maturing, activities, that is, that according to their nature are not specific events?"[35] Westermann is right to distinguish two spheres of divine activity but wrong to separate them. If anything, the sphere of blessing extending from creation through all time is the foundational one on which the soteriological builds, in order to bring people back to that foundation. To move back to the Old Testament, Deuteronomy has a place for the physical blessings of land and crops. One can speak of "family life blessings" imported into the nation, and these continue to have a place in worship along with "deliverance." One senses the power of blessing in the Wisdom books, as a thing that is part of what it is to be saved.

This "blessing" theme Westermann finds to be prominent at least in the Gospels with the language of the continuous activity of God, as in Mark 10. The New Testament "concept of blessing that came down from the Old Testament retained its meaning."[36] However, in Pauline texts such as Galatians 3, Acts 3, and Ephesians 1:3 "the blessing is identified with God's act of deliverance in Christ, in contrast to the subordination to the events of deliverance."[37] But even while subordinated, blessing is still not wholly absorbed into salvation. For blessing gets renewed in the earliest practices of primitive Christianity: "This making the sign of the cross involved calling on Christ, who died on the cross for us. But its use in times of peril shows that it does not call on the cross as a symbol of the justification of sinners. It is instead an appeal to the power of the Savior to protect, secure, defend. . . . The accompanying words show that the blessing is seen as life power, as the presence and protection of the divine Lord."[38] Even though Wolfgang Schenk[39] would identify blessing with justification, hence salvation, Westermann would counter that the Old Testament concept with which the New Testament would work remains as a significant voice (even if second fiddle) and can be seen in the content of what it means for the church to be built up.

Should a sharp distinction be drawn between "spiritual" and "material" blessing? Westermann is happy for there to be some kind of fusion of the two spheres in and through the cross of Christ, where supremely God is

35. Westermann, *Blessing in the Bible and the Life of the Church*, 82.
36. Westermann, *Blessing in the Bible and the Life of the Church*, 100.
37. Westermann, *Blessing in the Bible and the Life of the Church*, 90.
38. Westermann, *Blessing in the Bible and the Life of the Church*, 40–41.
39. Schenk, *Der Segen im Neuen Testament*.

to be understood in the middle of life.[40] In the Old Testament it is not so much about spiritual goods as material ones, whereas in the New Testament blessedness is depicted as giving the latter up. Since this is the case, the New Testament view of providence is one of returning God's gifts to him, while acknowledging a loose right to their possession. However, *pace* Westermann, one should also remember that for all the demands of Jesus to be materially poor (Luke 10:4; 12:33; 22:35), Jesus also says in Matthew 6:3, "And all these things will be added." Hence possessions are somehow secondary in sequence rather than "penultimate" and are to be received gladly, while one gives God glory, viewing the goods themselves as means to life (*Mittel zum Leben*) rather than as the content of life or as that which life is about (*Lebensinhalt*). But faith in "material" creation-providence is not jettisoned in the Christian life.

The verb *ḥāšab*, used for the brothers' plotting in Genesis 50:20, is also in the same verse ascribed to God, as one who makes deliberate schemes. Simeon and Levi will be disciplined, according to Genesis 49, but overall the result of God's plan is one of blessing through the presence of Joseph for the preservation of the nation, Egypt, and Israel. Yet it is clear that God had assisted Joseph (39:21), having worked through him as well as with him and around him. Here God himself seems to be the one who also "did" the work of Joseph's brothers in punishing his stubborn, proud people with exile. The same word *ḥāšab* appears in that equally well-loved one-liner ("plans for peace, not for evil" [AT]) from Jeremiah 29:11, which promises *peace* rather than the "good" of Genesis 50:20, a verse that speaks of plans that surprise. Again, there is a reciprocity of encounter and dialogue, even of a coming to terms. The promise in Jeremiah 29 is conditional on the fifty years of exile being over and on the people's penitence.

But whereas (as we have seen) "emplotment" matters to biblical narrative and there is at least meaning at a microlevel of the narratives themselves,[41] David Gunn thinks that to say this is to miss the point, which is that there is no point: "In Old Testament Studies critics have (in my view) sometimes too readily viewed these stories as simply prescriptive of a particular kind of seriousness—theological, political, historical—and, just because they are fundamentally only interested in prescriptions, read a drastically simplistic 'message' or 'purpose' from the narrative."[42] By contrast, while Robert Alter

40. Wehmeier, *Der Segen im Alten Testament*. Cf. Bonhoeffer, *Widerstand und Ergebung*, 182. Also Heckel, *Der Segen im Neuen Testament*.

41. Mimesis is overrated. See Alter, *Art of Biblical Narrative*, 80: "The ancient Hebrew writer will never tell us, say, that a character lazily stretched out his arms, simply out of an author's sheer mimetic pleasure in rendering a human gesture."

42. Gunn, *Fate of King Saul*, 12.

might think that mimesis of characters is not something the texts encourage (either to appreciate or imitate), he does at least believe in characters (and character) as drivers of the plots, rather than vice-versa. "On the restricted scale of their highly laconic narratives, the ancient Hebrew authors contrived to achieve something resembling Flaubert's aspiration in his seminal art-novel to 'achieve dramatic effect simply by the interweaving of dialogue and by contrasts of character' (*Letter to Louise Colet*, 12.10.1853)."[43] Now, this works better for some biblical narratives than others. Further, if one had to choose, even though the characters are memorable, they are more memorable for what they *do*, often without any observable reflection, and for what is done to them, than for what they say in terms of preaching a message. In that sense plot is at least the "warp" to character's "weft." The plot, not the realistic character (Alter) nor any "meaningful purpose" (Gunn's straw man), is the key. Character is not a project for the self, nor is there a telos for each character, but a divine or at least scriptural telos, a narrative or "provisional" script that is a "given," to which agents may respond.[44]

Unlike Homer, who liked to plunge *in medias res*, the Bible allows the order of events to unfold in sequence. Simultaneity and flashback are rare.[45] This can be called the "biblical revolution" in the history of literature. "This revolution largely turns on the foregrounding not only of new causes and new effects, nor simply of their interaction, but also of their straight, lawlike, irreversible, hence unmistakable enchainment under God."[46] This includes acceleration and slowing down, as is observed in streams. Asserting the difference between the "blind accident" of Sterne's *Sentimental Journey* and the Bible, Meir Sternberg concludes:

> Whether the characters meet or miss each other, whether the happenings manage or just fail to coincide and intersect, depends on precision work that is not so much the narrator's as God's. . . . It is the design to establish and glorify God's control over the plot that explains the features of juxtaposition here—from the drama itself to the discourse, from the very staging through the pinpoint synchronism to the language of these encounters or near-encounters.
>
> "Before" the servant "had finished speaking" his inward prayer, God silently grants it in the medium of action through "Rebekah coming out," so that the double time-relation combines the persuasive benefits of linearity and simulta-neity. Where a two-part sequence of request followed by advent would in itself

43. Alter, *Art of Biblical Narrative*, 86.
44. Ricoeur, *Temps et récit*, 3:356.
45. Sternberg, "Time and Space in Biblical (Hi)story Telling."
46. Sternberg, "Time and Space in Biblical (Hi)story Telling," 90. Genesis 24:15 and Judg. 3:23–24 evince an "omnipotence effect."

imply marvellous causality but still leave an aperture for chance—*propter hoc* or just *post hoc*? fulfilment or good fortune?—the intersection of events stamps the coincidence as providential, as well as demonstrating God's insight into the requester's heart and his approval of the request.[47]

A clear example of a plot-driven narrative is that of Israel in the wilderness. Already into the realm of special providence, God's covenantal concern for a people who are representative of humanity provides a framework for history. However, one should not overlook the place of "covenantal" institutions (law, tribe, cult) that extend the blessing of creation forward into history but with regularity. That is not to say that these cannot themselves evolve, but that is just it: change and adaptation will never claim to escape from the creation mandates. Moreover, these deep structures are not particular as a genus to Israel, but serve for all nations. What is different between the cases of Israel and the nations is the particular way of that blessing, which elevates and reconciles as well as orders and maintains. Fretheim puts this rather well: "Most basically, law helps order human life so that it is in tune with the creational order intended by God. . . . Law is given to serve the proper development of God's good but not perfect creation . . . towards its fullest possible life-giving potential."[48] To take but one example, providence includes the provision of purification from sin in the red cow (Day of Atonement) ceremony, which has to do with corpse contamination, with Moses's staff playing an important part (Num. 17:5), as providential actions not only provide for the people's needs but also serve to renew the wilderness, with an echo of Job 38:25–27. The point is that the human actor made no plan and thus possessed no true agency.

"It is on the basis of a deeper understanding of the divine plan that Moses attempts to convince God to pursue His initial intentions. His intercession is profoundly in tune with YHWH's nature and purposes."[49] As a result, YHWH changes his mind regarding the intended judgment (Exod. 32:14), with the upshot being (32:33–35) that the people will be punished but not exterminated. Numbers 14:18–20 reads likewise: "Moses never prayed for Israel's forgiveness in the sense of annulment of guilt and sin, but rather prayed for a state which enables the preservation of divine covenant loyalty."[50] This accords with David Jobling's structuralist distinguishing of YHWH's leading the people to the promised land and the *provision* along the way.[51]

47. Sternberg, "Time and Space in Biblical (Hi)story Telling," 107.
48. Fretheim, *God and World in the Old Testament*, 138.
49. Fretheim, *God and World in the Old Testament*, 342.
50. Fretheim, *God and World in the Old Testament*, 342.
51. Jobling, *Sense of Biblical Narrative*, 1:40.

Being given quail does not improve the people's salvific state, but through God's cooperating with their demands it keeps them going, the better to learn what salvation requires (cf. James 2:14–16; 1 John 3:17).[52] Gratefulness for the permission of less-suitable everyday things (e.g., quail), but also realizing their limitations (Num. 11:19–20), eventually leads to a readiness to participate in God's purposes, for the Lord's hand is not too short (v. 23). Moses's prayer helped to enable that state of readiness.[53] On the "judgment" side of history, again "visiting" is a theme that might be understood more in terms of God's response to the next generation in terms of a case-by-case basis. God is responsive and equitable. One should understand *pqd 'āwōn* in Exodus 34:7 and Numbers 14:18 in a strong, even adverse sense of "visiting."

It is hidden operation, not miracle, that is the norm in "ordinary" times. "Little in Holy Scripture is as unremittingly apocalyptic as is the book of Numbers."[54] This "harsh environment resembles . . . human life,"[55] and yet there is a theme of divine life over against and yet seeping through life, such that life becomes an oasis in wilderness.[56] On Numbers 17:5 and Moses's staff, Kate Sonderegger concludes: "These actions are providential, certainly, but they are more than that. The interpreter's focus should not be simply on the provision of the daily needs of the people; in addition, the wilderness itself is genuinely renewed."[57] These actions are not so odd as to be unnatural. Fretheim helpfully observes: "God's providence is often shown in leading Moses (and others) *to help that is already available in the world of creation.* Notably, one element of the creation is used to put right another element from that order (cf. the modern use of natural elements to develop medicines.)"[58] This is perhaps one of the things that the story of the bronze snake (Num. 21:9) is meant to reinforce.[59]

Numbers is "the present moment" in between the deliverance and the settlement.[60] The wilderness theme is refigured in the story of Elijah and also in the promises of Hosea 2:14–20[61] and in Ezekiel 20:36–47. "The wilderness country is ultimately for Ezekiel the place of God's judgement and only secondarily a source of purification."[62] The theme is echoed in Psalms 78, 95, and

52. Jobling, *Sense of Biblical Narrative*, 1:48.
53. Widmer, *Moses, God, and the Dynamics of Intercessory Prayer*, 333–34.
54. Sonderegger, *Systematic Theology*, 1:275.
55. Sonderegger, *Systematic Theology*, 276.
56. Sonderegger, *Systematic Theology*, 286.
57. Sonderegger, *Systematic Theology*, 127.
58. Fretheim, *God and World in the Old Testament*, 127–28.
59. Cf. Sonnet, "Ehyeh asher ehyeh (Exodus 3:14)."
60. Sonnet, "God's Repentance and 'False Starts' in Biblical History."
61. Mauser, *Christ in the Wilderness*.
62. Leal, *Wilderness in the Bible*, 148.

106. Yet God *does* repent, even if in a way unlike that of a human being (e.g., in Hosea 11:8–9; cf. Num. 23:19 and 1 Sam. 15:29). In a way similar to how God in Christ "suffered impassibly" on the cross (as per Cyril of Alexandria),[63] God changes his mind yet does not change. Commenting on 1 Samuel 15:29, Alter finds a clever way of explanation: "What Samuel says here is that God will not change His mind about changing His mind."[64] Or as Fretheim puts it: "Samuel bears witness to God's ethical consistency" so as "to install in the reader's mind the measure of ethical seriousness."[65]

Part of God's changing his mind is tied to the nature of covenant: God repented after the creation, at the opening of the flood narrative (Gen. 6:6); after the Sinai covenant, in the golden calf narrative (Exod. 32:14); after the adoption of kingship, at the end of the Saul narrative (1 Sam. 15:35). Even if God is unchanging, the structure of the relationship between him and his people is changeable, such being the nature of relationships, which are necessarily complex through being (at least) bipartite. Whatever the composition of Israel (and one could argue, as Paul does, that the covenants with Abraham are predicated on a faith relationship), in the case of the Noachic covenant God guarantees the perseverance of creation in some shape or form, for all generations, for as long as these last. The gist of Genesis 9:8–17 is that God has a covenant that is ultimately with the earth, even if it is mediated through Noah as a sort of spokesperson.

In these cases all leads to an arrangement of which, God promises, he will never repent. "Covenant forever" is the phrase used in Exodus 31:16–17, "forever" on the condition that certain sacrificial specifications are observed in sacred time and space, and meaning "indefinitely" rather than "eternally." In other instances as well God promises not to repent. In Jeremiah 33:20–22 he links the certainty of the covenant to that of day and night, comparing the certainty of the Davidic dynasty to that of night and day's mutual succession. And in Isaiah 54:9–10 the certainty of the promise to remnant Zion is compared favorably to the certainty of creation remaining, even although one senses that it is in some ways mutable, in other ways immutable.

> This is like the days of Noah to me:
>> Just as I swore that the waters of Noah
>> would never again go over the earth,
> so I have sworn that I will not be angry with you
>> and will not rebuke you.

63. Cyril of Alexandria, *Scholia on the Incarnation* 35.
64. Alter, *David Story*, 92.
65. Fretheim, *Exodus*, 488, 492.

> For the mountains may depart
> and the hills be removed,
> but my steadfast love shall not depart from you,
> and my covenant of peace shall not be removed,
> says the LORD, who has compassion on you.

God learns as well as knows, and so he dwells in the plot as well as above it, not least in the case of Abraham's obedience (cf. "for now I know" [Gen. 22:12]). Yet very often God is in the plot *so as to fix* it. As Elias Bickerman put it, although sometimes people have the opportunity to repent and God then will "change his mind" (so-called *fata conditionalia*, conditional doom), at other times it will be a case of *fata denunciativa* (condemnatory doom), as at Amos 1:3, 6, 9, 11, where the same verb, *'ăšîb*, is used each time but with a different word for "punishment."[66] In such cases there will be no change of mind by God. In the case of Jonah, "herald of God's wrath, Jonah declared the immutable and inevitable *fata denunciativa*—the sinfulness of Nineveh is described, as David Kimchi noted, in the same words as are used in Genesis about Sodom."[67] Jonah was of course embarrassed, yet he was not wrong, for Nineveh would indeed be destroyed, as Tobit saw occur, for with judgment comes the possibility of the *postponement* of severe decrees, as is patent in Hezekiah's story in Isaiah 38. It was Jeremiah who introduced the idea of prophecy that announces God's relenting, even where there is nothing more than lament on the side of the people, supremely in Jeremiah 29, before it was taken up in Ezekiel 38, and again by Joel (2:17), with its appeal to "pity," and by Malachi 3:6–12; 4:1–6.

God's relational activity is more than can be summed up by "covenant," even while the latter sets the direction of the course of that activity.[68] One might say that the God of the Old Testament is so much the God of guiding history that the term *providence* is but another name for God. Yet one sees enough divine-human synergy in the likes of Psalm 18:33–34, while that key "covenantal" text 2 Samuel 7:14 makes it quite clear that history happens especially through *people* who bind themselves to God, even as God takes hold of them.[69] Not only in the early chapters of Genesis can one say that history is the history of God with humanity as a whole, despite the errant behavior

---

66. Bickerman, *Four Strange Books of the Old Testament*, 31–32.

67. Bickerman, *Four Strange Books of the Old Testament*, 32.

68. One may think of the angels of the nations (*Volkerengel*), announced in the apparently "late" (redactional) Deut. 32:8–9, as in some of the OT versions (e.g., Greek Codex Vaticanus) and subsequent interpretations; those angels have the nations, while YHWH has Israel. It is affirmed in vv. 39–43 that God has power of life over all.

69. Hossfeld, "Wie sprechen die Heiligen Schriften?," 74.

of human beings. In general, history is one of meeting and seeing God's being for others, to Israel first but often of wider implication. [70] Hosea 11 informs us that God uses history to punish then restore, with anger only to the third and the fourth generation. In Ezekiel 20:33–44 mercy becomes a matter of God's reputation, and this can be seen as providing a way through to the New Things (Isa. 43:19). God's purposes are not exclusive or narrow. If with Abraham Genesis separates, it comes after genealogies (*tôlǝdôt*) that remind the reader of the common ancestry of all. It is also the case that Joseph plays his part in blessing the history of the nation of Egypt, and the exodus story in a sense includes all. It also reinforces the idea that God reverses things, in that he is not a respecter of primogeniture where blessing is concerned. Experiencing God as the God of promise is something that is "open": "a wandering [refugee?] Aramean was my ancestor" (Deut. 26:5) indicates the less-than-pure nature of the stock as well as the contingency of the ancestral history. Moreover, as Thomas Hieke puts it, in Exodus there is a sharpening to an exclusive point after an inclusive broadening out ("Zuspitzung nach Ausweiterung"); there is no chosen people from the beginning, but what is first formed is an "ethical unit" of those who choose to obey.[71] Nahum Sarna argues that in its use of the verb *pqd* or *pkd*, Genesis 50:24 refers back to Genesis 21:1 ("The Lord took note of Sarah" [AT]; cf. 1 Sam. 2:21 for Hannah). "The Hebrew stem *p-k-d* connotes the direct involvement or intervention of God in human affairs. This can be of a providential nature, or it can be judgmental or redemptive. The verb is a leitmotif of the divine promises of national redemption from Egyptian slavery. The birth of Isaac thus marks a new and momentous stage in the unfolding plan of history."[72] True, but God's intervention for the postexilic reader of the Tanakh dwells in very ordinary human affairs, and pleasure and pain are felt in those areas. Christoph Dohmen notes that Benno Jacob[73] translated the verb as "heimsuchen" in that "literal" sense of God's "visitation" as "coming to one's house," with all appropriate connotations of the domestic.[74] This is not experienced in an altogether pleasant way, as Egypt experiences it.[75] This is certainly an aspect of providence.

In picking up on Exodus 7:5 ("And the Egyptians will know that I am the LORD, when I stretch out my hand against Egypt and bring the Israelites out

---

70. Hossfeld, "Wie sprechen die Heiligen Schriften?," 79, 81.
71. Hieke, *Die Genealogien der Genesis*.
72. Sarna, *Genesis*, 145.
73. Dohmen, *Exodus 1–18*, 164.
74. Dohmen, *Exodus 1–18*, 165.
75. Exod. 7–11; Rev. 6:12–17. See Irenaeus, *Haer.* 2.30.4. Dohmen comments on the theme of God's visitation in *Exodus 1–18*, 216.

of it" [AT]), the prophecy of Isaiah adds that when God makes the desert fertile, he will do so with a purpose—namely, "so that people may see and know, may consider and understand, that the hand of the LORD has done this, that the Holy One of Israel has created it" (Isa. 41:20 AT). A God who remembers (Exod. 3:7, 17; 4:31) is a God who cares. The theme of "plucking up" followed by "building" in a proportion of two negatives to one positive is famously echoed in the beginning of Jeremiah (1:10: "to pluck up and to break down, and to destroy and to overthrow, to build and to plant" [AT]).

God's manipulating of human wills can be observed in the story of the two midwives in Exodus 1:15–22. "They make a difference, not only to Israel but to God! These women create possibilities for God's way into the future with his people that might not have been there otherwise."[76] Dohmen is surely right to emphasize that this is not so much "revelation" of who God is as an expression of a sensed experience of God's activity including prompting. When in Exodus 1:7 one is told that the Israelites multiplied, it is true that there is "not a word about God! But the agents are active indeed in the fulfillment of God's ancient promises. Their word is a profound witness to the activity of human agents and their success."[77] God is finally introduced as an actor in the story in 1:20–21 and responds to their initiative. God allows human agents to work and then reacts in order to use them. However, Moses himself is the one God needs to win over. As Fretheim puts it: "Perhaps most strikingly (Exod. 4:10–17), in the face of Moses' continued resistance, God adjusts the plan and chooses Aaron to be a co-leader rather than insisting on the original terms of the call or overpowering Moses. One might say that, in the face of Moses' resistance, God 'resorts to plan B,' calling Aaron to be Moses' voice."[78]

Exodus 34:7's word of grace declares that God has removed his anger through or by means of his mercy: the one God is merciful in both Testaments. God's people are also one people, even as the range of the provenance of its membership grows as God takes its members into his family. "Naming is an expression of the divine providence, the form of divine tending that extends throughout covenant history. Not so creation! This Act is unique, at the alpha and at the omega of created history, an absolute Origin of life, out of nothingness and out of death."[79] Sonderegger here rightly suggests that God's fatherhood in providence builds on his almighty character in creation, as God comes close, even as he did in Genesis 2 "after" Genesis 1.

---

76. Fretheim, "Issues of Agency in Exodus," 596.
77. Fretheim, "Issues of Agency in Exodus," 595.
78. Fretheim, "Issues of Agency in Exodus," 600.
79. Sonderegger, *Systematic Theology*, 1:301.

God's will, then, will overcome, even while working with the "passive" interaction of humans. This affirmation stands in opposition to the interpretation offered by Cornelius Houtman,[80] that there is no room for a human contribution, only for God's intervention and persistence, as much with Pharaoh as it had been with Moses. If Houtman thinks that "YHWH makes [Pharaoh] obstinate and stubborn, so that he only appears to be YHWH's opponent," then Fretheim's rejoinder is that "the three hardening verbs occur twenty times, God is the subject ten times, and Pharaoh/Pharaoh's heart ten times. Pharaoh hardens his own heart, and so does God. God does not actually harden Pharaoh's heart until after the sixth plague." It is a two-way thing. Fretheim is able to conclude: "God does not micro-manage the work of agents, but exercises constraint and restraint in relating to them."[81] When the story restarts after Passover, in Exodus 15:22–18:27, divine care is fully demonstrated. "From God's perspective, the theme of these stories is not 'murmuring in the wilderness' but 'care in the wilderness.'"[82] Likewise, as Thomas Dozeman comments, in Exodus 33 deliverance is past but settlement is still a future hope—wilderness is the present, and that is where the pillar of cloud and fire and manna show God's dedication to his people. Thus Exodus 33 has two main themes, including "the revelation of God at Sinai" and "the guidance of God in the wilderness."

Now, Exodus 32–34 emphasizes the transcendent distance of God as foundational—a distance bridgeable only by grace, as when in 33:19 God says: "I will have mercy."[83] Exodus 34:9–10 then provides a turning point where God makes a covenant in response to Moses' praying that he would accompany Israel with his presence. Yet the "My presence will go with you" that precedes, a few verses back in 33:14–15, is not just an assertion of mere presence: "Rather, it was an affirmation of God's powerful presence in times of trouble . . . a promise of help in times of great danger."[84] The verbs suggest a *protecting and enabling* presence. If this becomes reworked by the Priestly writer as an affirming presence in the tent or temple, then the judging side of God's *kābôd* (weight of glory) is emphasized in the later redactional parts of the Pentateuch, for those unprepared for his coming.[85] In any case, God's *kābôd* brings in his dynamically relational side, as he can be encountered

---

80. Houtman, *Exodus*, 1:325.

81. Fretheim, *Exodus*, 606.

82. Gowan, *Theology in Exodus*, 170.

83. Gowan, *Theology in Exodus*, 286.

84. Gowan, *Theology in Exodus*, 65: *ṣālaḥ* (Gen. 39:2, 3, 23; Josh. 1:8; 1 Chron. 22:11; 2 Chron. 13:12; 20:17–20); *śākal* (1 Sam. 18:14–15; 2 Kings 18:7).

85. Wagner, *Gottes Herrlichkeit*, 441, 443.

personally in a sort of visual perceptibility of brilliance, but also known through his operations, understood as his "honor."

The God of these narratives is morally constant in that he reacts and changes according to the circumstances in a consistent (open to those with intelligent hindsight) if not always predictable way. Thus "not only does His tendency towards grace and mercy belong to YHWH's constancy, but so too does His commitment to justice,"[86] although mercy might further "trump" this.[87] God's greatness includes accommodating human prayer in his will and plan.[88]

"Divine presence" means that God is not *only* in heaven; it is not merely his name that is in the temple, but his active presence that is there,[89] albeit a veiled one, with more of an emphasis on the whispered but definite verbal-aural communication aspect—for example, at Deuteronomy 5:4 or 4:36.

Unlike in Exodus, in Deuteronomy the Lord does not "need" to descend, because he has already descended and is in residence in his sanctuary and covenant people. If indeed the spirit of YHWH is intrinsic to presence, as God nudging people to recognize his presence,[90] this recognition seems to be more than the subjective awareness of presence as constituting "real" presence in any particular location, contra Ingolf Dalferth. Indeed, divine presence chooses where to realize itself. One might affirm that "covenant and presence go hand in hand"[91] and usually actively, in that "the divine presence was expected to be part of the life of an individual and to grant blessing, protection, salvation, life and health."[92] "The ambulatory nature of the theophanic elements hints that he [God] may come and go. . . . The glory seems to be a metonym that captures some of the divine essence."[93] There of course is a universal aspect,[94] but it is a transformative one in the way that the *šem* (name) accounts, and perhaps even the *kābôd* accounts, of divine presence are far less so.[95] Aniconic

---

86. Widmer, *Moses, God, and the Dynamics of Intercessory Prayer*, 346.

87. Miller, "Prayer and Divine Action," 221.

88. Widmer appeals to Barth here in *Kirchliche Dogmatik*, III/4, 119–20, on God to Moses.

89. Note Wilson, *Out of the Midst*, 214: "Rather than portraying YHWH as being in heaven and therefore not on the mountain, the verse represents him as being both in heaven *and* on the earth." See also Wilson's nuancing of the differences between Exodus and Deuteronomy at 85–104.

90. Dalferth, *Becoming Present*, 13–32, 160–62.

91. Tooman, "Covenant and Presence," 178.

92. Berjelung, "Divine Presence for Everybody," 89.

93. Hundlet, *Keeping Heaven on Earth*, 50–51.

94. MacDonald, "The Spirit of God," 101: "This universal perspective is expressed particularly in the description of yhwh as the 'God of the spirits of all flesh' (Num 16.22; 27.16). This title reflects the dependence of all human beings on yhwh for the breath of life."

95. MacDonald, "The Spirit of God," 116.

or nonhuman metaphors serve to prevent the divine from being "pinned down"; see, for example, the convoluted "likeness of the appearance of the presence of YHWH" at Ezekiel 1:28 (AT). It has recently been argued that the prohibition on images was at least in part a reaction against thinking of God as static and against not appreciating his relationship to the world as invisible activity.[96]

One could further argue that "the name" was part of Israel's coming to invoke that presence—asking it to be active—rather than essential to the presence itself. As Stephen Cook puts it: "God wills intermittent, potentially lethal encounters with God's servants and mysteriously preserves their lives through such encounters."[97] God in his action is communicative, yet forceful for all that. Ezekiel 43:7, 9 promises unconditional divine presence (cf. Exod. 29:45: "dwell in the midst" [AT]), while Deuteronomy 33:28 maintains that Israel's *škn* takes place "in safety" (*beṭaḥ*); "by itself is Jacob's fountain." As for the term "making to dwell": "Although the promise in Gen. 9:27 that Japheth will 'live in the tents of Shem' doubtless refers to a powerful presence, it by no means implies an enduring possession of the land."[98] These two aspects of divine presence, that of Yahweh as "enthroned" (*yšb*) and that of him as "dynamically present" (*škn*), stand in a mutual relationship of complementarity. For Janowski, it is all about God dwelling in people once the temple had been destroyed and being perceived closely, but Janowski downplays divine effect, or *Wirkung*.[99] Yet surely part of God's "dwelling" (Ps. 132:5) is his reordering and governing by the communication of his word, all the while in a subrational manner. In all this, Israel's coming to "own" as tradents of the name and nature of God extends the divine providence into the future.

Others would contest this evaluation of creaturely freedom and posit that secondary characters in Exodus are incapable of denying YHWH in terms of outcome, whatever "wiggle room" on details they have (Dozeman).[100] Yet surely he enacts his will only in relation to other characters, who then act toward his targeted end.

Saul and David

"For David, Yahweh is 'Providence'; for Saul, Yahweh is 'Fate.'"[101] The continuation of the narrative with David is under grace, and hence Saul's

96. Hartenstein and Moxter, *Hermeneutik des Bilderverbots*.
97. Cook, "God's Real Absence and Real Presence," 124. If it is indeed a *mysterium tremendum*, it is something powerful.
98. Görg, "שׁכַן," 697.
99. Janowski and Welker, "Vorwort."
100. Dozeman, *Exodus*, 178.
101. Gunn, *Fate of King Saul*, 116.

story is not a tragedy because the story moves on beyond him. In 1 Samuel 9:1–10:16 one can trace the intricate way in which Saul came to be chosen, where "the material is arranged in such a way that divine causation is revealed more subtly. Indeed, the initial story does not cite any explicit divine intervention but demonstrates that it is a series of coincidences that lead to Saul meeting Samuel."[102] In other words, by means of "third party" involvement God seems to work through Samuel and institutions despite Saul's reluctance, leading to his public installation (in 11:14–15). The Saul story is bigger than Saul and his intentions.

However, just a few chapters later, in 1 Samuel 15, Saul gets rejected. "The verses [10, 29, 35] pose a theological problem about the character of God, who does not change and yet who changes."[103] Brueggemann will not resolve the aporia on either side, but prefers to let the tension (or mystery) be. Yet God's "repentance," as Jörg Jeremias observed,[104] is not a primitive notion, nor does it indicate that God is weak, but with theological reflection it shows how he is responsible to save and that God can change his mind according to his self-control, as expressed to the uttermost in Hosea 11:8–9, where God considers destroying his people but recoils (v. 9: "I will not do [lōʾ ʾeʿĕśeh] the burning of my anger"), possibly because a long period of suffering can be substituted for repentance. Although God himself is said to have repented of crowning Saul (1 Sam. 15:10–11), and Saul then begs Samuel to help change YHWH's mind, Saul is then told, "also the Glory of Israel will not lie nor repent, for he *is* not a man, that he should repent" (v. 29 AT).[105] The Greek and 4QSamᵃ have "change mind" for the first verb, while the Masoretic Text has "play false." As Graeme Auld puts it: "Both elements of MT's distinctive text seem to belong together: it is the 'glory' or 'durability' (whatever exactly nēṣaḥ means) of Yahweh that would be impugned by any expression of deceit or falsehood. The point that Samuel makes, according to 4QSamᵃ and GT, is more local, which fits well into the argument of the whole dialogue: Yahweh may have regretted the original mistake over making Saul king but will neither turn from nor regret his decision to remove the kingship from this failed king."[106] It is not simply that although God might repent he will not *deceive*

---

102. Gilmour, *Representing the Past*, 65.
103. Brueggemann, *First and Second Samuel*, 116.
104. Jeremias, *Die Reue Gottes*, 48–58.
105. At v. 35: נִחָם; LXX: μετεμελήθη. Fretheim, "Repentance of God," 50: "nicham: the reversal of a decision previously made."
106. Auld, *I & II Samuel*, 179. Cf. Humphreys, "Tragedy of King Saul," 104. He refers to "the LXX's extended form of 10:1,5–6,8,10–13. The effect of this additional material is to stress the divine initiative and the prophet's essential part in the designation of Israel's first king, as well as to call attention to the role of the spirit in the exercise of even royal authority." Yet in

(the MT's way of trying to harmonize the two statements), but that he will simply not change a judgment other than on the basis of facts. The analogy of a retrial for new evidence comes to mind: there is to be no appeal on the basis of "law." Even if 1 Samuel 15:29 ("does not change his mind") is just Samuel's view of the matter, nevertheless the views expressed there and in verse 35 ("regret") are equally true.[107] One might compare with the Masoretic Text of Numbers 23:19, with its parallel of deceit and regret, which denies that God can ever be not true to his word. One might say that when Yahweh regrets, it is not as a human, even to the point that he *can* regret a past decision and change his approach thenceforth, but will not change once he knows the human heart is not inclined to turn.

Likewise Joel 2:13 ("Return to the LORD your God, for he is gracious and merciful, slow to anger, and abounding in steadfast love, and relents [*niḥām*] over evil") implies that the Lord is able to stand back from judgment even as it is in process and to stop it. This emphasizes the "priority of God's grace in dealing with the world"; humans must repent, but it is left open whether God will indeed stop the punishment, as in Joel 2:14 ("Who knows whether he will not turn and relent [*yāšûb wəniḥām*]?"), or, as in Zephaniah 2:3, whether the one threatened with punishment will be spared. "This is a way of saying that the human return is the necessary precondition, but not the ground, of God's repentant activity."[108]

> Thus this cycle of Saul's demise satisfies all the conditions required to merit the predicate *tragic* in the strict sense. As a king and war-leader he falls from high places to the bottomless depths, whereas with his charisma we might imagine him to be in an unassailable position after his success around Jabesh. We participate in the spectacle of a man harassed by God. . . . He [the writer] draws a development which represents Saul's growth process. It is a process which for a long time consists of its opposite, of being blocked and shattered, of resisting an unacceptable destiny.[109]

Sympathy for Saul is to be expected. The "tragic hero" tag certainly suits him when he dies in battle in 1 Samuel 31:1–7. Yet the whole point of kingship was to serve as a go-between or buffer between God and the people. Accordingly,

---

1 Sam. 16 a number of verses that present Saul in a negative light are missing from the LXX: it is quite possible that originally that material was a story about David.

107. Bar-Efrat, *Erste Buch Samuel*, 213.

108. Fretheim, "Repentance of God," 60–61; cf. 65: "Divine repentance means that the future is genuinely open. The future is not blocked out in advance." Cf. Barth, *Church Dogmatics*, II/1, 497–507.

109. Fokkelman, *Narrative Art and Poetry in the Books of Samuel*, 2:691.

Saul had been granted "another heart" (10:9) after a long and winding (in other words, "providential") road to his being anointed, with covenanted conditions imposed upon him as king (10:25).[110] Already in chapter 12 the prophet puts Saul on notice for his rash oath. The eventual judgment on Saul in chapter 15 (especially vv. 14–15) has to do with what would later be known as simony, and the fact that it is recast in the stories of Ananias and Sapphira (Acts 5) and Simon Magus (Acts 8) comes as no great surprise, given what 1 Samuel 12 makes all too clear.

Is this tragedy? Well, a tragedy is a narrative in which characters get caught up in something larger than their flaws or sins deserve, simply a guilt of existence (Karl Jaspers). Or, to be more "classical" about it, it is a narrative in which one who is "not us" is marked out, thus allowing the rest to feel under grace. The protagonist is made not so much a scapegoat as a lesson of how a little neglect and a misdirected attitude can result in disaster.[111] This can be a helpful grid for reading some biblical narratives.[112] Although one perceives divine fairness in the story of Samson, one finds nothing but oppressiveness in that of Saul, with knock-on effects for his family. Saul thought that knowing what was going to happen would help him (1 Sam. 28), as one who always "took matters into his own hands."[113] It seems that Saul could do nothing right. He got rebuked as a fool (13:13) and as one with an inferiority complex (15:17). He tried to get back at God by massacring the city of priests at Nob (1 Sam. 22). The evil spirit from the Lord replaced the Lord's spirit in Saul (as at 1 Sam. 16:14), and Saul fought his destiny till the end. The tragic vision is one of fundamental disorder and contingent "openness," and as such is true to reality. In Klaus-Peter Adam's view, Saul fell "'into affliction not because of evil and wickedness but because of a certain fallibility (*hamartia*)' . . . The tragic hero is misled and unable to make an educated decision after having considered different options."[114] "The description of Saul's guilt corresponds

110. Fokkelman, *Narrative Art and Poetry in the Books of Samuel*, 2:81.

111. I have learned much from Patrick Downey's throught-provoking study *Serious Comedy*. The point is that comedy teaches us by identification about our conventions, tragedy by repulsion at character. "As he [Plato] implies in Book V of the *Republic*, the role the lie plays in the city is the role the scapegoat plays in uniting and making the city one by excluding the 'other'" (67). Yet Adam, "Saul as a Tragic Hero," 162n156, claims that Aristotle's theories do not fit the tragedies of Sophocles: "The strongest objection against Schmitt and Lefèvre is that the tragedies of Sophocles do not focus on a specific guilt of the heroes. The focus is on tragic causation rather than on the pre-existing character flaw."

112. Exum has treated this in her *Tragedy and Biblical Narrative*.

113. Exum, *Tragedy and Biblical Narrative*, 25.

114. Adam, "Saul as a Tragic Hero," 161, quoting Aristotle, *Poetics* 13 from Halliwell, *Aristotle's Poetics*, 44; Adam makes further reference to Halliwell, *Aristotle's Poetics*, 146, on Aristotle, *Poetics* 6.

to the Aristotelian idea of a middle character. This idea of an unconsciously committed evil resulting in a (predicted) tragic destiny, could not be tolerated by later writers. Instead, both, the Deuteronomists and the Chronicler, plead Saul guilty of deliberately committed faults."[115] Saul's character does seem repeatedly to make poor moral choices: taking upon himself the role of prophet-priest, making rash vows, allowing Jonathan to do the fighting. It is not simply that he was ignorant, as Adam argues. The verb in 13:13 is *skl*, and this does not simply mean "an unwitting wrong action," but something more intentional.

Yet is Saul's end truly a suicide? Is it not a trope in battle scene descriptions to "fall on one's sword" in order to prevent ignominy and a crueler death? The alternative version given in 2 Samuel 1 by the Amalekite soldier to David contrasts with the noble pathos of 1 Samuel 31, true. There Saul has accepted his fate ever since the appearance of the witch of Endor. However, the text offers no reassurance as in the Joseph story that God is working it all out for good. Saul is fated even as he fails; failure and fate together necessitate his fall. King Lear–like, he stands rather as a deeply felt expression of a primal chaos in the face of which all assertions of order for good or for justice in this world must be made. In this tragic vision the secret terrors of the human condition surface for a moment with a force not to be denied.[116]

Once more, Saul can do no right for doing wrong and becomes the foil to David, who is further legitimated through Jonathan. For Jonathan "represents the extreme case of character being emptied into plot. . . . Jonathan knows the divine plan and acts in accordance with it."[117] Jonathan receives no revelation, and yet he knows. Somehow, mysteriously, the divine plan is clear to him. In 1 Samuel 23:17 he speaks as a prophet: "The hand of my father shall not find you; you shall be king over Israel, and I shall be next to you" (AT; cf. 20:13–16). Jonathan plays an insightful role and yet something akin to "a woman's role,"[118] one that is all about helping David; even the covenant (18:3; 20:16) is made at Jonathan's initiative. Jonathan is rather like Ruth and Abigail, who are allowed to initiate, with the men taking over when real decisions in the outside world are to be made. Yet Jobling's ideological approach fails to realize that the quiet characters who have adjunct roles are nevertheless extremely influential in the march of divine providence: they are not merely "walk-on parts." "The author depicts a succession of occurrences in which the chain of inherent cause and effect is firmly knit up—so firmly indeed that

115. Adam, "Saul as a Tragic Hero," 163.
116. Humphreys, "Tragedy of King Saul," 101.
117. Jobling, *1 Samuel*, 98–99.
118. Jobling, *1 Samuel*, 162; cf. Fewell and Gunn, *Gender, Power and Promise*, 150–51.

the human eye discerns no point at which God could have put his hand. Yet secretly it is he who has brought all to pass."[119] God is free to be merciful, to work with as well as around the human characters, and is not bound to mechanical laws of retribution.

The question "Who is in the know?" is a real one. It is such knowledge that makes Jonathan tragic, in a way one might say is similar to how Tiresias at Troy is tragic. For Jonathan "came to know the divine plan, and acted in accordance with it."[120] It is important for God's faithfulness that David is Saul's son-in-law who can acquire the promised succession, as Jonathan helps, even as he gives way to David.

Overall the Deuteronomistic History certainly does evidence a high degree of contingency, with its pairing of divine demand and divine grace: "Saul sins and must be rejected. But Yahweh made him a promise, which must be kept. Therefore, the passing of Saul's kingship must express the radical discontinuity caused by sin (the kingship is torn from him), but also the radical continuity guaranteed by grace—the kingship passes by legitimate means to the one who has become his heir."[121] Yet Robert Alter surely claims too much when he asserts "the dynamic interplay between two theologies, two conceptions of kingship and history, two views of David the man. In one, the king is imagined as God's instrument, elected through God's own initiative, manifesting his authority by commanding the realm of spirits good and evil, a figure who brings healing and inspires love. In the other account, the king's election is, one might say, ratified rather than initiated by God; instead of the spirit descending, we have a young man ascending through his own resourcefulness, cool courage, and quick reflexes, and also through his rhetorical skill."[122]

Alter here works with a presupposed separation of the private and the public, as promoted by Mieke Bal.[123] However, and *au contraire*, rather than seeing these as two sides of David, far less two literary sources in his story, we must recognize that the strands work together to remind us that divine use of human instruments nevertheless uses and amplifies human strength, even in the battles such as that versus the Ammonites, when the spirit is still with the house of Saul (1 Sam. 15). The resourceful David is every bit as much the instrument of—well, if not God himself, then at least the plot. Gunn rightly

---

119. Von Rad, "Beginnings of Historical Writing," 201.

120. Jobling, *Sense of Biblical Narrative*, 1:28.

121. Jobling, *1 Samuel*, 26.

122. Alter, *Art of Biblical Narrative*, 152–53. Cf. 147–48: "Logically, of course, Saul would have had to meet David for the first time either as music therapist in his court or as giant-killer on the battlefield, but he could not have done both. Both stories are necessary, however, for the writer's binocular vision of David."

123. On this story, see Schwartz, "Adultery in the House of David."

points out the contrast between the two figures as agents: whereas Saul is
controlled by fury to the point of having priests slain by a foreigner (22:18; he
had been more lenient in 15:3–9, before the Spirit departed), the "madness"
of David (Saul's "double") is something he feigns and controls. In a nutshell:
Saul experiences the dark side,[124] David the light side, of God's providence.
David gets sent back (the end of chap. 29), and, unlike Saul in the darkness,
sets out "in light" (Fokkelman).[125]

As 1 Samuel 29:9 presents him, David is a bit like an angel of God. He is
about to assume the role of "father of the nation." This is revealed to the
woman of Tekoa who claims to want to preserve the life of her fratricidal
son, although meaning Absalom (2 Sam. 14:11: "As the LORD lives, not one
hair of your son shall fall to the ground").[126] "The God who presides over
the beginning and the end of the narrative with such power is present to and
with David all the way through."[127] David gets protection from his own men
only by seeking clarity and order from God. Event is prior to character, and
hence the transition to kingship is bigger than Saul and what he is caught up
in.[128] One might say that God *is* somehow the event.

In his *The Story of King David* Gunn observes that David's prayer that
Ahithophel's advice will not be taken by Absalom is answered (2 Sam. 17:14:
"For the LORD had ordained to defeat the good counsel of Ahithophel").[129] The
text expresses a nostalgia in regard to loss that intensifies the sense of tragedy,
with a certain amount of collective guilt hanging over those watching. (Jobling
thinks that the causes of the biblical God and the oppressed are opposites.)[130]
Gunn quotes Brueggemann: "David dares to affirm that Yahweh's governance
of men's actions and destinies might not be in the precise calculating scale
as Shimei presumes." To which Gunn adds: "There would seem to be some
connection between David's gift of freedom to others and Yahweh's gracious
response to him, even in the context of a misfortune (the rebellion of Absalom)
which can be traced, via Nathan's prophecy, to David's prior sin (Bathsheba

124. Gunn, *Fate of King Saul*, 46; 116: "For David, Yahweh is 'Providence'; for Saul, Yahweh
is 'Fate.'" Crenshaw, *Samson*, 133, observes: "Samson can murder and fornicate, and God will
continue to bless him. But let him cut off his hair [a ritual matter], and God will depart from
him forthwith."
125. Fokkelman, *Narrative Art and Poetry in the Books of Samuel*, 2:578.
126. Brueggemann, *First and Second Samuel*, 293, quotes the Heidelberg Catechism, question 1: ". . . that he protects me so well that without the will of my Father in heaven not a hair
can fall from my head; indeed, that everything must fit his purpose for my salvation."
127. Brueggemann, *First and Second Samuel*, 357.
128. Jobling, *1 Samuel*, 254.
129. Gunn, *Story of King David*, 108.
130. Jobling, *1 Samuel*, 308.

and Uriah). Retribution and providential care are not, for David, mutually exclusive aspects of Yahweh's dispensation. Providence is not a matter of a mechanical predestination. . . . Blessing may come out of curse."[131]

Yahweh is the God of the unexpected.[132] As Erich Auerbach observed (and John Barton approved), these narratives are "fraught with 'background' and mysterious, containing a second concealed meaning."[133] Barton writes of

> the possibility that the ideas about God and his activity in the world which von Rad found in the Succession Narrative are primarily *a function of its narrative form or style*. It is not, we might say, that people in Israel unconsciously perceived God's hand in secular events, nor that the author of the Succession Narrative consciously wanted them to see it there, nor that Israel was committed to such a view of divine providence; it was simply that the narrative conventions available to the author resulted in the story's being told in this way rather than in any other.[134]

The whole story can be one that includes divine guiding and resolution even where the protagonists seem to get in the way. David, after all, is a serial murderer (and a "borrower" of wives[135] and a usurper). Soon indeed, *the Lord's presence is not with David*. Therefore, it is very hard to see his story as one of "salvation history" through and through, though neither is it all unholy history. In truth it is much more mundane even while purposeful. Violence in war seeps into court life; the taking of Rabbah (1 Sam 12:26) is followed by the rape of Tamar (13:14). David becomes a victim at least from the point of Absalom's revolt (2 Sam. 15) through to that of Adonijah's (1 Kings 1:5). A particular humiliation is inflicted on David by Shimei in 2 Samuel 16:5–8. Absalom's rising had been prophesied by Nathan as part of the punishment of David (12:11): this is the Lord's doing. The grim result of fighting in the wilderness and forest of Mahanaim (18:8) is, "The forest consumed more troops that day than the sword" (AT). This underlines the divine involvement. Sin and presumption have put nature out of joint. For in Genesis 50:24 the assurance is given: "God it is who will surely muster [*pqd*] you" (AT). In other words, the exodus was to be God's work. So that is why, in 1 Samuel

---

131. Gunn, *Story of King David*, 109, 110. Literally, at 2 Sam. 16:12: "It may be that the Lord will look on the wrong done to me, and that the Lord will repay me with good for his [Shimei's] cursing today." At this point David is penitent but also trusting.

132. Gunn, *Story of King David*, 110.

133. Barton, "Gerhard von Rad on the World-View of Early Israel," 321, quoting Auerbach, *Mimesis*, 15.

134. Barton, "Gerhard von Rad on the World-View of Early Israel," 320.

135. Halpern, *David's Secret Demons*, 100.

24:5, David was wrong to think he could take God's place in sounding out the troops, and with an intention to raise a standing army—rather than just count them (again *pqd*/"muster"): "to count" is designated more with *spr*.[136]

Is it an irony that Bathsheba's son becomes king? Now, of course 2 Samuel 12:24's "and YHWH loved him" (AT) raises some expectation of favor. However, it has been argued that Solomon's name suggests that he was Uriah's son and that there was never an unborn one. The point is that Ahithophel knew that Solomon was not David's son, and Bathsheba named him Solomon (which means "replacement") Jedidiah (12:24–25).[137] David ends up like Saul. History repeats. In turn, Nathan serves Solomon's interests and there is repetition again; taxation for building projects would be Solomon's downfall.[138] Even if one does not accept Baruch Halpern's and Joel Baden's reconstructions and prefers the plain meaning of the text as reflecting historical reality just as well as any reconstruction (or if one thinks the latter is not what discerning the meaning of a text is about), *nevertheless* the point is that the Lord is the one who is behind Solomon's actions and whose choices trump those of the greatest humans. Over a score of chapters the story winds its meandering way to the unlikely succession. This accords with a Christian reading, that the eventual, even "real," purpose of these narratives is Christ, a reading that casts the provisional purpose into more of an ancillary, and "providential," key.

Writing about 1 Kings 11–12, Brueggemann mentions Absalom's preferring Hushai to Ahithophel in 2 Samuel 17:14 ("The LORD had ordained to defeat the good counsel of Ahithophel"): "So for Israel, God has 'seen ahead' that the destruction of the Solomonic enterprise of acquisitiveness is a good to be accomplished through the course of public life. . . . If . . . we are more theologically attentive, we will say that these two chapters articulate Yahweh's providence, Yahweh's hidden way of shaping reality for the sake of Yahweh's purposes."[139]

Here it is God who has decided to divide the kingdom as per Ahijah's prophecy in 1 Kings 11:30–32. "It remains for human agents like Rehoboam to choose, unwittingly, the choices of Yahweh."[140] Behind the prophecy is the force of the overriding obligation of the law, to love Yahweh only. Something similar goes on with the downfall of Ahab (1 Kings 22:22–24). For Hezekiah,

136. Auld, "Reading Genesis after Samuel."
137. Halpern, *David's Secret Demons*, 400–403, claims Bathsheba is known to have been already pregnant. See also Baden, *Historical David*, 228–30; Baden goes back to Stanley L. Cook and the work of T. Veijola. In both cases (Saul and David) the kingdom was thrust upon them.
138. Halpern, *David's Secret Demons*, 248: reconstruction is required and obligated because biblical narrative has aporias.
139. Brueggemann, *1 & 2 Kings*, 157.
140. Brueggemann, *1 & 2 Kings*, 158. Cf. 176: "Public history is a working out of Yahweh's hidden intention."

the Lord rules over Sennacherib no less than over all creation (2 Kings 19:29–30), following this up with a delightful mixture of metaphor: "And this shall be the sign for you: This year eat what grows of itself, and in the second year what springs of the same. Then in the third year sow and reap and plant vineyards, and eat their fruit. And the surviving remnant of the house of Judah shall again take root downward and bear fruit upward" (AT).

It is clear that Hezekiah is no hero. In fact, 2 Kings 18 has modified the Isaianic account with its piety and its psalm—and brings Hezekiah right down to size. Yet even in the Isaiah account Hezekiah's healing is proleptic to the further-off salvation of Israel, and his is not full healing (cf. Pss. 22; 31; 41), for he just "sufficiently recovered to live out the promise made in the psalm, that he would spend his days praising God in the temple."[141] The royal house has let Zion down (Isa. 39:7), but God will bring Zion through. Here providence seems personal but on closer inspection is really "corporate." Brueggemann rightly emphasizes that it is the particular, concrete Jerusalem that here is promised salvation: "a real city facing a real Empire."[142]

In some ways comedy needs tragedy to grow around, like a vine wrapped around a tree: for example, Song of Songs may be viewed as an "answer" to the bitterness of life reported in Job 13. Perhaps, read in a "comical" context, the overriding concern of Job is "life-survival-offspring-fertility-continuity."[143] True, as J. William Whedbee admits, a trajectory of "fall" characterizes biblical history from Genesis 3 onward, but Scripture also contains moments and even patterns of transcendence and even transformations.[144] Comedy can allow "a narrow escape into faith" (out of despair),[145] and even Job with all its caricatures, irony, and resolution, or at least consolation, is more comic than it is tragic. The Bible loves to subvert the status quo while also celebrating life, although one might want to add that this "life,"[146] according to the Bible, includes a moral dimension over and above the naturalistic minimum. God changes ideas and minds so that people act differently from how they would have otherwise, acting instead according to his will, although this happens in long and deviating ways (as per Jonah, with a fair amount of bathos).[147] In

141. Seitz, *Zion's Final Destiny*, 171.
142. Brueggemann, *1 & 2 Kings*, 518. One might, however, have reservations about how freely Brueggemann wants to map these events onto those of modern American politics.
143. Fokkelman, "Genesis," 41.
144. Whedbee, *Bible and the Comic Vision*, 28.
145. Whedbee, *Bible and the Comic Vision*, 287.
146. Whedbee, *Bible and the Comic Vision*, 226.
147. Miles, "Laughing at the Bible," 174, points to the fact that Ps. 130's "Out of the depths . . ." is given full literalistic treatment in Jonah. Moreover, Jon. 4:2 contains a parody of Elijah at 1 Kings 19:4 (177).

fact, God's ability to remove a threat of unconditional judgment is part of the comedy.[148] Tragedy can be swallowed up in a bittersweet comedy: Joseph subsumes and sublates Cain-Abel.[149] Exodus can be read as a comedy of deliverance, with Moses as antihero saved by the "weaker sex," and tragedy is again transcended as God "toys" with Pharaoh. Providence is what God does through those who are not receiving salvation for the protection of those who are. The verbs for hardening (*kābēd, ḥāzaq*) can also be used positively with reference to the hearts of the prophets that God reinforces, such as Jonah's.[150]

However, whether Jonah is to be understood as full of parody (and Adele Berlin has disputed this) or not, the bigger point is that God is able to reverse his judgment, which was implicitly conditional, although not expressed that way formally in Jonah 3:4. One can find the theme in Jeremiah 18:7–8 ("At one instant I may speak concerning a nation, and concerning a kingdom, to pluck up and to break down and to destroy it; but if that nation turn from their evil, because of which I have spoken against it, I repent of the evil that I thought to do unto it" [AT]) and 26:18–19, where it is argued that the prophet Micah's prophecy of doom was not fulfilled because of Hezekiah's entreaty.

Northrop Frye has written of tragedy as prelude to comedy and in that sense subservient to it. In their joint article J. Cheryl Exum and J. W. Whedbee write: "Comedy indeed celebrates the rhythm of life with its times of play and joyous renewal, but frequently comedy must first resort to ridicule and bring down the boastful who block the free movement of life."[151] Tragedy shows isolation (often related to not being reconciled with God) and the terror of the irrational, as when Saul wrestles with his predestined fate. This might be contrasted with the "comic" Samson, who is both the hero and the one whose amoral and "picaresque" character sees little development through the mechanical plot, unlike a tragic protagonist (such as Saul, whose attempts at morality only heighten the poignancy of his tragic end). The coauthors' point is that biblical characters are more often like the first group, the amoral. Jacob and Esau and Isaac contribute to some comic scenes, arising out of basic appetites, as in Genesis 26:8 and 27:4. Genesis 22 was almost a tragedy, but Isaac, whose name reflects Sarah's laughter, is a survivor, and as such (contra Elie Wiesel) is not "most tragic" but "most comical."[152]

---

148. Bickerman, *Four Strange Books of the Old Testament*, 32.

149. Whedbee, *Bible and the Comic Vision*, 43.

150. See Dohmen, *Exodus 1–18*, 239.

151. Exum and Whedbee, "Isaac, Samson and Saul," 8. Cf. Robertson, *Old Testament and the Literary Critic*.

152. Exum and Whedbee, "Isaac, Samson and Saul," 10. Wiesel, "The Sacrifice of Isaac," 97.

Francis Landy objects to this valorization of humor, rather as Adele Berlin did to Jack Miles. For "Jacob still harbors rancor against Reuben, Simeon and Levi (Gen 49: 3–7). His wounds do not heal."[153] "History repeats itself as farce. Isaac's life is a continuation of Abraham's, but testifies to its thematic exhaustion. Why then is Isaac not a comic figure, unlike, say, Laban? First, because he is not laughed at or over in the text, *pace* Exum and Whedbee. . . . Secondly, because the liminal moments of his life are not funny, or at least have a gravity about them. . . . Thirdly, because a passive victim is not usually comic."[154] Yair Zakovitch would also argue that Samson does develop at least a little in character, for at Judges 15:18 the hero at least realizes it is God's doing. Now, the fact that he cannot fully learn his lesson makes him tragic, yet just as there is arguably (and as argued above) a kind of redemption for Saul in 2 Samuel 1:14, so too for Samson.[155] Comedy can be seriously moral because the universe's order is not overridden. It might be no coincidence that those who think that these plots are not amoral or absurd also tend to have a higher view of biblical authority and will tend to give the God of the Bible the benefit of the doubt.[156] Those who find comedy in the Bible to be mockingly hollow tend to appreciate the pure survival of life as something almost inbuilt, with those who don't fare so well being excluded through no fault of their own[157] and getting caught in the wheels of fate. This is well summarized by Gunn: Sarah laughs, but the reader does not laugh with her. Yet plot-wise, Sarah has the last laugh—namely, Isaac, if one remembers the etymology of his name. So whose happy ending, and what might happiness mean? Samson is a *nāzir* and is heroic, but he is hardly happy.[158] Biblical comedy is bittersweet, and partly because there is often an unfairness about who gets to survive. Gunn agrees with Whedbee and Exum: "The issue of the hero's so-called flaw is subordinate to the inexorable movement toward catastrophe and the increasing isolation of the hero in a cosmos that appears inhospitable and capricious."[159]

Yet that is not the whole story, since God is at work. "Such episodes as the fiery furnace and Daniel in the lions' den are by no means alien to comedy,"[160]

153. Landy, "Are We in the Place of Averroes?," 132. See also Landy, "Humour as a Tool for Biblical Exegesis."

154. Landy, "Are We in the Place of Averroes?," 139.

155. Zakovitch, "∪ and ∩ in the Bible," 111; cf. 109: "I nevertheless cannot overcome any impression that the terms 'comedy' and 'tragedy,' borrowed from the world of French drama, are entirely alien to biblical literature."

156. Cf. Nicholson, *Three Faces of Saul*.

157. "Saul is not disloyal to Yahweh." Gunn, *Fate of King Saul*, 124.

158. Gunn, "Anatomy of Divine Comedy," 117.

159. Gunn, "Anatomy of Divine Comedy," 124.

160. Good, "Apocalyptic as Comedy," 46.

if one likes one's comedy to be rough. Daniel is an *eirōn*, someone who helps usher in resolution, not a fool (*alazōn*), which is quite the opposite. Comedy, then, trades in virtue and vice, "goodies and baddies,"[161] although figuring out just who is more one than the other requires reading the whole story and with careful eyes. Commenting on Daniel, Edmund Good concludes:

> The entire story, then, is a comedy of subversion from the inside. . . . God is the Director, the off-stage manipulator of the comic plot. That makes the plot no less comic, though there are hints of a kind of inevitability in the successive failures of mighty kings to have their ways with underlings. . . . By the end of ch. 6, the previously temporary reconstitutions of successive absurd societies have given way to what looks like a permanent new age, when the pagans have irrevocably, according to the law of the Medes and Persians, as it were, committed themselves to the God they have resisted all along.[162]

Yet often survival is superimposed as a happy ending, even where there has been no sign of repentance. Indeed, the displacement into Babylonian exile and the period of painful punishment make up for the lack of godly sorrow. It is finally only the persistent "will" or "purpose" of God that holds the plot together and ensures the upswing of the closed and U-shaped comic structure. This divine enacted will is, of course, the implicit narrative, even the hidden narrative.

Esther

Esther begins with grim circumstances. The prophetic hope of a restored divine monarchy in Jerusalem, expressed in Zechariah 8:7–8, had not been gloriously fulfilled, and even with Ezra's going up to Jerusalem, the whole operation remained very much on a small scale, while Jerusalem's more segregated form of religious life contrasted with and even gave permission to diasporic Judaism to be more integrated in the host culture. The writers of Esther and the Aramaic Daniel saw God's providence no less at work among Jews in the East, the capital Susa included. These writers expressed confidence that God worked through the emperors, even when as personalities they could be unpredictable and unstable. Daniel was a more pious version of Joseph, although the reason for Joseph's silence about God is perhaps that he is in a

---

161. Even by Nebuchadnezzar and Darius God is recognized to be in charge: "The Good Guys are moved up the ladder of success, and the Bad Guys are either eliminated or brought around by reason and circumstance to being Good Guys." Good, "Apocalyptic as Comedy," 56.

162. Good, "Apocalyptic as Comedy," 55–56.

sense godlike, or one through whom God acted,[163] whereas in Daniel's case God worked indirectly through angels and other intermediaries.[164] Yet the Masoretic Text of Esther and Mordecai's story does not mention God at all, and the question is whether the Septuagint, with its "additions," introduced hints of the divine. In the basic text Esther is almost Machiavellian in her clever use of power and does not depend on supernatural, exodus-style deliverance. Fear of the Lord is replaced by fear of the Jews (Esther 8:17).[165] The silence of "God" and his absence given the distance from the temple were explained by talmudic sages with reference to the verse in Deuteronomy 31:18: "I will indeed hide my face on that day."[166] André Lacocque notes that the Masoretic Text must surely be more "original" since it is less religious and more serious than the Greek Alpha Text. The celebration is a far from a pious carnival. "But in Esther, there is no return to Jerusalem and no Passover, there is an entirely new celebration, Purim, a celebration of the happy Jewish implantation in the land of their 'exile.' The *people* has been substituted for land, Temple, and cult."[167] Adele Berlin classifies the book as "seriocomic" by genre, with plenty of bathos and use of the passive voice, almost a case of events without any agency divine or human.[168] Yet perhaps the fast at 4:16 implies that deliverance is in part a divine response to pious human initiative.[169] Moreover, human agents, while not totally in control, find themselves in places of influence for God to work through with a plan that has a look of the redemptive about it. It is "an intentional irony in the fact that in the story of Moses the people's clamor goes up to God's ears (Exod. 2:23), while in Esther's story the people's shouts reach Esther (4:13–17)."[170] With due pomposity Ahasuerus and Haman are determinists (1:19–8:8) in their beliefs regarding their laws, which maintain that an earlier command cannot be reversed. However, a reversal of fortune will bypass the fixity of legislation for the sake of the triumph of equity. Even the prophecy of Zeresh, Haman's wife, in 6:13 seems to indicate just that. Hence, "when fortune turns and the Jews are saved from annihilation, the city of Susa 'cries out in joy' (8:15)." Jews have found grace with the populace. "If Ishtar is 'queen of heaven,' the Jewess Esther becomes queen of Persia.

---

163. See Koller, *Esther in Ancient Jewish Thought*, 41–44.

164. Koller, *Esther in Ancient Jewish Thought*, 97. Levenson, *Esther*, 56, shows that Mordecai is linked to the house of Saul, hence very much non-Davidite.

165. Lacocque, *Esther Regina*, 91.

166. Koller, *Esther in Ancient Jewish Thought*, 204.

167. Lacocque, *Esther Regina*, 44–45.

168. Berlin, *Esther*, xxv.

169. Levenson, *Esther*, 19. Cf. Fox, "Religion of the Book of Esther," 147: "He is teaching a theology of possibility."

170. Fox, "Religion of the Book of Esther," 153n9.

If Marduk is compassionate, then Mordecai embodies compassion towards his people."[171]

Parallels between the Joseph and the Esther story were spotted by Ludwig Rosenthal in 1895 and more recently by Gabriel Hornung, who spots a "nuanced re-use" of "Joseph" by Esther. Both characters are good-looking and resort to playing on "luck," which really means that they are favored by God from the beginning, even as foreigners in influential positions. It might be that Mordecai and Esther share the role Joseph had. Certainly Mordecai is at points Esther's conscience, as at Esther 4:14: "For if you remain silent at this time, (will) relief and deliverance for the Jews arise from another place, and you and your family will perish?" (AT). Much has been written about whether this is an implicit reference to God, or simply to Esther being the agent. Is it an oblique reference to God's hidden activity, or is it rather the case that the answer to the question is no, that disaster will follow unless Esther acts: Esther is the only hope.[172] It is probably the latter, yet the latter does not exclude the former. As Carol Bechtel puts it: "It is left to Esther—with a lot of help from God and a little help from Mordecai—to get them out"[173] (of the mess). God's presence is also felt in the book's "coincidences," such as the king's insomnia in chapter 6.[174] True, as Fox's "humanistic" account of the story emphasizes: "The book is exploring and affirming the potential of human character to rise to the needs of the hour by whatever means and devices the situation demands. . . . It is not miracles, but inner resources—intellectual as well as spiritual—that one must call upon in a crisis."[175] Yet there are also links with Isaiah 54, which make it clear that this is a story about *Israel*'s destiny as the vehicle of salvation, which divine providential action both serves and works out from. God is unnamed but involved.[176] Nevertheless, by way of contrast with the Joseph story, in Esther it is more the case of Jews making their own luck.[177] If Joseph is instrument more than he is agent, then in the case of Esther the root selfishness that pervades human agency, including one's own, is taken up in God's purposes.

171. Lacocque, *Esther Regina*, 48–49.
172. These views are represented by McConville, *Esther*, 173, and Dunne, *Esther and Her Elusive God*, 42, respectively. Dunne continues: "The characters are not 'uncertain' about God's activity; they are oblivious" (114).
173. Bechtel, *Esther*, 55.
174. Bechtel, *Esther*, 57: "Author Frederick Buechner once said that a coincidence is just God's way of remaining anonymous."
175. Fox, "Three Esthers," 55. He notes that in the rewritten Alpha Text Esther is less heroic. Fox, *Character and Ideology in the Book of Esther*, 57.
176. Levenson, *Esther*, 15.
177. Cf. Meinhold, "Die Gattung der Josephsgeschichte und des Estherbuches II," 90.

"Thus we see Esther as a tale of *how good things happen to undeserving people.*"[178]

This chimes with a move in modern theology (mentioned in the discussion of Friedrich Graf above in chap. 2) to view providence as God's concurrence with the agency of humans (*concursus hominis*).[179] Mordecai and Esther use their gifts. God helps those who help themselves: "If the Jews were to wait for Passover for their deliverance, it would be too late. . . . If they were to survive, the Jews had to make their own story. . . . Esther is a story of how a people profoundly hurt by the absence of their hitherto faithful God may end up believing in themselves."[180] Yet this is not a case of action that deserves help as such. This is a situation of diaspora and not exile (cf. Daniel), where people must to some extent assimilate the surrounding culture and religion and get on with things. There is a "kenotic" aspect to Esther. The festival of Purim, unlike Passover, can represent an overaccepting of diaspora status.[181] Faith here is recognizing one's worth to take "bold steps that evince confidence in the Jews' place in history. Too much emphasis on God's action is in danger of diminishing the urgency and necessity of courageous contemporary steps from particular Jews. Too much exclusion of the shadowy purposes of God takes away the reason why the Jews are special and the guarantee that their destiny is unique."[182]

The emphasis on human agency, possibly at the expense of mystery, may well be reinforced. "Coincidence means that, once the Jews have shown courage and spirit by taking their destiny into their own hands, all kinds of allies begin to appear in the most unlikely of places. This is the diffused notion of providence that is the closest the narrative comes to identifying the ways of God."[183] However, this account (by Samuel Wells) swings the pendulum too far and sounds a little bit like reducing providence to plucky human action.

It seems almost a truism to write: "In the last portions of the Hebrew Bible, God is not present in the well-known apparent ways of the earlier books."[184] A clear exception, as already mentioned, is Daniel, which of course has miracles in the sense of warnings to pagans, as in Daniel 5's writing on the wall at Belshazzar's feast, which puts one in mind of 1 Corinthians 14:22's "tongues . . . are a sign . . . for unbelievers." Yet there seems to be a

---

178. Dunne, *Esther and Her Elusive God*, 125.
179. One thinks of Tanner, *God and Creation in Christian Theology*.
180. Wells, "Esther," 5, 11. The church is to act and live in an Acts 4 paradigm, argues Wells, by the church being itself, cherishing not control but faithfulness.
181. Wells introduces this key theme in his introduction ("Esther," 11).
182. Wells, "Esther," 57–58.
183. Wells, "Esther," 65.
184. Friedenthal, *Disappearance of God*, 7.

widespread view that in the "Second Temple" period God is relegated to the past or the eschatological future and not recognized in the present. "Now by moving the essence of divinity from the realm of nature to the realm of history, Israelite religion made it possible for a deity to recede."[185] Perhaps. Yet Jesus the "second-temple Jew" in Matthew 22:32 speaks of the God of the living, and the motto in Deuteronomy 29:29, "The hidden things belong to Yahweh our God, and the revealed things belong to us and to our children forever, to do all the words of the Torah" (AT), is of the essence of Pharisaic religion. Torah and temple do not block God off from his people; quite the opposite. The shuttling of conception of God between *absconditus* and *revelatus* (hidden and revealed) is a mark of post-Hebrew biblical literature. God is seen as far from absent.

The Prophetic Understanding of History and the Reality of "Cause and Effect"

Drawing on the work of H. H. Schmid, H.-D. Preuss concludes that biblical wisdom reflects the experience of reality's "communicativeness." But— echoing Martin Heidegger—this means a perceiving of life's "historicality" in the way humans talk about it, rather than in terms of a linear salvation history.[186] This sense of *Geworfenheit*, or landing where one falls, includes a calling to take charge of and responsibility for the world, and that requires wisdom, even when one must operate on a trial-and-error basis. For only in the historical repairing and enhancing of life is wisdom to be gained. All this calls into question Westermann's rather blithe assumption that life is mostly about giving and taking blessing.[187] No, the cosmic order is just a bit too shaky for that. Indeed, blessing is partial and requires one to depend on God in faith for his intervention and salvation, without thinking that this life is on the way to any sort of state of permanence. At least for most premoderns, the contingency of creation was a given, and divine providence was seen as having more to do with sustaining than progressing. Now, part of that sustaining meant pruning or judging.

On the matter of divine judgment two different positions were taken by Klaus Koch and Patrick D. Miller.[188] Koch gave an account of the biblical ethos whereby the results of actions were according to a natural law of deed and

185. Friedenthal, *Disappearance of God*, 26.
186. Preus, *Theologie des Alten Testaments*, 1:183.
187. Westermann, *Blessing in the Bible and the Life of the Church*.
188. Miller, *Sin and Judgment in the Prophets*; also Krüger, *Geschichtskonzepte im Ezechielbuch*, 86–89.

consequence that required no additional divine intervention: one reaps what one sows (cf. Gal. 6:7). Although beginning with Proverbs (mostly 25–28), Koch was quick to range across the Old Testament as a whole, turning next to Hosea (and then Psalms, then historical books). He observed how the juridical and "recompense" theme appears much more strongly in the "Hellenistic" Septuagint version(s).[189] Koch specified that "the deed" forms a sort of invisible sphere around the agent, through which one day a corresponding outcome will be produced. Divinity merely "watches over this inner-human order and constantly gives it power where it threatens to weaken."[190] Koch went on to say that the deeds return to the person in the form of this invisible cocoon (*Hülle*) that accompanies and pays back a corresponding result, thus representing a fortune-effecting "sphere of action." This of course *can* be positive, as in Proverbs 21:21 ("Whoever pursues righteousness and love finds life, prosperity and honor" [NIV]). The sphere very much belongs to the person. The outworking of such deeds does not immediately appear, but develops like a plant from a seed.[191]

Already on page 10 of his well-known essay Koch pointed to Hosea 8:4b–7 ("sowing the wind and reaping the storm" [AT]). Hans Walter Wolff followed the same line in his commentary on Hosea, when on 4:1–3 he wrote that the judgment is not owing to the Lord's direct action but from "an organic structure of order," "a sphere in which one's actions have fateful consequences," which "Yahweh puts into effect."[192] Koch argued that this is only about God bringing an already and independently caused deed to light, in its having its (dire) consequence. That guarantee of the consequences is YHWH's contribution, while the (secondary) causal connection that is going on invisibly is not his doing.[193]

In that way "Vergeltung" (retribution), which appears in the title of Koch's article "Gibt es ein Vergeltungsdogma im Alten Testament?," is not appropriate terminology to use, since that implies a causal action of recompense coming from outside, which does not do the subtlety of the texts justice. Koch's view thus fits with a more "scholastic" account of God as one who is not a causal agent among others in the universe but who nevertheless gives power to the process of reality.[194] Fortune springs from a person's own decision

189. Klaus Koch, "Gibt es ein Vergeltungsdogma im Alten Testament?"
190. Miller, *Sin and Judgement in the Prophets*, 135, quoting Koch, *Um das Prinzip der Vergeltung*, 140.
191. Klaus Koch, "Gibt es ein Vergeltungsdogma im Alten Testament?," 31–32.
192. Wolff, *Hosea*, 68.
193. Klaus Koch, "Gibt es ein Vergeltungsdogma im Alten Testament?," 13.
194. Koch and Roloff, "Tat-Ergehen-Zusammenhang," 493. Also, Klaus Koch, *Um das Prinzip der Vergeltung*.

and deeds. Yet Koch's account of things has been criticized in light of the growing awareness that recompense is part of a cosmic mechanism (1) in the cognate ancient Near Eastern material and (2) a fortiori in the biblical accounts of the "personal" God of the prophets.[195] Patrick D. Miller counters Koch's interpretation of the "sow-reap" metaphor *as used in the Prophets* by saying that what is meant is that there is a correspondence or nexus between the two, not a direct causal link.[196] Hosea contains passages where God seems to intervene directly, such as where it is indeed "YHWH" himself who catches the "bird" (Israel) in the net (Hosea 7:12). Or consider 12:2 (12:3 MT: וְלִפְקֹד עַל־יַעֲקֹב כִּדְרָכָיו), on which Koch had commented: "Yahweh brings the deed home [*pqd*] to the evildoer" (Jahwe sucht die Tat am Täter heim);[197] he also commented on Hosea 4:9, which he renders in German what may be translated into English as follows: "He will visit [*pqd*] them and repay them for their ways." There is no getting away from the juridical nature of divine involvement: for Miller, it is "Yahweh" himself who makes the link between deed and punishment; he does not merely make that already existing link explicit, as per Koch.[198] What Koch has done is to contextualize those verses without reference to God within their wider passages or cotext, where there *is* mention of divine involvement in judgment.

Reciprocity lies at the heart of *Vergeltung*, and this is also found in the Golden Rule (Matt. 7:12). Even a verse like Proverbs 26:27 ("Whoever digs a pit will fall into it") should not be pushed too far, for the consequence is not necessarily automatic; certain things have to happen for this to take place. Proverbs 28:18, on the other hand, speaks of divine activity "implicitly" in the respective outcomes for the Torah keeper (safety) and the Torah breaker (the pit). God and society combine to pay back the offender and the victim, respectively. Proverbs 25:21–22[199] tells of a recompense by God in the present life, and not just some mere confirmation of such. Janowski concludes that the lesson being taught is not about ontology but morality, urging humans to be drawn toward and to reach out toward right behavior.[200] The Septuagint

195. Janowski, "Die Tat kehrt zum Täter zurück," 253n31. Cf. Hausmann, *Studien zum Menschenbild der älteren Weisheit*, 244.

196. Miller, *Sin and Judgment in the Prophets*, 123.

197. Klaus Koch, "Gibt es ein Vergeltungsdogma im Alten Testament?," 11.

198. Miller, *Sin and Judgment in the Prophets*, 138: "There is no such trivialization of the notion of judgment in the passages studied. On the contrary, they reveal a kind of synergism in which divine and human action are forged into a single whole or the divine intention of judgment is wrought out through human agency. . . . The prophetic announcement is that Sennacherib's encampment against Jerusalem is Yahweh's encampment."

199. Janowski, "Die Tat kehrt zum Täter zurück," 269.

200. Janowski, "Die Tat kehrt zum Täter zurück," 271.

often has simply not understood this idea of inculcating interpersonal morality and often added in the message of recompense (*apo-/Lohn*) and turned
it into a legal term (*Rechtsbegriffe*). Truly, in Hebrew thought, this morality is not something inner and "habitual," as Johannes Pedersen seemed to
think, but a socially networked, hence external yet communal morality, civic
hence religious.[201] What connects deed and result is more a sphere of action
(*Tatsphäre*), one that is freely chosen to be entered into, and not one tied to
magic. So Janowski is more with Koch in the sense of action having its own
results, with God and society merely confirming this. He is right to steer away
from Koch's "Tendenz" (tendency), by concluding that there is little sense in
Proverbs or the Prophets of any eschatological or "end of life" judgment, but
if anything, this reinforces the idea that in watching over these processes God
is more than just a spectator.

Yet Koch is surely right that the later Old Testament and the New Testament do not *totally* abandon the nexus, even when a new age lies ahead.[202]
Daniel, too, and Paul believed in the idea of a deed that creates "fate," as in
Galatians 6:8–9, which employs the Old Testament image of the relationship between sowing and reaping.[203] Where is God in that? Well, perhaps
the "personal" intervention intensifies and affirms this impersonal process
in order to work in it to bring it to the completion of judgment, as the Lord
finds himself touched by the behavior.[204] As Paul said about ministry: it is
God who gives the growth (though not as per Koch: "who gives the harvest").
Morality requires a coming close to God and committing one's cause to him,
whether as a victim of injustice or in times of moral uncertainty, where one
feels tempted to do wrong. It also means for the one who has been affected
to give due response.[205] Hence Johannes Scharbert thinks that morality is
not about fulfilling but just returning what is due—as in Isaiah 57:18—as a
consolation for suffering. God is portrayed not as judge but as one affected,
hence more like a complainant.[206] H. H. Schmid, doubtful that the Hebrews
thought so differently from other cultures, adds that in any case YHWH's
fulfilling the schema surely signifies some amount of divine involvement.[207]

Natural law is the universal moral sense that takes the rights of all human
beings seriously, even corresponding to their dignity "according to the image"

201. Pedersen, *Israel*, 178.
202. Pedersen, *Israel*, 173–74.
203. See Schlier, *Der Brief an die Galater*, 204.
204. Scharbert, "Das Verbum *pqd* in der Theologie des Alten Testaments," 311.
205. Scharbert, "Das Verbum *pqd* in der Theologie des Alten Testaments," 312.
206. Scharbert, "Das Verbum *pqd* in der Theologie des Alten Testaments," 317.
207. H. H. Schmid, *Gerechtigkeit als Weltordnung*, 177–80.

qua human, and is also based on reflection on the nature of things. Thus, John Barton: "I am not specially concerned here to endorse the idea that 'wisdom' must lie at the back of such emphases, but simply to suggest that the attitude towards ethics which underlies them would seem to be like that of some parts of the wisdom tradition in that they are most easily explained as a coherent whole if we see them as deriving from belief in a kind of cosmic order."[208] This is patent in Isaiah 1:3 ("The ox knows its master") or 29:16 ("You turn things upside down") and is latent in Amos 6:12 ("Do horses run on rocks?")

There is also the question as to how merely "residual" in the culture these elements were and whether Hermann Gunkel was right to say that on the whole the contribution by the prophets of a principle of recompense was one of their glorious inventions.[209] Yet their achievement was more to make clear that there are such things as ethical rights and wrongs than to claim something about the mechanism. The Hebrew word for sin and punishment is *ʿāwōn*, "meaning both a sin and the penalty for sin," whereas the term *rāʿ* stands for "both moral evil and the physical evil with which it is rewarded (as in English, we might note with some discomfort)."[210]

To give a brief example of the Hebrew Bible's history-writing, it does seem that 1–2 Kings (and 1–2 Chronicles) are predicated on a "prophetic" view of history. Ahab's death is the place where he committed his worst crime, in the vineyard of Naboth (1 Kings 21:17–24; cf. the similar place of death of Ahab's son Joram at the hand of Jehu in 2 Kings 9:26). From the prophets it seems clear that God in his wrath can outdo human beings in posing a threat to life,[211] thereby breaking the shell of the material good for the sake of the spiritual one. God thus presses what is most real (something hypermoral) on humanity.[212]

Even the relatively early prophecy of Amos had some sense of world order. "However, with him this connection is not so much that of an independently functioning principle in a sphere of the ill-fated development of the sinful deed ('*Schicksal wirkende Tatsphäre*'—K. Koch), but in YHWH Himself. Amos does not first of all point his listeners in the direction of an inescapable world order but, rather, to the very nature of YHWH's actions."[213] God is himself the world order or, to be precise, God's activity is. The point is that there is no semiautonomous and automatic link between deed and justice, which would

208. Barton, "Natural Law and Poetic Justice in the Old Testament," 6.
209. Barton, "Natural Law and Poetic Justice in the Old Testament," 11, refers to Gunkel, "Vergeltung im Alten Testament."
210. Barton, "Natural Law and Poetic Justice in the Old Testament," 11.
211. Dietrich and Link, *Die dunklen Seiten Gottes*, 1:174.
212. See Dietrich and Link, *Die dunklen Seiten Gottes*, 1:179.
213. Paas, *Creation and Judgement*, 432.

bypass God's judgment and ordering. In Amos, creation power is "reversed" against the people (7:1–4; 9:11) as destruction looms. Amos emphasizes God's unpredictability as both creator and destroyer, and Hosea 4:1–3 shows that the ecological disaster is a result of Israel's sin, again not as a directly caused punishment, but as a meet one. People think that God does not see, when in fact it is his seeing that means there is no escape. With the prophets, whatever the case with "Wisdom," God is fully involved in the process of deed and consequence.

On the one hand, for Ezekiel, "needing no physical representation, YHWH could be present in exile in the form of כָּבוֹד ('glory'), even without a functioning cult. . . . For Amos, however, the specific incidents attributed to YHWH's initiatives were unrelentingly destructive."[214] Divine direct action in Amos is perhaps not as immediately recognizable as divine presence in Ezekiel is. Texts such as Amos 3:6b, "Does evil beset a city and YHWH has not done it?" (AT), are echoed by Isaiah 28:21 with its talk of God's alien work. "This teacher, it asserts, does not apply an arbitrary standard but follows the rule of law . . . , even when executing a strange deed. . . . In one way or another these two texts that presuppose nature's regularity and cold indifference place them under YHWH's sovereignty. Behind the mystery of nature rests one permanent reality, the texts assert, a divine teacher who communicates openly and clearly."[215] The strangeness of the action will be in some ways alleviated by the prophetic revelation that the Lord God is behind it.

The Isaianic "God" works to forcefully reimpose a created order, and the strangeness of his operating is in part due to how far the people have wandered in their hearts and minds.[216] The outcome of Jeremiah 36 is that the Word is living and cannot be destroyed by fire. Jehoiakim cannot stop the things the Word predicts from coming to pass. The only way to "nullify" a prophecy of doom is obedience. "In the burning of the scroll, Yahweh himself experiences a fiery death, a means of death that was especially ignominious for Old Testament sensibilities."[217] The one who suffers is God through the Word in its effacing, not least as the character of Jeremiah begins to fade from view in the narrative.

Again in Isaiah 40–66 the theme shifts from creation to new creation, with 56–66 feeding off 40–55.[218] "The emphasis of *bārā'* [a verb that appears

214. Crenshaw, "Theodicy and Prophetic Literature," 251, following Kutsko, *Between Heaven and Earth.*

215. Crenshaw, "Theodicy and Prophetic Literature," 254.

216. Paas, *Creation and Judgement,* 418.

217. Zimmerli, "Fruit of the Tribulation of the Prophet," 357.

218. Cf. Steck, "Beobachtungen zu Jesaja 56–59."

nineteen times in Isa. 40–55] lies first on the sovereignty of what God achieves rather than on the nothingness from which God starts."[219] God works in and with creation and for creation's sake. The covenant with Israel and its outworking in history may be understood as a subset of the covenant of creation, and it means that God works with the creation order for the sake of the people, constantly renewing *not* creation but its order.

As early as the Genesis creation story "this account of God's creation of humanity and God's words of blessing remind the chosen people(s) that God's choice of them is subordinate to a commitment to humankind as a whole."[220] When it comes to the use of creation as a metaphor in "Second Isaiah," the point is that the metaphorical exchange means that the division between creation and salvation gets blurred. "The belief that God created and is sustaining the order of the world in all its complexities, is not a peripheral theme of biblical theology but is plainly the fundamental theme."[221] Rather than see the two (creation and salvation) as "polarities" (John Goldingay's term),[222] one might prefer to see God's providential reenergizing of creation in historical mode through his gifts of peace and order as is given to his "saved" people.[223] It is not so much a plan for history as it is an ordering that God continuously imposes on errant creation, to check it and bring it back by a historical process, undoing and redoing. As with 2 Samuel 17:14b, the previous events are becoming realized once again as being part of a history of divine leading.[224] God, according to Jeremiah 23:23–44, fills heaven and earth, meaning that God fills nonhuman creation and that "God's presence to and relationship with the earth and its creatures is more than external; there is an inwardness or interiority characteristic of the earth and its creatures such that a genuine relationship with God exists."[225]

The "some kind of *internal* relationship" that Fretheim observes seems quite different from the standard Christian scholastic idea that God has no real relationship with his creation (e.g., Aquinas, *Summa theologiæ* I.28.1).[226] To take another example, God's anger means that his pathos is not sentimental but rather witnesses just how committed to the cause he is when provoked, his anger being "a divine response, not a divine attribute." If there were no

219. Goldingay, *Old Testament Theology*, 1:78. He reminds the readers that they are no longer in the 1930s: covenant must not be allowed to take over from creation (1:101).
220. Goldingay, *Old Testament Theology*, 1:101.
221. H. H. Schmid, "Creation, Righteousness and Salvation," 111.
222. Goldingay, *Old Testament Theology*, 1:289.
223. "His plan" (עֲצָתוֹ; "his counselor" in NRSV) in Isa. 40:13 is a way of righteousness. See Werner, *Studien zur alttestamentlichen Vorstellung vom Plan Jahwehs*, 295.
224. Werner, *Studien zur alttestamentlichen Vorstellung vom Plan Jahwehs*, 295.
225. Fretheim, *Jeremiah*, 32.
226. Fretheim, *Jeremiah*, 32.

sin, there would be no anger, and in God the latter is mixed with grief, as in Jeremiah 21:14 God declares: "I will visit upon you the fruit of your doings" (AT; cf. 14:10). "God enters deeply into the realities of sin and evil—including experiencing the very suffering that people and land experience . . .—and breaks them open from within."[227]

Yet divine wrath can be presented as impersonal, almost as if under God's supervision, as in Jeremiah 7:20; 10:25; 42:18, where it is "poured out upon" like the contents of a bucket. God's personal anger may be said to be expressed in a "seeing to" the moral order and in this movement from deed to consequence. It is ultimately personal, but at one remove from the wrath and judgment itself, which are functions of what creation receives as distinct from what God sends. As with Pharaoh in Exodus 12:30–32, one should not play down Babylonians as mere instruments, for they were often working in tandem with the divine will—for example, at Jeremiah 49:20, where God is said to have a "plan" and "purposes"; compare 49:30, where Nebuchadrezzar is said to have a "plan" and "purpose" (same phrase) of not pitying nor sparing. Nebuchadrezzar is not a puppet of God, since the former is able to overreach and go beyond God's instruction.[228] In 42:10 God says he is sorry for the disaster of the fall of Jerusalem, which may mean—and Fretheim believes it does[229]—that God does not take responsibility for the extent of the damage. However, the phrase "I relent of the evil I did to you" seems to take whole responsibility. It is perhaps better to see this as a case of primary and secondary causality. It would seem that God's power is not so much restrained as it is channeled and directed.

How should one view "providence" according to "the Prophets" as a whole?[230] Well, the prophetic theology seems to change in response to circumstances and Israel's behavior. Israel's vacillation can even serve as an explanation for *delay* of any God-delivered change.[231] Hence Isaiah 60–62 was written in response to a new situation, offering a relecture of Isaiah 40–55. The same goes for the later parts of Zechariah. This is because prophecy never stops speaking and making itself fit. The message is metahistorical (*Übergeschichte*),[232] in

---

227. Fretheim, *Jeremiah*, 35.

228. Fretheim, *Jeremiah*, 37, with reference to Jer. 25:11–14; 51:24; see Isa. 47:5–7.

229. Fretheim, *Jeremiah*, 37. Cf. Fretheim, "Authority of the Bible," 43: God sometimes regrets—"The judgment and its painful effects proved to be more severe than God had intended, or even thought they would be" (see, e.g., Jer. 3:19–20). See also Jer. 42:10 (cf. McKane, *Jeremiah*, 2:1033) and Zech. 1:15: "While I was only a little angry, they made the disaster worse" (one might ask: Who are "they" except agents who work along with and often against God?).

230. Steck, *Die Prophetenbücher und ihr theologisches Zeugnis*, 22.

231. Steck, *Die Prophetenbücher und ihr theologisches Zeugnis*, 149.

232. Klaus Koch, *Die Propheten*, 1:249–52; see also Steck, *Die Prophetenbücher und ihr theologisches Zeugnis*, 50.

the sense of not being stuck in time. Whereas Barton would resist trying to describe the invisible structures lying behind or underneath what is said in the Hebrew Bible, Steck is all for it: there are deep levels of meaning in the background of the history of events, experiences, and expectations.[233] There is scant sense that the later redactors of the prophets aimed to apocalypticize: in fact, these saw themselves in continuity with the prophetic glimpse into YHWH's counsel. The plan of God was adapting itself to the times.[234] Steck likes to think that this means that the process implies God himself changing, but a changeable theology, even if understood as "God's view of reality," does not imply that God himself undergoes change. And God's power to effect things remains constant throughout.[235]

Wisdom

"The belief that God has created and is sustaining the order of the world in all its complexities is not a peripheral theme of biblical theology, but is plainly the fundamental theme."[236] However, sometimes a theme can be so fundamental that where one would expect to find it, in Israelite Wisdom literature, it is well hidden.

Proverbs

Thus there is much less about world order in Proverbs than in the corresponding Egyptian wisdom.[237] Nor is there all that much about "cult" in the collection, for there is little sense of "man before God" needing atonement or to sense the divine presence. The theme of trust in God is repeated, but not love, service, or belief. Trust includes trust that things will work out well if the deed is done well.[238] Proverbs 10–24 shares a positive attitude to "life" and assumes that humans can achieve things. What there is in theological terms is a providential God who ensures order in the affairs of human existence.[239]

233. Steck, *Die Prophetenbücher und ihr theologisches Zeugnis*, 150n42.
234. Steck, *Die Prophetenbücher und ihr theologisches Zeugnis*, 179.
235. Steck, *Gott in der Zeit entdecken*, 70–71. Cf. Kaiser, "Jahwe, der Reichsgott Israels."
236. H. H. Schmid, "Creation, Righteousness and Salvation," 111.
237. Hausmann, *Studien zum Menschenbild der älteren Weisheit*, 363.
238. See Hausmann, *Studien zum Menschenbild der älteren Weisheit*, 247. Roland Murphy holds that wisdom is not so much about world order as about the quest to find patterns in human life. Murphy, *Tree of Life*, 85.
239. Dell, *Book of Proverbs in Social and Theological Context*, 146: "In Proverbs 1–9 itself the stress on creation as past and present event is much more marked. This suggests that the more basic and primitive view of God as creator in Proverbs is as orderer."

Whereas folly causes different types of sin, wisdom sums up all virtues. "Fear of Yahweh and trust in him are sufficient to motivate the search for wisdom and the avoidance of sin."[240] Proverbs 21:10 and 28:15 express skepticism about the idea that virtuous behavior is rewarded (again, the *Tun-Ergehen* [deed and result] principle; see "The Prophetic Understanding of History and the Reality of 'Cause and Effect'" in this chapter above). For it might be the malice of others that brings persecution to the one who does well, or one can suffer at least temporary setbacks after right behavior. Yet what is crucial to observe is that the Old Testament refuses the Egyptian "way out," that of deferring things to the afterlife (see Prov. 21:18; 22:8; 24:16).[241]

Now, often God is viewed as acting along *with* the right acting, but because God is trusted as just judge over all (cf. Rom. 3:6), Proverbs 25:21 urges the reader to offer help even to the enemy. Proverbs 13:13b ("he who reveres the commandment will be rewarded" [AT]) brings an unnamed party into play with the "divine passive." Reward doesn't just happen automatically, but the Lord often gets involved in equitable rearranging, especially where the community seems to be at risk. Wisdom has an appellative function: it expects ethical improvement and ethical engagement as part of God's providential scheme.[242]

However, nothing in life seemed guaranteed, as Proverbs 27:1 bears witness: "Do not boast about tomorrow, for you do not know what a day may bring" (cf. James 4:14). In Egypt reward was rather seen as something positive, certain, and guaranteed with reference to the life to come and the enduring community of this world. Jan Assmann has commented on how in Egypt the principle of *Ma'at* was not just about the famous *Tun-Ergehen-Zusammenhang* or a *do ut des* principle but was also or even more a "being connected in action" ("Aufeinanderbezogensein des Handelns"), which allows life in community, including the dead, to be tightly connected, and mostly for the good.[243] A statement such as 15:24, "For the wise man's path of life leads upward, in order to avoid Sheol beneath" (AT), addresses present responsibilities and potential benefits rather than the threat of eternal punishment for the transgressor of wisdom. The person who internalizes "fear of the Lord" in the present can expect a multitude of rewards, but he or she will meet the same fate as the fool, so the rewards, not least wisdom, are to be enjoyed in this life.[244] Yet getting wisdom and fear of YHWH are closely associated; there

---

240. Fox, *Proverbs 10–31*, 944.
241. Hausmann, *Studien zum Menschenbild der älteren Weisheit*, 234.
242. Hausmann, *Studien zum Menschenbild der älteren Weisheit*, 245.
243. Assmann, *Ma'at*, 137.
244. Boström, *God of the Sages*, 96. He concludes (242): "Our study has led to the conclusion that this belief in justice and the character-consequence relationship did not serve a primarily

is no Egyptian equivalent of this communicative biblical wisdom representing God on earth. The fear of God is distinctive to Israel and thus is to be viewed[245] as central to the faith.[246] Solidarity with the community is clearly a theme in Proverbs 10 especially. Living wisely gives one a *chance* (not certainty) of a happy life.[247] Part of that wisdom lies in trusting God to take care of consequences. There are enough cases in Proverbs where God is clearly intervening, such as in 16:7; 24:12; 25:22, which have God making a difference although in a hidden way toward a manifest outcome, plus the divine passives at 10:24b ("The desire of the righteous will be granted") and 11:31 ("If the righteous is repaid on earth . . ."), which have no mention of reward being in the afterlife. In fact, it is arguable that the notion of "death and afterlife" preoccupies the writers only in later Wisdom material and that Proverbs almost just ignores the issue. One cannot really give Proverbs' "predictability" a name like "world order"[248]—as though constant patterns were mediating between God and the world: it is more like a *social* order, configured horizontally from within.[249]

Certainly, there was *ma'at* or "death and afterlife/renewal" as a force, since really it is for humans to initiate and work out such a principle into the cosmos. Assmann's observation that the Egyptians viewed the cosmos less as "order" and more as a process offers a variation on H. H. Schmid's thesis and serves to play up the biblical distinctiveness.[250] Even then, the idea of "order of the whole" came much later in terms of the history of ideas. Cosmic "order" (*mišpāṭ*) follows human microcosmic order, meaning that history became the way of attaining the good and that along with it came a confidence that was lacking in Stoicism.[251] Schmid's thesis was that the idea of order became that of reordering, in the sense of trying to get a society in motion back to something corresponding to a primitive ethical ideal of *mišpāṭ*. So the meaning of "order" was more a "moral" one and was quite like the German idea of *Ordnung* (order), yet with the sense of "loyalty to covenant" as that which corresponded to a moral order that was both in motion and yet harmonious.[252] Cleaning up, controlling, resetting, proving—these seem to be biblical "distinctives."

---

theological purpose in the book of Proverbs, but rather was employed to provide a philosophical basis for the ethical teaching of the sages."

245. Dell, *Book of Proverbs in Social and Theological Context*, 93.

246. Fox, *Proverbs 1–9*, 71.

247. Hausmann, *Studien zum Menschenbild der älteren Weisheit*, 247.

248. Adams, *Wisdom in Transition*, 84.

249. See Janowski, "Die Tat kehrt zum Täter zurück."

250. Brague, *La sagesse du monde*, 32.

251. Brague, *La sagesse du monde*, 214. Cf. H. H. Schmid, *Wesen und Geschichte der Weisheit*, 151.

252. H. H. Schmid, *Gerechtigkeit als Weltordnung*, 180, speaking of the Prophets; see also 185.

When it comes to the will of God in the Old Testament, Proverbs 16:9 suggests the following relationship: human plans are of no little importance but are dependent finally on God's work to bring them to completion (*kûn*). This suggests not only that God works in and through human beings in the establishment of the divine purpose in the world but also that human involvement is real and effective to that end (cf. 16:1). God wills that this be so, taking human intentions into account.[253] What humans do affects God's own working, and that is why wicked human plans are an "abomination" to the Lord (6:16–18).[254] The term "works" usually has to do with serving as a witness to the nations concerning God's activity in their midst. Psalm 104:24 is a clear example of this. The point of the select aphorisms of this middle part of Proverbs is that human plans are established by God—that is, in the sense of being *reinforced* by him. This is clear from the Septuagint translation of Proverbs 16:9 (15:29b LXX). The Hebrew of that verse can be translated, "The human heart plans the way, (but) the LORD establishes [MT: "directs"] the steps." Fox thinks that the Hebrew of verse 9 here is quite "deterministic"[255] and that the Greek has softened it in making God confirm the human choice, as it also does on verse 33, where the Hebrew mentions the drawing of lots ("The lot is cast into the lap, but the decision is the LORD's alone") but the Septuagint has "for the wicked all things arrive into their laps [*eis kolpous*], but with the Lord all things are righteous," which is more about God being the reliable and upright one. But this does not mean that the sense of the Hebrew has to take the *waw* particle as adversative; rather, it is a case of God working along with the lottery. (How one translates the *waw* often depends on how one thinks of the place of lots in Israelite religion.)[256] It could also be that the pious Septuagint equivalent found at 15:29b ("Let the human heart plan righteous things, so that the Lord might correct his steps") is a guide to the interpretation of the Hebrew, which bears the sense of God's affirming human choices or lifestyles. Hence even in Proverbs 16:1 ("The plans of the mind

253. Cf. Fretheim, *Exodus*, 150: "The human situation makes a difference regarding God's possibilities."

254. Cf. d'Hamonville, *Les Proverbes*, 252, who suspects two different Vorlage to explain the semantic differences between the MT and LXX: "Face au groupement de proverbes 'yahvistes' des v.15,33–16,9 du TM, on remarque une curieuse série 'théiste' de la LXX aux v.15,29–16,7; l'analyse de ce phénomène suggère que l'ordre du TM reflète une reconstruction plus tardive." It seems the LXX accentuates human virtue and its reward and has more of the antithesis (cf., e.g., Prov. 16:21), between the righteous and the rest.

255. Fox, *Proverbs: An Eclectic Edition*, 247.

256. Fox, *Proverbs: An Eclectic Edition*, 253: so as not to give credibility to lot casting (which was a common way of inquiring of gods among foreign peoples but not in Hellenistic Judaism), the translator transforms the verse into a new proverb. See Fox's comment on 18:18 ("where 'lot' is replaced by 'silent man'").

belong to mortals, *and* the answer of the tongue is from the LORD" [AT]), it may be better to translate the *waw* not as adversative, as most, including Fox and Jutta Hausmann, think. God does not always deny or frustrate human initiative but acts in his own way to complement and direct human action, and has the last word over against the wicked's schemes, as is made clear at the end of that section of Proverbs. God works with and establishes the good deed but blocks the wicked deed.

Proverbs 19:21 seems to say that human plans are numerous but the single "counsel" of God will prevail, and that does seem to set up a contrast. Proverbs 20:24 does seem monist and deterministic: "From the LORD the steps of a man; what mortal can understand his path?" (AT).[257] Although the mortal takes the steps, the Immortal guides, like a parent helping a toddler. Moreover, in the case of 21:31 the activity of human and that of divine are not really antithetical: people prepare the horse, but God is the one who gives aid in battle. Yet this is not a call to resignation, implying that one is achieving nothing by getting the horse ready.

The larger question is whether God is partner or "other" to humans. Hausmann prefers to see God as the initiator at all times rather than the respondent[258] and believes that in the case of Proverbs 16:9 and 21 it is best not to speak of God's resistance to human plans but rather to say that he is the limit of human planning and knowing.[259] As becomes clear in the proverbs of Agur in chapter 30, God has already been "introduced," so that even though he is not mentioned in the cause-and-effect moral mechanism in the earlier Proverbs 25–29, he is implicitly behind it. God is immediately near to humans: he can interrupt.[260] He can even influence the outcome of lots, and even affairs where kings are concerned (16:3; 21:21). Thus God restrains people in society partly by his law giving, yet also he watches over them to judge their daily activity.[261] There is a tension between apparent "luck" and divine superintendence.

Bernd Schipper has argued that by adding Proverbs 10–30 and then Proverbs 2 to a core of Proverbs 1–9, the writers and collectors of Israel's scriptural traditions moved away from theologizing wisdom toward emphasizing the purely practical aspect of lived wisdom. Salvation requires intervention,

---

257. Evagrius Ponticus sees a "mortal" as one who has not died with Christ (*Schol. Proverb.* 218; cf. Origen, *Dial.* 25–27); see d'Hamonville, *Les Proverbes*, introduction.

258. See Prov. 10:22: "God's blessing makes rich / work adds nothing" (AT); this is meant as a corrective to illusions of self-determination and the concomitant stress.

259. Hausmann, *Studien zum Menschenbild der älteren Weisheit*, 257.

260. Kaiser, *Der Mensch unter dem Schicksal Studien zur Geschichte*, 76. Citing Prov. 17:5; 22:2; 16:33, Kaiser observes that even the poor have an elementary "Achtungsanspruch" (right to respect).

261. Kaiser, *Der Mensch unter dem Schicksal Studien zur Geschichte*, 79, 89.

and that is something wisdom cannot supply.[262] However, the theme of the testing of humans by a God who sees all suggests otherwise, for wisdom, as Torah internalized, is essential to salvation as Torah internalized. So there is something even of grace in 24:12–14, where God is said to judge by intentions as well as deeds, *yet* wisdom is like "honey for the soul," so that "your hope will not be cut off" (v. 14). Thus wisdom-led pleasing God does have consequences for standing before him.[263] What is being taught in 16:2 ("the LORD weighs the spirit")—and there might just be something of the gracious corrective in the verb "to weigh" (*tkn*) here—as in much of Proverbs 15, is that God is concerned less with consequences and reward for action than with evaluating the depths of the human heart. It seems clear that Proverbs 10–25 includes human creation in the Lord's providence overall.[264] "It is the work of the Creator that defines the limits of human potential. Created by God, the human finds his limitations manifest in his mortality and his fallibility."[265] Westermann thinks that the psalms develop the theme of fear of the Lord into that of "trust," but one can just as well ask precisely how far apart semantically the two terms are, and it would be unwise to assume Proverbs is underdeveloped.

Job

Job, too, has "lament" as its genre,[266] although it could also be classified as a sort of drama, albeit very much sui generis; it was indeed turned into drama, as in the late medieval morality play *La pacience de Job.*[267] The providence of God is explained in Job as something that is indeed real, but not in accordance with a teleology that is clear. What Arnold van Ruler wrote about the "surplus" of the Old Testament[268] is pertinent here. Not all roads from the Old Testament end in "Christian salvation," even if the most important ones do. The canonical Job says both yes and no to the resurrection as the final word. Hence what the ending of Job offers is really about being in conversation with God at all, with all the questions and half-understood

---

262. Schipper, *Hermeneutik der Tora.*
263. Schipper, *Hermeneutik der Tora,* 264.
264. Doll, *Menschenschöpfung und Weltschöpfung in der alttestamentlichen Weisheit,* 9–28.
265. Westermann, *Roots of Wisdom,* 125. Opposing this is the critical appraisal of human potential inherent to wisdom, where opportunity is afforded to address human limits. "This reference point to human limitation is one of the reasons why the early wisdom of Israel was preserved in the canon" (136).
266. Westermann, *Structure of Job.*
267. Mies, *L'espérance de Job,* 262.
268. Van Ruler, *The Christian Church and the Old Testament.*

answers, with some kind of reception, what might be called "seeing without seeing."[269] God repeats his lessons, a pattern of his presence that eventually gets acknowledged. Because of the "messiness" of Job one does not have to accept that Job's friends said what was right, but nor that their view of a "cause and effect" moral universe is necessarily wrong, any more than Newtonian physics was superseded by quantum physics. At 5:10 Eliphaz wants to accentuate the positive message that God replenishes, rescues, and corrects (cf. Zophar in 11:13–20). God is no hard Master, but Job needs to wait for the restoration: trust, and all will be forgotten.[270] Hence where Bildad says at 18:6–7, "Indeed, the light of the wicked is put out, and the flame of his fire does not shine" (AT), Carol Newsom comments: "Flames, of course, may be put out by an agent, but a flame goes out by itself when it has no fuel (Prov 26:20). The metaphorical claim is that the wicked is a self-limiting presence because he has no access to the fuel that would allow him to remain vital, a claim previously made by Bildad in the metaphor of the dry and well-watered plants (8:11–19)."[271]

Verses such as these affirm that evil will consume itself while good will persevere, since the good is more foundational in terms of being, and this is a presupposition of any attempts to build a moral society—to go, as it were, "with the grain of the universe"—and especially it is a presupposition of a way of life that tries to include prayer and self-transformation or reordering in this.[272] Although Job, both as character and as book, might seem to question this principle in terms of its ultimacy in explanatory power, he does not undermine it. Any truth claims in any speeches, especially those speeches that relate storied experience, are by definition partial and provisional, since they are spoken midstory, as is the case with all human life. Any hoped-for resolution and answers lie off in the distance of "resurrection" or the vindication of which Job speaks. Even the sublime is "an experience that must always be *construed* within a framework of meaning and value."[273] Resolution, then, is very much *in* God. For "God thunders wondrously with his voice; he does great things that we cannot comprehend" (Job 37:5).

Now, Elihu is a bit like the youth Neoptelemus in Sophocles's *Aias*, in that Elihu speaks to Job as one who has become sated with perfection and its hubris. Elihu is on to something here, that we should realize that God's knowledge, intention, providence, and rule are far from similar to ours.

---

269. Fornara, *La vision contraddetta*: "vedere senza vedere."
270. Balentine, *Job*, 117, 195.
271. Newsom, *Book of Job*, 120.
272. Newsom, *Book of Job*, 124–26.
273. Newsom, *Book of Job*, 237.

The thrust of Elihu's speech, the pivotal point that causes the "turn" (or *peripateia*, the reversal that moves "nonknowledge to knowledge," to use Aristotle's formulation), is his significant contention regarding the revelation of the divine *within* the human. In his first address (Job 33:15–20), Elihu declares that the divine is revealed to the human in two unique and "nonnatural" ways: in dreams and in disease.[274]

Therefore one might want to affirm (with Friedrich Schleiermacher):[275] "God's activity in the world is not to be depicted as a series of personal acts but as a spiritual influence"[276]—indeed, as a way of response to adversity.

Newsom has argued that the abrupt ending of Job, with its reversal of fortunes, means that the character Job doesn't receive eschatological blessing as the result of the long trial he underwent: Job is no bildungsroman. If Job's state of mind has any part to play in the reversal of his fortunes for the good, it is through a transformation of perception by sudden aesthetic experience, which by definition is no proper part of human life. In the meantime, through the pitting of human voice against voice in the poetic "drama" the reader has to learn that truth is dialogic and that there is no sure answer. Job is a site of ethical inquiry, not resolution, on account of which questions of morality are addressed.[277] "In this surprisingly philosophical tale, what is at stake is not simply the testing of a virtue but the testing of the conditions that make this virtue possible. . . . The interest rather lies in how Job will articulate a form of piety that persuasively resolves the threat of incoherency, to manifest a world in which piety and blessing exist in complementarity, not mutual subversion."[278]

As Newsom has observed, Elihu's point to the Promethean, Lear-like Job is, "God *does* speak"—through dreams, suffering, and even through angelic mediators,[279] as Elihu tries to persuade Job and others to contemplate creation in hymnic form so that order will work its therapeutic power. Job 33:15–16 mentions that God warns the prideful person through a dream, and Elihu magnifies the point by appealing to the overthrow of impenitent rulers (34:18–20). He argues that creation has purpose, within which a sort of dynamic

---

274. Hirschfeld, "Is the Book of Job a Tragedy?," 26, with reference to Maimonides (*Guide of the Perplexed* 3.23): ". . . the divine voice that is heard from within the internal human experience of being"—but it is couched in the conditional—this stops him from falling into the abyss. "The phrase בָּחַרְתָּ מֵעֹנִי ('chosen from affliction'—36:21) strikes the dominant chord of Elihu's words" (32–33).

275. See Schleiermacher, *Christian Faith*, section 4.

276. Bernhardt, "Abraham's Dice in the Flow of Life," 348.

277. Newsom, *Book of Job*, 38.

278. Newsom, *Book of Job*, 56.

279. Newsom, *Book of Job*, 209.

providence exists (36:28–33; 37:12–13). Yet with respect to 28:21, wisdom "is hidden from the eyes of all living, and concealed from the birds of the air"; that is, wisdom is concealed, not nonexistent; the point is that only God can see it. He expects humans to fear him and play their part as the property of wisdom, not its owners. That it exists some*where* is suggested by the description of it as "concealed" *from all the living (creatures)*, or "hidden" from the birds of the air (28:21). God can see wisdom (28:24), since he sees differently. In Newsom's summary:

> Wisdom, after all, is not in some place beyond place but in the wind, waters, rain, and thunderstorms, that is, in all the aspects of creation. But it is not "in" them as an object but in their construction and interrelationship, in their presence and limits ("weight," "measure," "limit," "way") with respect to other aspects of the created world. Thus, one realizes that the poem is in no sense saying that humans have no access to wisdom. They will not find it if they look for it as an object (even an intellectual object) but only if they also know it through a comparable mode of being, a way of acting. The disposition of piety and the moral habit of turning from evil are the way in which one will know wisdom and understanding.[280]

In other words, human beings come to know wisdom inasmuch as they act wisely. Yet of course one problem is that the divine speeches at the end of Job establish that creation in all its dimensions lacks purpose in itself, even if God by contrast has a surplus of purpose to share. This leads some to conclude that Job can rightly be called a tragedy in that the vision of the human universe is a bleak one, with mere existence as a consolation. Accordingly, the animals in the divine speeches have a better time of it and can see the comic side of things. Yet, as Newsom argues concerning the names of Job's daughters in Job 42: "Such playful names are a form of laughter—not heedless or anarchic laughter—but human and therefore tragic laughter. Read in dialogic tension, the sublimity of the divine speeches and the beauty of the prose epilogue gestures toward the human incorporation of tragedy into the powerful imperatives of desire: to live and to love."[281] For his part, David Clines prefers to see the lesson as "There is more to life than justice."[282] There is a plausible aesthetic argument: in the darkness the light seems to shine more brightly.

Even if Leviathan is rather identified with a God of terror,[283] "tragic" seems much too strong for the genre of Job, since one needs to bear in mind that

---

280. Newsom, *Book of Job*, 180.
281. Newsom, *Book of Job*, 258.
282. Clines, *Job 38–42*, 1242.
283. Keel, *Jahwes Entgegnung an Ijob*.

Leviathan is presented in God's eyes as one who is firmly on the leash. Thus Newsom's interpretation at the end of her book seems itself too bleak when she posits: "The only consolation is the obedience that consists in speaking the words of God, as Job comes to do, and in that a recognition of the deeply fractured nature of reality. . . . [Job is] one who grasps in the sublime experience the nature of a tragically structured world and his place in it."[284] In a passage slightly earlier Newsom seems to think that the Jobian sublime is not just a sobering experience, when she writes: "As Lap-chuen Tsang has argued, although the sublime is an experience and not an objective thing, it is an experience that must always be *construed* within a framework of meaning and value."[285] So which is it? Perhaps both. But if both, then can tragedy be even penultimate to divine comedy? The way that chapter 40 rolls into chapter 41 suggests that Behemoth and Leviathan are one and the same and that their depiction serves to show the figure of Satan as both terrifying and yet under divine control. Job 41:10–11 suggests that God is even more terrifying than Leviathan, and yet, as the master of this beast, here he is addressing Job. As Edmund Burke wrote: "Now, though in a just idea of the Deity, perhaps none of his attributes are predominant, yet to our imagination, his power is by far the most striking. . . . In the scripture, wherever God is represented as appearing or speaking, every thing terrible in nature is called up to heighten the awe and solemnity of the divine presence."[286] He is one made in the way that Job himself was: "Consider" (40:15) is another echo of Job 1. "On earth there is not his like, a creature without fear. . . . He sees everything that is high; he is king over all the sons of pride" (41:33–34 ESV; 41:25–26 MT). This is magnificence, but essential to the comedy is that the beast is truly a servant.

Nobody says in the Bible: "I have no hope, I despair." Whatever Job may have suffered, his words express a "blessed rage for order."[287] In contrast to the psalms, he places hope in something he has lost, and he is left to find all that sustained him oppressive: God was a rock, but now that rock crushes Job. Job looks for God himself in the absence of a certain number of expected goods. Job isn't just asking for his goods back.[288] God does not "appear" in Job's sufferings, so in that sense God in Job is not a providential God, certainly not a deus ex machina; he exists but absently. When God appears, it is because he has to break in,[289] supplying consolation that is communicated

---

284. Newsom, *Book of Job*, 255–56.
285. Tsang, *Sublime*, 45–48, quoted in Newsom, *Book of Job*, 237.
286. Burke, *Philosophical Enquiry into the Sublime and the Beautiful*, 56–57.
287. Mies, *L'espérance de Job*, 576.
288. Mies, *L'espérance de Job*, 585. See also 19, 25–27.
289. Mies, *L'espérance de Job*, 590. Cf. Mies, *Bible et littérature*.

purely through his pointing at the otherness of creation, not in the realm of history: it is a "consolation sans cause précédente" (consolation without a preceding cause; Ignatius of Loyola), although there is a light toward which the process of Job advances, like Abraham's hoping against hope.[290] Ultimately God might become present. Job expects from God forgiveness (7:21 and 9:28) as part of God's care. He lacks recognition from God and friends and lacks assurance that neither will evil last forever, nor will he feel so distant in relationship to God.[291]

In the divine speeches the discourse is of God's taking the burden of responsibility off the shoulders of humanity. God's care for wild creation is intended to encourage Job (and the reader). God's power reveals itself not in history but in creation, since the miracle of life is greater than humans can grasp or make sense, and it offers light on the horizon.[292] Robert Alter views Job 38–40 as a response to the "death-wish" of chapter 3 (where the external world's goodness is "cancelled" by imagery of darkness and "darkening counsel," more so than even in Ecclesiastes);[293] one realizes in these closing chapters that things seen for their own sakes, without reference to human appreciation, are truly beautiful. The theme of "energy" is prominent, since God is working with and within all that creation. Yet of course it remains true that whereas there is hope for a tree (Job 14:7), "mortals are at one with the dust of the decaying cosmos."[294] In Job 6 this seems to drive the argument toward a case for some sort of afterlife "in God." Job's alternative is more like "temporary asylum in the land of the dead until God's fury is abated and a fair trial is possible" (cf. 9:32–34; 13:18–22).[295] Job is ready for a lawsuit, a court case, even while waiting for God to prosecute. It is no small irony that the personal is replaced by the legal form of discourse for most of the poetic section.

Water is good for vegetation but not for rocks over time, and the image of military and personal physical disaster in chapter 19 is potent. Yet Clines views these verses as being about human hope: "Habel takes the images to signify that the reality of the universe, however solid it may appear, is toward decay rather than new life, more like a crumbling mountain than a tree. But is it human *hope* rather than human *fate* that they symbolize,"[296] before the speech finally gives way to complete negativity for Job himself in 19:19b?

---

290. Mies, *L'espérance de Job*, 590.
291. Heckl, *Hiob*, 478.
292. Keel and Schroer, *Schöpfung*, 211.
293. Alter, *Art of Biblical Poetry*, 97.
294. Habel, *Book of Job*, 237.
295. Habel, *Book of Job*, 242.
296. Clines, *Job 1–20*, 335.

Clines adds: "Most of the implausible interpretations reviewed here are swept away by the recognition (i) that there is a contrast between what Job *believes* will happen (his death before vindication, but vindication thereafter) and what he *wishes* would happen (a face to face encounter with God this side of death); and (ii) that what pleads for Job in the heavenly realm is nothing but his own protestation of innocence."[297]

Moreover, what we have in Job is not the Blakean assertion of the defiant individual. Wisdom literature often extrapolates from what God is to Israel in election as well as in creation, to what that means for his wider providence as expressed in Wisdom 6:7 and Job 10:12: "You have granted me life and steadfast love, and your care has preserved my spirit."[298] However, Job departs from any sense that divine justice for humans corresponds well to God's order of creation.[299] Against the God of the prophets, God can take away abruptly and arbitrarily even where there is no sin. Over against the Priestly writer's God, God here in the book of Job must be accepted as being as much absent as present and as allowing evil a very long leash.[300] It is a supremely theocentric vision that implies a relatively low anthropology. Job 28's skepticism about human enlightenment outdoes that of the Deuteronomic Jeremiah, if one compares Jeremiah 20:14 with Job 3:3. The goal of the narrative of Job is for Job to come to appreciate the personal relationship he has with God, through the process of being bent but not broken, softened by the test, not hardened.[301] Job 42:7 is about how Job's friends have spoken to God less than they have spoken about him (they were right). Theology should be "speaking to God" (*Rede zu Gott*), and one needs to live in texts.[302] Since C. G. Jung,[303] some have considered Job 42:6 to be ironic or containing double entendre.[304] Perhaps it means "I have changed my mind about dust and ashes" (i.e., in the spirit of Blake: "I am done with penitence"). Ulrich Berges translates the verse, "I feel aversion: I console myself with dust and ashes."[305] Another

---

297. Clines, *Job 1–20*, 465.

298. Röhser, *Prädestination und Verstockung*, 10–62.

299. K. Schmid, *Hiobs Weg*, 32.

300. Oeming, "Die Begegnung mit Gott," 125.

301. Oeming, "Die Begegnung mit Gott," 141–42: "Mit Gerhard Ebeling möchte ich Hiob 42,7 stark machen und festhalten: 'Das Phänomen des Gebets wird somit zum hermeneutischen Schlüssel der Gotteslehre. . . . Dass Hiob auf seinem Weg nicht zerbrochen ist, ist Zeichen göttlicher Führung und gnädiger Bewahrung.'"

302. Oeming, "'Ihr habt nicht recht von mir geredet wie mein Knecht Hiob,'" sees Job's message as theology in God's presence ("theologische Wissenschaft coram Deo").

303. Jung, *Antwort auf Hiob*.

304. Berges, "Hiob in Lateinamerika," 314.

305. Berges, "Hiob in Lateinamerika," 314.

possible sense of the Hebrew is "I repent *in* dust and ashes"[306]—refusing the Egyptian speculative idea of becoming like an Osiris on the way to join the gods via the court scene. Indeed, Job 14:7–9's "hope for a tree" may refer to a tree for Osiris, while echoing the grimly realistic Isaiah 6:13. The book of Job mimics sarcastically the promises of the prophets.[307] Yet it appeals to history as well as creation in the divine speeches.[308] God *moves* in mysterious ways.

Clines comments on the divine speeches in Job: "There is no dereliction from an original state of perfection; there is no eschaton toward which the universal order tends. God's in his heaven; all's well with the world. . . . Not only is there no problem with the world: every element in it is a source of constant delight to its maker."[309] Behemoth is a useless creature, but God is not bound to rules of utility, and so it, not Job, is presented as the crowning glory of creation, masterpiece.[310] "The absence of reference to humans is not to teach Job that the universe can survive without him[311] . . . but to show that the principles on which it is founded should be discerned from the realities of the natural world."[312] And these are summed up in the principle of divine provision for the nonhuman world: God sends rain on the desert (38:25–27) and provides for ravens in the sense of creating the system of hunting for food (v. 41). He by no means says that he himself "hunts" prey for the lion and its cubs (vv. 39–40). "Nor is it implied that though the ostrich may neglect its young Yahweh protects them (39:14–16); and the vulture's prey (39:27–30) is not said to be Yahweh's provision."[313] Rather, the Lord establishes and supervises the structures.[314] This is not a defense of providence in history or big ideas for "the future" but a declaration of the provision in creation that God constantly makes according to design (עצה).[315] One might agree with H. H. Schmid, who attempts to correct von Rad's subjugation ("Unterwerfung") of "creation" to "history," preferring to speak of an accommodation ("Zuordnung").[316]

---

306. Patrick, "Translation of Job 42:6."

307. See Dell, "'Cursed Be the Day I Was Born!,'" and also Kynes, "Job and Isaiah 40–55." These scholars disagree with the sequential order that Terrien offers, of Deutero-Isaiah answering Job; no, Job is parodying Deutero-Isaiah.

308. Kubina, *Die Gottesreden im Buche Hiob*, 122.

309. Clines, *Job 38–42*, 1090.

310. Clines, *Job 38–42*, 1084.

311. This contra Crenshaw, *Old Testament Wisdom*, 110.

312. Clines, *Job 38–42*, 1091.

313. Clines, *Job 38–42*, 1094.

314. Lévêque, *Job, ou le drame de la foi*, 512.

315. Lévêque, *Job, ou le drame de la foi*, 1096, contra Kubina, *Die Gottesreden im Buche Hiob*, 122–23, and Terrien, *Elusive Presence*, 375.

316. Schmid, *Gerechtigkeit als Weltordnung*.

Ecclesiastes

It seems that Proverbs 10–29 is the earliest layer of canonical biblical wisdom; Job replies, but Proverbs 1–9, in turn, replies to that as a sort of "from
above" prophetic-style answer, and then in terms of canonical order Qoheleth
gets to respond (Otto Kaiser). Whatever the state of Israel's history in all
its doom-ladenness, the canonical texts manage to remain more than hope-
ful, even if their claim to knowledge is modest.[317] For Qoheleth, God is the
maintainer as "your creator" (12:1). And he does all (11:5; 7:13; 8:17), even if
there is no sign of any possibility of having personal relationship with God,
who simply acts and judges without relating.[318] Something seems to hang over
human beings: the contingency of human life and the contingency (not to say
the apparent arbitrariness) of divine judgment over it.[319]

Yet the main reason humans cannot wholly understand God's works is
their inability to see these from their start to their end (Eccles. 3:11; 8:16–17).
Hebel ("meaningless"; used thirty-eight times in the book) does not mean that
all is objectively meaningless, just that it cannot be grasped owing to human
contingency, not to mention sin. Qoheleth has no illusions about human
goodness.[320] There is a semantic link, in the plural form of *hebel*, to false
gods.[321] Yet the core sense is that of ephemerality and limitation rather than
of absurdity. What is wise is to treat time as that which subjects all human
affairs to chance and limitation under God's gift and judgment. Work is merely
a means to joy but no guarantee of it. Joy is a share (2:10) but not a gain.[322]

Unlike the prophets, Ecclesiastes thinks that the future cannot be fore-
known (9:11–12) and that if prophecy has any role, then it has to do with
living in the now. Yet does not Qoheleth show an awareness that things have
changed even in an everyday, "nonprophetic" time? Time is changeable, after
all (3:1–9).[323] God has made all things for the right time. Our lack of knowing it and our inability to control it—that is something else. On 3:11a, "He
has made everything in its time" (AT), we must recognize that this time of
making is not restricted to the "mythische Urzeit" (mythical prehistory).[324]
The verse's tenses are perfect: God has established goodness and order to

---

317. Kreuzer, *Der lebendige Gott*, 256–68.
318. Kreuzer, *Der lebendige Gott*, 269.
319. T. Krüger, *Kohelet*, 13.
320. Admittedly, neither does the book of Ecclesiastes as a whole. On הבל, see Ingram,
Ambiguity in Ecclesiastes, 91–129. See also Enns, *Ecclesiastes*, 85; Fox, *A Time to Tear Down
and a Time to Build Up*, 262.
321. Ingram, *Ambiguity in Ecclesiastes*, 108.
322. T. Krüger, *Kohelet*, 15.
323. T. Krüger, *Kohelet*, 39.
324. T. Krüger, *Kohelet*, 171.

do the ongoing work of witness to his hidden part in it all.[325] God's creation stretches on into time, as Sirach 39:16 confirms.[326] In that verse it is not just from God's viewpoint that things are created with sequence and purpose. As Thomas Krüger argues, the state of the cosmos does not seem all so good.[327] For one cannot see the sweep of God's plans; only God can, or at least it takes a prophet to see it. Krüger points to Isaiah 46:10 here, yet the force of that is not so clear when it speaks of a purpose from of old:

> . . . declaring the end from the beginning
>   and from ancient times things not yet done,
> saying, "My purpose shall stand,
>   and I will fulfill my intention."

It does not seem that the prophet here thinks he is the first.

The point remains that the distinct gifts of this constant divine creativity are good and can be enjoyed as ends in themselves, to a large degree. Ecclesiastes 3:11 speaks of God as having made (perfect tense), and verse 14 speaks of what he now *makes* (imperfect tense), so as to bring past, present, and future together and thus define work that is enduring, sufficient, and "for good" ("unabänderlich"/*lə'ōlām*).[328] That which is inaccessible should not be spoken of, but this principle allows room for moving beyond that to a theological alternative in 3:1–4:12. Ecclesiastes 3:21 sounds an agnostic note: "Who knows?" It is hard to know whether he is here doubting his doubts or is reacting to some overly optimistic contemporaries. Ecclesiastes 12:7 supplies the final negative word: "And the dust returns to the ground it came from, and the spirit returns to God who gave it." "Eternity in their hearts" (3:11 AT) might be as well translated as "conscious of the passing of time."[329]

However, for our purposes the question is more that of what "good news" is built into creation and history, such that when prophets are speaking for revelation, this has more to do with an intensification of knowledge and application to a particular situation than with a different kind of knowledge, even if the

325. See Letter to Aristeas 210 ("God constantly moves everything") and 234 ("Everything is prepared and arranged by God according to his will"). Cf. Sir. 43:3: ἐν μεσημβρίᾳ αὐτοῦ ἀναξηραίνει χώραν, καὶ ἐναντίον καύματος αὐτοῦ τίς ὑποστήσεται;

326. Sir. 39:16: Τὰ ἔργα κυρίου πάντα ὅτι καλὰ σφόδρα, καὶ πᾶν πρόσταγμα ἐν καιρῷ αὐτοῦ ἔσται· οὐκ ἔστιν εἰπεῖν Τί τοῦτο; εἰς τί τοῦτο; πάντα γὰρ ἐν καιρῷ αὐτοῦ ζητηθήσεται.

327. T. Krüger, *Kohelet*, 174.

328. T. Krüger, *Kohelet*, 149. Krüger refers to skepticism ("Programm der Entwertung alles Unverfügbaren") as the common intellectual inheritance, which Ecclesiastes uses for a diagnosis. Cf. Hossenfelder, *Die Philosophie der Antike 3*.

329. Enns, *Ecclesiastes*, 55.

sources of knowledge include some visionary input. The prevalent consensus that Ecclesiastes is all about the *limits* to knowledge is actually open to challenge.[330] What might be inferred from this is perhaps not the only conclusion:

> Thus, for Qoheleth, the value of wisdom has been overstated; it is only a probabilistic enterprise. So Qoheleth states that the two usually good things to do to ensure success in life (righteousness and wisdom) are really not very effective. Rather, what Qoheleth has found good to do in life is to live life to the fullest in all of its ordinary and basic aspects and enjoy. "Whatever your hand finds to do, do it with all your might" (9:7–10). One should focus on being alive and on enjoying the present moment, because that is the only realm in which we have some power and control.[331]

That includes (9:1–12) generosity as the route to joy.[332] As Fox has written, Qoheleth is no nihilist.[333]

Addison Wright's analysis is attractive. Yet if Ecclesiastes expresses skepticism about the afterlife, then a fortiori it must express belief in providence in this life.[334] This corresponds to an ethic of sobriety, a joyful fatalism.[335] Indeed, Ecclesiastes can be viewed as receiving Torah as a classical text, not a canonical one.[336] Just what does that mean, however? A more liberal "room to maneuver" in selecting what is to be taken seriously? Krüger points to Ecclesiastes 8:6–7 as advocating a rational-critical ("vernünftig-kritischen Rezeption der TORA")[337] approach to the Law. He thinks that 3:11 reminds the reader that they have the capacity to know good from evil and that 12:13 notes that Torah is not to be taken quite literally, thus promoting along with Deuteronomy 4:6–8 a religion of the heart. God's judgment is already in the unpredictable contingency of time (8:6–7). Hence there can be some reassembling of meaninglessness into meaningfulness.[338] In epistemological sequence

---

330. Wright, "Ecclesiastes 9:1–12," 253. Of modern commentators only Loader (*Ecclesiastes*, 107) is of a similar view.

331. Wright, "Ecclesiastes 9:1–12," 258.

332. Wright, "Ecclesiastes 9:1–12," 262: "Qoheleth's observations therefore end on the two themes of enjoyment and death, which are the two themes in the center of the chiasm in 9:1–12 and at the center of his thought."

333. "He also builds up meaning, discovering ways of creating clarity and gratification in a confusing world." Fox, *A Time to Tear Down and a Time to Build Up*, 3.

334. Schwienhorst-Schönberger, *"Nicht im Menschen gründet das Glück" (Koh 2,24)*, 274. Here is a Jewish teacher focusing on the happiness of humanity. But the point is in the title.

335. Schwienhorst-Schönberger, *"Nicht im Menschen gründet das Glück" (Koh 2,24)*, 274.

336. T. Krüger, *Kohelet*, 321.

337. T. Krüger, *Kohelet*, 315.

338. T. Krüger, *Kohelet*, 314, understands this not so much as a process but rather as an epiphany.

the note of memento mori comes before that of carpe diem. Knowing God to be in charge, one should appreciate life and make something of it. Such joy is not presented as something superficial.[339]

Biblical monotheism and continuous creation form a keynote of Ecclesiastes, which concerns itself more with what God *does in the present*, and that includes God's holding present opposites together.[340] There is a pattern of repetition according to chapter 1: both in structure of world (rivers cannot fill the sea) and in human experience of it; yet in 1:8–11 human life is not so freeflowing. "As well as being insufficient, our sensing and communication are characterized by breaks and silences."[341] In 7:13–14, with its talk of making things crooked, there is an allusion to Genesis 1:31 ("See/consider what God has done") yet with a "spin": for bad days follow good days; just as at Ecclesiastes 3:11a, the "all" that God has made includes bad as well as good. Yet that is not to say that God harmonizes things, merely that a good part of his creation is experienced by humans as dark, even though it is good.[342] However, Ludwig Schwienhorst-Schönberger is surely right to claim that for Ecclesiastes, the goodness of God isn't necessarily what we think it is, and more than any other biblical book it emphasizes the inscrutability and mysterious nature of divine action (8:17). If Antoon Schoors is correct in saying that this God is impersonal,[343] that is not a bad thing, because for God to be personal in some ways would necessitate limitations of his will and judgment. Yet this is not a "Deist" God, for he maintains a connection with humans (see Prov. 12:2, 7).

Indeed, although Ecclesiastes contains no word for fortune nor for providence, it does use *miqreh*, which means "what comes up to meet one." This word can be found at 2:14–15; 3:19; 9:2–3 and is neutral at best. It connotes the following idea: "(1) The lives, at least of humans, move according to preset patterns. (2) The patterns are set and controlled by a superhuman force or forces. (3) The knowledge of these patterns and of the relationships among patterns is only partially accessible to humans at best. And (4) . . . there may be points where the patterns can be changed, whether by the superhuman force or by humans with its help."[344] So this is in no way randomness. However,

339. Zimmer, *Zwischen Tod und Lebensglück*, 154. This, contra Crüsemann, *Wie Gott die Welt regiert*, 80.

340. Schwienhorst-Schönberger, *Kohelet*, 93.

341. Bundvad, *Time in the Book of Ecclesiastes*, 54; cf. 187: "He argues that there is a lacking correspondence between, on the one hand, the temporal reality as it manifests itself in the cosmos and, on the other hand, the human experience of time."

342. Schwienhorst-Schönberger, *Kohelet*, 93.

343. Schoors, "Words Typical of Qoheleth."

344. Machinist, "Fate, *Miqreh*, and Reason," 160, with reference to Werner, *Vorstellung von Planes Jahwes*; Machinist further notes, "As Kaufmann has seen with particular force, the

in this justly famous article Peter Machinist ends up concluding: "The word *miqreh* is here, as its root would suggest, an 'occurrence'—not just any occurrence, but one that is predetermined and defines the life events of humans and animals. It becomes, thus, an abstract concept, and we are not wrong in translating it 'fate.' (2) The 'occurrence' in question is death. . . . (5) Humans are left, therefore, to enjoy as they can their *ḥēleq*, that is, what is granted to them by God as part of their activity while alive."[345]

Qoheleth then works backward from the one clear final point in the pattern, death. Only in Ruth 2:3 ("And her *miqreh* happened . . ." [AT]) do God and *miqreh* seem closely associated. More generally it means "a type of occurrence befalling humans that is beyond their control and understanding."[346] Yet it can be inferred from the existence of *miqreh* that there is a God who somehow guarantees it. "For, if *miqreh* is the end point of all patterns of activity (the *maʿăśeh*), God, affirms Qohelet, is the one in control of those patterns. See, for example, 3:11," where *maʿăśeh* means "a planned life pattern of activity characteristic of each individual and God" (3:11; 7:13; 8:14, 17),[347] albeit these things are unknowable. In 3:11 *ʿōlām* is not simply "eternity" but "ability to consider and reflect on the concept of eternity." "Thus it is the time at which the events will occur, rather than the fact they will occur, that is unpredictable."[348] This, a situation of bamboozlement, knowing that there is something hard to outline, is where faith as trust is the appropriate disposition of response. In each of the *Megilloth* a call to take initiative through trust in a hidden providence comes to the fore.[349] There is no "fate" outside of God. (*Ḥēleq*, which does seem external to God, tends to mean fortune in a positive but somewhat lighter sense or pertaining to less important matters.) Surely one cannot influence the mysterious *miqreh*/fate, for it is too strong a force. Humans cannot lengthen days, but they can shorten them. It might just mean that God has a plan that can then be varied later, but, more to the point, it is a *Fremdbestimmung*—that is, a determination of a

---

Bible is unusual in that it does not seem to reckon with an impersonal, metadivine realm, from which fate might emanate" (163).

345. Machinist, "Fate, *Miqreh*, and Reason," 166–67: *gad* and *mǝni* in Isa. 65:11 appear to be deities of fate, and even *ḥayyîm* can mean luck or well being, as in Mal. 2:5–6. Psalm 16:5 contains the synonyms *gôrāl*, *ḥēleq*, and *mǝnāt*, while Esther 3:7; 9:24 have *gôrāl* and *pûr*.

346. Machinist, "Fate, *Miqreh*, and Reason," 170. *Miqreh* occurs three times outside of Ruth 2:3: 1 Sam 6:9 ("if [the ark] does not [go up to Beth Shemesh], we shall know it was not his hand which reached out against us; it was a *miqreh* for us" [AT]); 1 Sam. 20:26 ("Saul thought, 'By a *miqreh* he [David] has become unclean'" [AT]); and Deut. 23:10–11 (which refers to a man who becomes unclean because of "a *qāreh* of the night" [AT]).

347. Machinist, "Fate, *Miqreh*, and Reason," 167n21, 171.

348. Melton, "*Miqreh* in Retrospect," 37.

349. Weeks, *Ecclesiastes and Scepticism*, 68.

stranger or even an alien in a pejorative sense.[350] Ruth 2:3 may seem to employ *miqreh* in the sense of blind chance, but the reader knows God has planned it. If Ecclesiastes 9:1 speaks of all being in God's hands, then this is a happy thing.[351] At Ecclesiastes 9:2 the term for "fate" has been understood simply to mean "death," but that presupposes a sudden shift of topic. Generally in Ecclesiastes *miqreh* can mean events in life, not just death. In this text the word "fate" clearly means not death at all, but rather what happens during life to the righteous and the wicked, because the text is restating the problem just mentioned five verses earlier in 8:14: "There are righteous people to whom it happens according to the deeds of the wicked, and there are wicked people to whom it happens according to the deeds of the righteous" (AT). So the context clearly indicates that "one fate" in 9:2 refers not to death but to the events of one's lifetime. There are two texts that suggest that human wishes and divine plans can coincide (5:18–20 and 9:7). For certainly moral freedom is *not* limited—*and that is the important kind of freedom.* To some extent—but only to some extent—is human freedom conditioned by God.[352] One can possibly trust in creation within the limits of its changeability.[353] Ecclesiastes affirms something quasi-personal, at least in comparison to the contemporary Greek philosophies.

According to Ecclesiastes 9:2, everyone "under the sun" is at the mercy of time and *miqreh*. God has set the world up this way so that randomness accompanies sameness and patterning; it is *not* chance that is the foundation of things in time. Instead, "*miqreh/qāreh* describes an occurrence that to humans is unexpected because they cannot foresee it or control it and cannot understand, *at least at the time of occurrence,* the reason for it."[354] Likewise the sense of *wayyiqer miqreâ* ("As it happened, she came") in Ruth 2:3 is that of something beyond human control, "something people cannot see or grasp"—though the narrator and God can; it is providential patterned time.[355] "Qoheleth does not consider chance to be a force operative in existence. . . . The term מקרה , contrary to its usage elsewhere in the Hebrew Bible, has the sense of '(unpredictable/uncontrollable) happening' rather than 'chance happening,' for it is used primarily of death, which is clearly stated by Qoheleth to be predetermined."[356] The certainty of death makes grasping life even more important.

---

350. Kaiser, "Determination und Freiheit beim Kohelet," 259.

351. Zimmer, *Zwischen Tod und Lebensglück*, 174.

352. T. Krüger, *Kohelet*, 77.

353. Cf. Lux, "Denn es ist kein Mensch so gerecht auf Erden," 281.

354. Machinist, "Fate, *Miqreh*, and Reason," 169, quoted in Melton, "*Miqreh* in Retrospect," 39 (emphasis added).

355. Machinist, "Fate, *Miqreh*, and Reason," 169.

356. Rudman, *Determinism in the Book of Ecclesiastes*, 200. Cf. 202: "Human beings have as little chance of breaking free of the divine decrees that determine the progress of their lives as have the elemental forces which bind the cosmos together."

It can be argued that there is no teleological thinking in the Hebrew Bible / Old Testament.[357] Or at least, if God has intentions, they are not always carried through. That might not be the case with Ecclesiastes. Part of the burden is that even though his purposes seem cyclical, God is just too much in charge and is at work frustrating lives, even cutting them and their dreamed-of long-lasting legacies short. The text is somewhat similar to Stoicism, yet "whereas the Stoic god is said to 'make crooked things straight,' Qoheleth's god does the exact opposite and makes that which is straight crooked. Qoheleth appears to demonstrate some knowledge of the deterministic mechanism which the Stoics called the *logos*."[358] This, however, may be an overstatement. God does not promise and then take away: it is clear from natural observation that human life is fragile and short at the outset. God cannot be indicted for misrepresentation. However, it does seem that humans have only limited control over their own destiny, and individuals are strongly influenced by connective chains of forces.

Ecclesiastes 3:18–22 is not really interested in cosmology but rather in the "givens" of anthropology, and with a pessimistic message, that there is no "help for good guys," that fate is blind and there is no human advantage over beasts. Adam is truly the dust of Genesis 3:19;[359] the situation is much more like that of Genesis 3 than that of Genesis 1. *Rûaḥ* as "guaranteed life" belongs to all creatures (cf. Ps. 104:22) but has nothing to do with postmortem existence. The tone set by the opening in Ecclesiastes 1:3–9, which declares that generations come and go, conveys that there is energy and movement but without a goal, and the passage questions whether there was even ever a beginning. In 9:11–12 a brutal alliance of time (determinism) and chance that comes to all is only slightly alleviated by the message of 9:4–5: knowing we will die is some sort of assurance, for there is not much advantage being alive except that one can make something small but meaningful out of existence and natural gifts.

Human beings are here viewed as very much part of the world: Is there nothing "fully new," or do they just have poor memories? There is a connection between the previously mentioned "positive" term *ḥēleq* (portion [Eccles. 5:18]) and "lot," in that they are both received rather than worked for, but at least one has a claim on a lot, and each portion (*ḥēleq*) is somewhat made to measure.[360] Yet even fate/*miqreh* can be received with joy, and sometimes

---

357. Spieckermann, "Wenn Gott schweigt," 108. Even the LXX's καὶ περιέπεσεν περιπτώματι at Ruth 2:3 plays the matter down.

358. Rudman, *Determinism in the Book of Ecclesiastes*, 199.

359. Rudman, *Determinism in the Book of Ecclesiastes*, 112.

360. Cf. Enns, *Ecclesiastes*, 132: "Our *ḥēleq* is what we can glean in the here and now."

in the case of an unlikely coincidence it can be implied that God may have been involved, even guiding, as in Ruth 2:3, and as in 1 Samuel 6:9, where the Philistines watched to see where the ark of the Lord would end up. However, with Qoheleth it is now pure fate in quite strong bleakness.[361] Qoheleth has no expectation of salvation or of all things being made new, as time repeats its cycle and nothing is to be hoped for in the "house of eternity": the teacher almost expresses a mocking irony in giving four euphemisms (silver cord snapped, etc.) for death in 12:6.[362] It might be argued that joy in keeping the law for its own sake, *Torahfrömmigkeit*, is the end goal, although it is not clear that this is the sense of Ecclesiastes 11:9 as it is of 12:13, which is clearly redactional. Life overall is vain and passing, and trying to make sense of it is vanity. Humanity is like a vapor (*hebel*) that cannot be held on to.

Certainly the gloominess is offset to some extent by the verses about love of life and community (Eccles. 9:9) and perhaps by the book's theme of happiness, as Schwienhorst-Schönberger has claimed.[363] Melanie Köhlmoos in turn tries to link or fuse the themes of "joy" and "the fear of the Lord." True fear of God is located in the perception of joy in life, because in that way of acceptance humans are in accordance with God's determination of creation. However, this combination is not made in the text, and perhaps it would be more accurate to see the two themes as the two pillars of the canonical form of the book, very much set apart from each other.[364] Joy might certainly incline one to be Torah-ethical, but this disposition generates no expectation of reward. Ecclesiastes 7:20 settles for low expectations ("Surely there is not a righteous man on earth who does good and never sins" [RSV]). God is no savior, but just a creator, and the text gives no hint of any requirement to improve or rescue any people at all.[365] All that is left is a mix of pure duty (here with Köhlmoos) *and* pure natural self-expression.

In Ecclesiastes *rûaḥ* and its cognates are best seen in parallel to *hebel* in such a way that the life-force is unsteady as a "desire/thought of wind." Indeed, in 2:17 "Qohelet deduces the absurdity and senselessness of the entirety of events."[366] One might act with purpose and constructively and yet get nowhere.

---

361. Köhlmoos, *Kohelet*, 108.

362. In Eccles. 12:1 there is "eine prononcierte Distanz zu allen Heilserwartungen" (Köhlmoos, *Kohelet*, 241–42); "Was sich wiederholt—and daher allein gedenkenswürdig ist—ist das Sterben" (244).

363. Köhlmoos, *Kohelet*, 69–80, 70.

364. Here (*Kohelet*, 55) Köhlmoos quotes S. Fischer, *Die Aufforderung zur Lebensfreude im Buch Kohelet und seine Rezeption*, 110–11.

365. See Köhlmoos, *Kohelet*, 57.

366. Fox, *A Time to Tear Down and a Time to Build Up*, 47. Fox's book is cited parenthetically hereafter in this paragraph and the next.

"When the belief in a grand causal order collapses, human reason and self-confidence fail with it" (49). Yet Fox can also affirm the solidity of God's side of the arrangement in Qoheleth's vision: "To say that God made everything fitting (*yapeh*) in its time (3:11) is an affirmation of the fundamental rightness of the divine order" (53). There is one kind of retribution that is natural, but 5:5b shows God clearly as one who gets angry and punishes ("Why should God be angry at your words, and destroy the work of your hands?"), in the context of an unfulfilled vow. "Qohelet speaks of a special *time of judgment* for everyone. This is not an apocalyptic day of judgment for the world, a concept foreign to Wisdom Literature, but the time in each individual's life when God will intervene to right the remaining wrongs. *Mishpat* means less 'universal order' and more a series of judgements (3:16)" (52). One could call this a place for providence in Qoheleth's universe.

"Judgment too has its time, but it sometimes comes too late to do any good" (58). Ecclesiastes 8:14 is aware of such problematic exceptions where bad outcomes happen to good people. In all this, Fox would like to compare Qoheleth to Camus, and certainly, from the human noetic point of view, this is plausible parallelism. Wisdom is deficient as it struggles to form principles for life through merely inductive means. "Qohelet asserts the irrationality of life and the impenetrability of God's will, but he also seeks to recover meanings, values and truths, to discern a way of Life through the murky wasteland" (11). Fox does not elaborate what is implicit here, that a search for meaning presupposes a sense that there is a meaningful, if mysterious, universe. God's control extends to the human heart. Taken together with the objectivity of the time for judgment and fitting arrangements, the account is hardly "existentialist" (for instance, Eccles. 2:26: "To the person who pleases him, God gives wisdom, knowledge and happiness" [NIV]).

"[God] is the maker of a problematic world, a *Deus absconditus*. He makes what is the way it is, but he is no factor in human knowledge of the world."[367] He is operating in the world but is the meaning of the world in a way unknowable to humans.[368] It seems clear that 11:9b ("and know that regarding all this God *puts you in that condition*" [AT]) is not about judgment; rather, the sense of "placing" is akin to that of *miqreh*.[369]

In Ecclesiastes there is endless repetition that doesn't need "fixing," for death is part of how things are. Krüger sees (e.g., at 3:19–22) the skepticism about the afterlife, indeed its clear denial, just as Sirach (chap. 41) would see

367. Schoors, "Theodicy in Qohelet," 409.
368. Michel, "Vom Gott, der im Himmel ist," 97.
369. For the use of *ntn* in Ecclesiastes, see 1:13; 2:26; 3:10; 5:18; 12:17.

death as a divine law. All that there is to creation is its present, not its future or past, although this is arguably an encouragement to think of God as interested in the present world and its maintenance, even if not in its transformation.[370] By contrast, the apostle Paul thinks that the world can be changed, even though his verdict or diagnosis might seem overly negative in that he sees its present state as one of corruption rather than (with the preacher) as one that is "good enough."

But the testimonies of the preacher and the apostle can be harmonized in the sense that it is necessary for God generously to grant his eternity for humans to possess eternity requiring a suspension and elevation of time (*Aufhebung der Zeit*), where God is all in all. In another season God's love will prevail so as to allow a sober joy in life and to allow a death in consolation, free from anxiety. A good life before death is possible only as a gift including the confidence that even the negative sides of things have their place and that God can handle all that—such confidence helps one to find joy in life and meet death in peace while not claiming to know too much. First Corinthians 8:1–2 echoes Ecclesiastes 8:17.[371] The voice of the preacher urges that accepting the limit of death can free people to live life well: "Do good and enjoy good," as it were, and don't put it off for any illusory future hope. Everything in its time means that the creation is a framework allowing for rich possibilities in event and action.[372] Joy can be an experience in which one transcends mortality for a moment and is enabled to grasp life as life in the presence of God, an experience that can be called "life before death."[373] But God is very much present even in the final verse: "For God will bring every activity into judgment" (AT). In other words, "God . . . will not allow any deed, even those hidden, . . . to evade his scrutiny."[374] The redactor or frame narrator affirms the reality of providence despite human ignorance about it. A canonical reading will acknowledge this counterpoint: God's deeds are hardly clear to us, but ours are transparent to God.

370. T. Krüger, "Leben und Tod nach Kohelet und Paulus," 212.

371. 1 Cor. 8:1–2: Περὶ δὲ τῶν εἰδωλοθύτων, οἴδαμεν ὅτι πάντες γνῶσιν ἔχομεν. ἡ γνῶσις φυσιοῖ, ἡ δὲ ἀγάπη οἰκοδομεῖ· εἴ τις δοκεῖ ἐγνωκέναι τι, οὔπω ἔγνω καθὼς δεῖ γνῶναι·

372. T. Krüger, "Leben und Tod nach Kohelet und Paulus," 213.

373. Zenger, *Einleitung in das Alten Testament*, 21.

374. Enns, *Ecclesiastes*, 115. Fearing God means recognizing that he is not at our disposal, according to Hieke, "Wie hast Du's mit der Religion?"

FIVE

Providence as Set Forth in the New Testament

Jesus

> These things I have spoken unto you, that in me ye might have peace. In the world ye shall have tribulation.
>
> John 16:33 (KJV)

The cross of Jesus was not simply about an innocent man coming up against evil, or even a prophet taking on the powers and failing while scoring a moral victory. He was aware that his death would have meaning, at least some weeks before it happened. At times martyrs have died on behalf of the people, but in Jesus's case this was allied with the notion of humanity's need to be delivered from the curse of sin more than from foreign oppression, its symptom. The unusual use of the word "ransom" in a world that might have understood it as to do with manumission of slavery reinforces the idea that the ideological background came from Isaiah 43:3–4, as one of exchange of a wider range of humanity for the sake of a saved people: "I give Egypt as your ransom, Ethiopia and Seba in exchange for you. Because you are precious in my sight, and honored, and I love you, I give people in return for you, nations in exchange for your life." Jesus was no foreign nation, but indeed someone whose life was exceedingly precious.

Also in earliest Christianity (cf. Acts 2:22–36 and elsewhere in recorded sermons) Jesus's death by itself seems meaningless, an offense against God, yet it is put right by God's raising of him, and hence is shown to be part of God's plan (v. 23). The view from Paul is more one of a theology driven by the conceptuality and imagery of the Old Testament cultic system (see Exodus, Leviticus, Numbers) to get across the message that all of humanity needs atonement with God and that this is made possible by Christ's willing, perfect death. Johannine theology and that of Hebrews present an account that shows that Jesus's once-for-all sacrifice nevertheless goes on being made afresh for those who trust. But it is Paul who puts Jesus's suffering in the context of a story of God justifying himself before the world. God is by definition just (Rom. 3:5–6), but Paul takes it upon himself to "exegete this"—to unpack it, unravel it. The world may go on being a "speculative Good Friday" (Hegel), but God, far from "making another mistake" in letting Christ be crucified, forges a way of making all evil work for good (Gen. 50:20; Rom. 8:28). Baptism makes possible an identification in a death that reaches lower than any of our tragedies. The man Jesus is found and betrayed and tried and condemned and crucified and left to die as a result of human violence and, behind that, human unbelief and suspicion. And yet, as with Moses, as with Jeremiah and other prophets, "The LORD has laid on him the iniquity of us all" (Isa. 53:6). This relates to the Bible's view of providence: "You meant evil against me, but God meant it for good" (Gen. 50:20 RSV). It is not God who punishes Jesus, but it is God who lets it happen and *in that sense* can be regarded as causing the punishment. Evil people, or good people with evil thoughts and deeds, punish Jesus. The Father is hardly pleased with this yet allows it to happen for the purpose of seeing moral order restored: his Son is the principle of the universe who also happens to be a perfect creature. Both Father and Son can be said to be pleased with the result. Nonetheless, the efficient cause of punishment is the action of people, and one might say that the final cause is the restoration of order and peace. Indirectly the providential God makes all this available. The cross reminds us of the sober news that something very much like original sin is our lot at the same time as reminding us of God's great estimation of our value. The Lord will provide.

In the Gospels (and Acts, and as reflected in the Epistles) providence goes underground. Matthew's Gospel does promote God as good: sixteen times in the Sermon on the Mount alone, which ends (7:7–11) with a patient appeal to trust the heavenly Father, Matthew refers to God as "your/our Father" (and twelve times elsewhere as redaction). As such, God is gracious and generous

(18:27).[1] Now, in Mark's Gospel God operates in a hidden way in and through the crucified one, in a case of revelation through contradiction.

In John's Gospel Jesus has a plan from which he must not deviate. Hence in 4:4, "But he had to go through Samaria" means, in light of Josephus's comments about crossing Samaria to get to Galilee from Jerusalem, avoiding the Jordan Valley.[2] But in any case the choice of route and place is made in service of time, or a schedule: Jesus is constrained. In the adjacent passage Jesus teaches of living water (3:5; 4:10). John 7:38–39 sees this identified with Holy Spirit and/or the divine life, and this might also be the case in 3:5, where in "by water and the Spirit" (AT) is a case of hendiadys. One might compare Sirach 24:21,[3] in which God gifts a new source of spiritual life that will be more real than the physical/corporeal life, in that it does not decay but endures through and beyond death.[4] What matters is that this force moves people in a way analogous to how the Johannine Jesus was made to move or made to stay (e.g., John 11:6: "So, when he heard that Lazarus was ill, he stayed two days longer in the place where he was"), or how the Markan Jesus was carried along by plot and Spirit via his baptism (Mark 1:10). Water may have cleansing and nourishing qualities, but it also is a stream by which to be carried.

Paul's theory of atonement stipulates that it was the divine and providential strategy that Jesus somehow managed to absorb the violence that is the expression of the universe's evil. God in Christ has reconciled humanity to himself (for God himself did not need to change). God justifies himself, or does his own "theodicy," in taking responsibility for that which is not his responsibility (cf. the good Samaritan). The new creation that Christ makes possible is more a pneumatological actuality,[5] where God acts on his creation to renew and free it, and less an ontological reality, whereby the stuff or structures of creation are affected. God is working his purposes out through

---

1. Feldmeier and Spieckermann, *Menschwerdung*, 273.
2. See Schnackenburg, *Das Johannesevangelium*, 458, commenting on Josephus, *Vita* 52.269.
3. οἱ ἐσθίοντές με ἔτι πεινάσουσιν, καὶ οἱ πίνοντές με ἔτι διψήσουσιν. Also, 1 En. 48.1: "In that place I beheld a fountain of righteousness, which never failed, encircled by many springs of wisdom. Of these all the thirsty drank, and were filled with wisdom, having their habitation with the righteous, the elect, and the holy."
4. Schnackenburg, *Das Johannesevangelium*, 466–67.
5. Hence I find less than helpful Colin Gunton's use of the term "actuality": "The metaphors of a universe out of joint, of an indelible stain, are ways of speaking of a world whose relationship to its creator is disrupted to such an extent that only the crucifixion of the incarnate Son is adequate to heal it. . . . At issue is the actuality of atonement: whether the real evil of the real world is faced and healed ontologically in the life, death and resurrection of Jesus." *Actuality of the Atonement*, 164–65.

and around his church.[6] This can and should include sacraments and the "worship" of the faith community. In an article, R. Messner argues on the basis of patristic witness that the Mass could be seen as the best place for intercession and votive prayer. It is all about joining oneself to the symbol/sacrament and thereupon offering not just thanks but intercession.[7] The Lord goes on providing.

Suffering is presented as a means to glory and is self-attesting evidence at least of being called, as per John 16:33 ("In the world you have tribulation; but be of good cheer, I have overcome the world" [RSV]). The position of the nonhuman creation (*ktisis*) is different from that of Christians, of course. Yet in the innocence of creation as subjected through the guilt of others (harking back to Genesis 3:17b's curse on the earth) there does seem to be a parallel in Romans 8 to Christians qua suffering martyrs. Providence is found in the overcoming of the danger of the trials.

"The idea that in Jesus God has undertaken to suffer together with the suffering world is not a notion for which much support can be found in the NT."[8] Jesus is not presented as a fellow sufferer. Instead, his suffering is an example (e.g., 1 Pet. 2:21) of how best to react to unjust suffering. One might see the parallels to Job that were so important for Gregory the Great's influential treatment of that book in his *Moralia*. Hebrews 2:18 is more about overcoming temptation than about suffering. "Therefore, as much as the texts can be said to deal with suffering, they specifically concern suffering resulting from testing and temptations that we encounter in this world and from weaknesses that make it difficult for us to abide by God's will."[9] This could well be the sense of Luke 18:7's μακροθυμεῖν, about God's seeming to be slow to bring justice to his people.[10] The experience of suffering is not so much about remorse as about struggle, thereby establishing that innocent suffering is not meaningless. Paul found a joy in God's pleasure: "I am content . . ." (*eudokō*), as in 2 Corinthians 12:10, relating back to Galatians 1:15, which speaks of God's plan to set him apart.

In a similar way in John's Gospel, Jesus's itinerary serves God's calendar of events, as exemplified in John 4:4's "But he had to go through Samaria."[11]

6. As argued by Hubbard, *New Creation in Paul's Letters and Thought*.

7. Messner, "Opfer."

8. Holmén, "Theodicean Motifs in the New Testament," 650. Cf. Karrer, *Jesus Christus*, 219–35.

9. Holmén, "Theodicean Motifs in the New Testament," 639. Cf. at 647: "The majority of the approaches are based on an eschatological solution."

10. Haacker, "Lukas 18:7 als Anspielung auf den Deus absconditus."

11. Josephus (*Vita* 52.269) observes that one went through Samaria to get to Galilee from Jerusalem avoiding the heat of the Jordan Valley. See also Schnackenburg, *Das Johannesevangelium*, 458.

Place and direction are chosen for the sake and in service of (sacred) time, partly en route to the cross, but also for meaningful encounters like the one at the well in Sychar. The use of *edei* is significant because it is susceptible of three levels of meaning: he had to go that way—to avoid a dangerous route; to meet the woman at the well; to fulfill his ministry and be ready for "his hour."

Providence and the Acts of the Apostles

The New Testament presupposes the resurrection of Jesus. Jesus's own resurrection faith, which is integral to the event and interprets it (as bequeathed to his disciples), is faith in the creator God who is faithful to his creation.[12] As already mentioned, Christ, as the one who will return, is the foundation as down payment of the promise of the movement of divine providence toward those who love God, as in Romans 8:28.[13]

Yet the Gospel of Luke evidences a form of presentist or realized eschatology that in a sense takes a believer or disciple out of historical reality into a space of "salvation reality." Salvation history might well be seen as an eschatological thread hidden within history.[14] For Luke, eschatology supplies a critique of history, as is implied in Acts 7:56, where, after recounting a history of spiritual failure, Stephen looks up to the open heaven, which in turn builds on Luke 22:69 (ὁ υἱὸς τοῦ ἀνθρώπου καθήμενος ἐκ δεξιῶν τῆς δυνάμεως τοῦ θεοῦ). Both passages describe a vision of the end, with judgment and eternity standing over the wicked plots of men. However, this needs to be balanced with the consideration that Luke sees Jesus's work as one of inverting Israel's disobedience so as to supply and complete her obedience. One might go further and say that, for Luke, it is still Jewish Israel's story.[15]

Does Jerusalem exercise a continuing pull on the action? Yes, until the very end. Yet only in the first missionary journey is there a return of Paul to the relatively nearby Antioch (Acts 14:26), and the forced return of Paul is just the prelude to one final departure. One might fancy that the church's "central management" had (providentially) to escape from Jerusalem to Rome just

12. Konradt, "Schöpfung und Neuschöpfung im Neuen Testament," 175.
13. Roloff, "Vorsehung," 531. For more on Pauline emphases, see chap. 1 of the present work, and also Barclay and Gathercole, *Divine and Human Agency in Paul*.
14. Bauspieß, "Die Gegenwart des Heils und das Ende der Zeit," 144. Bauspieß works with Flender, *Heil und Geschichte in der Theologie des Lukas*, and Klein, "Lukas 1,1–4 als theologisches Programm"; both Flender and Klein would resist the idea that Luke's leading idea is salvation in history.
15. Jeska, *Die Geschichte Israels*, 268; see Jeska's comments there with reference to Acts 13:17–25.

before the Neronic persecution struck that would kill James in the former city and before the eventual sack of Jerusalem, which would be even less discriminatingly destructive. Acts does have a strong sense of being, among other things, an apologetic toward diaspora Jews: they and Christians have a common enemy. That Paul gets through all his forensic scrapes and so can't be charged as a blasphemer and that he survives other forms of violence and danger indicate that he must actually be blessed. The earthly telos of this history is no longer that holy city, even while it continues to exert a gravitational pull.

There is a kind of dialectic between experienced reality—one still has to live in this world for now—and *future* salvation history.[16] One must have faith, and specifically faith in the promises and proclamation, before one can participate in and narrate history.[17] And this dialectic is part of world history, or operates within it as an in-breaking of salvation history in world history, visibly, even if not communicating revelation "publicly." Günther Klein (and Zimmerli) were right to argue against the "Pannenberg group," that history by itself is not revelation; recognizing it as one interprets it (*erkennen*) is crucial.[18] Yet the revelation has happened objectively in its events, and not in a corner (Acts 26:26).[19]

Yet just how "objectively" did the events "happen"? According to the influential critic Richard Pervo, Luke's aim in writing Acts was to entertain. Hence, "Luke turned Acts 21–28 into a cliffhanger by withholding the verdict again and again, despite assurances that this time it would be final."[20] Yet if Ernst Haenchen was right, then a providential history was somewhere *behind* what Luke wrote, and it was a history he tried to map. Indeed, sometimes truth can be stranger than fiction. He might have had some literary models, yes, although the likes of Lucian (whom Pervo prefers) is surely much later. Yet in this much is Pervo certain: "The verifiability of God's 'providence' is constitutive for the theology of Luke. All salvation history, all history, including the course of nature, is in God's hands. This providence is not a mystery but may be verified by reference to empirical

16. Jeska, *Die Geschichte Israels*, 147.
17. Bauspieß, *Geschichte und Erkenntnis im lukanischen Doppelwerk*, 303. See also Crabbe, "Luke/Acts and the End of History"; Crabbe, "Accepting Prophecy"; Crabbe, "Being Found Fighting against God."
18. Bauspieß, *Geschichte und Erkenntnis im lukanischen Doppelwerk*, 305–6; G. Klein, "Lukas 1,1–4 als theologisches Programm."
19. Bauspieß, *Geschichte und Erkenntnis im lukanischen Doppelwerk*, 198.
20. Pervo, *Profit with Delight*, 48. There is something a bit sneering about Pervo's assessment: "He has created, in Paul and others, the kind of heroes admired by upwardly inclined persons of modest education and resources" (80).

criteria, as Gamaliel made clear in 5:38–39. Success will distinguish between the human and divine wills. . . . Miracles may most visibly witness providence, but they are merely the tip of the iceberg (14:15–17)."[21] Yet Pervo's analysis contains this curious qualifier: "Missionaries move from place to place not so much by plan as through the compulsion of hostile powers."[22] However, Luke would have responded, if asked, that the divine plan is more than able and certainly most willing to make use of such powers. "The hero of this relentless expansion is not any single individual, but 'the church' (8.1) or perhaps 'the Word.' And secondly, the thrust of this expansive movement is centrifugal: Acts, seen as a whole, does not share the outward-and-return structure of the novels."[23] The plot of Acts is not resolved, unlike the plots of romances. The book *does* express a presumption of shared religious experience, with "a committed narrative of a type unusual in Greek prose literature."[24] Acts is epic in its grandeur and heroism, in its elements of journey (even for Peter), and in its rival empire-foundation; but it is even more like the Septuagint than it is like any epics.

It is true that one experiences God's providence firstly in terms of his plan for salvation and that then one can see God's action more widely.[25] This is to give God's decree or plan its own subjectivity in the Christian sanctified understanding, as many Acts scholars recognize. Luke mentions only once the election of individuals (Acts 13:48), because it is the salvation of a people out of the nations that matters. The mission is all part of a closed history.[26] Yet this need not mean that the whole thing is just a display of divine power and little human character or agency, as though it were by Euripides; and even Greek tragedy has some place for human agency, albeit at a high price.[27] In all this, free will is lost; hence Paul cannot hit out against the pricks or spurs, and Peter cannot wrestle with God. However, this kind of "necessitarian"

---

21. Pervo, *Profit with Delight*, 74: the first-century AD novelist Chariton is like that, as is the fourth-century Heliodorus. Haenchen, *Acts of the Apostles*, 362, was right to describe the action in Acts 10–11 as "the twitching of human puppets"; cf. Auerbach, *Mimesis*, 443; Rohde, *Der griechische Roman*, 296–306; Kerényi, *Griechisch-orientalische Romanliteratur*. Pervo concludes: "Rather than seeking growth of character through acceptance of responsibility for one's fate, the 'immature reader' prefers a beneficent providence, not least a providence partial to youth and beauty. Works that establish causal links through a god rather than by characterization reflect a certain view of life" (74). Needless to say, this seems extremely unfair toward Acts.

22. Pervo, *Profit with Delight*, 28.

23. Alexander, *Acts in Its Ancient Literary Context*, 73.

24. Alexander, *Acts in Its Ancient Literary Context*, 163.

25. Schulz, "Gottes Vorsehung bei Lukas," 105.

26. Concerning Acts 13:46, see Schulz, "Gottes Vorsehung bei Lukas," 108–9.

27. Schulz, "Gottes Vorsehung bei Lukas," 111.

interpretation is somewhat exaggerated, to say the least, and shows a huge insensitivity toward the text. Neither apostle (after the earliest resistance) seems inclined to see things otherwise than God's way, and that freely. Where Barnabas and Paul are prevented from preaching any further into Asia, they concur with it as meant for a positive thing, and indeed it is the very words of their preaching, as the likes of Sigfried Schulz admits, that make the difference to events being received as divinely ordered.[28]

God may be said to help those who help those who help themselves, as in the commentary by Chrysostom on the passage in Acts 10 where Cornelius comes to faith.[29] This was a key passage in Acts for the providential advance, according to Chrysostom. The whole episode demonstrates the perfect administration of providence. The later (sixth-century) Christian poet Arator, too, seems to have viewed Cornelius's conversion as some sort of reward. Bovon adds that for Irenaeus, Cornelius already knew the Father, although not the Son, so that what went on was more an adding to knowledge the degree of faith.[30] This note of "continuity" between creation—with its natural religiosity in response to and as part of providence—and fuller Christian redemption marks the early reception of Acts.

Particularly significant, and worthy of closer attention, are Acts 5:34–39 and 17:25–28. On Acts 5:34–39, in his Regensburger commentary Joseph Zmijewski shows some pious appreciation where he writes that today's Christian readers can learn from Gamaliel to learn from history.[31] By contrast, Pervo is scathing about Gamaliel's advice: "The learned Pharisee suggests leaving the matter in God's hands. This was scarcely responsible advice, for it urges the council to abrogate the duties for which they have been truly appointed, and as noted, his examples were not truly relevant."[32] The rabbi, concludes Pervo, was moreover quite wrong about the revolutionary Theudas. Consequently, he was rightly ignored (despite what 5:39c clearly says, "They were convinced by him"), and the apostles were duly punished. Gamaliel was no Christian, but pragmatic about (not) fighting God.

Daniel Marguerat is much more forgiving or even appreciative of Gamaliel and thinks his was a wisdom of which providence availed itself.[33] Indeed, *Pirqe Avot* 4.11 has similar advice from the mouth of R. Johanan. But, notes Marguerat, one should recognize that that second alternative, that the Christian

28. Schulz, "Gottes Vorsehung bei Lukas," 116.
29. Bovon, *De vocatione gentium*, 53.
30. Bovon, *De vocatione gentium*, 34–44.
31. Zmijewski, *Die Apostelgeschichte*, 254.
32. Pervo, *Acts*, 148.
33. Marguerat, *Les Actes des apôtres (1–12)*, 200.

movement might come from God (as compared with the possibility, stated in the previous line, that it has come from humans), is couched, grammatically speaking, in less hesitant terms, as though Gamaliel thought it the more likely probability that God was on the side of the Christian movement. A good Pharisee, he was following the test of Deuteronomy 18. Marguerat does not quite say, but implies, that Gamaliel is not far from the kingdom of God. One might add that this kingdom is a "providential" one, according to a guided sequence of events, with a spatial ("ends of the earth") rather than a temporal ("end of the world") destination (Acts 1:8).[34] The alert reader will, of course, remember the connection with the Saul who became Paul, as per Acts 22:3 ("educated at the feet of Gamaliel according to the strict manner of the law of our fathers" [AT]). The apostles were punished, but perhaps with a degree of leniency.

God's providential and sovereign movement of people and events in Acts is what is at issue throughout the book. As Torsten Jantsch helpfully summarizes:

> In Acts 14:15αβ, we encounter the motif of God as the creator of everything: ". . . the living God who made the heaven and the earth and the sea and everything within them." This formulation alludes to Ex 20:11 (see also Ps[LXX] 145:6), with the relative clause clarifying that God is the living one, *because* he is the creator of all things. This motif occurs regularly in Luke-Acts.
>
> Next, Acts 14:16–17 emphasizes God's continuous caring for man rather than the initial act of creation. God did beneficial acts, giving rain and "fruitful seasons" to satisfy human "hearts with food and gladness."[35]

One might also compare God's being "not far" in Acts 17:27.[36]

In a monograph from 2002 Marguerat strongly hints at what could be called a trinitarian reading of Acts when he writes: "This impressive Christological concentration of the gospel makes way in Acts for a theology offering more balance between the poles of Christology (the resurrection kerygma and miracles), pneumatology (the launch of missions) and theo-logy (God as the agent of the history of salvation). . . . The decisive question then becomes the interpretation of the theophanic signs. It is to this task that the author of

---

34. Wolter, "'Reich Gottes' bei Lukas," 561.

35. Jantsch, "God of Glory," 201–2. He argues that humans (in their natural state, presumably) do not have such access as to amount to a full recognition of God; rather, they have a "feeling" (204). Cf. Jantsch, *Jesus, der Retter*. Also, Salmeier, *Restoring the Kingdom*: Luke assumes the reality of divine action rather than argues for it.

36. ζητεῖν τὸν θεόν, εἰ ἄρα γε ψηλαφήσειαν αὐτὸν καὶ εὕροιεν, καί γε οὐ μακρὰν ἀπὸ ἑνὸς ἑκάστου ἡμῶν ὑπάρχοντα.

Acts applies himself. . . . To read the work *ad Theophilum* is to learn to name God."[37] Marguerat insists that divine interventions have more the aspect of the revelatory, in terms of a communication of meaning, than of the causal, in terms of events.

> From the point of view of the plot of the narrative, divine interventions can have three distinct functions. In some cases, they precede events and take on a *programmatic* function (in the form of a vision, a dream or an oracle), for example, when Paul is led off to Macedonia (16. 6–10). On other occasions, they exercise a *performative* function, at the moment that God intervenes by saving, punishing, or guiding the course of the events, for example, the Damascus road incident (9. 1–19a). They can also fulfil an *interpretative* function, when they are situated after the events in order to indicate their meaning or to justify them, for example, Stephen's vision (7. 55–6).[38]

Yet in a revealing movement God also acts providentially, even if the movement bears revelation. The theme of the agency of God as key to Acts has made its way into some recent commentaries. "In addition, by depicting dramatic escapes, two aspects of Acts reinforce the theme of providential protection: (1) God's status as active agent, and (2) the Holy Spirit as the manifestation of God's presence or agency. . . . Acts consistently attributes a remarkably active role to God. God is an active agent, another character and participant in the narrative rather than an inscrutable deity whose actions are obscured by hiddenness and mystery. . . . God is presented as being in the forefront, leading the movement forward,"[39] and, not least, overriding opposition as well as making provision, as at 15:14, where the verb *episkeptomai* is "make provision."[40] However, this conclusion, indebted to Scott Shauf, seems exaggerated. God indeed does act in Acts, but not in such a visible way as to become a dramatis persona. As Shauf himself concludes, Paul is the hero of Acts 15:36–19:40, even as he is doing God's work. At least within New Testament church history, "human events take on divine meaning."[41]

Then, to turn to Acts 17:28 and that famous line: "In him we live and move and have our being." Jacob Jervell is convinced that Luke here reflects a biblical Jewish idea of God as creator and of humans being made as the image

37. Marguerat, *First Christian Historian*, 88, 89, 91.
38. Marguerat, *First Christian Historian*, 92.
39. Holladay, *Acts*, 62, with reference to Shauf, *Theology as History*, 171–72.
40. Holladay, *Acts*, 301.
41. Shauf, *Theology as History*, 325. The argument is that the continuity with Jewish identity requires a commitment to the divine in history, for all the expression in Hellenistic terms for a wider audience.

of God, in whom is the source of human life.[42] Hence any pagan idolatry is harshly judged for its presumption that we can put ourselves above creation. On the other hand, Jürgen Roloff[43] thinks that Luke here received pagan sources favorably—since Aratus gets cited with authority—and that Luke is thinking of the whole Zeus hymn of Cleanthes. Roloff also contends that ἐν αὐτῷ clearly means "in him" rather than "by Him," since the sense of verse 25 reinforces the idea that God is the guarantor of all life. A middle way is offered by Rudolf Pesch, who argues that for Aratus of Cilicia (ca. 370 BC), perhaps a local hero in Paul's homeland, the idea would have been more of humans existing "through [ἐν] him" rather than "in him."[44] Paul was making common cause with something the pagans knew deep down, and his critical rebuke comes only in verse 29; they are without excuse, as Wisdom 13:2–8 teaches, because so much has been given to them through reason. Pesch reminds us that although the tradition through to and including Reformation-era Lutherans like Johannes Brenz viewed the employment of Aratus favorably (Brenz: pagan poets are *theologi prophetae*); Calvin insisted that Aratus was cited as a witness to the Athenian shame ("beschämendes Zeugnis")—that is, a louche poet is as good as it gets where their authorities and teachers are concerned.[45] Pervo is not far from Pesch when he writes: "Humanity's relationship to this God is characterized with a triad: vitality, movement and existence."[46] This triad is the common source of all humans, an idea that would become part of Christian apologetic tradition, which is the very reason for the attack on idolatry that immediately follows in verse 29. If humans are in the image of God, they are not to obscure who they are and who God is by fixating on some idolatrous intermediary in the form of an image.

Thankfully, although the commentaries are sometimes wanting—sometimes simply due to lack of space to discuss everything of theological import well, given all that commentaries have to do these days—there are monographs and articles that are more welcome, and on Luke-Acts there is no shortage. One thing most scholars agree on is that Luke-Acts was intended as an orderly account (*kathexēs* [Luke 1:3]) that reflects the perceived order of the events. Luke arranged his episodes with relation to cause and effect, as Carl Holladay puts it.[47] Luke wanted to inform Theophilus not just of things that happened, but of the *things* "that have been fulfilled among us"

42. Jervell, *Die Apostelgeschichte*, 449.
43. Roloff, *Die Apostelgeschichte*, 263–64.
44. Pesch, *Die Apostelgeschichte*, 141.
45. Calvin, *Commentary on the Acts of the Apostles* 2.170.
46. Pervo, *Acts*, 438.
47. Holladay, "Interpreting Acts," 247.

(Luke 1:1). The use of the term translated as "things" (*pragmata*, "actions") suggests that Luke is referring back to a beginning of action that was carried to completion in Jesus's ministry, along with the security coming from traditional and truthful words that Luke wants Theophilus to have. That means not just the reported facts of the fulfillment of the Old Testament in the New Testament, but a step further, the theological significance.

In Acts the divine plan is understood as having been announced in the Old Testament and now having been revealed. The plan is not a necessity that cancels human freedom. Among pagan historians a note had already been sounded that the divine will would work itself out but that human cooperation was preferable. "For the historian Sallust, Fortune (*Fortuna*) provides not a deterministic fate but an opportunity for intellectual powers (*animus*; *ingenium*) to lead to full excellence of character (*virtus*)."[48] Pamela Hedrick is confident that Luke thought little different. The emphasis on δεῖ and its connotation of the ineluctability of the divine will in Acts is considerable.[49] But as Mark Reasoner notes—building on the work of Charles Cosgrove, who "helpfully nuances this example of 'the divine δεῖ' by noting that Ps 109:8 is used in Acts 2 as an '*ante eventum* divine imperative'"[50]—this is an early clue in Acts that the divine necessity at work is not a rigid plan in which humans play robotic roles; this necessity at times calls humans to obedience. Thus human activity is demanded as part of the summons of providence. Reasoner declares to have changed his mind, from the position represented by, for example, Hubert Cancik,[51] who posited that Acts recounts an "institutional history" (i.e., of the church), to the view that Acts is about divine action at every turn. Reasoner concludes: "The point repeatedly made in Acts, that the word of Jesus and those who proclaim it are in continuity with the prophetic ministry of the past, feeds directly into its main theme, that divine necessity plays out in the lives of those who proclaim and encounter the word of Jesus."[52]

Clare Rothschild also thinks that Acts cannot be an institutional history, because, as she puts it, "The ἐκκλησία (church) as depicted in Acts does not consistently refer to a universal entity, but to various churches (Acts 9:31 alone may have a broader than local sense)."[53] However, the word could still be

48. Hedrick, "Fewer Answers and Further Questions," 298, speaks of divine plans that can be discerned and that use cooperators and noncooperators, with reference to Polybius and Dionysius Halicarnassus.
49. Fascher, "Theologische Beobachtungen zu δει," 246.
50. Reasoner, "Theme of Acts," 638, concerning Cosgrove, "Divine *Dei* in Luke-Acts."
51. Cancik, "History of Culture, Religion, and Institutions."
52. Reasoner, "Theme of Acts," 649.
53. Rothschild, *Luke-Acts and the Rhetoric of History*, 55.

referring to the institution at local level. Rothschild concedes: "Organizing, however, might be seen as the central subject of the book."[54] Beyond that, one might see organization in the church as a response to the organizing activity of God. And if Reasoner is going to emphasize Christian ethics in Acts, then he cannot conclude that the narrative is *uniquely* about divine action. Of course there is so much direct discourse from divine beings—twenty-two times, in fact, but that is precisely the point—discourse that demands human action to give the plan of providence its legs.

Rothschild objects that Reasoner wants to perpetuate a facile theology/history dichotomy. Instead, "theology—a component of every ancient historian's worldview—is integrated in the warp and woof of each historical work."[55] Or, as Shauf puts it: "Divine activity is woven into the fabric of human history."[56] However, Rothschild is somewhat hoisted by her own petard when she argues that Luke wants to be taken seriously as a historian. Her claim is that Luke was first and foremost trying to establish his account as history. To summarize her case in her own words: "This chapter, thus, endorses that Luke-Acts contains a strong expression of necessity, not however, as a means of persuading audiences that God guides history or that the present account of origins was divinely led—ideas of which they are surely convinced—rather to certify his own version of what took place through the ultimate and indisputable rhetoric of necessity."[57] If Luke really means "iron necessity," she writes, then he uses terms like *anagkaios*—for example, at Acts 13:46. Now, she does not explain why *anagkaios* has to be anything other than a synonym for *dei*. She prefers to see δεῖ as one step down from *anagkaios* in terms of strength, with a subtle sense of "it had to be." "In conclusion, the author of Luke-Acts regularly inserts the impersonal verb δεῖ to strengthen the credibility of his historical claims."[58] Does an impersonal verb imply "impersonality" in Luke's view of providence? No, there is nothing necessarily impersonal about the use of *dei*. Does his employment of *dei* for rhetorical ends mean that we should harbor prima facie suspicions about the validity of his case, as Rothschild implies?

Furthermore, it is not that Luke was trying hard to be a historian's historian. It is not the research but the ordering of it that matters, and behind that,

---

54. Rothschild, *Luke-Acts and the Rhetoric of History*, 55.
55. Rothschild, *Luke-Acts and the Rhetoric of History*, 59.
56. Shauf, *Theology as History*, 299.
57. Rothschild, *Luke-Acts and the Rhetoric of History*, 189.
58. Rothschild, *Luke-Acts and the Rhetoric of History*, 208; cf. 212: "not to mention that where the divine will of God is explicit in Luke-Acts, δεῖ is conspicuous by its absence (Lk 7:30; Acts 2:23; 4:28; 13:36; 20:27)."

what it meant theologically.[59] One is aware of the title of a book from a few decades back by I. H. Marshall, *Luke: Historian and Theologian*. Acts 1:1 is hardly a prologue at all, and certainly by verse 2 the reader is in medias res, so that one must look to *Luke* 1, in its much more abstract but theological terminology, as functioning as a prologue for Acts as well as for Luke. And there, in that prologue, one finds theological direction. As for the beginning of Acts, well, the one clue concerning the sovereignty of God is contained in the phrase *basileia tou theou* in Acts 1:3, about which Jesus spoke to his disciples during the forty days. Just as important: "In summary, Luke integrates without hesitation the fulfillment of the purpose of God (cf. the importance of the term βουλὴ τοῦ θεοῦ) into the lives of humans. It is this junction, for lack of a better term, we call salvation history."[60] God takes his time to develop in believers an appreciation of a kingdom that is spatial ("to the ends of the earth") and yet is more than that, as something that can be imagined and is also to be understood metaphorically, linking the mind to the heavenly realm, which is demarcated by divine action and placed in the "narrated world."[61]

In his monograph *The Plan of God* John Squires has to rely on a chapter as late in the book as Acts 26, and hence he does not really prove that "God's plan" as he detects it there is *programmatic* for Acts. He relates that, for Josephus, "Fortune's inconsistency and unpredictability are grounds for repudiating her power. It is divine providence which actually guides history."[62] One does not really encounter the relationship between God's providence and "fortune" as an issue in Luke, any more than one found it operative in the Hebrew Bible / Old Testament. Peter in his sermon (Acts 2:14–36) speaks much of God's foreordaining and even doing events in Jesus's life.[63] In Acts 19 the obviously divine events are best viewed as the hermeneutical key for the mundane ones.[64] One such "divine event" is the bestowal of the Spirit on the disciples in 19:1–7, although one only understands these divine events in turn in relation to the order of the narrative. The point is made in 19:20: "Thus the Word of the Lord was powerfully growing and prevailing" (AT). One

59. Backhaus, "Lukanische Geschichtsschreibung im Rahmen des antiken Wahrheits-diskurses."

60. Bovon, *Luke the Theologian*, 86. Cf. Schneider, *Lukas Theologie als Heilsgeschichte*. The theme of salvation as an overlooking and rectifying of ignorance is treated by Hagene, *Zeiten der Wiederherstellung*, in her comments on Acts 3:17.

61. Cf. Blumenthal, *Basileia bei Lukas*, 40–42. "Ereigneten unerhörten Begebenheit" (Goethe). Contra Prieur (*Die Verkündigung der Gottesherrschaft*), the two *basileia* references in Acts (28:23, 31), with reference back to Luke 1–4, are at the heart of Lukan theology.

62. Squires, *Plan of God in Luke-Acts*, 52.

63. Squires, *Plan of God in Luke-Acts*, 65.

64. Shauf, *Theology as History*, 300–301.

should compare Acts 12:24: "But the word of God continued to spread and was fulfilled" (AT). Acts 19:20 sums up Paul's activity prior to arrest, hence coming at the end of his missionary activity, just as Acts 12:24 rounded off the account of Peter's part. Perhaps the difference is that through Paul God consolidated what was fulfilled by God through Peter and the Twelve. Paul was a chosen *instrument* in a real sense, even as he lived the apostolic life as testimony to the resurrection and to the oversight of providence. Churches are grown by the Word "from above."[65] In Luke's account of Paul's journeys, the speeches of outsiders are used to further the message, even while the church is the continuing people of God: God is working his purpose out through unwitting characters such as Gamaliel, and then Gallio in Acts 18 (whose dramatically ironic defense ensures that Paul stays in Corinth), and finally Tertullus and Festus (Acts 24 and 25: Paul is innocent, like Jesus).[66] One might want to call the pattern of acts a *theopraxis* in which humans participate. Marguerat takes issue with Jervell, who argues: "God is the only *causa*, the motor and the driving force in history, the only master in history. . . . Humans are forced to bring about all the things God has foreordained."[67] No, opines Marguerat: Scriptures legitimize retrospectively, and they do not compel, in keeping with a view of the prophetic *dābār* (Hebrew: "word") as illuminative of minds rather than causative of events. Of course we may still observe irony as God's triumph mocks those who by opposing his Word advance it unwittingly.[68] Hence the Word leaves room for human maneuvering. Following "the Gamaliel principle,"[69] we can say that "it [the Lukan view of history] assigns the reader the course of day-by-day history as a place to discover and to celebrate the ways of God."[70] Subtle irony appears also in Luke's telling of events, such as at Acts 12:7 (*pataxas*) and 12:23 (*epataxen*), where the same term is used for Peter's liberation and the effecting of Herod's demise. There is irony, too, in the use of *ekklēsia* for the mob in 19:32.[71]

65. Roloff, *Die Apostelgeschichte*, 306.
66. Uytanlet, *Luke-Acts and Jewish Historiography*, 41: "A dominant theme in Jewish historical narratives is the kingship of Yahweh. Yahweh is king by virtue of being the creator . . . with Israel to be constituted as kingdom of priests."
67. Jervell, "Future of the Past," 106.
68. Jervell, "Future of the Past," 108: "Neither Gamaliel, when he pleads in favour of the liberation of the apostles, nor the magistrates of Philippi, when they imprison Paul and Silas, nor even Claudius, the tribune, when he takes Paul to Caesarea under escort, realize their collaboration with the divine plan. The irony of God consists in integrating even the actions of his enemies in order to make them contribute to the advancement of the Word 'to the ends of the earth' (1. 8)."
69. Aletti, *Quand Luc raconte*, 5.
70. Aletti, *Quand Luc raconte*, 38–39.
71. Wolter, "Das lukanische Doppelwerk als Epochengeschichte."

Paul's "prophetic" knowledge of providence contributes to providence's being not completely determined. Indeed, the point of Luke's sad, or at least downbeat, final chapter is driven home by the penultimate chapter's portrayal (Acts 27) of the gentiles in Malta as the complete opposite to the Jews in Rome (and, it might be said, beyond Joshua Jipp's argument,[72] opposite to the gentiles in Rome too). Yet the end of Acts operates not simply to highlight "the bad guys and the good guys," nor even to show what an extraordinary kind of human being Paul was, even as he headed to the imperial capital, where he apparently would find his hands figuratively and perhaps literally tied. No, the main point is to describe the workings of God's providence in his preserving and leading Paul and others in such a way that valuable lives are kept safe. This takes place as a subplot so closely tied together with the geographical plot of the advance of the gospel and the strengthening of the church that this providential subplot becomes hard to separate from the soteriological-ecclesiological plot, so much that it hardly makes sense to describe the latter as "plot." Marguerat touches on how Luke lovingly traces this.

However, God's protection does not shield his envoys from failure, humiliation, flagellation, and martyrdom. The route of the missionaries is a "via dolorosa." Marguerat has a section heading "*A God who arranges and withdraws.*"[73] In no sense is God caught up in any reverses of the movement, but rather he initiates, then waits to use the human response in making his next moves. The heavens can be silent: "Jesus . . . will come in the same way as you saw him go" (Acts 1:11), but the narrative strongly suggests that in the meantime the disciples are to get on with things as the Spirit empowers and directs. The arrangement reflects a pattern or ordering for Theophilus and his successors today to follow: it is the ordering, not the research, that provides the reliability (*asphaleia* [Luke 1:4]).[74] *Orientation* might be the right English word. (Knut Backhaus uses "in der Geschichte zurechtzufinden.") In that sense Acts 7 (Stephen's speech) is programmatic: God is the Lord of universal history, not to be limited to the cult, even if the term "Father" is not used for addressing gentiles, to avoid confusion with Zeus.[75]

72. Jipp, *Divine Visitations and Hospitality to Strangers in Luke-Acts*.

73. Marguerat, *First Christian Historian*, 97. Cf. 102: "It is striking that the narrator never says 'God did' or 'God said'; he lets one of the characters in the narrative say it, not without having shown, in some cases, the correct reading of the event. There is a divine discretion, which indicates the theology that Luke draws on: *a theology of the hidden God, who reveals himself by veiling himself: it is the word of the witness that must pierce the uncertainty.*" Cf. Gaventa, *From Darkness to Light*, 107–25; also Neyrey, "Acts 17, Epicureans and Theodicy."

74. Backhaus, "Lukanische Geschichtsschreibung im Rahmen des antiken Wahrheits-diskurses," 107–8.

75. As argued in Zimmermann, *Die Namen des Vaters*.

Hebrews 11

Here, having looked at a large unit within the canon (Acts) in some detail, we shall consider a small but significant part of the New Testament.

How might providence be involved in salvation history? If Acts 7 offers a story of judgment, then Hebrews 11, with its story of faith to faith under God, is its counterpoint. To that extent it is quite correct for exegetes from as different corners as Erich Grässer and Pamela Eisenbaum to highlight the passivity of the faith of the heroes to the point where "heroic" might be the wrong epithet: these are *not* self-made heroes at all. These people in the list are somehow *less* heroic because they are *more* indebted to grace. Thomas Aquinas would suggest that Moses was also motivated by a hoped-for reward.[76] The "reproach of Christ" is simply an expression for passivity in having adverse things done to one by God through unpleasant creaturely agencies. The title "Christ" here, as elsewhere in early Christianity, is solidly connected with the aspect of suffering.[77] The idea of messianic woes is patent. The key messianic-time virtue is patience, waiting, hoping.

Well, yes and no. For in verses 8–9 we are told: "[Abraham] . . . went out, not knowing where he was to go. By faith he sojourned in the land of promise" (AT)—this is hardly a case of digging in and waiting. In the same way Moses, for all his standing fast, was forever on the move. "Stasis" is not quite right. Being carried about hither and thither and obediently taking the brakes off is more like it. And the Christian experience of faith was not all that different, not least where Hebrews speaks of the pilgrim people of God seeking rest (4:9). In fact, a lot of the stories in Hebrews 11 are about providence. The last ones—verse 35b onward—are more about things suffered and endured; yet just prior to that we read of *action* (vv. 33–34): ". . . who through faith conquered kingdoms, enforced justice, received promises, stopped the mouths of lions, quenched raging fire, escaped the edge of the sword, won strength out of weakness, became mighty in war, put foreign armies to flight" (RSV). This seems all quite "active," in the sense of pressing movement. There is, as Hans-Friedrich Weiss puts it, a mutual connection of faith and the experience of the marvelous action of God.[78]

So faith is an action, or at very least a disposition moving toward action. Grässer's view of faith seems "static," because its object for him is also static.[79] However, the God who moves is the God who is believed in. Grässer possibly

---

76. Aquinas, *Commentary on the Epistle to the Hebrews*, 252.
77. Weiss, *Der Brief an die Hebräer*, 607n21.
78. Weiss, *Der Brief an die Hebräer*, 612.
79. Grässer, *Hebräer*, 3:117. Cf. 108.

equates Hebrews too much with Philo here. For even as the martyrs' witness is passive, we may truly say they express that witness actively, even while we understand that God is moving to link first, middle, and last in the historical sequence.

Providence means God is making history turn out right; it is not primarily about his giving reassurance to believers. Moreover, God must be the focus. Hebrews 11 traces the arc of divine action from protology to eschatology. The plural form (νοοῦμεν [v. 3: "we know"]) of the verb entails that Jewish patriarchs and Christians are included in the one covenant. If covenant separates (liturgically, in its forms of worship at least), then history and providence and faith unite the Testaments.[80] As Markus Bockmuehl sagely comments: "But it is clear that here the superiority of the New Covenant introduces not a new *people* of God so much as a newly energized *worship* of God—constituted around the definitive and permanently efficacious sacrifice."[81]

So Hebrews 11 is not specifically Christian in its content.[82] Its genre can be considered to be a Hellenistic Jewish list, where "believers" are commended for remaining true to the covenant, with an echo of Sirach 44. As Backhaus sums up the chapter, we have the whole history of Israel and beyond reinterpreted as a drama of faith ("die gesamte Geschichte . . . als Glaubensdrama reinterpretiert").[83] And what's more, faith is a virtue, but that means it is active as *virtus*, with the connotation of power. And the fact that the chapter reads like a drama means that the narratives about the former people in Hebrews 11 are meant to inform the exegete's understanding of 11:1–3.

In my view Pamela Eisenbaum seems on the wrong track when she argues: "The author uses the retellings to describe the past, i.e., the state of the world before Christ, while the citations of speech determine the present, i.e., the post-Christ world."[84] This, I suspect, is at least to exaggerate the contrast: for the relationship of Testaments is no adversative one, for all the contrasts. One consequence of this move is that she reads 11:2 (*en tautē gar emartyrēthēsan hoi presbyteroi*) in rather a strange way: "This means that scripture—that which constitutes the *record* [emphasis added] of the ancestors' lives—was provided by faith."[85] This, Eisenbaum believes, is a case of the superimposition of a Christian way of reading by the writer; she does not countenance the possibility that the writer of Hebrews located faith *in* the realities of

---

80. Backhaus, *Der sprechende Gott*, 163.
81. Bockmuehl, "Abraham's Faith in Hebrews 11," 368.
82. Grässer, *Hebräer*, 3:102.
83. Backhaus, *Der Hebräerbrief*, 380.
84. Eisenbaum, *Jewish Heroes of Christian History*, 133.
85. Eisenbaum, *Jewish Heroes of Christian History*, 147.

those lives, and not just in the written or spoken record of them. Further, she thinks that for Hebrews "Abraham and Moses are not Israelites or Jews, they are *Christians*."[86] That is, they are interpreted as such, so as to lose their identity. She thinks their heroism is devalued and the characters presented as individuals, more in a Hellenized manner, "to denationalize the history of Israel."[87] A strong case for her thesis concerns Moses, since he "considered the reproach of Christ to be greater wealth" (11:2),[88] which seems to be making a Christian out of Moses. Yet immediately thereafter the text refers to Moses suffering with his people, Israel, and so his figure is in no way deracinated from them. Moses is a Jew, or at least the forefather of Jews, whatever "the reproach of Christ" might mean. Or to take the case of Abel, it is worth hearing the tenth-century writer Oecumenius commenting how Abel's sacrifice was the occasion of his own death,[89] with allusion to Christ as both priest and sacrifice. This typology helps to intensify the quality of his act of faith that should not be allowed to be forgotten, but does not thereby Christianize it.

In fact, included in what Jews and Christians share is their creation faith. If the order of being moves from the invisible to the visible, then in the order of knowing the movement goes in reverse. Hence visible creation is a model for invisible things; creation faith can do a lot to ground Christian faith (what other faith did patriarchs have to begin with?). Grässer sees this "invisible reality" as that which the believer is put in touch with through the visible creation, and he considers the believer to be thus enabled to live "eschatologically."[90] Faith means looking through outward reality to the foundation that bears it and persevering in resistance until one reaches the heavenly goal, being true realists in the sense of seeing through appearances.[91] The change was much less a noetic one, leading to a New Testament faith that is different from Old Testament faith, than it was a new reordering of *realia* as part of God's overall providence. So what is faith, according to Hebrews? One answer is that it is a motioned, mobile response to the moving providence of God. In Hebrews 11 providence includes spiritual training (*paideia*) as a subset of it.

---

86. Eisenbaum, *Jewish Heroes of Christian History*, 220. She claims that Josephus loves to moralize (205), yet this is related to "providence" as the theme singled out by Attridge, *Interpretation of Biblical History*, with reference to Josephus, *A.J.* 1.1.3.14: history is a warning against vice and an encouragement to virtue.

87. Eisenbaum, *Jewish Heroes of Christian History*, 188. On p. 187: "The heroes derive their status from πίστις, not from any national role or office. πίστις allows the author to establish a non-national, salvation-historical trajectory which includes the Hebrews community."

88. Eisenbaum, *Jewish Heroes of Christian History*, 188.

89. Oecumenius, *Commentarius in Epistulam ad Hebraeos* 11 (PG 119:404).

90. Grässer, *Hebräer*, 3:99. (Cf. Calvin, *Institutes* 3.2.4, 1.)

91. Backhaus, *Der Hebräerbrief*, 378.

A metaphysical "top and tailing" of the history of the faithful witnesses
can be seen in Hebrews 11:3 and 12:1. In his discussion of 11:3 Christian
Rose comments that he favors the patristic interpretation that viewed the
verse as providing a statement about creation out of nothing and tied it to
2 Maccabees 7:28: "from what was not God made these things" (AT).[92] In
other words, the early Christian interpreters spotted the connection with the
Maccabees passage and read Hebrews 11:3 in light of that. Rose is sure that
this was justified, for the particle *mē* goes with *phainomenōn*, and together
these should be understood as meaning "nothing," not just "invisible." Further, the "out of" implies not a place called "Nothing" but rather that the
creation—as in 2 Corinthians 4:6—took the place of nothing: God's Word
set reality where there was nothing before. So along with the early Christian
interpretation, one can, without being more precise, interpret this as creation
out of nothing.[93] Rose is not sure that Hebrews 11:3 can mean this in its plain
or historical sense but admits there's something about the eyes of faith that
pushes in that direction.[94] Thus, through faith we acknowledge that *aiōnes*
were created by the Word of God (1:2), so that in the place of the imperceivable
(in the sense of nonexistent) the visible has stepped in, although only for the
eyes of faith.[95] Surely the *visible* things of creation are visible not only to the
eyes of faith, so it must be rather the belief in the dawning visibility of new
creation that Rose ascribes to the writer.

On this "cosmogenetic" reading, 11:3 simply teaches that the visible did
not come from anything visible, not that "the visible came from that which
cannot be seen." It is anti-Aristotelian rather than pro-Platonic. Martin Karrer
notes that the technical term *aoratos* (invisible) is avoided.[96] Yet Weiss had
argued quite the contrary, claiming that Hebrews 11:3 means exactly that the
invisible gave rise to the visible—in other words, that the view in this verse
resembles a Platonic view.[97]

Yet perhaps it is nothing to do with the original creation except by analogy.
More recently Wilifried Eisele has discussed this and convincingly concluded
that Hebrews here is thinking of a visible, material world being formed out
of and subsequent to an invisible one. Here are located the promised invisible
goods to be tasted after death, although even in the highest heaven they are
made accessible in Christ and after his coming—through the curtain. Philo

92. Rose, *Die Wolke der Zeugen*, 157.
93. Rose, *Die Wolke der Zeugen*, 159.
94. Rose, *Die Wolke der Zeugen*, 276.
95. Rose, *Die Wolke der Zeugen*, 160.
96. Karrer, *Der Brief an die Hebräer Kapitel 5,11–13,25*, 275.
97. Weiss, *Der Brief an die Hebräer*, 574.

taught an active principle in the mind of God, but also a passive one—in connection with the perceptible world (*Opif.* 26: the parts of the world mentioned in the first three verses are intelligible things), and that allows time to begin within creation while remaining foreign to and distinct from God. What God created first of all in the beginning, according to Philo, and what is echoed in Hebrews 11 was order of an intellectual and structural sort. There is nothing until there is invisible order, and as with Philo (*Opif.* 29), so in Hebrews, the invisible provides a model for the other.[98] What is needed is not a material cause but an immaterial model; the *mē phainomena* are invisible things, not "nihil," which would make creation have its origins in rather unreliable stuff or nonstuff.

What does the cloud (of witnesses [12:1]) do? It gives *guidance* as the pillar of cloud did, as well as encouragement through remembrance of these heroes. Remembering those and looking toward the realities above might well help with "satellite" navigation. The tradition, to take Oecumenius once more as an example, regarded this cloud as that which offers shade from the sun's heat,[99] since those who were once evaporated by the heat now form a cloud for the sake of those remaining. This works through their beseeching God for the latter saints' sake, but subjectively also: the remembrance of the martyrs cools the heat of the Christian's temptation. Here one is well on the way to the Eastern doctrine of the intermediate state. Or, to give full value to the sense of *epikeimenōn* (literally, lying-around), it is simply that the cloud, unlike that in Exodus, does nothing to give believers any idea of where they are going, for, like Abraham, they remain pretty blind, having to feel their way by faith. This faith looks not only forward to hope but also back to the past, and in the present, faith allows God's power and invisible realities in providential motion to lead and encourage.

James 4:13–17

This text is too richly relevant to the task to overlook. The tradition of interpretation takes this text as applying more widely to the human condition as such: the rich merchants are simply stark and colorful examples of this. Arguably, that is exactly what verse 14 in particular means. Many commentators[100] want to reduce James 4:13–17 to a prelude to the main attack in 5:1–6 on rich people. But although James doesn't call either group in either passage

---

98. Eisele, *Ein unerschütterliches Reich*, 185.
99. Oecumenius, *Commentarius in Epistolam ad Hebraeos* 12 (PG 119:424).
100. Burchard, *Jakobusbrief*, 182; Konradt, *Christliche Existenz nach dem Jakobusbrief*, 154.

brothers,[101] and in fact makes the latter group seem way beyond penance and saving, James wants to remind the former in 4:13–17, who may yet be called back, to remember the demand of true *charity*. They are to spend more time and resources on the needs of the community, rather than on amassing capital.[102] They are the "wanna-be rich through hard work" kind, those who want to be literally self-made men. James here is bringing to their attention just who made and who keeps them.

Now some, such as Dale Allison, take this passage to be a momentary deviation in the letter's argument, one that tells one of the fragility of life, the better to underline the thin ice on which the rich are skating. "The ephemeral nature of human existence or of evildoers was a commonplace in the Jewish and Graeco-Roman worlds."[103] Allison then proceeds to give Old Testament verses that also insist that "everyone is a mere breath." The very "shortness and uncertainty of life is reason for repentance," as per 1 Chronicles 29:15 (LXX): "Our days are as a shadow on the earth, and there is no permanence" (AT).[104] The Peshitta of this verse makes this vivid: "We are comparable to the smoke of a pot, and we sojourn with you (God) and are of little account in the world" (AT). Also, 1 Clement 17.6 has Moses calling himself the *atmis* (smoke) of a pot.[105] There are no close rabbinic parallels. "The ἐάν presumes that God's will is in some sense unknown."[106] James would have been familiar with some idea of providence from the Pentateuch. Allison makes a good job of suggesting a common Jewish tradition behind the passage and the "in sha'a Allah" of Islam.

While this is all interesting, it shines a light much more on the human situation of weakness than on the capability of God. If life is merely a breath, without substance, how consoling is it that God's will is constant? What is the point of being moral if one's life is just a breath? Is this not more Stoic in its worldview? Perhaps the clue is in verses 15–16a: "Instead of you saying, 'If the Lord will, then we shall live and do this or that,' you are now boasting with your foolish words [*alazoneiais*]" (AT). The text does not have "you ought to say instead." James is still being critical of what they do (boast, but

---

101. Burchard, *Jakobusbrief*, 182.
102. Burchard, *Jakobusbrief*, 189.
103. Allison, *James*, 657.
104. Allison, *James*, 657.
105. 1 Clem. 17.5–6: "Moses was called faithful in all his house, and by his ministry God judged his people Israel by stripes and punishment. But he, though he was greatly glorified, spake not haughtily, but said, when the oracle was given him out of the bush, Who am I that thou sendest me? I am weak of voice and slow of tongue. And again he saith, I am but as the smoke from a pot."
106. Allison, *James*, 660.

now in the name of the Lord) and is not advocating an alternative. Yet the meaning comes pretty much to the same thing. The point is that the Lord is the one who sustains and offers all possibilities.

What we get in the Byzantine treatment (the commentary of Oecumenius once again, which is then republished under the name of Theophylact)[107] rings out in a similar key. God's will does not take away human *exousia* (authority or power) but shows that what happens does not lie in one's own hands but comes through the grace from above. For it is perfectly permissible to strive and run and do business and all things for life, so long as we do not reckon success to our own efforts but to the mercy of God. The way of a person is not in themselves but in the Lord. This Byzantine exegesis is happy to generalize, such that the precise nature of what the protagonists in James 4:13–17 were up to is not particularly relevant. Getting a lesson for the church is more important, and that lesson is that the Lord wishes human agents to align their wills with his. Hence, for the Byzantine exegesis, David (in Ps. 38:7) speaks about that which has no substance (NRSV: "no soundness"), only image. A vapor without substance. Oecumenius concludes: the fool (*alazōn*) is the one who lives with wandering (*alēs*)—that is, with instability.[108] One must learn not to use words arrogantly, but only to boast in the Lord, who says himself that the one who does then teaches is greater (Matt. 13:23).

What one can discern in this Byzantine exegesis is perhaps true to the spirit of the passage, for as Knut Backhaus has put it, James 4:13–17 expresses a fundamental theme of an everyday ethic ("theonomen Alltagsethik"), behind which lies a theonomous anthropology—namely, that humans are bound in their existence to the divine will.[109] This apparently tangential passage concerns the ontological and anthropological foundation for ethics that is Christian existence before God (*coram Deo*). It is neither a statement about rich and poor (so, Hubert Frankemölle)[110] nor a critique of Pauline missionary planning (so, Hengel), nor anything quite so particular. Instead, the will of God is presented as the material criterion of human action, as the limit of human autonomy and as the mover of the human constitution. As Backhaus concludes, Jewish-Christian bells are here playing the melody that Jesus proclaimed in the Sermon on the Mount, with some debt to Sirach especially. James can thus function as a bridge between Testaments, providing some theological continuity of subject ("theologische Sachkontinuität" [Frankemölle]).

---

107. Oecumenius, *Commentarius in Epistolam Jacobi* (PG 119:455–509) = Theophylact, *Expositio in Epistolam Jacobi* (PG 125:1131–90). Here PG 119:501.
108. Oecumenius, *Commentarius in Epistolam Jacobi* (PG 119:501).
109. Backhaus, "*Condicio Jacobaea*," 138. Cf. 144.
110. Frankemölle, *Der Brief des Jakobus*, 45–54.

Conclusion: The New Testament and Providence

Can "blessing" be considered as a further stage in salvation, one that builds on the gift of creation yet requires some amount of a restored relationship with God, such that assurance of God's interest in the life of family, community, and world follows from one's assurance of salvation and belonging to the body of Christ? In receiving the power of salvation the community is afforded an excess of life. One should thus unite the theme of ongoing natural gift and supernatural rescue.[111] Blessing and salvation are tied together, in such a way that *šālôm* means both cessation of hostility and the dividend of peace. James Loader has argued that as well as the beauty of Moses and David playing a part in the salvation of Israel, in Psalm 48 Zion's beauty, her providential ordering, contributes to her salvation from her enemies.[112] The contingency of createdness and "thisness" (*haecceitas*, in scholastic language) comes to the fore. Many of the Reformed theologians speak of a common-grace kingdom established by the Noachic covenant.[113] Rule by Logos and rule by Christ are distinct, even if they are to be integrated. "The imperatives of the Noahic covenant . . . come to people not as redeemed by God but as created and preserved by him . . . not as believers but as human beings."[114] Now, if believers or the people of God are further blessed because, as those with faith, they are aware of providence, this is not to say that only such people are the recipients of providence, even if only they have their providential care shaped according to the fact of their being on the way to full salvation.

---

111. Loader, "Schönheit zwischen Segen und Errettung," 165.
112. Loader, "Schönheit zwischen Segen und Errettung," 173.
113. VanDrunen, *Living in God's Two Kingdoms*.
114. VanDrunen, "Two Kingdoms and the Social Order," 448.

SIX

Systematic Considerations in the Light of Biblical Theology

Providence is not a doctrine that lacks the promise of therapeutic effects. For example, Job 23:10 ("But he knows the way that I take; when he has tested me, I will come forth as gold" [AT]) offers a reassuring reminder that divine surveillance followed by testing through suffering (cf. Ps. 26:2: "Test me and try me" [AT]) is for one's personal benefit. Yet, as Susannah Ticciati notes, this is not a case of searching out so as to bring people to themselves, but just as in Psalm 139:23–24 ("Search me, God, and know my heart; test me and know my anxious thoughts. See if there is any offensive way in me, and lead me in the way everlasting" [NIV]), it is more about the therapy of being brought *out of* oneself. The world is to be delighted in, but even more, God's way is to be welcomed.[1] She adds: "When [*ḥqr* (explore, search out) is] used of God's searching out of persons, then, a sense of the boundless, even aporetic, depths of the self is present—their *un*searchable nature being strongly connoted."[2] Perhaps, but more to the point, it is God who is the agent of change, pointing things out and correcting by leading in the right way. The

1. For that reason, Ticciati's claim, which owes something to Jung, has little foundation in the text: "His activity . . . for Job involves, not only his engagement in trial with Job, but his engagement in trial against himself. God's continual disruption of history, in other words, presupposes the more fundamental disruption within God." *Job and the Disruption of Identity*, 178.
2. Ticciati, *Job and the Disruption of Identity*, 177.

original (whether MT or LXX) refers not to human psychological depths but merely the seat of the moral will.

Well, is providence a doctrine that relates primarily to the human condition rather than to the doctrine of God? John Webster offered a dissenting voice amidst this trend: "The creaturely act of faith is the work of the Holy Spirit, a point at which reason is caught up in an antecedent, gracious causality which enables the intellect to see God and all things in God by locating its operations *coram Deo.* This is why faith in providence is only derivatively 'subjective,' an interpretation of and attitude toward the world. Primarily and strictly it is *objective*, generated and sustained by a movement from outside reason."[3] Likewise, obsession with the human condition has been at the root of the problem of mislocating the doctrine, according to David Burrell: "Redemption . . . has so overshadowed creation in the Christian sensibility that Christians generally have little difficulty adopting a naturalistic attitude toward the universe. Rather than approaching it and responding to it as a *gift*, they can easily treat it simply as a *given.* Three factors appear to have been decisive in fixing this stance: the liturgical shift from the sabbath to the 'day of the Lord,' connotative fallout from the medieval distinction of *supernatural* from *natural*, and the nineteenth-century cleavage of history from nature."[4] Burrell thinks that wisdom can be found in the Dominican Middle Ages: "Thomas incorporated into his synthesis the results of three centuries of prior labor by Muslim and Jewish thinkers."[5] The former are not altogether determinist: al-Ghazali, for instance, emphasizes mutual love between God and the intellect, and the Jewish sage Maimonides can affirm that providence "is constantly watching over those who have obtained this overflow, [and] that individual can never be afflicted with evil of any kind. For he is with God and God is with him."[6]

However, most theologians today think otherwise. Providence is less something divine, accessed by faith seeking understanding, than it *is* that very faith seeking understanding. Providence is a construct of faith to keep the

3. Webster, "Providence," 154; "Like the history of redemption that it accompanies and supports, providence is ubiquitous" (150). It is thus a "distributed doctrine" (150), connecting with many if not all other doctrines. Webster insists it remain firmly connected to the (trinitarian) doctrine of God. *Pace* Zwingli, providence is not a necessary "thing," necessitated by God's supremacy of being. In arguing that the history of the creation serves the order of grace, or that general providence serves special providence for the church, Webster comes too close to failing to distinguish their spheres of operation.

4. Burrell, *Freedom and Creation in Three Traditions*, 3.

5. Burrell, *Freedom and Creation in Three Traditions*, 95–96.

6. Maimonides, *Guide for the Perplexed* 3.51, quoted in Burrell, *Freedom and Creation in Three Traditions*, 132.

soul feeling consoled with a sense that there is meaning in life, a new sort of theodicy. As David Fergusson justly notes: "The vexed relationship of the theology of providence to theodicy is unavoidable. Questions of suffering and evil haunt the margins of every paragraph written on divine providence."[7] Yet that which is marginal need not always be front and center. Further, are not these "soul-making" theodicies unhappy attempts to make sense of suffering, when after all the lesson of Job is that "metaphysical evil" is a surd, and the New Testament affirms that only a radical change to creation will do? If that is the case, then more attention will be paid to what God is said to have done, is doing, could do, and will do. We shall indeed attempt this, after considering the "subjective" approaches.

Subjectivization

Like Fergusson and the other theologians alluded to above, some philosophical theologians, too, have recently been subjectivizing providence. For instance, John Polkinghorne: "I have come to believe that *the Creator's kenotic love includes allowing divine special providence to act as a cause among causes. . . .* However, there is theological attraction in identifying the working of the Spirit with pure information input."[8] This last phrase means that providence is more a concept that helps us adjust our interpretations and reactions to events than it is a claim being made about providence being at work in the events themselves. Moreover, theodicy is typically making sense of providence from the human side. If Polkinghorne suggests providence as something given in the form of information of an inspirational sort to humans, then, in a similar mode, Reinholdt Bernhardt argues that this providence is something rather powerful: "Providence is the field of force of God's Spirit which can be experienced in various forms: as spiritual guidance, as the power of resurrection in the midst of life, as a vigor of resilience, as the growing of new confidence and hope, and so on—especially in situations we experience as tragic. . . . God's activity in the world is not to be depicted as a series of personal acts but as a spiritual influence."[9] Hence, with Polkinghorne and Bernhardt, the Holy Spirit is cast as the *effector providentiae*,[10] in the sense of inspiring a response to adversity. One might call this an aesthetic-spiritual interpretation of providence.

7. Fergusson, *Providence of God*, 302–3.
8. Polkinghorne, "Kenotic Creation and Divine Action," 104–5.
9. Bernhardt, "Abraham's Dice in the Flow of Life," 334, 348.
10. Calvin, *Zacharias* 6.5, p. 206. Krusche (*Das Wirken des Heiligen Geistes nach Calvin*, 13) uses this term, which is not in the text, although the Spirit as *effector providentiae* well sums up Calvin's interpretation here.

A second form of the subjective model is a therapeutic and virtue-ethical one. This accords with what Eleonore Stump points to in the "life-story" of Teresa of Ávila, who learned to acquire "stern-mindedness," and therein lay divine providence for her.[11] As Fergusson recently commented: "What we find in the recent literature instead is a concentration on strategies of discipleship. These are set in dialectical opposition to the classical theodicies, the experiential being preferred to the theoretical. . . . But the drift towards an instrumentalisation of evil should be resisted. Its capacity for destruction cannot be wholly contained or resolved by a worldview in which it constitutes a necessary part of divine design."[12] Fergusson is surely right that not all that happens can be said to be God's will, however equivocally one glosses it as a dark means to a happy ending. In part human resistance (moral evil) and ontological fragility (metaphysical evil) conspire to make life shot through with what can be called "tragic" in the expanded sense of wasteful of potential and mocking of the good. It is thus correct to caution against looking to providence for a remedy or consolation for an evil, in terms of "instrumentalisation." The therapeutic model, where the self is to the fore, can be viewed in Richard Swinburne's comment that while general providence includes all that is good and effective about a person, "God's dealings with particular individuals, however, in response to their particular needs and requests, not in accordance with any general formula, manifest God's 'special providence.' This involves his intervening in the natural order of things"—although this is simply "a matter of inclining things to behave" in a certain way on a certain occasion rather than God's direct steering of creatures. Also, human beings are like subatomic particles—less predictable and more mysterious—such that divine intervention violates fewer rules of nature than one might think.[13] Special providence in Swinburne's account no longer has the connection with redemption and the church, but "the parable of Dives and Lazarus represents the good situation of Lazarus in the afterlife not as reward, or where he naturally fits because of his goodness, but as compensation for a bad life on Earth" (Luke 16:25).[14] For Swinburne, Lazarus is the disadvantaged everyman or even the troubled "I," discomfited by the plight of many. In the modern world is Lazarus not to be cared for by ethical human beings: is his evil even a spur to our moral growth? Is that where providence is truly found and expressed, in its cognate "prudence," as humans virtuously provide care for each other and thereby for themselves? All very well, but from this view the ecclesial

11. Stump, *Wandering in the Darkness*, 424.
12. Fergusson, *Providence of God*, 338, 341.
13. Swinburne, *Providence and the Problem of Evil*, 116.
14. Swinburne, *Providence and the Problem of Evil*, 116.

dimension, the notion that special providence is firstly for the people of God as a whole, is missing; likewise, any link with soteriology.

Cooperating with God: Prudence and Providence

For Giambattista Vico and the Enlightenment, world history, now having moved into the era of human reason and moral character, could "no longer" respectably think of itself as on its way to any goal. Any providence in the sense of purposeful, caring action was rather to be located in people's own deeds, and these attributable to the common nature of human beings. Fortunes come and go cyclically.[15] Vico still believed in some sort of determining progress that lent a hand, whereas a generation later, Voltaire believed that progress could be attained only if humans bettered themselves. Yet the point that human ethical action could *contribute* to providence was not disputed in the earlier Christian tradition. One thinks here of Melanchthon and, before him, Aquinas. It is worth appreciating that Aquinas says the following in the context of speaking about grace and supernatural ends: "Now He so provides for natural creatures, that not merely does He move them to their natural acts, but He bestows upon them certain forms and powers, which are the principles of acts, in order that they may of themselves be inclined to these movements, and thus the movements whereby they are moved by God become natural and easy to creatures, according to Wis. 8:1: 'she . . . ordereth all things sweetly.'"[16]

Law provides a rational rule that gives human action a reason, and not so much a "cause." It serves to direct action toward the flourishing of all the community and includes a corrective aspect. From *Summa theologiæ* I-II.90 one can learn that natural law as the image of eternal law on the human heart means that humans are "hardwired to seek happiness."[17] Here is a subjective element in providence, but it is less about illumination or some special form of intervention than about regular, natural operations in which humans are more the beneficiaries before they become agents.

Overall, then, it seems that Aquinas equates the natural law more or less with the Old Testament law, and this had an earthly goal primarily, with a heavenly goal only secondarily. The New Testament then comes along and reverses that order: heavenly goals first ("seek ye first the kingdom of God") and earthly ones second ("these things shall be added" [Matt. 6:33 KJV]). Nevertheless, even in the Old Testament that earthly goal had to

---

15. Rohls, *Geschichte der Ethik*, 397.
16. Aquinas, *Summa theologiæ* I-II.110.2.
17. Eardley and Still, *Aquinas*, 78.

be considered in light of "the good"—including heavenly beatitude—as a goal to which it half-blindly points and leads. It is a bit like the train line from Edinburgh to St. Andrews, Scotland: it is the line for St. Andrews, even though it stops four miles short of that goal, such that a new form of grace is needed to get there. The II-II section of the *Summa* records that, as the letter of the Old Testament law falls away, it is replaced by the internalized spiritual law, which provides grace and infused virtues for any virtuous life on its way freely and lovingly to meet Christ, who is "met" in the final, third part of the *Summa*. There this very Christ works like a head to his body, resourcing and improving it.[18] Yet prior to this third part—and this is important—the spiritual laws of Christianity, mediated spiritually in the context of love and freedom, are part of divine providence, for the assistance of *all* reasonable creatures, not just those in the church. In hard moral decisions it is never a case of honoring rules above values. In hard cases a human agent must sometimes leave the balancing of goods to providence and await further illumination in God's time—for the kingdom is "under construction."[19] "Prudence extends divine providence so that it reaches even to the most particular of moral actions."[20] The objective works through the subjective, even while not being reduced to it; the principle is similar to one that applies to machines, in that operating a machine is not so much about the action of supplying and oiling the various parts as about allowing the machine to run most efficiently.

This was grasped by a number of Scottish *philosophes* of the early Enlightenment. George Turnbull, the teacher of Thomas Reid, was the Aberdeen equivalent of a "providential naturalist," who "railed against the notion that man is fundamentally depraved and powerless against sin."[21] For Turnbull, Jesus's ministry was to tidy up creation and reveal clearly the universal good will of God.[22] Likewise for Reid himself, divine order meant that humans are called to order: providence implies prudence. (For Kant, these two objects of wonder—cosmic order and moral order—were equal, but not linked together.) The manifest goodness of the universe and the goodness of the God who created the universe and sustains it in existence were a major theme of the final work of Turnbull's contemporary Frances Hutcheson, the posthumously published *System of Moral Philosophy* (1755). In the *System* the moral sense is shown to be an essential means to the realization of God's providential

18. See Cessario, *Moral Virtues and Theological Ethics*, 38–39.
19. Balthasar, *Principles of Christian Morality*, 12.
20. Cessario, *Moral Virtues and Theological Ethics*, 92.
21. Suderman, *Orthodoxy and Enlightenment*, 213.
22. Turnbull, *Impartial Enquiry into the Moral Character of Jesus Christ*.

purpose.[23] Admittedly, as formulated by Adam Smith, the "impartial specta-tor" of the moral agent's "imaginative, sentimental reflection" has become the ideal (not the actual) moral society rather than the Deity.[24]

Providence and Eschatology

Most of "*general* providence" concerns God's constraining the natural order and keeping it going—although it can extend to history, in which God's activ-ity can be called "conservation" or restraint of active creatures. In some ways, while no means undisputed, this is the least controversial aspect of providence. To hear Fergusson once more: "A polyphony of providential themes is un-dergirded by one historical sequence that reflects a particular and definitive form of divine action."[25] Perhaps not much more can be said than that the ongoing basic goodness of creation should be affirmed. Kathryn Tanner offers a paraphrase of Barth, but in a way that brings out the distinctive emphases of her own work.[26] The incarnation brings humans closer to God than as mere partners. God's providence toward Israel leads them on the way to that partnership in the incarnation,[27] and providence's nature is pretty much determined by that way in which God determines to be God in Jesus Christ.

Finally, creation and providence are distinct from each other yet related to the grace of Christ as subordinate preconditions or presuppositions for a far more important given fact. They are the road or means to it. In this sense, creation and providence are the external bases for what God has always in-tended to do in Christ. God's being for us in Christ requires the existence of the world as a theater or space for its occurrence and requires the existence of created subjects who are to be God's partners made over in that special way by him.[28]

However, one might add that the biblical witness calls us also to have faith in an eschatology beyond incarnation, and that element seems missing in most twentieth-century accounts as well as in the Thomist one.[29] The problem is

23. Harris, "Shaftesbury, Hutcheson and the Moral Sense," 334.
24. Smith, "Smith and Bentham," 358: "Many assume that Smith's argument in the *Wealth of Nations* encourages a morality grounded in self-interest and utility calculation. But nothing could be further from the truth. Smith acknowledges that self-interest is a powerful motive in human life and argues that, when properly bounded by a sympathetically generated moral code, it forms itself into the useful virtue of prudence."
25. Fergusson, *Providence of God*, 316.
26. Notably her *God and Creation in Christian Theology*.
27. Tanner, "Creation and Providence," 117.
28. Barth, *Church Dogmatics*, III/1, 97. See Tanner, "Creation and Providence," 121.
29. Cf. Link, *Schöpfung*, 334.

that classical Christian eschatology has not always seemed like good news for those who suffer. Traditionally it has seemed to present the statistical probability of *not* being consoled, and that very anxiety promotes one more (and possibly extremely significant) source of misery. Moreover, eschatology is problematized by its speculative nature. One might argue that if we cannot be more than, say, 25 percent sure of what life after death will look like, even if we do believe that it will be favorable to all human creatures (and perhaps other creatures), how can such an uncertainty be consoling? Yet even if not consoling, it is, all the same, something one has to reckon with as part of the deposit or content of Christian faith. Although assurance of one's own salvation is not of the essence of faith—and one might add the corollary, that assurance of God's love toward oneself is not of the essence of faith— nevertheless, to have faith one needs to have faith that God is a God of love and therefore that he will bring salvation. It is not so much that all that is good must be saved and thereby has a claim on God, but that salvation of what is to be saved attests to its goodness as created. If there is some theology of hope informed by an eschaton that one can trust, then that theology has to do more than "realize" that eschatology in the soul, in idealist fashion. One needs a faith that "he shall come again to judge the living and the dead, and his kingdom shall have no end," and that this relates to and connects somehow with world history and the lives of those dead and alive. Jürgen Moltmann summarizes many decades of this thinking:

> Through the presence of his Wisdom and his Spirit the creator impels his creation towards its goal: it is destined to become the temple of his indwelling glory, as the prophet Isaiah saw in his call vision: "The whole earth is full of his glory" (6.3). All things are created, sustained and further developed so that they may become the shared house of created being, the eternal house of God. . . . The heavenly and the earthly will interpenetrate each other without intermingling. God in all things and all things in God: that is what is meant biblically by the kingdom of God. . . . If this is the church's all-embracing hope for the kingdom of God, then its universal mission is to prepare the way for this future.[30]

So the heavenly vision is an inspiration for Christian ethics. It requires future resurrection for the hope to become a reality. Up until then, humans are to take the initiative, it would seem, and so Moltmann's system lacks grace and providence. However, Moltmann is right to show the tie between that aspect of providence that is not simply about conservation and the goal of

30. Moltmann, *Sun of Righteousness, Arise!*, 31–32.

the eschaton.[31] This is preferable to the situation of his Lutheran colleagues who prefer to see a hiatus with the cross. Linearity and story continue in his scheme, with life becoming new life.

Not everyone is so sanguine. Walter Dietrich and Christian Link rejoice that already Schleiermacher excluded *Vorsehung* (providence) from his 1830 *Die Christliche Glaube*, 37.2, 164.2, since for him the divine purpose remained far too much darkened. "Providence," they think, has little biblical basis and at best offers a way for how things should be, which humans need to pursue. Yet if one thinks humans have that responsibility, this need not sound too Pelagian, if there is a place for God's accompaniment through presence. But, they claim, providence can no longer be a key to explaining the world.[32] For it presupposes "Stoic" omnipresence, omnicausality, and omnipotence. Yet Dietrich and Link admit (reminded by Helmut Gollwitzer) that life was no easier for the two Pauls, Fleming or Gerhardt, who endured the Thirty Years' War and very much were able to believe in providence. Accordingly, faith that does not need proof of providence before one's eyes, and may even seem "counterfactual": that indeed is what is required in such dire circumstances. Hence this faith cannot be taught as a doctrine, nor can we think of divine power as providing an explanation for anything. If one wants to keep "early modern" certainty, this must be done through a willed faith, not by a worldview.[33] One cannot *know* God's providence. It is better and more "biblical," they conclude, to focus on God's weakness. Yet Dietrich and Link are prepared to say that God's plans can be traced *in hindsight*, where he has worked in a hidden, subversive way, as his agents or instruments embrace weakness, whether David or Isaiah. God suffers in his people. A brief exegesis of Jeremiah and the Isaianic Servant Songs aligns with a "process" view of God, who gives his creation room, who is the latent possibility of creation, but is not guiding it.

Yet whoever claimed *certainty* about providence (*Providenzgewissheit*)? One might add that a little more acknowledging of God, a little more certainty of his providential rule (even if not of its content—in other words, *that* God reigns, not what God reigns over) might have stopped the crisis of faith in providence in the twentieth century and, consequently, a number of atrocities committed in the name of *homo deus*. Nonetheless, the two authors seem resigned to it, even to revel in it. We cannot sense God quietly at work in this technological, fast-living age, but suffering makes us value what is truly

31. Moltmann, *Das Kommen Gottes*, 46.
32. Dietrich and Link, *Die dunklen Seiten Gottes*, 2:254.
33. Dietrich and Link, *Die dunklen Seiten Gottes*, 2:255.

good and makes us long for help to regain it. Barth supplies a corrective by describing how the kingdom comes through prayer, reaching out to call in the divine purpose.[34] It is not enough to think that the New Testament answer[35] is simply the powerlessness of the cross, which continues to have effect as it offers humans a way to call for God's justice.[36] Yet of course "hidden working" does not imply "powerless working," as is suggested by Dietrich and Link: God does not use evil, but endures it while condemning it and annihilating it. The modern world is not simply an endless "Good Friday" (*Karfreitag*), where hope intensifies pain—as they claim.[37] One cannot confess Easter without mentioning God's vindication of Jesus Christ and the implications of that.

Dietrich and Link further consider how God's end judgment is not a reckoning up of where past events were leading or a denial of primal life but is a new affirmation of that life. God will put things right, but not in this world. Yet this denial of the ends of history swaps a modern problem for a postmodern one: before the Judge of the world the whole creation sinks into nothing, from which God once called it.[38] For this Lutheran theology, it is only in the eschaton that God rediscovers his power, to free creation from evil and powerlessness. This reduces God to a Deist shadow, who sends his Son and Spirit only to withdraw again. Informed by the hope witnessed to by prophets and apostles, we might well say that God is working his purposes out in a cruciform manner, but he is still working (John 5:17) on his way to full salvation.

Mode of Divine Operation

The second question is: Assuming God *is* even now at work, how does this working happen? According to the Lutheran Scholastic Johannes F. König, a general influence (*influxus generalis*) works in all things: the immediate presence of God mixed with secondary causes.[39] God's plan becomes more something worked from bottom upwards, not from the top down. The earth can be explained without recourse to a bigger plan or to a cosmological fixing of things.[40] Special providence, starting with a group of people who,

34. See Svinth and Põder, *Doxologische Entzogenheit*, 93.

35. Svinth and Põder, *Doxologische Entzogenheit*, 268.

36. Svinth and Põder, *Doxologische Entzogenheit*, 314; cf. 310.

37. Svinth and Põder, *Doxologische Entzogenheit*, 309, with reference to Hegel, *Glauben und Wissen*, 124.

38. Svinth and Põder, *Doxologische Entzogenheit*, 345.

39. Ratschow, *Lutherische Dogmatik zwischen Reformation und Aufklärung*, 209. Cf. Ratschow, *Von den Wandlungen Gottes*.

40. See Deuser, "Vorsehung," 312.

filled with the Spirit, have "Christ in [them], the hope of glory" (Col. 1:27), can be extended from a category that concerns only the church to a wider category of "kingdom" (God's particular interactions with the unfolding course of creation's history).[41] Hence there is a salvation history in a wider, more implicit sense, reaching out to join forces with a wider providence. The history of salvation is the not-quite-so-hidden (assuming lives transformed, witness given) core of providence as the hidden dimension of all history. It is coextensive with profane history yet *knowable* only from the vantage point of the special ecclesial history of salvation, which is constituted by the Word of God. In distinguishing between general and special providence one is made to place only the nonhistorical aspects—the regularities of planetary life—in the former "box."[42] Even while the visible history of the church is interminably mingled with history in general, that ecclesial history that is hidden within history lies behind all of history, even if only accessible with help from the "sacramental" church history, which provides necessary though not sufficient "information." While one can argue about how objective "history" or "church history" is, any account of "hidden history" or "providence" is subjective, speculative, and in flux, because it springs from a faith that one is being led (Pannenberg: "Führungsglaube") and lives in a "betweenness," from Adam to the Second Adam.[43] Even Augustine did not give up on the history of the world so as to ignore it, but saw it as the sphere of battle between good and evil and believed in a prophetic gift that could read trajectories of despair, but also of hope: the salvation of God appeared in Jesus once and can again appear in the world through human action as the power of God inspiring such.[44] On this view of providence *God is* providing a good for humans to reach toward—and that can be a form of inspiration that also promotes humility, so that the human cooperation in ethical form is visible human history too, but with an invisible inspiration.

"Our complaint against historicism is that it has made every act of providence by definition an act of salvation."[45] Yet "we must not champion 'saving history' so zealously that the kingdom of God ceases to be the purpose and destiny of all history."[46] What Oliver O'Donovan means here seems

41. Polkinghorne, "Kenotic Creation and Divine Action," 101.
42. Pannenberg, "Weltgeschichte und Heilsgeschichte," 362.
43. Pannenberg, "Weltgeschichte und Heilsgeschichte," 363. This movement is for Pannenberg happening within all religions, at the level of religious consciousness in a sort of "Glaubensgeschichte" (history of faith).
44. Pannenberg, "Weltgeschichte und Heilsgeschichte," 366.
45. O'Donovan, *Resurrection and Moral Order*, 66.
46. Gregory, "Boldness of Analogy," 76, quoting O'Donovan, *Resurrection and Moral Order*, 65–66.

to be that the kingdom of God is more than just the truth of Christ being witnessed to and souls being saved; it includes purposes that are neither properly salvific nor simply natural ends, but are goods somehow related to salvation. Eric Gregory, noting that Augustine did have room in his theology for making the world a better place, asks: "But might an Augustinian vision admit something like infused civic virtues in light of salvation history? Can we differentiate yet also analogize civic and theological virtues? Might some civic virtues, including justice and courage, participate in, and have as their object, some type of redemptive end?"[47] One could certainly admit this, but only if one has a positive account of providence and believes that God is at work at all. It is this very premise that has been disputed at least since the Enlightenment, even by theologians: "History, as a strictly causal sequence, has no salvific power, reflects no universal or providential order, has no metaphysical yield. In a sense the eschatological liberates time from the burden of history."[48] There is no necessity in the sense that there are no ends constraining history. What is given in the eschaton is the giving-back of creation.

Indeed, Giorgio Agamben has criticized post-Enlightenment theology for aping philosophy and propounding a Christology that is almost nontheological. The Hegelian version of incarnation has driven God's will from the field by viewing it as absorbed by human initiative.[49] Yet the world abhors a vacuum. Hence micromanaging human government has stepped in to fill the void and mirrored an absolute will through its acting in the name of the people, but in effect, as Foucault suggested, this has meant the arrogating of divine-like powers to governmental authorities. "La providence, qui trouve son origine dans l'oikonomia trinitaire" (providence, which finds its origin in the trinitarian economy)[50] becomes overidentified with the world, and the modern "God" becomes a *Deus otiosus* (redundant God). Of course the Bible suggests that God is interested in the details, as opposed to the view of Alexander of Aphrodisias, for whom any deity who reigned would leave the world to its own purposes. Proclus anchored providence in nature as being the divine knowledge of wholes and individuals. This knowledge necessitates things without thereby causing them, so that liberty would be excluded. Nevertheless, there is a noble biblical and philosophical tradition that insists that only the God of the universe can be the one who is powerful enough to engage with details while preserving creaturely freedom.

47. Gregory, "Boldness of Analogy," 83.
48. Hart, *Beauty of the Infinite*, 397.
49. Agamben, *Le règne et la gloire*, 421.
50. Agamben, *La règne et la gloire*, 178.

Nobody seems to appreciate an "occasionalist" God with a constant "hit and run" modus operandi.[51] Hence it behooves the theologian to be more subtle as God is subtle within his creation, not at all coming at it from without. "Providence refers to the ways in which God *provides* for human (and other) creatures to achieve their proper ends in the face of the threat posed by evil."[52] Ian McFarland rightly notes the occasionalistic problem of the *creatio continua* idea, that creation does not have sufficient autonomy and that God's constant coming down and keeping things going does not give creatures enough of their own causal capacity; the God described by this view might fairly be described as a "tinkering deity." The providence that God gives creatures is the help to move forward on their own feet. In *De potentia Dei* 3.3.6 Aquinas speaks of the continuous shining of a light source, rather than "discrete acts of re-creation." "Creatures' preservation, no less than their creation, is thus a matter of grace."[53] One might only want to question whether that light cannot act in a discrete manner, unless one thinks only subjectively, in terms of "information." To act constantly and by way of *concursus* (as well as by preservation and governance) need not mean "occasionalism," but complements the constant work of preservation. The use of the language of grace is not totally unwelcome, for providence is over and above what is given in creation and is in that sense an antidote to sin, but it is wider than that. Perhaps the language of grace might better be avoided, in light of what follows.

Grace Is Already Given in Nature?

Let us take two examples where "grace" might be seen to do the work of providence. First, Henri de Lubac insisted that for Thomas Aquinas the desire to see God was certainly a desire of human nature, and so it remains to show how this desire is still always by grace, irrespective of matters of sin and pardon. The power of seeing God is the *potentia obedientialis* (potential to obey).[54] *Potentia* here is not as an inherent potency, but exists as a possibility to come to one, which will depend on some form of encounter for its fulfillment, according to God's good pleasure. In that state of affairs there is something providential, presoteriological. It is grace, but not, as Fénelon

51. "Occasionalism" is an aspect of the thought of Malebranche and Jonathan Edwards that has not been well received in recent times.
52. McFarland, *From Nothing*, 136.
53. McFarland, *From Nothing*, 142.
54. De Lubac, *Le mystère du surnaturel*, 85.

said, "a debt under the name of grace."[55] The modern hypothesis says that God has decided for this world to make it as it is, such that there is no place for such a "more humble" destiny. However, grace was not simply "given" in Adam but remains there as an invitation to each one in a providential offer of happiness.

For de Lubac, this ongoing gift is relational and personal, not merely "natural," and that means (as in Augustine) that there is no essential order beyond what is historical; but to be historical is part of the metaphysics of creation. This means no pure empiricism, even though we speak out of the experience of providence traced and made clear by experience of the protagonists in Scripture: "Ex legibus divinae praesentis Providentiae, Scripturarum revelatione manifestis."[56]

For grace to be gratuitous another end must be possible in theory, and that end is not damnation but that of purely natural vision. Yet in actuality God gives himself[57] in such a way that grace is prior (temporally and logically) to any faith or conversion.[58] Thus there exists no pure nature at all, but a situation of being offered transformation into a new creation. God wills the liberty of humans to glimpse their true destiny.[59] One cannot comprehend truth even when it can be tacitly "understood." When Thomas Aquinas[60] says that all creatures are made for God's sake ("universa propter semetipsum operatus est Dominus"), he quotes Proverbs 16:4.[61] In everything God is first. "Before they call, says the Lord, I will respond" (in de Lubac's French: "En tout, Dieu est premier. 'Avant qu'ils appellent, dit le Seigneur, je répondrai' [Isa. 65:24]").[62] Zechariah 1:3's "Turn back to me, . . . and I will turn back to you" (AT) has to be complemented by the less Pelagian-sounding verse from Lamentations 5:21: "Make us return to you, Lord, and we will return!" (AT).

Humans have a spiritual nature (albeit with a physical finality), one that was purely natural to Adam, but lost by Adam in such a way that fallen man felt no longer "called," even though the calling remains and a trace of it can be felt. This nature may have been a *donum superadditum* (additional gift) with Adam that was then withdrawn (this was developed out of Cajetan by Suarez to the point that this state of nature is the case for all humans qua humans),

55. De Lubac, *Le mystère du surnaturel*, 89, citing Fénelon, *Réponse à la Relation sur le Quiétisme*.
56. De Lubac, *Le mystère du surnaturel*, 91–96.
57. De Lubac, *Le mystère du surnaturel*, 106.
58. De Lubac, *Le mystère du surnaturel*, 106.
59. De Lubac, *Le mystère du surnaturel*, 132.
60. Thomas Aquinas, *In II Sententiarum*, distinctio 19, 1.2.
61. Prov. 15:3 Vulg.: "In omni loco oculi Domini contemplantur malos et bonos."
62. De Lubac, *Le mystère du surnaturel*, 129.

but, no, that is not the end of the story within creation. Aquinas speaks of a gift made by love and love itself as maintaining that gift. Bonaventura saw this in Psalm 103:30 (Vulg. [104:30 EV]: "Emittes spiritum tuum et creabuntur et instaurabis faciem terrae"; You send out your spirit and renew the face of the earth) as a second creation of grace.[63] The imprint of a Spirit-made capacity *and* a lack (hence *not* "natural" but "graced") is how it all operates, but is inchoate in that it is made by grace, which will render it ready for operations of the divine. Although this grace is not from within our nature and never becomes part of us even when "habitual"—for there is freedom and not necessity on either side—nevertheless it attaches to our nature. God has made us for himself, so the image of God serves to pull us up, unlike the image of God in the thought of the Belgian theologian Michael Baius (1513–89), for whom it was something necessary within us to get us going. As Cajetan put it, that love that Aquinas spoke of is beyond us and outside us.[64]

In many ways this account of human gifting and capacity is welcome, and yet it feels all too anthropocentric. Theological anthropology almost replaces the realms of creation, providence, and salvation. At points, the graciousness of grace is not altogether maintained in de Lubac's system, and because this account represents grace as "potential," it ends up representing the human spirit as retreating from the God of creation and history to the higher ground of "soul," with action in the world still to be realized by human endeavor. Some recent interpreters have offered a modified version of de Lubac, which speaks about grace *as* the desire, in the sense of a restless "felt lack." This makes it truly anthropological and therefore without pretensions as a pseudoprovidence, a built-in motor for human spiritualization. Yet this seems a retreat from history, from life.

A recent interpretation of de Lubac is offered by Jean-Yves Lacoste, who comments that "pure nature" is only *philosophically* possible. It has no place *in theology*; for in the state of nature the soul would not feel troubled by the lack of a vision of God. "Hegel disenchants the future so that the present can accommodate the fullness of time and the fullness of man's relation with God; and with that it is goodbye to history—goodbye, at any rate, to history's pretensions to carry ontophanic and ontopoetic responsibilities."[65] So much for actual providence: the moment of *knowing* is all. Heidegger had only philosophy as consolation. De Lubac saw human beings feel a natural sense

63. De Lubac, *Le mystère du surnaturel*, 123, with reference to Pseudo-Dionysius, *On the Celestial Hierarchy*, and the commentary thereon by John Scotus Eriugena with reference to James 1:17: datum optimum = natura; donum perfectum = gratia.

64. De Lubac, *Le mystère du surnaturel*, 289.

65. Lacoste, "Henri de Lubac and a Desire beyond Claim," 362.

of lack and a desire that outreaches "claim." "In talk of 'provisionality' we are concerned with something different: the dependency of present reality upon an absolute future, exposed to its measure and critique."[66] Such provisionality does not claim definitive presence: "I am not master of my desires; what I desire I do not truly know. I might even say, in a manner of speaking, that there is something that desires *within* me, rather than that 'I' desire for myself."[67] It is hard to *know* anything in this provisionality. It allows joy while knowing that this cannot be perpetual, only "moments": this is a restlessness that can counter or overwhelm petty anxiety. However, the coming end "is the only thing that can put an end to the logic of instability that governs every joy within the world, not excepting *true* joys, as when one senses the nearness of God here and now."[68] God is not an end deducible from what we already know—since we cannot know that which is beyond our experience and reason without that knowledge becoming a projection of what has been learned from this world. Also, as Cyril O'Regan insists, the church is the carrier of a mysterious history; yet it is only the vehicle: "It is not progressively teleological in the way that an acorn will in due course yield an oak." One must beware idealism; the church only *carries* the kingdom.[69] In sum, this version of *surnaturel* does not seem either to overwhelm nature or to triumphantly postulate human nature as containing a graced identity that might make faith and baptism unnecessary. That is reassuring, but in all the "negative," qualifying talk of provisionality one misses the positivity of providence, that God is working something out on the basis that his creation as he made it is already good in and for itself. Against Jean-Luc Marion's idea of "meaning-saturated experience," Ephraim Radner proposes: "I am suggesting the converse here: when God acts creatively and self-sufficiently, this world—and ourselves—is what we get."[70] Yet one can also allow providence to absorb too much, as when Radner paraphrastically quotes 1 Corinthians 6:19–20 ("I am not my own—I am bought at a price"), then comments: "Among other things, this statement of Paul means that I am a temporal being." It seems to rob soteriology of its discrete place in God's working. Yet the overall point—that this temporality, understood as God using his creation, does not require pure passivity but a reaching out and up by human creatures to know more of grace—is apposite, as when Radner adds: "Temporal being, from a moral standpoint, is all about

66. Lacoste, "Henri de Lubac and a Desire beyond Claim," 365.
67. Lacoste, "Henri de Lubac and a Desire beyond Claim," 366.
68. Lacoste, "Henri de Lubac and a Desire beyond Claim," 368.
69. O'Regan, "A Theology of History," 297. Mention should be made of de Lubac's *La posterité spirituelle de Joachim de Fiore.*
70. Radner, *Chasing the Shadow*, 11.

searching after, discerning, and embracing the purpose of divine grace in the existence of all things. Our lives are in part themselves a vocation to search for this connection."[71] The critique of de Lubac offered by recent Catholic writers seems often on target, not least their assumption that theology *must* be able to speak a common language with natural science.[72] However, in my view, the language of "providential order" is to be preferred to that of "pure nature" in some diachronic extension since creation, concurrent with the history of grace.

Second, and in Protestant style, one can use the language of "blessing" rather than of "graced nature." David Kelsey writes that blessing is fully realized due to some kind of dialectic of creation and reconciliation, but for fuller blessing beyond that, eschatology could be the key to a third story line. This "line" is one that is unlike the narratives of God's deeds of deliverance, which concern episodes. No, it is more like the Bible's accounts of God relating to his people in creative blessing. Scripture's narratives of actualized eschatological blessing describe an ongoing steady-state relationship between God and creatures. For Kelsey, the irruption into history of the end time and the circumambience of the Spirit are a blessing on creation from the God beyond time who also related outside of himself in order to create. That is part of the fore of the technical theological formula that is "the Father" who "sends" the Spirit. Kelsey calls as his witness for the Old Testament "Claus Westermann, who has pointed out that 'blessing' is understood in two distinctive ways in Scripture. First, God's blessings are distinct from God's mighty deeds of deliverance. . . . In blessing God relates continuously and creatively. . . . Second, although many deeds of divine deliverance occur in history, there are two abiding conditions of history: creation as the blessing expressed by stories of a primal time, and consummation expressed by stories of the blessing of the end time."[73]

One might want to interject: Just which are these narratives of consummate blessing in the Bible? If only a few early chapters of Genesis, then it is hardly a story line. For Westermann himself has described Genesis 1–11 as prehistorical, communicating existential and everlasting truths about creation and humanity.[74] It is better to think in terms of providential "discourse" in a number of genres, operating in various biblical books. Moreover, Kelsey's account of eschatology sounds almost static and impersonal, like a coating on top of creation, only lent personality by its being tailored to individual

---

71. Radner, *Chasing the Shadow*, 30.
72. See Long, *Natura Pura*; Mulcahy, *Aquinas's Notion of Pure Nature*.
73. Kelsey, *Eccentric Existence*, 1:447.
74. See Westermann, *Genesis 1–11*.

human circumstances. This leaves the soteriological "deeds of deliverance" as the only locus of "personal" divine action.

Kelsey, who is perhaps overly indebted to the Old Testament or a particular reading of it as being a book of hoping rather than a book about the thing hoped for, believes that the eschatological consummation narrative absorbs the creation one and the salvation one, joining them as it does so. Salvation is not the fundamental purpose of incarnation, he thinks, for *that* is more about communion. However, stories of God's relation to all else on the way to eschatological consummation are absorbed into this salvation narrative, not as stories of a distinct and different way in which God relates, but actually all as stories of the final moment of God relating by way of incarnation. (He claims this to be both Irenaean and Schleiermacherian.)[75] It does not even follow that the Spirit is primarily located in the church. The storied presence of eschatological blessing does not mean progressive improvement, for the apocalyptic vision reminds us that there is not a process from within, not even a liberal form of liberation,[76] whatever one wishes to argue about "continuity." So, Kelsey thinks, it might be better to affirm: "What God relates to in eschatological blessing is what is constituted by God relating creatively."[77] In other words, for Kelsey, it is something established transcendently and transcendentally that draws out possibilities from what is actual, taking them out of the historical flow.

Yet surely providence also comes *before* salvation *as well as following it*, and is very much *in* history. Providence accompanies salvation like a strand woven through it, although salvation has a confirmatory, revelatory, explicit aspect to it. Providence is thus in the equipping toward the calling of apostles and teachers for the sake of the kingdom/evangelism. It includes building up the church: special providence is that which is ecclesial in scope, as distinct from the *providentia specialissima* of individuals. Hence, if salvation is shaped by Christ's story toward sanctification, then providence is the human story shaped or given an imprint by that of the church qua people of God, and that includes Christians qua ordinary people. There is in all this a place for creativity—not something we possess as reflecting the image and then exercise in such a way that as recreation it excludes God, although we do have our secularity: culture is allowed as a good. But while distinct, culture does not so much point away toward the transcendent God as witness to the joy of the

75. Kelsey, *Eccentric Existence*, 1:466.
76. Kelsey, *Eccentric Existence*, 1:490. The New Testament scholar J. Louis Martyn (*Galatians*) helps him here to see that the tension between good and evil builds as history progresses, yet nobody knows what the goal of history is.
77. Kelsey, *Eccentric Existence*, 551.

Creator as present (*creator presens*). That is perhaps to be seen by some as an invasive and oppressive presence, but that is to confuse the *Deus revelatus* with the *Deus absconditus*.[78]

Yet mere presence is not what providence is for, if "mere presence" means simply the securing of a relatively peaceful life for the average person, although it might *include* that. Olivier Boulnois reminds us that Matthew 10:16–31, which warns disciples to expect persecution, is full of tragic irony because martyrdom is expected, but the consolation comes from laying weight on the happiness of the soul rather than that of the body. Sudden bad luck in Luke 13:5 ("unless you repent, you too will all perish" [NIV]) is viewed as in fact being cast by the shadow of eschatological condemnation. Here providence seems directed toward the action of judgment—of the hidden God;[79] or perhaps the idea is more that like that expressed by the fig tree of verses 8–9: a last chance is being given; and even that disaster at Siloam (vv. 4–5) is pedagogical—appealing to our freedom, to prepare us for end, to seek pardon and reconciliation.[80] John 9, the counterpoint to Luke 13:5, reinforces the converse of what seems like bad luck so that the bad luck becomes an opportunity for God to work. Things (states of blessing or curse) are not what they seem.[81] In all this God knows not to cure too quickly, for some amount of human dispositional and ethical responsibility is a prerequisite for God's action to care and save. As Origen saw (*Or.* 29), God's care could actually be excessive in a negative way, in order to treat his people with a sort of aversion therapy.[82]

The Story of Providence: Comedy, Tragedy, or Neither?

The "theater of God's glory" metaphor goes back beyond Calvin to John of Salisbury, and possibly further back.[83] One could argue that by placing "God in his providential economy" into a theater and a dramatic schema, where there is resolution, then a pleasing finality might be made too much into a "god," or God becomes not even a *deus ex machina* as simply one of the players, albeit an all-knowing and very influential one. Yet the point of tragedy is that God's character seems to underachieve. There are no resolutions. In fact, Rowan

78. Hürliman, *Das Einsiedler Welttheater*, 96.
79. Boulnois, "Unser Gottesbild und die Vorsehung," 309.
80. Boulnois, "Unser Gottesbild und die Vorsehung," 310.
81. Thissen, "Schöpfungsbejahung und Kreuzesnachfolge."
82. Stritzky, *Studien zur Überlieferung und Interpretation*, 175.
83. John of Salisbury, *Policraticus*, chap. 3, "De mundana comedia vel tragedia." Cf. Pieper, "Unter dem Schirm des Höchsten?," 353, concerning the case of Calderon.

Williams argues that tragedy is a sobering genre, meant to instruct people in the art of becoming more self-aware, even at the expense of tidy and happy endings. Hence Euripides stopped the chorus from having a "normalizing" function by commenting on the tragic narrative from a position of collective sanity. The bleaker it is, the better for us, if we can only stand to be challenged by it.[84] The tragic hero finds that "in his passion to be 'good' without cost or shadow he has guaranteed that he cannot now be good at all."[85] His problem is that he is no longer a stranger to himself. Tragedy teaches us to be realistic about conflict and not to be complacent about our own capacity. To be able to tell of or represent loss is to manage it.[86] So it was unhelpful of George Steiner to set tragedy against Christianity, since the latter's vision is at least *partly* tragic. The tradition of German *Trauerspiel* in the early modern era, with all its easy certainties, was arguably a contamination of the genre of tragedy. There are limits to what God can do. So says Williams, who thinks that it is perhaps better to say that God comes onstage only after the play is finished, at the dawn when the nightmare is over. "The last thing Hegel is saying is that everything is all right really, that individual wreckage is smoothed over by universal benefit. . . . It is about sustaining the conviction that what has happened is, precisely, outrageous, menacing, and yet at the same time capable of contemplation and of being represented in speech."[87] And that aesthetic, by stretching our thinking, even as truth and self fall apart, might lead to transformation, not least, one might wish to add, by enabling us to become "the less deceived" through less misrecognition.

Steiner's antithesis of Christianity and tragedy has been recently reinforced by David Bentley Hart in the name of a more robust Christian faith. He complains that the tragic (Christian) outlook overaccommodates itself to evil, whereas in truth evil is not sewn together with good creation, but has absolutely no place in it. For Hart, the cross was merely a political accident, not something necessitated. Whereas tragedy universalizes the status quo,

84. Williams, *Tragic Imagination*, 11 (in agreement with Nussbaum, *Fragility of Goodness*): "The further implication is that tragedy obliges us to pay attention to sheer *circumstance*, to the different pressures and impulses that are at work on actual agents in the world." For Hegel, tragedy has to do with the self's misrecognition and the ethical implications of that misrecognition. Tragedy allows one to re-view one's self, the better not to be too easily caught up in mass movements.

85. Williams, *Tragic Imagination*, 12. See Edith Hall's review, "Rowan Williams's Tragic Mistake," where she writes: "It leaves an agnostic such as myself still failing to understand how such a committed Christian as Williams can reconcile his faith with what seems to be a complete lack of belief in a 'happy ending' for any individual or for the human race as a whole."

86. Williams, *Tragic Imagination*, 15.

87. Williams, *Tragic Imagination*, 71.

Jesus and the resurrection challenge it. Tragedy assumes a fixed universe bearing down on poor human individuals. John Milbank, too, has challenged this "deterministic" worldview in the name of a better order and some common decent morality (*Sittlichkeit*), which good Christian drama calls for.[88] But Williams goes further: the crucifixion will not be purified of its less salutary effects "until the Second Coming," and before then there will be a history of, for example, Christian anti-Semitism. As he puts it, "resurrection does not cancel crucifixion," at least not for now. In a too-quickly-letting-go of past identities and their sober home truths, one can lose growth. Rather than always looking ahead, one should always be aware that one's "past actions have been 'released' into a world of both consequences and meaning in which countless other processes, decisions and determinations are at work," whatever one's "good intentions."[89]

The ending of Job is not restoration or reward, for the moral world resists this idea of having to pay exactly for sin or that of obliging God to pay up. Williams would speak of "healing without cure," where there is neither erasing nor explanation nor again compensation for injury. This is reminiscent of Donald MacKinnon, for whom, because he resists Hegel, tragedy demands a belief in transcendence through a sense of nonresolution here below.[90]

Tragedy, while a vehicle for mourning, also teaches us that debt and calculus don't determine outcomes, such that appropriate mourning in the confusion means "affirming neither absolute guilt nor absolute innocence." Tragedy does strongly imply that the lives of human beings are under necessity.[91] Tragic knowledge involves a reconciliation of the self with the incompatibility of competing demands and forces, the collision of competing rights.[92] Of course tragedy in the Christian vision does not exclude the presence of comedy in and through the resurrection of Jesus. By itself meaningful human existence can go no further; yet with grace, as Williams concludes, the blow can be softened: "But damage matters because *what is damaged* or lost or wounded matters, and matters lastingly and ineradicably. . . . Tragedy points towards a comedy

88. See Hart, *Beauty of the Infinite*, 374–83.

89. Williams, *Tragic Imagination*, 114.

90. Wallace, *Cambridge Introduction to Tragedy*, 188: "But as far as Mackinnon was concerned, any attempt to 'move beyond tragedy,' by explaining the mystery or seeing in it a 'traceable providential order,' was deeply suspect." See MacKinnon, "Some Reflections on Hans Urs von Balthasar's Christology."

91. Williams, *Tragic Imagination*, 119. "There is therefore a multiple necessity to the story of Jesus's suffering: the cross stands where it does because of God's eternal purpose and character, because of Jesus's identity as 'sent' on behalf of God's purpose, embodying divine gift, and because of the world's self-inflicted closure against God" (122).

92. Roche, *Tragedy and Comedy*.

that imagines a restored body where the wounds are not ignored or belittled or explained away, healed rather than cured, to go back to Nussbaum's terms."[93] It might be better to coin the term "comi-tragedy." It still remains tragic, whatever else. This despite Hart's assurance that "in the light of Easter, the singularity of suffering is no longer tragic (which is to say, ennobling), but merely horrible, mad, everlastingly unjust."[94] No, God is able to handle it.

Terry Eagleton has argued that modernity has made things worse, since more people expect to achieve more, and this in itself is indeed tragic. The world is not in our control, but we are answerable to it. He cites Northrop Frye: "Tragedy seems to elude the antithesis of moral responsibility and arbitrary fate."[95] Steiner transposes this into theological terms: "This nucleus (*Ur-grund*) is that of 'original sin.' Because of that fall or 'dis-grace,' in the emphatic and etymological sense, the human condition is tragic. It is ontologically tragic, which is to say, in essence."[96] Yet for Eagleton, this is far too much like resignation for a moral religion like true Christianity.

Yet one could argue, along with Williams that far from simply overwhelming tragedy with comedy, Christian theology made the tragic go deeper, to an original hopelessness, a fall from grace. "In Adamic and Calvinistic monotheism, punishment emanates from an offended, vengeful deity."[97] Seventeenth-century Jansenist playwright Jean Racine might well have thought that Christ would be in agony till the end of time, and indeed the silence of the character Berenice was deafening. "The Sun watches her throughout the play: silent, remote to the point of absence, but of piercing intensity, like the *Deus absconditus* of Jansenism."[98] The character Phèdre cannot even die, and she will go on suffering in Hades. Sure, Racine's tragedy was antipolitical in its utter rejection of the political temporal world, and Eagleton reckons that Racine was "sub-Christian" here. Again, against Steiner's views Eagleton complains: "Even the author of the last act of *Lear* fails to be glum enough to qualify for kosher tragic status." As humans we need hope for things to get better: progress, although not "Progress." Although Aristotle found tragedy useful, he did not build his "ethical" worldview on it (so, Stephen Halliwell),[99] and nor should we. Yet the darkness in eschatology is not something to be left behind,

93. Williams, *Tragic Imagination*, 157.
94. Hart, *Beauty of the Infinite*, 393.
95. Frye, *Anatomy of Criticism*, 211.
96. Steiner, "Tragedy Reconsidered," 30.
97. Steiner, "Tragedy Reconsidered," 33. Cf. 44: "Desiderated: an adequate theory of comedy, of the riddles of grief, singular to man, in the merriment of *Twelfth Night* or the finales of *Così fan tutte*."
98. Critchley, "I Want to Die, I Hate My Life," 171.
99. Halliwell, "Unity of Art without Unity of Life?"

but to be remembered, as Aquinas (and painters in his wake) articulated the resurrected Christ still bearing his wounds.

Eagleton caricatures Steiner's position but then shows that worse is postmodern escapism: "The resurrection annuls the crucifixion, resolving it into eschatological comedy. Steiner does not see that the cliché 'all's well that ends well' is just as much a banal half-truth now as it was when Shakespeare misguidedly adopted it as a play title. Which is not to say that discontinuities cannot be overdone as well. What else, one might inquire, is postmodernism, which celebrates discontinuities (in non-tragic spirit, to be sure), while demonising continuity?"[100] Yet to be fair to him, Steiner was clear that tragedy and comedy do coexist within the Christian vision. Shakespeare's vision is of the "tragi-comic weave of the world, its refusal to be one thing at a time," although Timon of Athens is an exception: "Here the universe itself is made pestilential."[101]

Eagleton, railing against Steiner's view that glumness and a hope for another world, not this world, are the hallmark of tragedy, argues that one should recognize tragedy in the ordinary, nonreligious life in order to ameliorate it.[102] Likewise, Martha Nussbaum: "In short, instead of conceding the part of ethical space within which tragedies occur to implacable necessity or fate, tragedies, I claim, challenge their audience to inhabit it actively, as a contested place of moral struggle, a place in which virtue might possibly in some cases prevail over the caprices of amoral power, and in which, even if it does not prevail, virtue may still shine through for its own sake."[103] Pity means action. It seems as though Eagleton's concern that there be a recognition of the value of the ordinary regards eschatology as simply an upgrade of the mundane, rather than the total transformation of renewal, as in 1 Corinthians 15:42–44, where the seed and the crop are very different in status. Renewal is very much God's work, as much as there is ethical cooperation.

Whatever Christ is the telos of, Christ is not a culmination and fulfillment of all tragedy, "the heir of all tragedy" (Balthasar),[104] but he can be a model

---

100. Terry Eagleton, "A Response," 133. Cf. 135: "As far as rupture goes, Jesus's death is absolutely final—which is to say that only by accepting that this is the last word can it somehow cease to be so, and a form of life in continuity with it be inaugurated. It is this dialectic of acceptance or letting go, on the one hand, and transfiguration, on the other, that we find at the core of a great deal of tragic art. And this is at the same time a revolutionary continuity between the special and the common, as an act of extremity becomes the foundation of the ordinary."

101. Steiner, "Tragedy Reconsidered," 12.

102. On this, see Eagleton, "Commentary," 344.

103. Nussbaum, *Fragility of Goodness*, xxxvii.

104. Taylor, *Hans Urs von Balthasar and Christ the Tragic Hero*, chap. 7. Cf. Balthasar, *Creator Spirit*, 400.

of how to live in it. "What does take time and repeated good fortune to heal is the corruption of desire, expectation, and thought that can be inflicted by crushing and prolonged misfortune."[105] Yet precisely that is possible, although it requires a trusting faith in a Christocentric resolution of the tragicomedy in which providence can find its place.

Conclusion

One sees the outworking of providence overreaching into soteriology in the universalist tendency in Eilert Herms's *Systematische Theologie*. Communion ("Gemeinschaft") with Jesus becomes the community of humanity, and vice versa, as a further extension of the trajectory of inclusion operating from "OT" to "NT."[106] Such communion involves securing the confidence of and in "life," uniting a link back to the originary power ("Ursprungsmacht") and to "common life."

Yet Christian faith *trusts* in the living God, with a very sober form of ecstasy that is located in the ground for hope, in that God is more forgiving and more in control of events than we will ever be. Faith has to have a cognitive element, that which is the ground of trust: creed for sake of trust in God at all times.[107] Yet it relies on and presupposes God's trusting initiative, one that has brought life out of death and light out of darkness, most creatively.[108] Trust corresponds to and latches on to trustworthiness of the Other. Life relationships are a context for good things to get done.[109] God is encountered in the world not least in the meshing of vocations and the forming of community.[110] Trusting confidence (*Vertrauen*) may be better than belief or faith (*Glauben*) to get at what Paul means in Romans 3:28. Yet the text is about reaching out to the providential God for help in the life of faith rather than salvation from sin.[111] Hans Weder thinks that it is divine *Vertrauen* that resonates with human trust. The Word creates this. One can think here either of Thomas Aquinas on the concept of faith in Hebrews or Wilhelm Herrmann's distinction between the ground and the content of faith; the former is the growing

105. Nussbaum, *Fragility of Goodness*, 337.
106. He sums this up with "Die Christusoffenbarung ist der Anfang der Erfüllung dieser Verheißung und Erwartung" (cf. Herms, *Systematische Theologie*, 1:481). See §§13–16 generally.
107. Dalferth and Peng-Keller, *Gottvertrauen*, 15.
108. Dalferth, "Vertrauen und Hoffen," 421. Cf. Weder, "Glaube, Hoffnung, Vertrauen," 89.
109. Weder, "Glaube, Hoffnung, Vertrauen," 102.
110. Jenkins, *Experiment in Providence*, 20–24.
111. Koch, "Geleitwort," 19. See also Dalferth and Peng-Keller, *Grundvertrauen*; Lassak, *Grundloses Vertrauen*.

confidence through the personal life of Jesus. Faith allows thankfulness for salvation, yes, but equally for creation, for which all people could be thankful. It is seeing the God of creation providentially giving a guarantee of his commitment to creation in his self-determination in Christ.[112] One believes when one gets that God somehow even puts trust in us (cf. the parable of the talents in Matt. 25:14–30), and one in return resolves to live life as thankful for life as gift.[113] Faith is thus a critical standpoint to life, one that considers counterfactuals and is open to new possibilities in trust. It does not balk at the stern words of Jesus in Luke 13:4: "Or those eighteen upon whom the tower in Siloam fell and killed them, do you think that they were worse offenders than all the others who dwelt in Jerusalem?" (RSV).

Length of years as sign of blessing is not so prominent in the New Testament. Long and healthy life is a good thing, and the Old Testament helps us to remember the gift of existence along with somehow the dignity and calling of "in the image of God" and "life together," but this existence is a penultimate good, as death, like birth, comes through a narrow space.[114] Yet, again the New Testament message is to embrace or at least stand easy about suffering in the shadow of death. One has gone there before; as for him, so also for Peter and for us, a time will come when we will be carried to where we do not want to go, but in that trustful surrender we may go. "Shall we receive the good at the hand of God, and not receive the bad?" says Job (Job 2:10), whom the early church saw as a martyr because, although his suffering seemed unlike that of martyrs, its motivation and execution was satanic dislike of a godly witness. The apocalyptic side to Christianity allows for judgment as something through which new life comes (pruning, the green wood, etc. as a favorite metaphor), so that when love emerges, it is purer, stronger, ready to embrace opposites as though alike.

As seen in the parable of the prodigal son, part of God's fatherly providence is that he extends trust to his human children enough to wait for them to come to trust him. That trust includes obeying his commands (Eccles. 12:13; John 14:15). This is not quite the same as "desire of the heart" being broken and remade into desire for God, as Stump has argued,[115] but rather is a disposition that is content with "Our Father . . . , your kingdom come."

---

112. Dalferth, "Vertrauen und Hoffen," 427.
113. Dalferth, "Vertrauen und Hoffen," 433.
114. Luther, *Sermon von der Bereitung zum Sterben*, 1521.
115. Stump, *Wandering in the Darkness*, 481.

Bibliography

Adam, Klaus-Peter. "Saul as a Tragic Hero: Greek Drama and Its Influence on Hebrew Scripture in 1 Samuel 14,24–46 (10,8; 13,7–13A; 10,17–27)." In *For and against David: Story and History in the Books of Samuel*, edited by A. Graeme Auld and Erik Eynikel, 123–85. BETL 232. Leuven: Peeters, 2010.

Adams, Samuel L. *Wisdom in Transition: Act and Consequence in Second Temple Instructions*. JSJSup 125. Leiden: Brill, 2008.

Agamben, Giorgio. *Le règne et la gloire*. Vol. 2, part 2 of *Homo sacer*. Translated from Italian by Joël Gayraud and Martin Rueff. Paris: Seuil, 2008.

Aitken, James K. "Divine Will and Providence." In *Ben Sira's God: Proceedings of the International Ben Sira Conference, Durham-Ushaw College, 2001*, edited by Renate Egger-Wenzel, 282–304. BZNW. Berlin: de Gruyter, 2002.

Aletti, Jean-Noël. *Quand Luc raconte*. Paris: Cerf, 1998.

Alexander, Loveday. *Acts in Its Ancient Literary Context*. LNTS 289. London: T&T Clark, 2007.

Allen, Leslie. *Psalms 101–150*. WBC 21. Waco: Word, 2002.

Allison, Dale. *James: A Critical and Exegetical Commentary*. ICC. London: Bloomsbury T&T Clark, 2013.

Alter, Robert. *The Art of Biblical Narrative*. New York: Basic Books, 1981.

———. *The Art of Biblical Poetry*. New York: Basic Books, 1985.

———. *The David Story: A Translation with Commentary of 1 and 2 Samuel*. New York: Norton, 1999.

André, Gunnel. *Determining the Destiny: PQD in the Old Testament*. ConBOT 16. Lund: Gleerup, 1980.

Anselm, Rainer. "Systematische Theologie: Schöpfung als Deutung der Lebenswirklichkeit." In *Schöpfung*, edited by Konrad Schmid, 225–94. Themen der Theologie 4. Tübingen: Mohr Siebeck, 2012.

Aquinas, Thomas. *Commentary on the Epistle to the Hebrews*. South Bend, IN: St. Augustine's Press, 2006.

―――. *Summa theologiæ*. Blackfriars ed. 61 vols. 1963–75. Reprint, New York: Cambridge University Press, 2006.

Assmann, Jan. "Das Doppelgesicht der Zeit im altägyptischen Denken." In *Die Zeit*, edited by A. Peisl and A. Mohler, 189–223. Schriften der Carl Friedrich von Siemens Stiftung 6. Munich: Oldenbourg, 1983.

―――. *Ma'at: Gerechtigkeit und Unsterblichkeit im Alten Ägypten*. Munich: Beck, 1990.

―――. "Vergeltung und Erinnerung." In *Studien zu Sprache und Religion Ägyptens*, festschrift for W. Westendorf, edited by F. Junge, 2:687–701. Göttingen: Vandenhoeck & Ruprecht, 1984.

Attridge, Harold. *The Epistle to the Hebrews: A Commentary on the Epistle to the Hebrews*. Hermeneia. Philadelphia: Fortress, 1989.

―――. *The Interpretation of Biblical History in the "Antiquitates Judaicae" of Flavius Josephus*. Missoula, MT: Scholars Press, 1976.

Auerbach, Erich. *Mimesis*. Princeton: Princeton University Press, 1952.

Auld, A. Graeme. *I & II Samuel*. OTL. Louisville: Westminster John Knox, 2011.

―――. "Reading Genesis after Samuel." In *The Pentateuch*, edited by Thomas Dozeman, Konrad Schmid, and Baruch Schwartz, 459–69. Tübingen: Mohr Siebeck, 2011.

Avemarie, Friedrich. "Heilsgeschichte und Lebensgeschichte bei Paulus." In *Heil und Geschichte: Die Geschichtsbezogenheit des Heils und das Problem der Heilsgeschichte in der biblischen Tradition und in der theologischen Deutung*, edited by Jörg Frey, Stefan Krauter, and Hermann Lichtenberger, 357–83. WUNT 1/248. Tübingen: Mohr Siebeck, 2008.

Backhaus, Knut. "*Asphaleia*: Lukanische Geschichtsschreibung im Rahmen des antiken Wahrheitsdiskurses." In *Wahrheit und Geschichte: Exegetische und hermeneutische Studien zu einer dialektischen Konstellation*, edited by Eva Ebel and Samuel Vollenweider, 79–108. ATANT 102. Zürich: TVZ, 2012.

―――. "*Condicio Jacobaea*: Jüdische Weisheitstradition und christliche Alltagsethik nach Jak 4:13–17." In *Schrift und Tradition: Festschrift für Josef Ernst zum 70 Geburtstag*, edited by Knut Backhaus and Franz Georg Untergassmair, 135–58. Paderborn: Schöningh, 1996.

―――. *Der Hebräerbrief*. 2nd ed. RNT. Regensburg: Pustet, 2009.

―――. *Der sprechende Gott: Gesammelte Studien zum Hebräerbrief*. WUNT 1/240. Tübingen: Mohr Siebeck, 2009.

―――. "Lukanische Geschichtsschreibung im Rahmen des antiken Wahrheitsdiskurses." In *Wahrheit und Geschichte: Exegetische und hermeneutische Studien zu einer dialektischen Konstellation*, edited by Eva Ebel and Samuel Vollenweider, 79–108. ATANT 102. Zürich: TVZ, 2012.

Baden, Joel. *The Historical David: The Real Life of an Invented Hero.* New York: HarperCollins, 2013.

Balentine, Samuel. *The Hidden God: The Hiding of the Face of God in the Old Testament.* OTM. Oxford: Oxford University Press, 1983.

———. *Job.* SHBC 10. Macon, GA: Smyth & Helwys, 2006.

———. "The Poet as Intercessor: A Reassessment." *JBL* 103 (1984): 161–73.

Balthasar, Hans Urs von. *Creator Spirit.* Translated by Brian McNeil. Vol. 3 of *Explorations in Theology.* San Francisco: Ignatius, 1993.

———. *Principles of Christian Morality.* St. Bonaventure, NY: Franciscan Institute, 1954.

Barclay, John. "Grace within and beyond Reason: Philo and Paul in Dialogue." In *Paul, Grace and Freedom: Essays in Honour of John K. Riches,* edited by Paul Middleton, Angus Paddison, and Karen J. Wenell, 9–20. London: T&T Clark International, 2009.

Barclay, John M. G., and Simon J. Gathercole. *Divine and Human Agency in Paul and His Cultural Environment.* London: Bloomsbury, 2007.

Bar-Efrat, Shimon. *Erste Buch Samuel: Ein narratologisch-philologischer Kommentar.* Translated from modern Hebrew by Johannes Klein. Stuttgart: Kohlhammer, 2007.

Barnard, Jody A. *The Mysticism of Hebrews: Exploring the Role of Jewish Apocalyptic Mysticism in the Epistle to the Hebrews.* Tübingen: Mohr Siebeck, 2012.

Barr, James. *The Semantics of Biblical Language.* London: SCM, 1961.

Barth, Karl. *Church Dogmatics.* Edited by G. W. Bromiley and T. F. Torrance. Translated by G. W. Bromiley, G. T. Thomson, et al. 4 volumes in 13 parts. Edinburgh: T&T Clark, 1936–77.

———. *Kirchliche Dogmatik.* 4 vols. in 13 parts. Munich: Kaiser, 1932; Zürich: Evangelischer Verlag, 1938–65.

———. *Offene Briefe, 1945–1968.* Edited by D. Koch. Gesamtausgabe V.15. Zürich: TVZ, 1984.

Barton, John. "Gerhard von Rad on the World-View of Early Israel." *JTS* 35 (1984): 301–23.

———. "Natural Law and Poetic Justice in the Old Testament." *JTS* 30 (1979): 1–14.

Baumgartner, Hans Michael. *Kontinuität und Geschichte: Zur Kritik und Metakritik der historischen Vernunft.* Frankfurt am Main: Suhrkamp, 1972.

Bauspieß, Martin. "Die Gegenwart des Heils und das Ende der Zeit: Überlegungen zur lukanischen Eschatologie im Anschluss an Lk 22,66–71 und Apg 7,54–60." In *Eschatologie—Eschatology: The Sixth Durham-Tübingen Research Symposium; Eschatology in Old Testament, Ancient Judaism and Early Christianity,* edited by Hans-Joachim Eckstein, Christof Landmesser, and Hermann Lichtenberger, 125–48. WUNT 272. Tübingen: Mohr Siebeck, 2011.

————. *Geschichte und Erkenntnis im lukanischen Doppelwerk.* Arbeiten zur Bibel und ihrer Geschichte 42. Leipzig: Evangelische Verlagsanstalt, 2012.

Beale, G. K. *The Book of Revelation: A Commentary on the Greek Text.* NIGTC. Grand Rapids: Eerdmans, 1999.

Bechtel, Carol. *Esther.* IBC. Louisville: Westminster John Knox, 2002.

Becker, Jürgen. "'Bei dir ist die Quelle des Lebens' (Ps 36,10): Lebensverständnis und Lebensgestaltung in biblischer Sicht." In *Leben. Verständnis. Wissenschaft. Technik. Kongressband des XI. Europäischen Kongresses für Theologie, 15.–19. September 2002 in Zürich,* edited by Eilert Herms, 52–69. Gütersloh: Gütersloher Verlagshaus, 2005.

Beer, Gillian. *Darwin's Plots: Evolutionary Narrative in Darwin, George Eliot and Nineteenth-Century Fiction.* London: Routledge & Kegan Paul, 1983.

Beinert, Wolfgang. "Weltgericht und Weltvollendung bei Paulus." In *Weltgericht und Weltvollendung—Zukunftsbilder im Neuen Testament,* edited by Hans-Josef Klauck, 85–105. QD 150. Freiburg: Herder, 1994.

Berges, Ulrich. "Hiob in Lateinamerika." In *The Book of Job,* edited by W. A. M. Beuken, 297–317. BETL 114. Leuven: Peeters, 1994.

Berjelung, Angelika. "Divine Presence for Everybody." In *Divine Presence and Absence in Exilic and Post-exilic Judaism,* edited by Nathan MacDonald and Izaak J. de Hulster, 67–93. FAT 2/61. Tübingen: Mohr Siebeck, 2013.

————. "Weltbild/Kosmologie." In *Handbuch theologischer Grund Begriffe zum Alten und Neuen Testament,* edited by Angelika Berlejung and Christian Frevel, 65–72. Darmstadt: Wissenschaftliche Buchgesellschaft, 2006.

Berlin, Adele. *Esther.* JPS Bible Commentary. Philadelphia: Jewish Publication Society, 2001.

Bernhardt, Reinhold S. "Abraham's Dice in the Flow of Life." In *Abraham's Dice: Chance and Providence in the Monotheistic Traditions,* edited by Karl W. Giberson, 333–52. Oxford: Oxford University Press, 2016.

————. *Was heißt "Handeln Gottes"? Eine Rekonstruktion der Lehre von der Vorsehung.* Gütersloh: Gütersloher Verlagshaus, 1999.

Bickerman, Elias. *Four Strange Books of the Old Testament: Jonah, Daniel, Koheleth, Esther.* New York: Schocken Books, 1967.

Black, Matthew. "The Interpretation of Romans viii 28." In *Neotestamentica et patristica: Eine Freundesgabe, Oscar Cullmann zu seinem 60 Geburtstag,* edited by W. C. van Unnik, 166–72. NovTSup 6. Leiden: Brill, 1962.

Block, Daniel. *Judges, Ruth.* NAC 6. Nashville: Broadman & Holman, 1999.

Blumenthal, C. *Basileia bei Lukas: Studien zur erzählerischen Entfaltung der lukanischen Basileiakonzeption.* HBS 84. Freiburg: Herder, 2016.

Böckler, Annette. *Gott als Vater im Alten Testament.* Gütersloh: Güterslöher Verlagshaus, 2000.

Bockmuehl, Markus. "Abraham's Faith in Hebrews 11." In *The Epistle to the Hebrews and Christian Theology*, edited by R. Bauckham, N. MacDonald, and D. Driver, 355–70. Grand Rapids: Eerdmans, 2009.

Bonhoeffer, Dietrich. *Widerstand und Ergebung: Briefe und Aufzeichnungen aus der Haft*. Munich: Kaiser, 1955.

Boring, M. Eugene. *Revelation*. IBC. Louisville: John Knox, 1989.

Boström, Lennart. *God of the Sages: The Portrayal of God in the Book of Proverbs*. ConBOT 29. Stockholm: Almqvist & Wiksell, 1990.

Boulnois, Olivier. "Unser Gottesbild und die Vorsehung." *Communio: Internationale Katholische Zeitschrift* 31 (2002): 303–23.

Bovon, François. *De vocatione gentium: Histoire de l'interprétation d'Act. 10, 1–11, 18 dans les six premiers siècles*. Tübingen: J. C. B. Mohr (P. Siebeck), 1967.

———. *Das Evangelium nach Lukas II (9:51–14:35)*. EKKNT 3/2. Neukirchen-Vluyn: Neukirchener Verlag, 1996.

———. *Luke the Theologian*. 2nd ed. Waco: Baylor University Press, 2006.

Brague, Rémi. *La sagesse du monde: Histoire de l'expérience humaine de l'univers*. Paris: Fayard, 2001.

Brown, Stewart J. *Providence and Empire: Religion, Politics and Society in the United Kingdom, 1815–1914*. Harlow: Pearson Longman, 2008.

Brueggemann, Walter. *1 & 2 Kings*. SHBC. Macon, GA: Smyth & Helwys, 2001.

———. *First and Second Samuel*. IBC. Louisville: Westminster John Knox, 1990.

———. "From Hurt to Joy, from Death to Life." *Interpretation* 28 (1974): 3–19.

———. "The God Who Gives Rest." In *The Book of Exodus: Composition, Reception, and Interpretation*, edited by Thomas Dozeman, Craig A. Evans, and Joel Lohr, 565–90. VTSup 164. Leiden: Brill, 2014.

Bundvad, Mette. *Time in the Book of Ecclesiastes*. Oxford: Oxford University Press, 2015.

Burchard, Christoph. *Der Jakobusbrief*. HNT 15/1. Tübingen: Mohr Siebeck, 2000.

Burke, Edmund. *A Philosophical Enquiry into the Sublime and Beautiful*. Oxford: Oxford University Press, 2015.

Burrell, David. *Freedom and Creation in Three Traditions*. Notre Dame, IN: University of Notre Dame Press, 1993.

Butler, Trent C. *Judges*. WBC 8. Grand Rapids: Zondervan, 2014.

Calvin, John. *Commentary on the Book of Psalms*. Translated by James Anderson. Edinburgh: Calvin Translation Society, 1848.

———. *Institutes of the Christian Religion*. Edited by John T. McNeill. Translated by Ford Lewis Battles. Philadelphia: Westminster, 1960.

————. *Sermons de Iehan Calvin sur le Cantique que feit le bon roy Ezechias après qu'il eut este malade & affligé de la main de Dieu: Selon qu'il est contenu en Isaie, chapitre XXXVIII.* Geneva: François Estienne pour Estiene Anastase, 1562.

————. *Zacharias.* In *Ioannis Calvini Opera Quae Supersunt Omnia,* vol. 44, edited by Guilielmus Baum, Eduardus Cunitz, and Eduardus Reuss, 125–392. Brunsvigae: C. A. Schwetschke et Filium, 1890.

Camponovo, Odo. *Königtum, Königsherrschaft und Reich Gottes in den frühjüdischen Schriften.* OBO 58. Freiburg: Universitätsverlag, 1984.

Cancik, Hubert. "The History of Culture, Religion, and Institutions in Ancient Historiography: Philological Observations concerning Luke's History." *JBL* 116 (1997): 673–95.

Cessario, Romano. *Moral Virtues and Theological Ethics.* 2nd ed. Notre Dame, IN: University of Notre Dame Press, 2008.

Childs, Brevard S. *Biblical Theology of the Old and New Testaments: Theological Reflection on the Christian Bible.* Minneapolis: Fortress, 1992.

Clayton, Philip. "Creation *ex Nihilo* and Intensifying the Vulnerability of God." In *Theologies of Creation: Creatio Ex Nihilo and Its New Rivals,* edited by Thomas Jay Oord, 17–30. New York: Routledge, 2015.

Clines, David. *Job 1–20.* WBC 17. Waco: Word, 1989.

————. *Job 21–37.* WBC 18A. Nashville: Thomas Nelson, 2006.

————. *Job 38–42.* WBC 18B. Nashville: Thomas Nelson, 2011.

Colish, Marcia L. "Stoicism and the New Testament: An Essay in Historiography." *ANRW* 26.1: 334–79. Part 2, *Principat,* 26.1. Edited by H. Temporini and W. Haase. Berlin: de Gruyter, 1992.

————. *The Stoic Tradition from Antiquity to the Early Middle Ages.* 2 vols. Leiden: Brill, 1985.

Colson, F. H., ed. and trans. *Philo.* 10 vols. Loeb Classical Library. Cambridge, MA: Harvard University Press, 1929–62.

Cook, Stephen L. "God's Real Absence and Real Presence." In *Divine Presence and Absence in Exilic and Post-exilic Judaism,* edited by Nathan MacDonald and Izaak J. de Hulster, 121–50. FAT 2/61. Tübingen: Mohr Siebeck, 2013.

Cosgrove, Charles. "The Divine *Dei* in Luke-Acts: Investigations into the Understanding of God's Providence." *NovT* 26 (1984): 168–90.

Crabbe, Kylie. "Accepting Prophecy: Paul's Response to Agabus with Insights from Valerius Maximus and Josephus." *JSNT* 39 (2016): 188–208.

————. "Being Found Fighting against God: Luke's Gamaliel and Josephus on Human Responses to Divine Providence." *ZNW* 106 (2015): 21–39.

————. "Luke/Acts and the End of History." DPhil thesis, Oxford University, 2017.

Craigie, Peter. *Psalms 1–50.* WBC 19. Waco: Word, 1983.

Crenshaw, James L. "The Birth of Skepticism in Ancient Israel." In *The Divine Helms-man: Studies on God's Control of Human Events*, edited by James Crenshaw and Samuel Sandmel, 1–19. New York: Ktav, 1980.

———. *Old Testament Wisdom: An Introduction*. Louisville: Westminster John Knox, 1998.

———. *Samson: A Secret Betrayed, a Vow Ignored*. Atlanta: John Knox, 1978.

———. "Theodicy and Prophetic Literature." In *Theodicy in the World of the Bible*, edited by Antti Laato and Johannes C. de Moor, 236–55. Leiden: Brill, 2003.

Critchley, Simon. "I Want to Die, I Hate My Life—Phaedra's Malaise." In *Rethinking Tragedy*, edited by Rita Felski, 170–98. Baltimore: Johns Hopkins University Press, 2008.

Crüsemann, Frank. *Wie Gott die Welt regiert: Bibelauslegungen*. Munich: Kaiser, 1986.

Cruz, Juan. *"Who Is like Yahweh?" A Study of Divine Metaphors in the Book of Micah*. FRLANT 263. Göttingen: Vandenhoeck & Ruprecht, 2016.

Dalferth, Ingolf. *Becoming Present: An Inquiry into the Christian Sense of the Presence of God*. Studies in Philosophical Theology 30. Leuven: Peeters, 2006.

———. "Vertrauen und Hoffen: Orientierungsweisen im Glauben." In *Gottvertrauen: Die ökumenische Diskussion um die Fiducia*, edited by I. Dalferth and S. Peng-Keller, 406–34. QD 250. Freiburg: Herder, 2012.

Dalferth, Ingolf, and Simon Peng-Keller, eds. *Gottvertrauen: Die ökumenische Diskussion um die Fiducia*. QD 250. Foreword by Kurt Cardinal Koch. Freiburg: Herder, 2012.

———. *Grundvertrauen: Hermeneutik eines Grenzphänomens*. Leipzig: Evangelische Verlagsanstalt, 2013.

Dell, Katharine J. *The Book of Job as Sceptical Literature*. BZAW 197. Berlin: de Gruyter, 1991.

———. *The Book of Proverbs in Social and Theological Context*. Cambridge: Cambridge University Press, 2006.

———. "'Cursed Be the Day I Was Born!' Job and Jeremiah Revisited." Chap. 8 in *Reading Job Intertextually*, edited by Katharine Dell and Will Kynes. LHBOTS 574. New York: Bloomsbury T&T Clark, 2013.

de Lubac, Henri. *Le mystère du surnaturel*. Paris: Aubier, 1965.

———. *La postérité spirituelle de Joachim de Fiore*. 2 vols. Paris: Lethielleux, 1979–81.

Deuser, Hermann. "Vorsehung: Systematische Theologie." *TRE* 35:302–23.

de Vaux, Roland. *Les institutions de l'Ancient Testament*. Paris: Cerf, 1958. Translated by John McHugh as *Ancient Israel: Its Life and Institutions*. London: Darton, Longman & Todd, 1961.

D'Hamonville, David-Marc. *Bible d'Alexandrie: Les Proverbes*. Paris: Cerf, 1986.

Dietrich, Walter, and Christian Link. *Die dunklen Seiten Gottes*. 2 vols. Neukirchen-Vluyn: Neukirchener Verlag, 1995–2000.

Dillon, Richard J. "Ravens, Lilies, and the Kingdom of God (Matt. 6:25–33/Luke 12:22–31)." *CBQ* 53 (1991): 605–27.

Dilthey, Wilhelm. *Poetry and Experience*. Vol. 5 of *Selected Works*. Princeton: Princeton University Press, 1985.

Döhling, Jan-Dirk. *Der bewegliche Gott: Eine Untersuchung des Motivs der Reue Gottes in der Hebräischen Bibel*. HBS 61. Freiburg: Herder, 2009.

Dohmen, Christoph. *Exodus 1–18*. HTKAT. Freiburg: Herder, 2015.

———. *Exodus 19–40*. HTKAT. Freiburg: Herder, 2004.

Doll, Peter. *Menschenschöpfung und Weltschöpfung in der alttestamentlichen Weisheit*. Stuttgart: Katholisches Bibelwerk, 1985.

Downey, Patrick. *Serious Comedy: The Philosophical and Theological Significance of Tragic and Comic Writing in the Western Tradition*. Lanham, MD: Lexington Books, 2001.

Dozeman, Thomas. *Exodus*. ECC. Grand Rapids: Eerdmans, 2009.

Dunne, John. *Esther and Her Elusive God*. Eugene, OR: Wipf & Stock, 2014.

Duthie, Charles. "Providence in the Theology of Karl Barth." In *Providence*, edited by Maurice F. Wiles, 62–76. London: SPCK, 1969.

Eagleton, Terry. "Commentary." In *Rethinking Tragedy*, edited by Rita Felski, 337–46. Baltimore: Johns Hopkins University Press, 2008.

———. "A Response." *Literature & Theology* 19 (2005): 132–38.

Eardley, Peter S., and Carl N. Still. *Aquinas: A Guide for the Perplexed*. London: Continuum, 2010.

Ebeling, Gerhard. *Dogmatik des christlichen Glaubens*. Vol. 1, *Prolegomena: Der Glaube an Gott, den Schöpfer der Welt*. Tübingen: Mohr Siebeck, 1979.

Eberlein, Karl. *Gott der Schöpfer—Israels Gott*. 2nd ed. Frankfurt: Lang, 1989.

Ego, Beate. *Im Himmel wie auf Erden: Studien zum Verhältnis von himmlischer und irdisscher Welt im rabbinischen Judentum*. WUNT 2/34. Tübingen: Mohr Siebeck, 1989.

Eichrodt, Walther. *Theology of the Old Testament*. 2 vols. Philadelphia: Westminster, 1961–67.

———. "Vorsehungsglaube und Theodizee im AT." In *Festschrift Otto Procksch: Zum sechzigsten Geburtstag am 9. August 1934 überreicht*, edited by Albrecht Alt, 45–70. Leipzig: A. Deichert'sche Verlagsbuchhandlung, 1934.

Eidevall, Göran. *Amos: A New Translation with Introduction and Commentary*. AYB 24G. New Haven: Yale University Press, 2017.

Eisele, Wilifried. *Ein unerschütterliches Reich: Die mittelplatonische Umformung des Parusiegedankens im Hebräerbrief*. BZNW 116. Berlin: de Gruyter, 2003.

Eisenbaum, Pamela. *The Jewish Heroes of Christian History: Hebrews 11 in Literary Context*. SBLDS 156. Atlanta: Scholars Press, 1997.

Elliott, Mark W. *The Heart of Biblical Theology: Providence Experienced*. London: Routledge, 2016.

Engberg-Pedersen, Troels. *Cosmology and Self in the Apostle Paul: The Material Spirit*. Oxford: Oxford University Press, 2010.

———. *John and Philosophy: A New Reading of the Fourth Gospel*. Oxford: Oxford University Press, 2017.

Enns, Peter. *Ecclesiastes*. THOTC. Grand Rapids: Eerdmans, 2011.

Essen, G. "Gottes Treue zu uns: Geschichtstheologische Überlegungen zum Glauben an die göttliche Vorsehung." *Communio: Internationale Katholische Zeitschrift* 36 (2007): 382–98.

Exum, J. Cheryl. *Tragedy and Biblical Narrative: Arrows of the Almighty*. Cambridge: Cambridge University Press, 1992.

Exum, J. Cheryl, and J. William Whedbee. "Isaac, Samson and Saul: Reflections on the Comic and Tragic Visions." *Semeia* 32 (1984): 5–40.

Fackenheim, Emil L. *God's Presence in History*. New York: New York University Press, 1970.

Fascher, Erich. "Theologische Beobachtungen zu δεῖ." In *Neutestamentliche Studien für Rudolf Bultmann zu seinem siebzigsten Geburtstag am 20. August 1954*, 228–54. BZNW 21. Berlin: Töpelmann, 1954.

Feldmeier, Reinhard. *Der Höchste: Studien zur hellenistischen Religionsgeschichte und zum biblischen Gottesglauben*. WUNT 1/330. Tübingen: Mohr Siebeck, 2014.

———. "Gott und die Zeit." In Feldmeier, *Der Höchste*, 337–55.

———. "Wenn die Vorsehung ein Gesicht bekommt: Theologische Transformationen im Neuen Testament." In *Vorsehung, Schicksal und göttliche Macht: Antike Stimmen zu einem aktuellen Thema*, edited by Reinhard G. Kratz and Hermann Spieckermann, 147–70. Tübingen: Mohr Siebeck, 2008.

Feldmeier, Reinhard, and Hermann Spieckermann. *Der Gott der Lebendigen: Eine biblische Gotteslehre*. Tübingen: Mohr Siebeck, 2011. Translated by Mark E. Biddle as *God of the Living: A Biblical Theology*. Waco: Baylor University Press, 2011.

———. *Menschwerdung*. Tübingen: Mohr Siebeck, 2017.

Fergusson, David. *The Providence of God: A Polyphonic Approach*. Cambridge: Cambridge University Press, 2018.

Fewell, Dana Nolan, and David M. Gunn. *Gender, Power, and Promise: The Subject of the Bible's First Story*. Nashville: Abingdon, 1982.

Fisch, Harold. *Poetry with a Purpose: Biblical Poetics and Interpretation*. Bloomington: Indiana University Press, 1990.

Fischer, Georg. "Biblical Theology in Transition: An Overview of Recent Works, and a Look Ahead at How to Proceed." In *Biblical Theology: Past, Present and Future*, edited by Carey Walsh and Mark W. Elliott, 79–90. Eugene, OR: Cascade Books, 2016.

————. "Die Josefgeschichte als Modell für Versöhnung." In *Studies in the Book of Genesis: Literature, Redaction and History*, edited by André Wénin, 243–71. BETL 155. Leuven: Peeters.

Fischer, S. *Die Aufforderung zur Lebensfreude im Buch Kohelet und seine Rezeption.* Frankfurt: Lang, 1999.

Fitzmyer, Joseph A. *First Corinthians: A New Translation with Introduction and Commentary.* AYB 32. New Haven: Yale University Press, 2008.

Flender, Helmut. *Heil und Geschichte in der Theologie des Lukas.* BEvT. Munich: Kaiser, 1965.

Fohrer, G., et al., eds. *Hebräisches und Aramäisches Wörterbuch zum Alten Testament.* Berlin: de Gruyter, 1971.

Fokkelman, Jan. "Genesis." In *The Literary Guide to the Bible*, edited by Robert Alter and Frank Kermode, 36–55. Cambridge, MA: Harvard University Press, 1987.

————. *Narrative Art and Poetry in the Books of Samuel.* Vol. 2, *The Crossing Fates (I Sam. 13–31 & II Sam. I)*. Assen: Van Gorcum, 1986.

Folliet, G. "Deus omnia cooperatur in bonum: Rom. 8,28 chez Augustin." *SacEr* 37 (1997): 35–55.

Fornara, Roberto. *La vision contraddetta: La dialettica fra visibilità e non-visibilità divina nella Bibbia ebraica.* Rome: Pontificio Istituto Biblico, 2004.

Fox, Michael V. *Character and Ideology in the Book of Esther.* 2nd ed. Grand Rapids: Eerdmans, 2001.

————. *Proverbs: An Eclectic Edition with Introduction and Textual Commentary.* Atlanta: SBL Press, 2015.

————. *Proverbs 1–9: A New Translation with Introduction and Commentary.* AYB 18A. New Haven: Yale University Press, 2000.

————. *Proverbs 10–31: A New Translation with Introduction and Commentary.* AYB 18B. New Haven: Yale University Press, 2009.

————. "The Religion of the Book of Esther." *Judaism* 39 (1990): 135–47.

————. "Three Esthers." In *The Book of Esther in Modern Research*, edited by Sidney White Crawford and Leonard J. Greenspoon, 50–60. London: T&T Clark International, 2003.

————. *A Time to Tear Down and a Time to Build Up: A Rereading of Ecclesiastes.* Grand Rapids: Eerdmans, 1999.

————. "Wisdom in the Joseph Story." *VT* 51 (2001): 26–41.

France, R. T. *The Gospel of Matthew.* NICNT. Grand Rapids: Eerdmans, 2007.

Frankel, David. *The Murmuring Stories of the Priestly School.* VTSup 89. Leiden: Brill, 2002.

————. "Two Priestly Conceptions of Guidance in the Wilderness." *JSOT* 81(1998): 31–37.

Frankemölle, Hubert. *Der Brief des Jakobus.* Oekumenischer Theologischer Kommentar 17.1. Gütersloh: Gütersloher Verlagshaus, 1994.

Fretheim, Terence. "The Authority of the Bible, the Flood Story, and Problematic Images of God." In *Hermeneutics and the Authority of Scripture,* edited by Alan H. Cadwaller, 29–47. Task of Theology Today. Adelaide, Australia: ATF, 2011.

———. *Exodus.* IBC. Louisville: Westminster John Knox, 1991.

———. *God and World in the Old Testament: A Relational Theology of Creation.* Nashville: Abingdon, 2005.

———. "Issues of Agency in Exodus." In *The Book of Exodus: Composition, Reception, and Interpretation,* edited by Thomas Dozemann, Craig A. Evans, and Joel Lohr, 591–609. VTSup 164. Leiden: Brill, 2014.

———. *Jeremiah.* SHBC. Macon, GA: Smyth & Helwys, 2002.

———. "The Repentance of God: A Key to Evaluating Old Testament God-Talk." *HBT* 10 (1988): 47–70.

Frevel, Christian. *Mit Blick auf das Land die Schöpfung erinnern: Zum Ende der Priestergrundschrift.* HBS 23. Freiburg: Herder, 2000.

Frey, Jörg. *Die johanneische Eschatologie.* Vol. 3. WUNT 117. Tübingen: Mohr Siebeck, 2000.

———. "Was erwartet die Johannesevangelium?" In *Die Johannesapokalypse: Kontexte, Konzepte, Wirkungen,* edited by Jörg Frey, James A. Kelhoffer, and Franz Tóth, 473–552. WUNT 1/287. Tübingen: Mohr Siebeck, 2012.

Frick, Peter. *Divine Providence in Philo of Alexandria.* TSAJ 77. Tübingen: Mohr Siebeck, 1999.

Friedenthal, Richard. *The Disappearance of God: A Divine Mystery.* Boston: Little, Brown, 1995.

Frye, Northrop. *Anatomy of Criticism: Four Essays.* Princeton: Princeton University Press, 1957.

Gäckle, Volker. *Das Reich Gottes im Neuen Testament.* BTSt 176. Göttingen: Vandenhoeck & Ruprecht, 2018.

Gaventa, Beverly R. *From Darkness to Light: Aspects of Conversion in the New Testament.* Philadelphia: Fortress, 1986.

Geyer, C. F. "Zur Bewältigung des Dysteleologischen in Alten und Neuen Testament." *TZ* 37 (1981): 219–35.

Gignilliat, Mark. "Working Together with Whom? Text-Critical, Contextual, and Theological Analysis of συνεργεί in Romans." *Biblica* 87 (2006): 511–15.

Gilmour, Rachelle. *Representing the Past: A Literary Analysis of Narrative Historiography in the Book of Samuel.* VTSup 143. Leiden: Brill, 2011.

Goldingay, John. *Old Testament Theology.* Vol. 1, *Israel's Gospel.* Downers Grove, IL: InterVarsity, 2003.

Good, Edmund. "Apocalyptic as Comedy." *Semeia* 32 (1984): 41–70.

Görg, M. "שָׁכַן." *TDOT* 14:691–702.

Gowan, Donald E. *Theology in Exodus: Biblical Theology in the Form of a Commentary.* Louisville: Westminster John Knox, 1994.

Graf, Friedrich Wilhelm. "Von der creatio ex nihilo zur Bewahrung der Schöpfung." *ZTK* 87 (1990): 206–23.

Grappe, Christian. "Main de Dieu et mains des apôtres." In *La main de Dieu / Die Hand Gottes*, edited by René Kieffer and Jan Bergman, 117–34. WUNT 1/94. Tübingen: Mohr, 1997.

————. *Le royaume de Dieu: Avant, avec et après Jésus.* Geneva: Labor et Fides, 2001.

Grässer, Erich. *An die Hebräer.* 3 vols. EKKNT 17. Neukirchen-Vluyn: Neukirchener Verlag, 1990–97.

————. "Das Seufzen der Kreatur (Röm 8,19–22)." *JBTh* 5 (1990): 93–117.

Gregory, Eric. "The Boldness of Analogy: Civic Virtues and Augustinian Eudaimonism." In *The Authority of the Gospel: Explorations in Moral and Political Theology in Honour of Oliver O'Donovan*, edited by Brent Waters and Robert Song, 72–85. Grand Rapids: Eerdmans, 2015.

Grohmann, Marianne. *Fruchtbarkeit und Geburt in den Psalmen.* FAT 53. Tübingen: Mohr Siebeck, 2007.

Guelich, Robert. *The Sermon on the Mount: Foundation for Understanding.* Waco: Word, 1982.

Gunkel, Hermann. *Genesis.* Mercer Library of Biblical Studies. Macon, GA: Mercer University Press, 1997.

————.*Genesis, übersetzt und erklärt.* Göttingen: Vandenhoeck & Ruprecht, 1902.

————. "Vergeltung im Alten Testament." *RGG* 5:1529–33.

Gunn, David M. "The Anatomy of Divine Comedy: On Reading the Bible as Comedy and Tragedy." *Semeia* 32 (1984): 115–29.

————. *The Fate of King Saul: An Interpretation of a Biblical Story.* JSOTSup 14. Sheffield: JSOT Press, 1980.

————. *The Story of King David: Genre and Interpretation.* JSOTSup 6. Sheffield: JSOT Press, 1978.

Gunton, Colin. *The Actuality of Atonement: A Study of Metaphor, Rationality, and the Christian Tradition.* Edinburgh: T&T Clark, 1988.

Haacker, Klaus. "Lukas 18:7 als Anspielung auf den Deus absconditus." *NovT* 53 (2011): 267–72.

Habel, Norman. *The Book of Job: A Commentary.* OTL. London: SCM, 1985.

Haenchen, Ernst. *The Acts of the Apostles.* Translated by Bernard Noble, Gerald Shinn, and R. McL. Wilson. Oxford: Blackwell, 1971.

Hagene, Sylvia. *Zeiten der Wiederherstellung: Studien zur lukanischen; Geschichtstheologie als Soteriologie.* Münster: Aschendorff, 2003.

Hahn, Ferdinand. "Die Schöpfungsthematik in der Johannesoffenbarung." In *Eschatologie und Schöpfung: Festschrift für Erich Grässer zum siebzigsten Geburtstag*, edited by Martin Evang, Helmut Merklein, and Michael Wolter, 85–93. BZNW 89. Berlin: de Gruyter, 1997.

Hall, Edith. "Rowan Williams's Tragic Mistake." *Prospect*, November 17, 2016. https://www.prospectmagazine.co.uk/magazine/rowan-williamss-tragic-mistake.

Halliwell, Stephen. *Aristotle's Poetics*. London: Bloomsbury, 1998.

———. "Unity of Art without Unity of Life? A Question about Aristotle's Theory of Tragedy." In *Renaissances de la Tragédie*, edited by M.-A. Zagdoun and F. Malhomme, 25–39. Naples: Accademia Pontaniana, 2013.

Halpern, Baruch. *David's Secret Demons: Messiah, Murderer, Traitor, King*. Grand Rapids: Eerdmans, 2001.

Hardy, Thomas. *The Collected Letters of Thomas Hardy*. Vol. 5, *1914–1919*. Oxford: Oxford University Press, 1985.

Harris, James. "Shaftesbury, Hutcheson and the Moral Sense." In *The Cambridge History of Moral Philosophy*, edited by S. Golob and J. Timmerman, 325–35. Cambridge: Cambridge University Press, 2017.

Hart, David Bentley. *The Beauty of the Infinite*. Grand Rapids: Eerdmans, 2004.

———. *The Doors of the Sea: Where Was God in the Tsunami?* Grand Rapids: Eerdmans, 2005.

Hartenstein, Friedhelm. "Die Geschichte JHWHs im Spiegel seiner Namen." In *Gott Nennen: Gottes Namen und Gott als Name*, edited by Ingolf U. Dalferth and Philipp Stoellger, 73–95. Tübingen: Mohr Siebeck, 2008.

———. "JHWHs Wesen im Wandel: Vorüberlegungen zu einer Theologie des Alten Testaments." *TLZ* 137 (2012): 3–20.

Hartenstein, Friedhelm, and Michael Moxter. *Hermeneutik des Bilderverbots*. Leipzig: Evangelische Verlage, 2016.

Hartin, Patrick. *James*. SP 14. Collegeville, MN: Liturgical Press, 2003.

Hasker, William. "The Problem of Evil in Process Theism and Classical Free Will Theism." *Process Studies* 29, no. 2 (Fall–Winter 2000): 194–208, https://www.religion-online.org/article/the-problem-of-evil-in-process-theism-and-classical-free-will-theism/.

———. *Providence, Evil and the Openness of God*. Routledge Studies in the Philosophy of Religion. London: Routledge, 2004.

———. *The Triumph of God over Evil*. Downers Grove, IL: InterVarsity, 2008.

Haskins, Minnie. "God Knows." In *The Oxford Dictionary of Modern Quotations*, 3rd ed., edited by Elizabeth Knowles, 147. Oxford: Oxford University Press, 2007.

Hauerwas, Stanley. *With the Grain of the Universe: The Church's Witness and Natural Theology*. Grand Rapids: Baker Academic, 2001.

Hausmann, Jutta. *Studien zum Menschenbild der älteren Weisheit*. FAT 7. Tübingen: Mohr Siebeck, 1994.

236 *Bibliography*

Heckel, Ulrich. *Der Segen im Neuen Testament: Begriff, Formeln, Gesten; Mit einem praktisch-theologischen Ausblick.* WUNT 150. Tübingen: Mohr Siebeck, 2002.

Heckl, Raik. *Hiob: Vom Gottesfürchtigen zum Repräsentanten Israels.* FAT 70. Tübingen: Mohr Siebeck, 2010.

Hedrick, Pamela. "Fewer Answers and Further Questions: Jews and Gentiles in Acts." *Interpretation* 66 (2012): 294–305.

Hegel, G. W. F. *Glauben und Wissen, oder Die Reflexionsphilosophie der Subjektivität.* PhB 62b. 1802/1803. Reprint, Hamburg: Meiner, 1962.

Hegermann, Harald. *Die Vorstellung vom Schöpfungsmittler im hellenistischen Judentum und Urchristentum.* TUGAL 82. Berlin: Akademie Verlag, 1961.

Held, Klaus. "Phänomenologische Begründung eines nachmetaphysischen Gottesverständnisses." In *Phänomenologie und Theologie*, edited by T. Söding and K. Held, 9–27. QD 227. Freiburg im Breisgau: Herder, 2009.

Heligenthal, Roman. "Werke der Barmherzigkeit oder Almosen? Zur Bedeutung von ἐλεημοσύνη." *NTS* 25 (1983): 289–301.

Hengel, Martin. "Die Finger und die Herrschaft Gottes in Luke 11,20." In *La main de Dieu / Die Hand Gottes*, edited by René Kieffer and Jan Bergmann, 87–106. WUNT 1/94. Tübingen: Mohr Siebeck, 1997.

Herms, Eilert. *Systematische Theologie: Das Wesen des Christentums; In Wahrheit und auf Gnade leben.* Vol. 1. Tübingen: Mohr Siebeck, 2017.

Hettema, Theo L. *Reading for Good: Narrative Theology and Ethics in the Joseph Story from the Perspective of Ricoeur's Hermeneutics.* Kampen: Kok Pharos, 1996.

Hieke, Thomas. "'Er verschlingt den Tod für immer' (Jes 25,8a): Eine unerfüllte Verheißung im Alten und Neuen Testament." *Biblische Zeitschrift* 50 (2006): 31–50.

———. *Die Genealogien der Genesis.* HBS 39. Freiburg: Herder, 2003.

———. "Wie hast Du's mit der Religion? Sprechhandlungen und Wirkintentionen in Kohelet 4,17–5,6." In *Qohelet in the Context of Wisdom*, edited by A. Schoors, 319–38. BETL 136. Leuven: Peeters, 1998.

Hildebrandt, Kurt. *Leibniz und das Reich der Gnade.* Heidelberg: Springer, 1953.

Hirschfeld, Ariel. "Is the Book of Job a Tragedy?" In *The Book of Job: Aesthetics, Ethics, Hermeneutics*, edited by Leora Batnitzky and Ilana Pardes, 9–35. Berlin: de Gruyter 2015.

Hoffman, Yair. "The Relation between the Prologue and the Speech-Cycles in Job: A Reconsideration." *VT* 31 (1981): 160–70.

Hofius, Otfried. "Einer ist Gott—Einer ist Herr." In *Eschatologie und Schöpfung: Festschrift für Erich Gräßer zum siebzigsten Geburtstag*, edited by Martin Evang, Helmut Merklein, and Michael Wolter, 95–108. Berlin: de Gruyter, 1997.

———. *Katapausis: Die Vorstellung vom endzeitlichen Ruheort im Hebräerbrief.* WUNT 1/11. Tübingen: Mohr Siebeck, 1970.

Holladay, Carl. *Acts: A Commentary.* NTL. Louisville: Westminster John Knox, 2016.

————. "Interpreting Acts." *Interpretation* 66 (2012): 245–58.

Holmén, T. "Theodicean Motifs in the New Testament." In *Theodicy in the World of the Bible*, edited by Antti Laato and Johannes C. de Moor, 605–51. Leiden: Brill, 2003.

Holtz, Traugott. *Die Offenbarung des Johannes: Neubearbeitung.* NTD 11. Göttingen: Vandenhoeck & Ruprecht, 2008.

Hommel, H. "Erwägungen zu Römer 8,28." *ZNW* 80 (1989): 126–30.

Hossenfelder, Malte. *Die Philosophie der Antike 3: Stoa, Epikureismus und Skepsis.* Vol. 3 of *Geschichte der Philosophie.* 12 vols. Munich: Beck, 1985.

Hossfeld, Frank-Lothar. "Wie sprechen die Heiligen Schriften, insbesondere das Alte Testament, von der Vorsehung Gottes?" In *Vorsehung und Handeln Gottes*, edited by Theodor Schneider and Lothar Ullrich, 72–93. QD 115. Freiburg: Herder, 1988.

Hossfeld, Frank-Lothar, and Erich Zenger. *Die Psalmen I: Psalm 1–50.* NEchtB. Würzburg: Echter, 1993.

————. *Psalms 3: A Commentary on Psalms 101–150.* Hermeneia. Minneapolis: Fortress, 2011.

Houtman, Cornelius. *Exodus.* Vol. 1. HCOT. Leuven: Peeters, 1993.

Hubbard, Moyer V. *New Creation in Paul's Letters and Thought.* SNTSMS 119. Cambridge: Cambridge University Press, 2002.

Hüffmeier, Wilhelm. "Deus providebit? Eine Zwischenbilanz zur Kritik der Lehre von Gottes Vorsehung." In *Denkwürdiges Geheimnis: Beiträge zur Gotteslehre; Festschrift für Eberhard Jüngel*, edited by Ingolf U. Dalferth, Johannes Fischer, and Hans-Peter Grosshans, 237–58. Tübingen: Mohr Siebeck, 2004.

Humphreys, W. Lee. "The Tragedy of King Saul: A Study of the Figure of Saul and the Development of 1 Samuel." *JSOT* 22 (1982): 95–117.

Hundlet, Michael B. *Keeping Heaven on Earth: Safeguarding the Divine Presence in the Priestly Tabernacle.* FAT 2/50. Tübingen: Mohr Siebeck, 2011.

Hürliman, Thomas. *Das Einsiedler Welttheater.* Zürich: Ammann, 2007.

Hurst, L. D. *The Epistle to the Hebrews: Its Background of Thought.* SNTSMS 65. Cambridge: Cambridge University Press, 2005.

Ingram, Doug. *Ambiguity in Ecclesiastes.* LHBOTS 431. London: T&T Clark, 2006.

Janowski, Bernd. *Arguing with God: A Theological Anthropology of the Psalms.* Louisville: Westminster John Knox, 2013.

————. "Die Tat kehrt zum Täter zurück: Offene Fragen im Umkreis des 'Tun-Ergehen-Zusammenhangs.'" *ZTK* 91 (1994): 247–71.

————. *Ein Gott, der straft und tötet? Zwölf Fragen zum Gottesbild des Alten Testaments.* Neukirchen-Vluyn: Neukirchener Verlag, 2013.

————. *Gott des Lebens: Beiträge zur Theologie des Alten Testaments.* Neukirchen-Vluyn: Neukirchener Verlag, 2003.

Janowski, Bernd, and Michael Welker. Foreword to "Einheit und Vielfalt biblischer Theologie." Special issue, *JBTh* 1 (1986): 5–10.

Jantsch, Torsten. "The God of Glory: Explicit References to God in Discourses in the Acts of the Apostles (7:2–53; 14:15–18; 17:22–31)." *STJ* 4, no. 2 (2018): 197–222.

———. *Jesus, der Retter: Die Soteriologie des lukanischen Doppelwerks.* WUNT 1/381. Tübingen: Mohr Siebeck, 2017.

Jenkins, Timothy. *An Experiment in Providence: How Faith Engages the World.* London: SPCK, 2006.

Jeremias, Jörg. *Das Königtum Gottes in den Psalmen: Israels Begegnung mit dem kanaanäischen Mythos in den Jahwe-König-Psalmen.* FRLANT 141. Göttingen: Vandenhoeck & Ruprecht, 1987.

———. *Die Reue Gottes: Aspekte alttestamentlicher Gottesvorstellung.* Neukirchen-Vluyn: Neukirchener Verlag, 1975.

———. *Studien zur Theologie des Alten Testaments.* FAT 99. Tübingen: Mohr Siebeck, 2015.

Jervell, Jacob. *Die Apostelgeschichte.* KEK 3. Göttingen: Vandenhoeck & Ruprecht, 1998.

———. "The Future of the Past: Luke's Vision of Salvation History and Its Bearing on His Writing of History." In *History, Literature, and Society in the Book of Acts,* edited by Ben Witherington III, 104–26. Cambridge: Cambridge University Press, 1996.

Jeska, Joachim. *Die Geschichte Israels in der Sicht des Lukas Apg 7,2b–53 und 13,17–25 im Kontext antik-jüdischer Summarien der Geschichte Israels.* FRLANT 195. Göttingen: Vandenhoeck & Ruprecht, 2001.

Jipp, Joshua. *Divine Visitations and Hospitality to Strangers in Luke-Acts: An Interpretation of the Malta Episode in Acts 28:1–10.* NovTSup 153. Leiden: Brill, 2013.

Jobling, David. *1 Samuel.* Berit Olam. Collegeville, MN: Liturgical Press, 1998.

———. *The Sense of Biblical Narrative: Structural Analyses in the Hebrew Bible.* Vol. 1. 2nd ed. JSOTSup 7. Sheffield: JSOT Press, 1986.

Johnson, Dan G. *From Chaos to Restoration: An Integrative Reading of Isaiah 24–27.* JSOTSup 61. Sheffield: JSOT Press, 1988.

Johnson, Luke Timothy. *Hebrews: A Commentary.* NTL. Louisville: Westminster John Knox, 2006.

Joseph, Simon J. "'Seek His Kingdom': Q 12,22b–31, God's Providence, and Adamic Wisdom." *Biblica* 92 (2011): 392–410.

Jung, Carl Gustav. *Antwort auf Hiob.* Zürich: Rascher Verlag, 1952. Translated by R. F. C. Hull in *Psychology and Religion,* vol. 11 of *Collected Works of C. G. Jung.* Princeton: Princeton University Press, 1973.

Jüngel, Eberhard. "Gottes ursprüngliches Anfangen als schöpferische Selbstbegrenzung: Ein Beitrag zum Gespräch mit Hans Jonas über den 'Gottesbegriff nach

Auschwitz.'" In *Wertlose Wahrheit: Zur Identität und Relevanz des christlichen Glaubens*. Theologische Erörterungen 3. Tübingen: Mohr Siebeck, 1990.

Kaiser, Otto. *Der Mensch unter dem Schicksal: Studien zur Geschichte, Theologie und Gegenwartsbedeutung der Weisheit*. BZAW 161. Berlin: de Gruyter, 1985.

———. *Des Menschen Glück und Gottes Gerechtigkeit*. Tübingen: Mohr Siebeck, 2007.

———. "Determination und Freiheit beim Kohelet/Prediger Salomo und in der frühen Stoa." *NZSTh* 31 (1989): 251–70.

———. "Jahwe, der Reichsgott Israels als Wächter der Menschlichkeit und Gerechtigkeit." Chap. 2 in *Der eine Gott Israels und die Mächte der Welt: Der Weg Gottes im Alten Testament vom Herrn seines Volkes zum Herrn der ganzen Welt*. Göttingen: Vandenhoeck & Ruprecht, 2013.

———. *Studien zu Philo von Alexandrien*. BZAW 501. Berlin: de Gruyter, 2016.

Karrer, Martin. *Der Brief an die Hebräer Kapitel 5,11–13,25*. Edited by Rudolf Hoppe and Michael Wolter. ÖTKNT 20/2. Gütersloh: Gütersloher Verlagshaus, 2008.

———. *Jesus Christus im Neuen Testament*. Grundrisse zum Neuen Testament 11. Göttingen: Vandenhoeck & Ruprecht, 1998.

Käsemann, Ernst. *The Wandering People of God: An Investigation of the Letter to the Hebrews*. Translated by Roy A. Harrisville and Irving L. Sandberg. Minneapolis: Augsburg, 1984.

Keel, Othmar. *Jahwes Entgegnung an Ijob*. FRLANT 121. Göttingen: Vandenhoeck & Ruprecht, 1978.

Keel, Othmar, and Silvia Schroer. *Schöpfung: Biblische Theologien im Kontext altorientalischer Religionen*. 3rd ed. Göttingen: Vandenhoeck & Ruprecht, 2008.

Kelsey, David. *Eccentric Existence: A Theological Anthropology*. 2 vols. Louisville: Westminster John Knox, 2009.

Kerényi, Karl. *Die griechisch-orientalische Romanliteratur in religionsgeschichtlicher Beleuchtung: Ein Versuch*. Tübingen: Mohr Siebeck, 1927.

Kertelge, Karl. "'Neue Schöpfung': Grund und Maßstab apostolischen Handelns (2 Kor. 5,17)." In *Eschatologie und Schöpfung: Festschrift für Erich Grässer zum siebzigsten Geburtstag*, edited by Martin Evang, Helmut Merklein, and Michael Wolter, 139–44. Berlin: de Gruyter, 1997.

Klaiber, Walther. Review of *Der Gott der Lebendigen*, by Reinhard Feldmeier and Hermann Spieckermann. *TLZ* 137 (2012): 651–54.

Klein, Günther. "Über das Weltregiment Gottes: Zum exegetischen Anhalt eines dogmatischen Lehrstücks." *ZTK* 90 (1993): 251–82.

———. "Lukas 1,1–4 als theologisches Programm." In *Zeit und Geschichte: Dankesgabe an Rudolf Bultmann zum 80. Geburtstag*, edited by Erich Dinkler and Hartwig Thyen, 193–216. Tübingen: Mohr Siebeck, 1964.

Klein, Hans. "Die Schöpfung in der Botschaft Jesu." In *Theologies of Creation in Early Judaism and Ancient Christianity: In Honour of Hans Klein*, edited by Tobias Nicklas and Korinna Zamfir in collaboration with Heike Braun, 253–65. DCLS 6. Berlin: de Gruyter, 2010.

Knierim, Rolf P. "Cosmos and History in Israel's Theology." *HBT* 3 (1981): 59–123.

———. "The Task of Old Testament Theology." *HBT* 6 (1984): 25–57.

———. *The Task of Old Testament Theology: Substance, Method, and Cases.* Grand Rapids: Eerdmans, 1995.

Knohl, Israel. *The Sanctuary of Silence: The Priestly Torah and the Holiness School.* Minneapolis: Fortress, 1995.

Koch, Klaus. "Gibt es ein Vergeltungsdogma im Alten Testament?" *ZTK* 52 (1955): 1–42.

———. *The Prophets.* Vol. 1. Minneapolis: Fortress, 1983.

———, ed. *Um das Prinzip der Vergeltung in Religion und Recht des Alten Testaments.* Darmstadt: Wissenschaftliche Buchgesellschaft, 1972.

Koch, Klaus, and Jürgen Roloff. "Tat-Ergehen-Zusammenhang." In *Reclams Bibellexikon*, edited by Klaus Koch et al., 493–95. Stuttgart: Reclam, 1987.

Koch, Kurt Cardinal. "Geleitwort." In *Gottvertrauen: Die ökumenische Diskussion um die Fiducia*, edited by I. Dalferth and S. Peng-Keller, 11–17. QD 250. Freiburg: Herder, 2012.

Köckert, Matthias. "Literargeschichtliche und religionsgeschichtliche Beobachtungen zu Ps 104." In *Schriftauslegung in der Schrift: Festschrift für Odil Hannes Steck zu seinem 65. Geburtstag*, edited by Reinhard G. Kratz, Thomas Krüger, and Konrad Schmid, 259–79. BZAW 300. Berlin: de Gruyter, 2000.

Köhlmoos, Melanie. *Kohelet: Der Prediger Salomo.* Alte Testament Deutsch 16/5. Göttingen: Vandenhoeck & Ruprecht, 2014.

Koller, Aaron. *Esther in Ancient Jewish Thought.* Cambridge: Cambridge University Press, 2014.

Konradt, Matthias. *Christliche Existenz nach dem Jakobusbrief: Eine Studie zu seiner soteriologischen und ethischen Konzeption.* Novum Testamentum et Orbis Antiquus 22. Göttingen: Vandenhoeck & Ruprecht, 1998.

———. "Schöpfung und Neuschöpfung im Neuen Testament." In *Schöpfung*, edited by Konrad Schmid, 121–84. Themen der Theologie 4. Tübingen: Mohr Siebeck, 2012.

Kratz, R. G. "Die Gnade des täglichen Brots: Späte Psalmen auf dem Weg zum Vaterunser." *ZTK* 89 (2000): 1–40.

———. "Das Sh^ema' des Psalters: Die Botschaft vom Reich *Gottes* nach Psalm 145." In *Gott und Mensch im Dialog: Festschrift für Otto Kaiser zum 80. Geburtstag*, edited by Markus Witte, 2:623–38. BZAW 345. Berlin: de Gruyter, 2004.

Kraus, H.-J. *Psalmen.* 2 vols. Biblischer Kommentar, Altes Testament 15/1–2. Neukirchen-Vluyn: Neukirchener Verlag, 1958.

———. *Theology of the Psalms.* Minneapolis: Fortress, 1986.

Kreuzer, Siegfried. *Der lebendige Gott: Bedeutung, Herkunft und Entwicklung einer alttestamentlichen Gottesbezeichnung.* BWANT 6/16. Stuttgart: Kohlhammer, 1983.

Krötke, Wolf. *Beten heute.* Munich: Kösel, 1987.

———. "Gottes Fürsorge für die Welt: Überlegungen zur Vorsehungslehre." In *Die Universalität des offenbaren Gottes: Gesammelte Aufsätze.* BEvT 94. Munich: Kaiser, 1985.

Krüger, Annette. *Das Lob des Schöpfers: Studien zur Sprache, Motivik und Theologie.* WMANT 124. Neukirchen-Vluyn: Neukirchener Verlag, 2010.

Krüger, Thomas. *Geschichtskonzepte im Ezechielbuch.* BZAW 18. Berlin: de Gruyter, 1989.

———. *Kohelet.* BKAT 19. Neukirchen-Vluyn: Neukirchener Verlag, 2000.

———. "Leben und Tod nach Kohelet und Paulus: Leben trotz Tod." *JBTh* 19 (2004): 195–216.

Krusche, Werner. *Das Wirken des Heiligen Geistes nach Calvin.* Forschungen zur Kirchen- und Dogmengeschichte 7. Göttingen: Vandenhoeck & Ruprecht, 1957.

Kubina, Veronika. *Die Gottesreden im Buche Hiob: Ein Beitrag zu Diskussion um die Einheit von Hiob 38,1–42,6.* FrThSt 115. Freiburg im Breisgau: Herder, 1979.

Kutsko, John F. *Between Heaven and Earth: Divine Presence and Absence in the Book of Ezekiel.* Winona Lake, IN: Eisenbrauns, 2000.

Kynes, Will. "Job and Isaiah 40–55: Intertextualities in Dialogue." Chap. 9 in *Reading Job Intertextually,* edited by Katharine Dell and Will Kynes. LHBOTS 574. New York: Bloomsbury T&T Clark, 2013.

Lacocque, André. *Esther Regina: A Bakhtinian Reading.* Evanston, IL: Northwestern University Press, 2008.

Lacoste, Jean-Yves. "Henri de Lubac and a Desire beyond Claim." Chap. 15 in *T&T Clark Companion to Henri de Lubac,* edited by Jordan Hillebert. London: Bloomsbury T&T Clark, 2017.

Landy, Francis. "Are We in the Place of Averroes?" *Semeia* 32 (1984): 131–48.

———. "Humour as a Tool for Biblical Exegesis." In *On Humour and the Comic in the Hebrew Bible,* edited by Yehuda T. Radday and Athalya Brenner, 101–17. JSOTSup 92. Sheffield: Almond Press, 1990.

Lang, Bernhard. *Joseph in Egypt: A Cultural Icon from Grotius to Goethe.* New Haven: Yale University Press, 2009.

Lassak, Andrea. *Grundloses Vertrauen: Eine theologische Studie zum Verhältnis von Grund- und Gottvertrauen.* Religion in Philosophy and Theology 83. Tübingen: Mohr Siebeck, 2016.

Lauster, Jörg. *Die Verzauberung der Welt: Eine Kulturgeschichte des Christentum.* Munich: Beck, 2014.

Leal, Robert Barry. *Wilderness in the Bible: Toward a Theology of Wilderness.* New York: Lang, 2004.

Leproux, Alexis. "L'ἐπιείκεια divine ou la mesure du jugement selon Sg 11,15–12,27." In *Wisdom for Life: Essays Offered to Honor Prof. Maurice Gilbert, SJ, on the Occasion of His Eightieth Birthday*, edited by N. Calduch-Benages, 272–89. BZAW 445. Berlin: de Gruyter, 2014.

Leuenberger, Martin. *Konzeptionen des Königtums Gottes im Psalter: Untersuchungen zu Komposition und Redaktion der theokratischen Bücher IV–V innerhalb des Psalters.* ATANT 84. Zürich: TVZ, 2004.

Levenson, Jon. *Creation and the Persistence of Evil.* Princeton: Princeton University Press, 1994.

———. *Esther.* OTL. London: SCM, 1997.

Lévêque, Jean. *Job, ou le drame de la foi.* LD 216. Paris: Cerf, 2007.

Liess, Katrin. *Der Weg des Lebens: Psalm 16 und das Lebens- und Todesverständnis der Individualpsalmen.* FAT 2/5. Tübingen: Mohr Siebeck, 2004.

Link, Christian. *Schöpfung: Ein theologischer Entwurf im Gegenüber von Naturwissenschaft und Ökologie.* Neukirchen-Vluyn: Neukirchener Theologie, 2012.

Loader, James. *Ecclesiastes: A Practical Commentary.* Grand Rapids: Eerdmans, 1986.

———. "Job—Answer or Enigma?" *OTE* 2 (1984): 1–38.

———. "Schönheit zwischen Segen und Errettung." *ZAW* 124 (2012): 163–79.

Lohfink, Gerhard. "Der praexistente Heilsplan: Sinn und Hintergrund der dritten Vaterunserbitte." In *Neues Testament und Ethik: Für Rudolf Schnackenburg*, edited by Helmut Merklein, 110–33. Freiburg: Herder, 1989.

Lohfink, Norbert. "Exodus 32,7–11.13–14 (24. Sonntag des Jahres)." In *Die alttestamentlichen Lesungen der Sonn- und Feiertage: Auslegung und Verkündigung; 20. Sonntag des Jahres bis Christkönig; Lesejahr C/3*, edited by J. Schreiner, 47–60. Würzburg: Echter, 1971.

———. *Theology of the Pentateuch: Themes of the Priestly Narrative and Deuteronomy.* Translated by Linda M. Maloney. Minneapolis: Fortress, 1995.

Löhr, Winrich. "Heilsgeschichte und Universalgeschichte." In *Heil und Geschichte: Die Geschichtsbezogenheit des Heils und das Problem der Heilsgeschichte in der biblischen Tradition und in der theologischen Deutung*, edited by Jörg Frey, Stefan Krauter, and Hermann Lichtenberger, 535–58. WUNT 1/248. Tübingen: Mohr Siebeck, 2008.

Long, A. A. *Epictetus: A Stoic and Socratic Guide to Life.* Oxford: Oxford University Press, 2002.

Long, Stephen A. *Natura Pura: On the Recovery of Nature in the Doctrine of Grace.* New York: Fordham University Press, 2010.

Longacre, Robert E. *Joseph: A Story of Divine Providence; A Text Theoretical and Textlinguistic Analysis of Genesis 37 and 39–48*. 2nd ed. Winona Lake, IN: Eisenbrauns, 2003.

Louw, J. P., and E. Nida. *Greek-English Lexicon of the New Testament Based on Semantic Domains*. 2 vols. Swindon, UK: United Bible Societies, 1996.

Lux, Rudiger. "Denn es ist kein Mensch so gerecht auf Erden, daß er nur Gutes tue: Recht und Gerechtigkeit aus der Sicht des Predigers Salomos." *ZTK* 94 (1997): 263–87.

Luz, Ulrich. *Das Evangelium nach Matthäus (Mt 18–25)*. EKKNT 1/3. Neukirchen-Vluyn: Benziger, 1997.

MacDonald, Nathan. "The Spirit of God: A Neglected Conceptualization of the Divine Presence in the Persian Period." In *Divine Presence and Absence in Exilic and Post-exilic Judaism*, edited by Nathan MacDonald and Izaak J. de Hulster, 95–120. FAT 2/61. Tübingen: Mohr Siebeck, 2013.

Macgregor, G. H. C. "The Concept of the Wrath of God in the New Testament." *NTS* 7 (1961): 101–9.

Machinist, Peter. "Fate, *Miqreh*, and Reason: Some Reflections on Qohelet and Biblical Thought." In *Solving Riddles and Untying Knots: Biblical, Epigraphic, and Semitic Studies in Honor of Jonas C. Greenfield*, edited by Ziony Zevit, Seymour Gitin, and Michael Sokoloff, 159–75. Winona Lake, IN: Eisenbrauns, 1995.

MacKinnon Donald. "Some Reflections on Hans Urs von Balthasar's Christology with Special Reference to *Theodramatik* Ii/2 and Iii." In *The Analogy of Beauty: The Theology of Hans Urs von Balthasar*, edited by John Riches, 164–79. Edinburgh: T&T Clark, 1986.

Malherbe, Abraham. *Light from the Gentiles: Hellenistic Philosophy and Early Christianity*. VTSup 150. Leiden: Brill, 2013.

Marcus, Joel. "Entering into the Kingly Power of God." *JBL* 107 (1988): 663–75.

———. *The Way of the Lord: Christological Exegesis of the Old Testament in the Gospel of Mark*. Edinburgh: T&T Clark, 1992.

Marguerat, Daniel. *Les Actes des apôtres (1–12)*. Geneva: Labor et Fides, 2007.

———. *The First Christian Historian: Writing the "Acts of the Apostles."* Translated by Ken McKinney, Gregory J. Laughery, and Richard Bauckham. Cambridge: Cambridge University Press, 2002.

Martyn, J. Louis. *Galatians: A New Translation with Introduction and Commentary*. AB 33A. New York: Doubleday, 1997.

Mathias, Dietmar. *Die Geschichtstheologie der Geschichtssummarien in den Psalmen*. BEATAJ 35. Frankfurt: Lang, 1993.

Mauser, Ulrich. *Christ in the Wilderness: The Wilderness Theme in the Second Gospel and Its Basis in the Biblical Tradition*. SBT 39. London: SCM, 1963.

McConville, Gordon. *Esther*. Louisville: Westminster John Knox, 2006.

McDermott, John M. *Love and Understanding: The Relation of Will and Intellect in Pierre Rousselot's Christological Vision*. Roma: Gregoriana, 1983.

McFarland, Ian A. *From Nothing: A Theology of Creation*. Louisville: Westminster John Knox, 2014.

McKane, William. *Jeremiah*. 2 vols. ICC. Edinburgh: T&T Clark, 1986–96.

Meinhold, Arndt. "Die Gattung der Josephsgeschichte und des Estherbuches II." *ZAW* 88 (1976): 72–93.

Melton, Brittany M. "*Miqreh* in Retrospect: An Illumination of *Miqreh* in Light of Ecclesiastes 3:1–8 and the Book of Ruth." In *Megilloth Studies: The Shape of Contemporary Scholarship*, edited by Brad Embry, 30–42. HBM 78. Sheffield: Sheffield Phoenix, 2016.

Messner, R. "Opfer: IV. Theologiegeschichtlich u. systematisch-theologisch." In *Lexicon für Theologie und Kirche*, 3rd ed., edited by Michael Buchberger and Walter Kasper, 7:1067–68. Freiburg im Breisgau: Herder, 1998.

Michel, Diethelm. "Vom Gott, der im Himmel ist." *ThViat* 12 (1973–74): 87–100.

Mies, Françoise. *Bible et literature: L'homme et Dieu mis en intrigue*. Naumur: Lessius, 1999.

———. *L'espérance de Job*. BETL 193. Leuven: Leuven University Press, 2006.

———. "Job et la main de Dieu." In *Wisdom for Life: Essays Offered to Honor Prof. Maurice Gilbert, SJ, on the Occasion of His Eightieth Birthday*, edited by N. Calduch-Benages, 61–83. BZAW 445. Berlin: de Gruyter, 2014.

Miles, Jack. "Laughing at the Bible: Jonah as Parody." *JQR* 65 (1975): 168–81.

Miller, J. Hillis. *The Disappearance of God: Five 19th-Century Writers*. Cambridge, MA: Harvard University Press, 1963.

Miller, Patrick D. *Israelite Religion and Biblical Theology: Collected Essays*. JSOTSup 267. Sheffield: Sheffield Academic Press, 2000.

———. *The Lord of the Psalms*. Louisville: Westminster John Knox, 2013.

———. "Prayer and Divine Action." In *God in the Fray: A Tribute to Walter Brueggemann*, edited by Tod Linafelt and Timothy K. Beal, 211–33. Minneapolis: Fortress, 1998.

———. "Prayer as Persuasion: The Rhetoric and Intention of Prayer." In *Israelite Religion and Biblical Theology: Collected Essays*, 337–54. JSOTSup 267. Sheffield: Sheffield Academic Press, 2000.

———. *Sin and Judgment in the Prophets: A Stylistic and Theological Analysis*. SBLMS 27. Chico, CA: Scholars Press, 1982.

Miskotte, Kornelis H. *When the Gods Are Silent*. London: Collins, 1967.

Moberly, R. W. L. "On Interpreting the Mind of God: The Theological Significance of the Flood Narrative (Genesis 6–9)." In *The Word Leaps the Gap: Essays on Scripture and Theology in Honor of Richard B. Hays*, edited by J. Ross Wagner, C. Kavin Rowe, and A. Katherine Grieb, 44–65. Grand Rapids: Eerdmans, 2008.

Moltmann, Jürgen. "Gespräch mit Christian Link." *EvT* 47 (1987): 93–95.

———. *Gott in der Schöpfung: Ökologische Schöpfungslehre.* Munich: Kaiser, 1985.

———. *Das Kommen Gottes.* Gütersloh: Gütersloher Verlagshaus, 1995.

———. "Schöpfung, Bund und Herrlichkeit." *EvT* 48 (1988): 108–27.

———. *The Spirit of Life: A Universal Affirmation.* Translated by Margaret Kohl. Minneapolis: Fortress, 1992.

———. *Sun of Righteousness, Arise! God's Future for Humanity and the Earth.* Translated by Margaret Kohl. London: SCM, 2010. Originally published as *Sein Name ist Gerechtigkeit: Neue Beiträge zur christlichen Gotteslehre.* Gütersloh: Gütersloher Verlagshaus, 2009.

Mulcahy, Bernard. *Aquinas's Notion of Pure Nature and the Christian Integralism of Henri de Lubac: Not Everything Is Grace.* New York: Lang, 2011.

Murphy, Francesca. *The Comedy of Revelation: Paradise Lost and Regained in Biblical Narrative.* Edinburgh: T&T Clark, 2002.

Murphy, Roland E. *The Tree of Life: An Exploration of Biblical Wisdom Literature.* 2nd ed. Grand Rapids: Eerdmans, 1990.

Mußner, Franz. "JHWH, der sub contrario handelnde Gott Israels." In *Der Lebendige Gott Israels: Studien zur Theologie des Neuen Testaments; Festschrift für Wilhelm Thüsing zum 75. Geburtstag,* edited by Thomas Söding, 25–33. Münster: Aschendorff, 1996.

Newsom, Carol. *The Book of Job: A Contest of Moral Imaginations.* Oxford: Oxford University Press, 2003.

Neyrey, Jerome H. "Acts 17, Epicureans and Theodicy." In *Greeks, Romans and Christians: Essays in Honor of A. Malherbe,* edited by D. L. Balch, E. Ferguson, and W. A. Meeks, 118–34. Minneapolis: Fortress, 1990.

Nicklas, Tobias. "Schöpfung und Vollendung in der Offenbarung Johannes." In *Theologies of Creation in Early Judaism and Ancient Christianity: In Honour of Hans Klein,* edited by Tobias Nicklas and Korinna Zamfir in collaboration with Heike Braun, 389–414. Berlin: de Gruyter, 2010.

Nicolson, Sarah. *Three Faces of Saul: An Intertextual Approach to Biblical Tragedy.* JSOTSup 339. Sheffield: Sheffield Academic Press, 2001.

Nolland, John. *The Gospel of Matthew.* NIGTC. Grand Rapids: Eerdmans, 2005.

———. *Luke 18:35–24:53.* WBC 35C. Dallas: Word, 1993.

Norin, Stig. "Das Hand Gottes im Alten Testament." In *La main de Dieu / Die Hand Gottes,* edited by René Kieffer and Jan Bergman, 49–63. WUNT 1/94. Tübingen: Mohr Siebeck, 1997.

Nussbaum, Martha C. *The Fragility of Goodness: Luck and Ethics in Greek Tragedy and Philosophy.* 2nd ed. Chicago: University of Chicago Press, 2001.

O'Donovan, Oliver. *The Desire of the Nations: An Outline for Political Theology.* Cambridge: Cambridge University Press, 1996.

————. *Finding and Seeking: Ethics as Theology.* Vol. 2. Grand Rapids: Eerdmans, 2014.

————. *Resurrection and Moral Order: An Outline for Evangelical Ethics.* Leicester: Inter-Varsity, 1986.

Oeming, Mannfred. "Die Begegnung mit Gott." In *Hiobs Weg: Stationen vom Menschen im Leid*, edited by Manfred Oeming and Konrad Schmid, 121–42. Neukirchen-Vluyn: Neukirchener Verlag, 2001.

————. "'Ihr habt nicht recht von mir geredet wie mein Knecht Hiob': Kritische Anfrage an die moderne Theologie?" *EvT* 60 (2000): 103–16.

Opelt, I. "Erde." *RAC* 5:1113–79.

O'Regan, Cyril. "A Theology of History." Chap. 12 in *T&T Clark Companion to Henri de Lubac*, edited by Jordan Hillebert. London: Bloomsbury T&T Clark, 2017.

Osburn, Carroll D. "The Interpretation of Romans 8:28." *WTJ* 44 (1982): 99–109.

Paas, Stefan. *Creation and Judgement: Creation Texts in Some Eighth Century Prophets.* Oudtestamentische studiën 47. Leiden: Brill, 2003.

Pannenberg, Wolfhart. "Weltgeschichte und Heilsgeschichte." In *Probleme biblischer Theologie: Gerhard von Rad zum 70 Geburtstag*, edited by Hans Walter Wolff, 349–66. Munich: Christian Kaiser, 1971.

————. *Wissenschaftstheorie und Theologie.* Frankfurt am Main: Suhrkamp, 1973.

Patrick, Dale. "The Translation of Job 42:6." *VT* 26 (1976): 369–71.

Pedersen, Johannes. *Israel: Its Life and Culture.* Oxford: Oxford University Press, 1926.

Perlitt, Lothar. "Die Verborgenheit Gottes." In *Probleme biblischer Theologie: Gerhard von Rad zum 70 Geburtstag*, edited by Hans Walter Wolff, 367–82. Munich: Christian Kaiser, 1971.

Pervo, Richard I. *Acts: A Commentary.* Hermeneia. Philadelphia: Fortress, 2009.

————. *Profit with Delight: Literary Genre of the Acts of the Apostles.* Philadelphia: Fortress, 1987.

Pesch, Rudolf. *Die Apostelgeschichte.* EKKNT 5/2. Neukirchen-Vluyn: Neukirchener Verlag, 1994.

Peterson, Erik. *Ausgewählte Schriften.* Vol. 4, *Offenbarung des Johannes und politisch-theologische Texte.* Würzburg: Echter, 2004.

Philonenko, Marc. "Main gauche et main droite de Dieu." In *La main de Dieu / Die Hand Gottes*, edited by René Kieffer and Jan Bergman, 135–40. WUNT 1/94. Tübingen: Mohr Siebeck, 1997.

Pieper, Irene. "Unter dem Schirm des Höchsten? Welttheater und Vorsehung." *Communio: Internationale Katholische Zeitschrift* 31 (2002): 351–57.

Piper, R. A. "Wealth, Poverty, and Subsistence in Q." In *From Quest to Q: Festschrift James M. Robinson*, edited by J. M. A. Asgeirsson, 219–26. BETL 146. Leuven: Peeters, 2000.

Platzer, Franz. *Geschichte, Heilsgeschichte, Hermeneutik: Gotteserfahrung in geschichtsloser Zeit.* Bern: Lang, 1976.

Pola, Thomas. 'Was ist 'Leben' im Alten Testament?' *ZAW* 116 (2004): 251–52.

Polkinghorne, John. "Kenotic Creation and Divine Action." In *The Work of Love: Creation as Kenosis,* edited by John Polkinghorne, 90–106. Grand Rapids: Eerdmans, 2001.

Prato, G. L. *Il problema della teodicea in Ben Sira.* AnBib 65. Rome: Pontifical Biblical Institute, 1975.

———. "L'universo come ordine e come disordine." *RivB* 30 (1982): 51–77.

Preuss, H.-D. *Theologie des Alten Testaments.* Vol. 1, *JHWHs erwählendes und verpflichtendes Handeln.* Stuttgart: Kohlhammer, 1991.

Priebatsch, H. *Die Josephsgeschichte in der Weltliteratur.* Breslau: M. & H. Marcus, 1937.

Prieur, Alexander. *Die Verkündigung der Gottesherrschaft: Exegetische Studien zum lukanischen Verständnis von* basileia tou theou. WUNT 2/89. Tübingen: Mohr Siebeck, 1996.

Prigent, Pierre. *L'Apocalypse de Saint Jean.* Geneva: Labor et Fides, 2000.

Radner, Ephraim. *Chasing the Shadow: The World and Its Times.* Eugene, OR: Wipf & Stock, 2018.

Ramelli, Ilaria. "Luke 16:16: The Good News of God's Kingdom Is Proclaimed and Everyone Is Forced into It." *JBL* 127 (2008): 737–58.

Ratschow, Carl Heinz. *Lutherische Dogmatik zwischen Reformation und Aufklärung.* Vol. 1. Gütersloh: G. Mohn, 1964.

———. *Von den Wandlungen Gottes: Beiträge zur systematischen Theologie; zum 75. Geburtstag.* Edited by Christel Keller-Wentorf, Carl Heinz Ratschow, and Martin Repp. Berlin: de Gruyter, 1986.

Reasoner, Mark. "The Theme of Acts: Institutional History or Divine Necessity in History?" *JBL* 118 (1999): 635–59.

Reumann, John. "*Oikonomia* = 'Covenant': Terms for *Heilsgeschichte* in Early Christian Usage." *NovT* 3 (1959): 282–92.

Richter, Gerhard. *Der Gebrauch des Wortes* oikonomia *im Neuen Testament, bei den Kirchenvätern und in der theologischen Literatur bis ins 20. Jahrhundert.* AKG 90. Berlin: de Gruyter, 2005.

Ricoeur, Paul. *Temps et recit.* Vol. 3. Paris: Seuil, 1985.

Ringgren, H. "חָיָה." *TDOT* 4:324–44.

Ritschl, Albrecht. *Die christliche Lehre von der Rechtfertigung und Versoehnung.* Vol. 3, *Die positive Entwickelung der Lehre.* Bonn: Marcus, 1874.

Robertson, David. *The Old Testament and the Literary Critic.* Minneapolis: Fortress, 1977.

Roche, Mark William. *Tragedy and Comedy: A Systematic Study and a Critique of Hegel.* Albany: State University of New York Press, 1998.

Rogerson, John. "Can a Doctrine of Providence Be Based on the Old Testament?" In *Ascribe to the Lord: Biblical and Other Essays in Memory of Peter C. Craigie*, edited by Lyle M. Eslinger and Glen Taylor, 529–43. JSOTSup 67. Sheffield: JSOT Press, 1988.

———. *The Supernatural in the Old Testament.* Guildford: Lutterworth, 1976.

Rohde, Erwin. *Der gri echische Roman und seine Vorläufer.* Leipzig: Breitkopf & Härtel, 1876.

Rohls, Jan. *Geschichte der Ethik.* 2nd ed. Tübingen: Mohr Siebeck, 1999.

Röhser, G. *Prädestination und Verstockung: Untersuchungen zur frühjüdischen, paulinischen und johanneischen Theologie.* TANZ 14. Tübingen: Mohr Siebeck, 1994.

Roloff, Jürgen. *Die Apostelgeschichte.* NTD 5. Berlin: Evangelische Verlagsanstalt, 1988.

———. "Vorsehung." In *Reclams Bibellexikon*, edited by Klaus Koch et al., 531. Ditzingen: Reclam, 1978.

Rose, Christian. *Die Wolke der Zeugen: Eine exegetisch-traditionsgeschichtliche Untersuchung zu Hebräer 10, 32–12,3.* WUNT 2/60. Tübingen: Mohr Siebeck, 1994.

Rosenthal, Ludwig A. "Die Josephsgeschichte mit den Büchern Ester und Daniel verglichen." *ZAW* 15 (1895): 278–84.

———. "Nochmals der Vergleich Ester, Joseph, Daniel." *ZAW* 17 (1897): 125–38.

Rosenzweig, Franz. *Der Stern der Erlösung.* Frankfurt: Suhrkamp, 1993.

Rothschild, Clare K. *Luke-Acts and the Rhetoric of History.* WUNT 2/175. Tübingen: Mohr Siebeck, 2004.

Rowe, C. Kavin. *One True Life: The Stoics and Early Christians as Rival Traditions.* New Haven: Yale University Press, 2016.

Rudman, D. *Determinism in the Book of Ecclesiastes.* JSOTSup 316. Sheffield: Sheffield Academic Press, 2001.

Runia, David T. "From Stoicism to Platonism: The Difficult Case of Philo of Alexandria's *De Providentia* I." In *From Stoicism to Platonism: The Development of Philosophy, 100 BCE–100 CE*, edited by Troels Engberg-Pedersen, 159–78. Cambridge: Cambridge University Press, 2017.

Ruppert, Lothar. *Genesis: Ein kritischer und theologischer Kommentar.* Vol. 4, *Genesis 37,1–50,26.* Würzburg: Echter, 2008.

Sakenfeld, Katharine Doob. "Theological and Redactional Problems in Numbers 20.2–13." In *Understanding the Word: Essays in Honor of Bernhard W. Anderson*, edited by James T. Butler, Edgar W. Conrad, and Ben C. Ollenburger, 133–54. JSOTSup 37. Sheffield: JSOT Press, 1985.

Salmeier, M. A. *Restoring the Kingdom: The Role of God as the "Ordainer of Times and Seasons" in the Acts of the Apostles.* PTMS. Eugene, OR: Pickwick, 2011.

Sarna, Nahum. *Genesis*. JPS Torah Commentary. New York: Jewish Publication Society of America, 1989.

Satake, Akira. *Die Offenbarung des Johannes*. Edited by Thomas Witulksi. Translated and with commentary by Akira Satake. KEK 16. Göttingen: Vandenhoeck & Ruprecht, 2008.

Scharbert, Johannes. "Das Verbum *pqd* in der Theologie des Alten Testaments: *SLM* im Alten Testament." In *Um das Prinzip der Vergeltung in Religion und Recht des Alten Testaments*, edited by K. Koch, 278–324. Darmstadt: Wissenschaftliche Buchgesellschaft, 1972.

Scharbert, Josef. "Formgeschichte und Exegese von Ex 34,6 f und Seiner Parallelen," *Biblica* 38 (1957): 130–50.

Schenk, Wolfgang. *Der Segen im Neuen Testament: Eine begriffsanalytische Studie*. Theologische Arbeiten 25. Berlin: Evangelische Verlagsanstalt, 1967.

Schimanowski, Gottfried. *Die himmlische Liturgie in der Apokalypse des Johannes: Die frühjüdischen Traditionen in Offenbarung 4–5 unter Einschluss der Hekhalotliteratur*. WUNT 2/154. Tübingen: Mohr Siebeck, 2002.

Schipper, Bernd. *Hermeneutik der Tora: Studien zur Traditionsgeschichte von Prov 2 und zur Komposition von Prov 1–9*. Berlin: de Gruyter, 2012.

Schleiermacher, Friedrich. *The Christian Faith: A New Translation and Critical Edition*. Translated by Terrence N. Tice, Catherine L. Kelsey, and Edwina Lawler. 2 vols. Louisville: Westminster John Knox, 2016.

Schlier, Heinrich. *Der Brief an die Galater*. 15th ed. Göttingen: Vandenhoeck & Ruprecht, 1989.

Schlosser, Jacques. *Le règne de Dieu dans les dits de Jésus*. Paris: Gabalda, 1980.

———. "Die Vollendung des Heils in der Sicht Jesu." In *Weltgericht und Weltvollendung: Zukunftsbilder im Neuen Testament*, edited by H.-J. Klauck and Rudolf Schnackenburg, 54–84. QD 150. Freiburg: Herder, 1994.

Schmid, Hans Heinrich. "Creation, Righteousness and Salvation." In *Creation in the Old Testament*, edited by Bernhard W. Anderson, 102–17. London: SPCK, 1984.

———. *Gerechtigkeit als Weltordnung: Hintergrund und Geschichte des alttestamentlichen Gerechtigkeitsbegriffes*. BHT 40. Tübingen: Mohr, 1968.

———. "Schöpfung, Gerechtigkeit und Heil: Schöpfungstheologie als Gesamthorizont biblischer Theologie." *ZTK* 70 (1973): 1–19.

———. *Wesen und Geschichte der Weisheit*. BZAW 101. Berlin: de Gruyter, 1966.

Schmid, Konrad. "Einführung." In *Schöpfung*, edited by Konrad Schmid, 1–15. Themen der Theologie 4. Tübingen: Mohr Siebeck, 2012.

———. "Fülle des Lebens oder erfülltes Leben? Religionsgeschichtliche und theologische Überlegungen zur Lebensthematik im Alten Testament." In *Leben, Verständnis. Wissenschaft. Technik. Kongressband des XI. europäischen Kongresses für Theologie, 15.–19. September 2002 in Zürich*, edited by E. Herms, 154–64. VWGTh 24. Gütersloh: Gütersloher Verlagshaus, 2005.

————. *Hiobs Weg: Stationen der menschlichen Leid*. BTSt 45. Neukirchen-Vluyn: Neukirchener Verlag, 2001.

————, ed. *Schöpfung*. Themen der Theologie 4. Tübingen: Mohr Siebeck, 2012.

————. *Schriftgelehrte Traditionsliteratur: Fallstudien zur innerbiblischen Schriftauslegung im Alten Testament*. FAT 77. Tübingen: Mohr Siebeck, 2011.

————. "Wenn die Vorsehung ein Gesicht bekommt: Theologische Transformationen einer problematischen Kategorie." In *Vorsehung, Schicksal und göttliche Macht: Antike Stimmen zu einem aktuellen Thema*, edited by Reinhard G. Kratz and Hermann Spieckermann, 147–70. Tübingen: Mohr Siebeck, 2008.

————. "Zeit und Geschichte als Determinanten biblischer Theologie." In *Schriftgelehrte Traditionsliteratur: Fallstudien zur innerbiblischen Schriftauslegung im Alten Testament*, 299–322. FAT 77. Tübingen: Mohr Siebeck, 2011.

————. "Zum Alten Testament." In *Schöpfung*, 71–120.

————. "Zusammenschau." In *Schöpfung*, 325–46.

Schnackenburg, Rudolf. *Das Johannesevangelium*. HTKNT. Freiburg: Herder, 1980. Translated by K. Smyth et al. as *The Gospel according to John*. 3 vols. New York: Crossroad, 1990.

Schneider, G. *Lukas Theologie als Heilsgeschichte*. BBB 59. Bonn: Peter Hanstein, 1985.

Schnocks, Johannes. *Vergänglichkeit und Gottesherrschaft Studien zu Psalm 90 und dem vierten Psalmenbuch*. BBB 140. Berlin: Philo, 2002.

Schoors, Antoon. "Theodicy in Qohelet." In *Theodicy in the World of the Bible*, edited by Antti Laato and Johannes C. de Moor, 375–409. Leiden: Brill, 2003.

————. "Words Typical of Qoheleth." In *Qohelet in the Context of Wisdom*, edited by A. Schoors, 17–39. BETL 136. Leuven: Peeters, 1998.

Schrage, Wolfgang. *Der erste Brief an die Korinther*. Vol. 2, *1. Kor 6,12–11,16*. EKKNT 7/2. Ostfildern: Patmos, 1995.

————. *Vorsehung Gottes? Zur Rede von der providentia Dei in der Antike und im Neuen Testament*. Neukirchen-Vluyn: Neukirchener Verlag, 2005.

Schulz, Siegfried. "Gottes Vorsehung bei Lukas." *ZNW* 54 (1963): 104–16.

Schürmann, Heinz. "Das hermeneutische Hauptproblem der Verkündigung Jesu." In *Traditionsgeschichtliche Untersuchungen zu den synoptischen Evangelien*, 13–35. Düsseldorf: Patmos, 1968.

————. *Gottes Reich—Jesu Geschick: Jesu ureigener Tod im Licht seiner Basileia-Verkündigung*. Freiburg: Herder, 1983.

Schwartz, Regina. "Adultery in the House of David: The Metanarrative of Biblical Scholarship and the Narratives of the Bible." *Semeia* 54 (1991): 35–55.

Schwienhorst-Schönberger, Ludwig. *Kohelet*. HTKAT. Freiburg: Herder, 2004.

———. *"Nicht im Menschen gründet das Glück" (Koh 2,24): Kohelet im Spannungsfeld jüdischer Weisheit und hellenistischer Philosophie*. HBS 2. Freiburg: Herder, 1994.

Seebass, Horst. *Genesis*. 3 vols. Neukirchen-Vluyn: Neukirchener Verlag, 1996, 1999, 2000.

———. *Numeri*. BKAT 4/2. Neukirchen-Vluyn: Neukirchener Verlag, 2003.

Seitz, Christopher. *Zion's Final Destiny: The Development of the Book of Isaiah; A Reassessment of Isaiah 36–39*. Minneapolis: Fortress, 1991.

Shauf, Scott. *Theology as History, History as Theology: Paul in Ephesus in Acts 19*. BZNW 133. Berlin: de Gruyter, 2005.

Siegert, Folker. "Philo and the New Testament." In *Cambridge Companion to Philo*, edited by A. Kamesar, 175–209. Cambridge: Cambridge University Press, 2009.

Ska, J.-L. *The Exegesis of the Pentateuch: Exegetical Studies and Basic Questions*. FAT 66. Tübingen: Mohr Siebeck, 2008.

Smalley, Stephen. *The Revelation to John: A Commentary on the Greek Text of the Apocalypse*. Downers Grove, IL: InterVarsity, 2005.

Smith, Craig. "Smith and Bentham." In *The Cambridge History of Moral Philosophy*, edited by S. Golob and J. Timmerman, 352–64. Cambridge: Cambridge University Press, 2017.

Smith, Mark S. "'Seeing God' in the Psalms: The Background to the Beatific Vision in the Hebrew Bible." *CBQ* 50 (1988): 171–83.

Sommer, Benjamin D. *The Bodies of God and the World of Ancient Israel*. Cambridge: Cambridge University Press, 2009.

Sonderegger, Kate. *Systematic Theology*. Vol. 1, *The Doctrine of God*. Minneapolis: Fortress, 2015.

Sonnet, Jean-Pierre. "Ehyeh asher ehyeh (Exodus 3:14): God's 'Narrative Identity' among Suspense, Curiosity, and Surprise." *Poetics Today* 31 (2010): 331–51.

———. "God's Repentance and 'False Starts' in Biblical History." In *Congress Volume Ljubljana 2007*, edited by André Lemaire, 469–94. Leiden: Brill, 2010.

Sparn, W. Review of *Johann Gerhards lutherische Christologie und die aristotelische Metaphysik*, by Richard Schröder. *TLZ* 112 (1987): 825–27.

Spieckermann, Hermann. *Heilsgegenwart: Eine Theologie der Psalmen*. FRLANT 148. Göttingen: Vandenhoeck & Ruprecht, 1989.

———. "Wenn Gott schweigt: Jüdische Gedanken zu Schicksal und Vorsehung aus hellenistischer Zeit." In *Vorsehung, Schicksal und göttliche Macht: Antike Stimmen zu einem aktuellen Thema*, edited by Reinhard G. Kratz and Hermann Spieckermann, 104–24. Tübingen: Mohr Siebeck, 2008.

Squires, John T. *The Plan of God in Luke-Acts*. SNTSMS 76. Cambridge: Cambridge University Press, 1993.

Staerk, W. *Vorsehung und Vergeltung: Zur Frage nach der sittlichen Weltordnung.* Berlin: Furche, 1931.

Steck, Odil Hannes. "Beobachtungen zu Jesaja 56–59." In *Studien zu Tritojesaja*, edited by O. H. Steck, 169–86. BZAW 203. Berlin: de Gruyter, 1991.

———. *Gott in der Zeit entdecken: Die Prophetenbücher des Alten Testaments als Vorbild für Theologie und Kirche.* BTSt 42. Göttingen: Vandenhoeck & Ruprecht, 2001.

———. *Die Prophetenbücher und ihr theologisches Zeugnis: Wege der Nachfrage und Fährten zur Antwort.* Tübingen: Mohr Siebeck, 1996.

———. *Welt und Umwelt.* Stuttgart: Kohlhammer, 1978.

Steiner, George. "Tragedy Reconsidered." *New Literary History* 35 (2004): 1–15.

Sterling, Gregory. *Historiography and Self-Definition: Josephos, Luke-Acts and Apologetic Historiography.* NovTSup 64. Leiden: Brill, 1989.

Sternberg, Meir. "Time and Space in Biblical (Hi)story Telling: The Grand Chronology." In *The Book and the Text: The Bible and Literary Theory*, edited by R. Schwartz, 81–145. Oxford: Blackwell, 1990.

Still, Todd, ed. *God and Israel: Providence and Purpose in Romans 9–11.* Waco: Baylor University Press, 2017.

Stritzky, Maria-Barbara von. *Studien zur Überlieferung und Interpretation des Vaterunsers in der frühchristlichen Literatur.* Münster: Aschendorff, 1989.

Stump, Eleonore. *Wandering in the Darkness: Narrative and the Problem of Suffering.* Oxford: Oxford University Press, 2010.

Suderman, Jeffrey. *Orthodoxy and Enlightenment: George Campbell in the Eighteenth Century.* Montreal: McGill-Queen's University Press, 2001.

Svinth, Christine, and Vaerge Põder. *Doxologische Entzogenheit: Die fundamentaltheologische Bedeutung des Gebets bei Karl Barth.* Berlin: de Gruyter, 2009.

Swinburne, Richard. *Providence and the Problem of Evil.* Oxford: Clarendon, 1998.

Tanner, Kathryn. "Creation and Providence." In *Cambridge Companion to Karl Barth*, edited by John B. Webster, 111–26. Cambridge: Cambridge University Press, 2000.

———. *God and Creation in Christian Theology: Tyranny or Empowerment?* Minneapolis: Fortress, 1998.

Taylor, Kevin. *Hans Urs von Balthasar and Christ the Tragic Hero.* London: Bloomsbury T&T Clark, 2013.

Tengström, S. "רוּחַ." *TDOT* 13:365–402.

Terrien, Samuel. *The Elusive Presence: Toward a New Biblical Theology.* New York: Harper & Row, 1978.

Thissen, Werner. "Schöpfungsbejahung und Kreuzesnachfolge: Christsein in Spannungseinheit von Nähe und Distanz zur Welt." In *Der lebendige Gott: Studien zur Theologie des Neuen Testaments*, edited by Thomas Söding, 361–67. Münster: Aschendorff, 1996.

Ticciati, Susannah. *Job and the Disruption of Identity: Reading beyond Barth*. Oxford: Oxford University Press, 2005.

Tooman, William A. "Covenant and Presence." In *Divine Presence and Absence in Exilic and Post-exilic Judaism*, edited by Nathan MacDonald and Izaak J. de Hulster, 151–82. FAT 2/61. Tübingen: Mohr Siebeck, 2013.

Tsang, Lap-chuen. *The Sublime: Groundwork towards a Theory*. Rochester: University of Rochester Press, 1998.

Turnbull, George. *An Impartial Enquiry into the Moral Character of Jesus Christ*. London, 1740.

Twain, Mark. "Providence." Chapter 53 in *Roughing It*. Chicago: American Publishing Company, 1872.

Uytanlet, Samson. *Luke-Acts and Jewish Historiography: A Study on the Theology, Literature, and Ideology of Luke-Acts*. WUNT 2/366. Tübingen: Mohr Siebeck, 2014.

Vance, Norman. *Bible & Novel: Narrative Authority and the Death of God*. Oxford: Oxford University Press, 2013.

VanDrunen, David. *Living in God's Two Kingdoms: A Biblical Vision for Christianity and Culture*. Wheaton: Crossway, 2010.

————. "Two Kingdoms and the Social Order: Political and Legal Theory in Light of God's Covenant with Noah." *Journal of Markets & Morality* 14 (2011): 445–62.

van Oorschot, J. *Gott als Grenze: Eine literar- und redaktionsgeschichtliche Studie zu den Gottesreden des Hiobbuches*. BZAW 170. Berlin: de Gruyter, 1987.

van Ruler, Arnold. *The Christian Church and the Old Testament*. Grand Rapids: Eerdmans, 1972.

Vögtle, Anton. "Der 'eschatologische' Bezug der Wir-Bitten des Vaterunser." In *Offenbarungsgeschehen und Wirkungsgeschichte: Neutestamentliche Beiträge*, 35–48. Freiburg: Herder, 1985.

————. "'Theologie' und 'Eschatologie' in der Verkündigung Jesu?" In *Offenbarungsgeschehen und Wirkungsgeschichte: Neutestamentliche Beiträge*, 11–34. Freiburg: Herder, 1985.

Vollenweider, Samuel. *Freiheit als neue Schöpfung: Eine Untersuchung zur Eleutheria bei Paulus und in seiner Umwelt*. FRLANT 147. Göttingen: Vandenhoeck & Ruprecht, 1989.

————. "Wahrnehmungen der Schöpfung im Neuen Testament." *Zeitschrift für Pädagogik und Theologie* 55 (2003): 246–53.

von Rad, Gerhard. "The Beginnings of Historical Writing." In *The Problem of the Hexateuch, and Other Essays*, translated by Eric William Trueman Dicken, 166–204. Edinburgh: Oliver & Boyd, 1966.

————. "Die theologische Stellung des Schöpfungsglaubens bei Deuterojesaja." *ZTK* 51 (1954): 3–13.

————. *Theologie des Alten Testaments*. Munich: Kaiser, 1957.

Wagner, Thomas. *Gottes Herrlichkeit: Bedeutung und Verwendung des Begriffs* kābôd *im Alten Testament*. VTSup 151. Leiden: Brill, 2012.

Wallace, Jennifer. *The Cambridge Introduction to Tragedy*. Cambridge: Cambridge University Press, 2007.

Watson, Francis. *Text and Truth: Redefining Biblical Theology*. Grand Rapids: Eerdmans, 1997.

Webster, John. "On the Theology of Providence." In *The Providence of God: Deus Habet Consilium*, edited by Francesca Aran Murphy and Philip G. Ziegler, 158–75. London: T&T Clark, 2010.

————. "Providence." In *Christian Dogmatics: Reformed Theology for the Church Catholic*, edited by Michael Allen and Scott R. Swain, 148–64. Grand Rapids: Baker Academic, 2016.

Weder, Hans. "Glaube, Hoffnung, Vertrauen: Beobachtungen aus neutestamentlich-hermeneutischer Perspektive." In *Gottvertrauen: Die ökumenische Diskussion um die Fiducia*, edited by I. Dalferth and S. Peng-Keller, 80–104. QD 250. Freiburg: Herder, 2012.

————. *Die Gleichnisse Jesu als Metaphern*. Göttingen: Vandenhoeck & Ruprecht, 1987.

Weeks, Stuart. *Ecclesiastes and Scepticism*. London: Bloomsbury, 2011.

Wehmeier, Gerhard. *Der Segen im Alten Testament: Eine semasiologische Untersuchung der Wurzel brk*. ThDiss 6. Basel: Reinhardt, 1970.

Weidemann, Hans-Ulrich. "The Victory of Protology over Eschatology? Creation in the Gospel of John." In *Theologies of Creation in Early Judaism and Ancient Christianity: In Honour of Hans Klein*, edited by Tobias Nicklas, Korinna Zamfir, and Heike Braun, 299–334. Berlin: de Gruyter, 2010.

Weiss, Hans-Friedrich. *Der Brief an die Hebräer*. 15th ed. KEK 13. Göttingen: Vandenhoeck & Ruprecht, 1991.

Wells, Samuel. "Esther." In *Esther & Daniel*, by Samuel Wells and George Sumner, 1–91. BTCB. Grand Rapids: Brazos, 2013.

Wénin, André. *Joseph ou l'invention de la fraternité*. Brussels: Lessius, 2005.

Werner, W. *Studien zur alttestamentlichen Vorstellung vom Plan Jahwes*. BZAW 173. Berlin: de Gruyter, 1988.

Westermann, Claus. *Blessing in the Bible and the Life of the Church*. Minneapolis: Fortress, 1978.

————. *Genesis 1–11*. CC. Minneapolis: Augsburg, 1984.

————. *Genesis 37–50*. CC. Minneapolis: Augsburg, 1986.

————. *The Praise of God in the Psalms*. Edinburgh: Oliver & Boyd, 1966.

————. *Roots of Wisdom: The Oldest Proverbs of Israel and Other Peoples*. Edinburgh: T&T Clark, 1995.

————. *The Structure of Job*. Minneapolis: Fortress, 1981. Originally published as *Der Aufbau des Buches Hiob*. Stuttgart: Calwer, 1977.

Whedbee, J. William. *The Bible and the Comic Vision*. Cambridge: Cambridge University Press, 1998.

White, Vernon. *Purpose and Providence: Taking Soundings in Western Thought, Literature and Theology*. London: Bloomsbury T&T Clark, 2015.

Wicke-Reuter, Ursel. "Ben Sira und die Frühe Stoa." In *Ben Sira's God: Proceedings of the International Ben Sira Conference, Durham, Ushaw College, 2001*, edited by Renate Egger-Wenzel, 268–81. Berlin: de Gruyter, 2002.

————. *Göttliche Providenz und menschliche Verantwortung bei Ben Sira und in der Frühen Stoa*. BZAW 298. Berlin: de Gruyter, 2000.

————. "Zusammenfassung." In *Göttliche Providenz und menschliche Verantwortung bei Ben Sira und in der Frühen Stoa*, 275–85. BZAW 298. Berlin: de Gruyter, 2000.

Widmer, Michael. *Moses, God, and the Dynamics of Intercessory Prayer: A Study of Exodus 32–34 and Numbers 13–14*. FAT 2/8. Tübingen: Mohr Siebeck, 2004.

Wiesel, Elie. "The Sacrifice of Isaac: A Survivor's Story." In *Messengers of God: Biblical Portraits and Legends*, 69–97. New York: Random House, 1972.

Wilckens, Ulrich. "Das Offenbarungsverständnis in der Geschichte des Urchristentums." In *Offenbarung als Geschichte*, edited by W. Pannenberg, 42–90. 4th ed. Kerygma und Dogma 1. Gottingen: Vandenhoeck & Ruprecht, 1970.

————. *Der Brief an die Römer*. 3 vols. EKKNT 6. Zürich: Benziger, 1978–82.

Williams, Rowan. *The Tragic Imagination*. The Literary Agenda. Oxford: Oxford University Press, 2016.

Wilson, Ian. *Out of the Midst of the Fire: Divine Presence in Deuteronomy*. SBLDS 151. Atlanta: Scholars Press, 1995.

Wischmeyer, Oda. "PHYSIS und KTISIS bei Paulus." *ZTK* 93 (1996): 352–75.

Witte, Markus. *Von Ewigkeit zu Ewigkeit: Weisheit und Geschichte in den Psalmen*. BTSt 146. Göttingen: Vandenhoeck & Ruprecht, 2014.

Wolff, Hans Walter. *Hosea: A Commentary on the Book of the Prophet Hosea*. Hermeneia. Minneapolis: Fortress, 1974.

Wolter, Michael. "Das lukanische Doppelwerk als Epochengeschichte." In *Die Apostelgeschichte und die hellenistische Geschichtsschreibung: Festschrift für Eckhard Plümacher zu seinem 65. Geburtstag*, edited by Cilliers Breytenbach and Jens Schröter, 253–84. AGJU 57. Leiden: Brill, 2004.

————. *Das Lukas-Evangelium*. Tübingen: Mohr Siebeck, 2008.

————. *Der Brief an die Römer*. EKKNT, NF 6/1. Ostfildern: Patmos, 2014.

————. "Die Unscheinbarkeit des Reiches Gottes." In *Reich Gottes*, edited by W. Härle and R. Preul, 103–16. Marburger Jahrbuch Theologie 11. Marburg: Elwert, 1999.

————. "'Reich Gottes' bei Lukas." *NTS* 41 (1995): 541–63.

————. "Was heisset nu Gottes Reich?" *ZNW* 86 (1995): 5–19.

Wright, Addison. "Ecclesiastes 9:1–12: An Emphatic Statement of Themes." *CBQ* 77 (2015): 250–62.

Yarbro Collins, Adela. *The Apocalypse*. Collegeville, MN: Liturgical Press, 1990.

———. *The Combat Myth in the Book of Revelation*. Eugene, OR: Wipf & Stock, 2001.

Yates, John. *The Spirit and Creation in Paul*. WUNT 2/251. Tübingen: Mohr Siebeck, 2008.

Young, Frances. *God's Presence: A Contemporary Recapitulation of Early Christianity*. Cambridge: Cambridge University Press, 2013.

Zakovitch, Yair. *On the Conception of Miracle in the Bible*. Tel Aviv: MOD, 1991.

———. "∪ and ∩ in the Bible." *Semeia* 32 (1984): 107–14.

Zehnder, Markus Philip. *Wegmetaphorik im Alten Testament: Eine semantische Untersuchung der alttestamentlichen und altorientalischen Weg-Lexeme mit besonderer Berücksichtigung ihrer metaphorischen Verwendung*. BZAW 268. Berlin: de Gruyter, 1999.

Zenger, Erich. *Einleitung in das Alten Testament*. 7th ed. Stuttgart: Kohlhammer, 2012.

———. *Mit meinem Gott überspringe ich Mauern: Einführung in das Psalmenbuch*. Freiburg: Herder, 1989.

Zimmer, Tilmann. *Zwischen Tod und Lebensglück: Eine Untersuchung zur Anthropologie Kohelets*. BZAW 286. Berlin: de Gruyter, 1999.

Zimmerli, Walter. "The Fruit of the Tribulation of the Prophet." In *A Prophet to the Nations: Essays in Jeremiah Studies*, edited by Leo G. Perdue and Brian W. Kovacs, 349–65. Winona Lake, IN: Eisenbrauns, 1984.

Zimmermann, Christine. *Die Namen des Vaters: Gottesbezeichnungen vor ihrem frühjüdischen und paganen Sprachhorizont*. AJEC 69. Leiden: Brill, 2007.

Zmijewski, J. *Die Apostelgeschichte*. RNT. Regensburg: Pustet, 1994.

Author Index

Scripture Index

Subject Index

Manufactured by Amazon.ca
Bolton, ON